STARLADY

The True Story of Valérie and Mr. Dickens
and other lifetimes spent with John Barrow

Valérie Judith Barrow

First published in Australia by Aurora House
www.aurorahouse.com.au

This edition published 2019

www.valeriebarrow.com

Typesetting and e-book design: Aurora House
Cover design: Simon Critchell

ISBN number: 978-0-6485216-3-1 (paperback)

Lightning Source has received Chain of Custody (CoC) certification from:
The Forest Stewardship Council® (FSC®)
Programme for the Endorsement of Forest Certification® (PEFC®)
The Sustainable Forestry Initiative® (SFI®)

Distributed by: Ingram Content: www.ingramcontent.com
Australia: phone +613 9765 4800 | email lsiaustralia@ingramcontent.com
Milton Keynes UK: phone +44 (0)845 121 4567 | email enquiries@ingramcontent.com
La Vergne, TN USA: phone +1 800 509 4156 | email inquiry@lightningsource.com

Gardners UK:
www.gardners.com
phone +44 (0)132 352 1555 | email sales@gardners.com

Bertrams UK:
www.bertrams.com/BertWeb/index.jsp
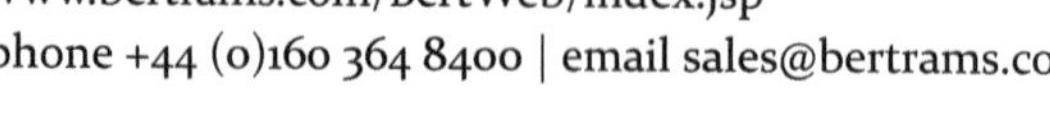
phone +44 (0)160 364 8400 | email sales@bertrams.com

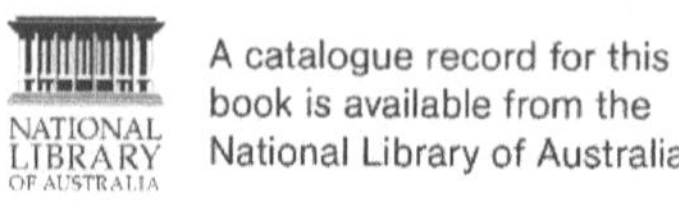

Valérie Barrow – Starlady

and 8th White Sister, Egarina
Who Has Returned From the Pleaides

I have absolutely NO DOUBT about the existence of Starpeople. I remember being one. In fact, I am one...who has walked into an Earth body (with God's permission). A lot of us have come to assist with raising consciousness on Earth with love and service.

When you come here you forget quite a bit, but the memory comes back as the frequency of the Earth raises—that is why there is so much more TALK about Starpeople now. The younger ones coming into Earth bodies can remember more easily.

Way back when Atlantis fell, the earth was in the fourth dimension (about what we are now) and Starpeople used to come and go easily, but they had different bodies. Not Earth bodies. Or Earth race bodies—if that makes sense...

People have asked why they don't come now. Or are they all coming into Earth bodies this time?

And I can say yes, they do come and go all the time, but in a different frequency that Earth people cannot see as yet. AND they are coming into Earth bodies also, which is much harder for them. BUT they want to help us. They are our brothers and sisters—OUR FAMILY.

Even though there is a mixture of DNA that makes us look different from their races, WE, meaning the Earthen race, are a mixture of all the types of DNA that came from the stars in the first place. Some are from a heavier frequency, ready to learn, and many more are from an advanced frequency, ready to move into the fifth dimension; when we finally leave our Earth bodies, we all return to the stars.

The Starpeople would come now, straight away, with greetings, if they were welcomed. But, at the moment, they are not being welcomed! Advanced Starpeople can easily disappear out of Earth people's sight by changing their frequency.

The fifth dimension is the frequency of where all on Earth, and the Earth herself, are heading—it has the same energy frequency of Crystal or Christ or Christos—and it is the level playing field for all Souls to attain in consciousness. It is known as the GOLDEN AGE.

*****

This is a true story of Valérie and her husband, remembering many past lives together and how they came to remember.

Valérie also speaks of a green crystal known as a Moldavite, which 'advised that she would be going home'. That was the beginning of her mission as a messenger.

Some time after that, a sacred stone wrapped in paperbark and then covered with cloth and tied with string was lent to her. It belonged to the Australian Aborigine—its role was to come to Valérie and introduce her to Alcheringa, who is well known to the Indigenous people as an ancestral creator spirit, and share with her knowledge about the evolution of the Earth and its creation.

Shortly after, she learnt of the mission she was asked to write about, as the returned 8th Sister from the Pleiades, nearly 1 million years ago in ancient time, when Starpeople from the Pleiades came to this planet to establish a civilisation with a raised consciousness in this dark corner of the Milky Way. Their huge mothership was attacked and destroyed, and the survivors, using genetic engineering, managed to uplift the ape-like, weapon-wielding form of slave MAN, to a man of light—our HU-MAN ancestors.

It is the missing link to the evolvement of humanity.

The age-old disagreement between the Evolutionists and the Creationists, of whether man evolved or was created, in my mind has been clarified—they are both right.

Dedication

This book is dedicated with endless love to our Creator ancestral spirit, well known to the Indigenous people. He tells us he resides at the sacred and mysterious monolith ULURU, living in the red desert centre of Australia.

ALCHERINGA

Acknowledgements

A big thank you is given to my beloved husband John and all my family.

And to Linda Lycett for her tireless support and understanding, along with her crew at Aurora House.

Contents

Living in France for Six Months

PART TWO

The Book of Love - Leading to the missing manuscript written by John the Divine

PART THREE

Foreword

Valérie's book is a chronicle of events and experiences both spiritual and physical. Over the last forty years, it has bonded our minds, bodies, and souls to an astonishingly profound degree.

Valérie has probably been an enlightened soul from birth or soon thereafter and has, as a consequence, developed extraordinary psychic powers and healing skills over the past forty years—a truly enlightened soul.

Unfortunately, I cannot claim the same track record. Until I first met Valérie in 1976, I was a spiritual mess, with my soul well and truly entrenched in my lower chakra—the only spirit I knew was generally poured from a bottle.

From the time I first met Valérie, my whole physical and spiritual being has been lifted from darkness into light and my consciousness has been elevated to a level that hopefully allows me to call Valérie my true soulmate.

This is our soul story, but the book is Valérie's—read and enjoy.

~ *John Barrow*

***John Wynford Grey Barrow** is a direct descendant of Charles Dickens. His great, great, great aunt was Elizabeth Barrow—Charles Dickens' mother. John's parents used to attend 'Dickensian Dinners' during the 1920s—only relations were invited.*

Barrow Coat of Arms

Poussez en Avant

"Push on Ahead"

Barrow

Preface

In the past two years, 2017/2018, I have been introduced to the galaxy M31 Andromeda. This is a major uplift for me and not one that happened without experiencing yet another initiation—an emergency visit to hospital—but I survived and live to tell yet more stories. Only after first experiencing a Divine Encounter and embracing my parents in a raised dimension – Sanat Kumara and the Lady Venus.

I have now been introduced to my Oversoul, who is androgynous, both male and female. They are Creators—meaning they have no limit—and they are 6,000 years into our future. They operate in a much higher frequency of light.

My inner knowing and vision about Andromeda is that it is a beautiful place with lots of white light, or golden at times, with jewel-coloured flowers, green trees and grass. Animals, such as lions and tigers, giraffes, elephants, and other wildlife we see on Earth, are all friendly, and all are white—including birds.

Where my Oversoul is from a race with a very human-like appearance: they have white hair and stand seven to eight feet tall. They are known as the Adonis race.

Everyone is respectful to each other and would not dream of raising a weapon to sort out a problem. If there are differences, they accept the differences and come to agreement with consensus.

We are advised the Angelic Realms in Andromeda M31 created our planet Earth in the first place. It was created to take the place of a previous planet that was destroyed and there was need to keep balance in the rotation of the solar system within the Milky Way galaxy.

We are also advised that 144,000 volunteers have come to Earth from Andromeda as healers, peacemakers, and light workers. They are here to assist the evolution of Mother Earth.

In the overview, our galaxy the Milky Way is being prepared for the uplifted level of consciousness in preparation for the huge galaxy Andromeda M31 to gently embrace the Milky Way galaxy, a long, long time into our future.

In the meantime, the beings from Andromeda want us to smoothly raise in consciousness without fear: to telepathically connect to them and other benevolent races of other worlds, joining with them in the United Planetary Nations. We are advised the colour MAGENTA is the vibration that will assist telepathic connection with them. It is the first colour on the electromagnetic spectrum.

I would like to share a reading that a clairvoyant gave me after I had been working with these beautiful benevolent beings for twelve years. I am sharing it because it may help others to realise who they are. Helen sent the reading without my asking for it.

"As I tune in, I see you in a state of spiritual enlightenment and illumination. You have been released from the cycle of birth, suffering, and death, and other forms of worldly bondage.

Your destiny called for the surrender of the personal for the impersonal. This destiny is being fulfilled because of your preparedness to substitute self-centeredness for the welfare of humanity as a whole. It is a difficult destiny to follow. Much self-adjustment was necessary, through suffering and disappointment. You have accepted the worthiness of this humanitarian life path by following your inner guidance.

You are stirred up by an emotional core, high ideals, and visions. You are an ambassador for the spirit world. Your refined vibrations enable you to express your fine sensitivity into high-minded thoughts. There is a strong urge within you to become a universal sister.

I see you being in communication with many light beings. Because of this, you have the need to impart this knowledge while on Earth.

You appear to me now as you are on the Other Side. Tall, slim, glowing with beauty, and immaculate skin. I am now being given to understand that you have taken on psoriasis to ease the burden of three other people. Two have already returned to the Other Side. You will not be free of this disease while this person is still on Earth.

Your higher self is actually very proud to have taken on this task because much pain and suffering was held away from those three persons.

I am being transported now to the other Other Side. I see the Hall of Memories—I see you communicating by thoughts alone. I see you 'nursing', so to speak, those who have recently arrived from the Earthly realm. I see several astral worlds.

Things are as real as on Earth; actually, they appear to me to be more substantial because of the extra senses, extra abilities, extra colours, and extra sounds. I am being given to understand that there are as many astral worlds as there are vibrations. Astral worlds are different planes of existence, having different frequencies.

I am being given an explanation. There are many radio stations all over the world. If those stations tried to share a common wavelength or frequency, everyone would interfere with everyone else. I am being shown that the lower astral is the meeting place for people of different races and creeds and different worlds! It is very similar to life on Earth.

As you progressed on the Other Side, your frequencies became purer and purer. You are doing a kind of voluntary work by helping those who pass over. You are a kind of midwife awaiting the birth of a new baby. With tender loving care you help them to adjust, you show the Hall of Memories, and you care for them.

You also counsel people who have to return to Earth. You question them about where would they like to go, what parents do they want, and what sort of conditions would enable them to do the task they plan to do.

I see you working alone—and yet, you are part of a group of six. By this I am referring to the Other Side. You, as a light being, are a kind of collective being. There are about three more people on Earth who come from the same group as you. Three are already on the Other Side.

If you feel that you have a deep affinity with a certain person on Earth, then it is likely that the person is a member of that group. Although I asked for names to be given, they were not provided. From this, the understanding was given that all six incarnated lives contributed to the welfare of one. (Oversoul is given to me.) The circle is not complete until the last one returns to the source.

When I asked for your name as a light being, I was being given to understand that names are vibrations and you are known by various vibrations, depending on the various vibrational levels you find yourself in. There is no Earthly sound that can even come close to express it. I experienced a very beautiful sound, but it is like explaining music to a deaf person. However, I was given to understand that the "V" has significance.

Valda, Vania, Velda, Victoria, and Vita were names chosen while incarnated on Earth...They each brought a certain quality into your lives...

I am now being shown that your husband John works with you on the Other Side. There is a kind of opposition and a kind of total unity present, which is hard to put into words. With this brief glimpse—I returned. With much love and light. Helen."

When I was given the above information, I chose not to take it too seriously, wanting to concentrate on my life here on Earth and to do the best I could.

Since my most recent introduction to the feminine side of my Oversoul, she has been named Andromeda Val, short for Valoel. She has adapted to speaking through my voicebox and sometimes speaks in her own language—that she will eventually translate, she advises.

She also advises she hopes to present herself at a meeting, the same way she presented herself to me one night. It was like science fiction in that a beam of light formed a hologram, allowing her image to appear beside my bed. She stood about 7ft tall, looking human and happy, smiling and excited to make her visit. When she visits me, it is out of joy and the true love of a wise sister.

So, at eighty-six years of age, here is my swan song I have been asked by my spirit mentors to write about—my soul journey and how I have shared many past lives with my husband John, but in particular Mr Charles Huffman Dickens.

*****

I briefly died while in hospital in 1969. The experience changed my life. Not long after that event, I was awakened with a male voice speaking to me, an authoritative but kindly voice, asking me to keep a writing pad and pen beside my bed, and the voice added, "You will be awakened from time to time and taught many things."

This has happened. It was a 'calling'.

Now, as I write much later, I have become an experienced medium and an advanced meditation teacher and have developed an understanding of how 'regression' and past-life therapy can heal our soul and our body. I know I have still much to learn on my soul journey.

I am often asked socially, "What do you do?" or "What are your interests?" I hesitate and think, *what can I say*? I am an ordinary grandmother who has extraordinary experiences. Can I tell them, "Well, I am awakened at night and a person I cannot see is training me to stand up, be over-lighted by its spirit energy, and then speak through me with a deep male sound by borrowing my voice box?" It is a bit confronting, isn't it? So how can I explain it without sounding like I have lost my mind?

Announcing, "I am a medium" helps. It opens up conversation with people who begin speaking of paranormal experiences they haven't had the courage to speak about to others. Often, they whisper, "I have never told anyone before...," but then go on to tell a story I am able to clarify and give reassurance they are not imagining. Our soul spirit physicality is real. Our physical Earth body would not stay alive without it.

This book is to demonstrate that everyone can 'channel' as a medium to some degree. We all have this gift—some call it intuition, inspiration, a feeling, or a 'creative thought' that seems to come from nowhere, 'out of the blue' one could say. It is from that place we recognise people we have known from past lives and, in particular, our soulmate.

Sometimes, we instinctively do not trust someone and another we may meet and feel we know them well, even though we have just met for the first time in this life. That special 'inspirational' or 'creative thought' does not come from the brain. It comes from soul consciousness that exists, whether or not we are in a physical Earth body or whether we are dead or alive.

While we are in an Earth body, it comes with a nice feeling, one of knowing deep within our heart that we are meant to take notice of the special 'intuitive thought'. With that conscious connection to our soul, we can even receive messages from other 'evolved' spirit entities from other worlds. There are worlds upon worlds upon worlds.

Once we connect to our soul consciousness, we can heal aspects of our past lives that are still affecting us. There are many ways to do this, such as meditation, dreams, or past-life regression. We can also draw from abilities and knowledge we have gained from other lives, embracing them into this life. This life is the one to focus on.

Our oversoul, also known as our God Self, holds together aspects of our other personality lives and guides us through our present life. We come with a soul blueprint that is born with spirit into our physical Earth body and prompts us throughout our life. It makes negotiating life much easier if we 'listen' to our inner guidance or our intuition; it assists us to build our character.

Something we all need to accept, or at least give thought to, is 'where do we come from before we come to Earth?' and 'where do we return to when we leave our Earth body?'

Science tells us that everything is ENERGY—and that can never be destroyed, but it can change its form. Thus, when our Earth body, along with its brain, returns to dust, where does our light body go to? Our life force. John and I have come to know we return to the stars. In fact, every soul does, with a consciousness that is eternal.

William Shakespeare said, "All the world is a stage, and all the men and women merely players. They have their exits and their entrances, and one man in his time plays many parts." The great bard then goes on to speak of one man's acts as being seven ages. The suggestion, of course, is one life. He wrote in the Renaissance period—was he hinting that we have other lives as well, with many exits and entrances?

This is something people would not dare speak about in the dark ages and begin to only hint at in his time.

We do 'play' out a story that has been written with other souls with various choices along the way before our sojourn on Earth. This is, as I have said, our soul blueprint. It is a stage play, designed to give opportunity for previous emotional trauma or hurt to be healed. Then, we go on to live with love, compassion, and understanding. Some choices we are free to make, allowing slight changes to what has been written. Other events in our lives are made with certainty; we have no choice.

Sometimes our soul blueprint is not played out as it is written and we, meaning our self or the other players in the story, 'fluff' our lines or our actions and miss opportunities, so to speak. Our life is played out in seven-year cycles. There is a reason and a purpose for everything that happens to us.

Our life has many mansions: many layers of knowledge and understanding. We no longer need to fear being 'burned at the stake' or 'stoned to death' or 'dunked in a pond' for speaking about having many lives and many masters, or paranormal experiences.

As a medium, I have been awakened from sleep many times by my spirit mentor, who is a light being, asking me to allow myself to be trained for another spirit to over-light my body and speak through my voice box. This, I am told, shows people ethereal beings really do exist. Those witnessing the event say it is apparent it is not me speaking.

My face changes, and the sound of my voice and my stance changes, depending upon whether it is male or female presenting itself; the messages have always been informative and uplifting. I do not readily remember what has been said until I transcribe it from the audio recording.

We have five senses—touch, sight, hearing, smell, and taste—in our Earth body that are duplicated in our spirit. This gives us insight to clearer sensitive touch, clairsentient; clear seeing, clairvoyance; clear hearing, clairaudience; clear smell, and clear taste, which can hold memory or alert us. This spirit connection is often referred to as psychic abilities.

When we regress into an altered state of consciousness, our memory and thinking is very clear and alert and enables us to connect directly to our soul thinking. It is our sixth sense; it is our soul spirit self that needs to be synchronised with our Oversoul or God Self.

I hope you will enjoy reading about John, the love of my life, and our story about the many lives we have shared. In one life we were enemies, but mostly we have been lovers, married, friends, associates, brother and sister, father and daughter, his mistress and roles reversed in that I was the husband and he the wife—but I have never been his mother, or so I thought, until we were given a strong past-life memory while living in France!

I was standing on the Great Pyramid of Giza in Egypt when I heard a voice asking me to write about the many, many lives that John and I have shared through time. I was also asked to write about the family of Jesus and a little of our planet's evolvement. I even questioned the point of it all but was told people would find it intriguing. I must confess it has taken some courage to 'bare my soul', so to speak. However, not for John; he is a total extrovert!

We have lived many lives, not always together and one might say seemingly insignificant at times, but always for a reason. I remember a life as a 'leper' and the dreadful suffering that existed as an outcast and the overwhelming feeling of not belonging. This caused me to feel resentment and understand how another feels when ostracised, rejected, and in the sense, "Why should this happen to me?" You build character from an experience such as that, if you accept the life with grace.

My soul partner and I did consider writing our story together, but John is an avid reader and finds books written by more than one person can be disjointed. I decided to interview him and write his story as he tells it. He is a natural raconteur and loves telling jokes.

The past lives we have shared together that I have written about in this memoir are those that have been recorded in history. For this reason, it should make an interesting read.

Our research has released information in our memory that has not been previously recorded in history. There have been other lives we have shared that are not recorded in history and I have not written about. Our sacred journey together will help to exemplify that souls really do exist first and foremost, and that our spirit, our personality, overlays our Earth physical body.

Our objective in writing this book is to give insight to another consciousness that is always within us that is infinite. It is our Eternal Self.

Everybody on Earth has soul stories within them. As mediums, we can bridge the path between our Earth brain thinking and our soul thinking that holds our blueprint for the journey in this life. Our inner guidance! No experience is ever wasted; this is the way to build our character and enter into an ascended state of consciousness, with our feet firmly planted on the ground.

John was born in England and I was born in Australia. We were destined to eventually meet. It was written in our soul blueprint and agreed long before either of us came to this Earth.

~ Valérie Barrow
8th White Sister

PART ONE

Memories of Soul Exchange

1

It is a second marriage for both of us. It had to be that way, for each of us had experienced a soul exchange in our Earth body. We were no longer the same personalities who had married our first partners.

It may seem strange to speak like this. From my point of view, I briefly died in the 1960s, after which I realised I was not the same person.

The person before me had followed a doctor's advice to try a new diet published in their Australian Medical Association Journal. The diet was to eliminate tryptophan, one of the basic amino acids in protein. This had proven to be helpful to people who suffered from a skin disease known as psoriasis. Suffer they do, in physical discomfort and emotional trauma. Nerve endings in the body seemed to be attacked, causing itching, sometimes a severe itching, and when scratched would bleed. The sores would become hot and red, with rough scabs covering the body.

The diet was adhered to religiously for a period of six months, even though the doctor was questioned if it could be making her feel unwell. He brushed her concerns away and because her skin had healed, she kept eating the same way. It came to a point when she really wasn't aware of how low in energy she was, and she kept ...falling asleep far too much.

She collapsed one day, unable to move at all. Her doctor called for an ambulance to rush her to intensive care at the hospital. The diagnosis was severe malnutrition, which did not show in her body until the doctor had given her a large dose of potassium. The potassium worked almost immediately, draining excess fluid from the flesh and muscles, leaving the body almost like a skeleton with absolutely no muscle strength.

Slipping into an altered state of consciousness memory of when my soul first took over the body, *I became aware of her soul remembering the feeling of a chilled stillness inside of the Earth body as it was slowly shutting down. A feeling of cold iciness steadily moved from the tips of the fingers and toes and deep into the body. It was as if electric lights were being turned off slowly inside each limb. She could not move the body, nor the fingers, toes, or eyelids...there was barely a breath.*

She lay, expecting to hear the heart stop beating; it was the only part of the body left with a feeling of a little warmth. She did not feel any fear. My soul wanted to live in this body and I prayed to God to give it life. I wanted to look after the Earth body's three children. So, I made a deal with God: "Please God, if you let me stay and assist me, I will do anything you ask of me."

The body's heart had stopped. There was no longer any spirit/soul lying there. For a short time after this, I realised I was above the body, experiencing the wonderful freedom. I could fly and I was conscious! An overwhelming feeling of joy swept over me with unlimited weightlessness.

A gentle voice, a deep authoritative sounding voice, said in my ear, "You can stay." Meaning my soul could now live in the body; the first soul had finally left. Then everything went black and I lost consciousness.

It took some weeks to adjust to my new body. The muscles were still very weak. I could not hold the head up high, nor move the arms or legs. I had to be pushed around the hospital in a wheelchair until the body was strong enough to stand alone.

When I came home from hospital, I was still weak and needing rest. The house, the garden, and my then husband felt like strangers. I remember spending a lot of time looking at photos of the body's childhood, her travels overseas from the age of twenty-one onwards, and a working life in Europe and Canada, her marriage in Canada, the family and holiday places. It all felt as if I were a visitor, and yet I knew and deeply loved the children.

The three little boys were the only reality that seemed familiar. I was unsure at the time of what had happened to me, but I knew I was a very different person.

A few years later, a medium/clairvoyant explained to me I had experienced a soul exchange with the former owner of the body and that it had been done with agreement long before either of us had come from the World of Light.

It meant I still walked in the Earth body created by the original soul, but I was a different personality and a different soul. I had inherited her Earth body, heavy with unhappy emotion but not her spirit/soul, which had finally returned to the World of Light. I was required to work at healing her emotional body and physical body and combine that with my own spirit/soul. Her soul, much lighter now, had returned to the World of Light and was not my responsibility. The children were still mine, for they had come from the Earth body.

The former soul loved singing, cooking, knitting, and sewing new clothes and even curtains and lounge covers. The embarrassment of her skin disease all over her body caused problems and rejection from people at times. It made it harder for her to deal with because some people thought it was contagious and would draw away from her with repugnance.

When she was only three years old, a specialist examined her on a table without her clothes, saying it was the worst case he had ever seen. He ordered her hair to be shaved off to treat her scalp. The mother was crying and the child felt she was the worst little girl the doctor had ever seen. A deep sense of insecurity had come from an unhappy childhood. Her mother was often crying, saying her father was mean to her, and the child's skin disease was her mother's fault, and there was a genetic inheritance. Her mother would sometimes just disappear; there had been talk of 'nervous breakdowns'.

The child believed she had caused all her mother's problems, leading her to confusion and shyness. Her self-worth wasn't helped when at eighteen years old, an aunt told her that a man would not want to marry her because of her skin disease. As an adult, she did marry and loved her children but was deeply unhappy with her life. After collapsing, and her emergency admission to hospital at age thirty-seven, when she returned home her friends and loved ones knew Valerie had changed dramatically.

My soul personality was more concerned about the quality of water, soil, and food grown in it, along with deep concern for the purity of air and what mankind was doing to it. I wanted to study more, and I prayed every day for World Peace.

The clairvoyant had said, "You are on a mission, along with many other souls who have come to Earth at this time, some as 'walk-ins', to help lift the consciousness of the Earth's soul and humanity's soul, weight and measure, readying all to move into an ascended state of being."

My destiny was to meet with my soul partner, one who had been designated by the Karmic Board in the Cosmos to assist me with my work and to support, love, and protect me. Unknown to me then, my soul partner arrived on the shores of my country almost at the same time I became the new caretaker of this body. It was 1969.

It would be another seven years until I met John, the debonair Englishman, and my future second husband.

We, at first, were business associates. He was selling dried fruit and nuts and called his warehouse business 'The Fruit & Nut Case'. I operated a popular health food store.

The first day John came into my store, he introduced himself saying, "I love chillies," and promptly grabbed a bottle of small red Bird's Eye dried chillies. He unscrewed the lid, took a handful of the enticing items, and threw them into his mouth. I was dumbfounded because they really are very hot; he completely ignored my protestations.

He began running up and down the store, fanning his mouth, and claiming, "Oh God, they are hot."

I could not stop laughing at his antics and secretly thought he was quite mad. I gave him a tub of cooling plain yoghurt to eat. I liked him and felt I knew him.

He kept coming back to the shop and bragging about all the different girlfriends he was taking out after his divorce. He made me laugh a lot, but I intuitively knew he was deeply unhappy with his life after giving up work as a Company Executive Officer in the commercial business world.

I knew he was capable of bigger thinking than selling goods to shopkeepers. I also 'knew' he did not trust women.

My marriage eventually broke up—it had to be that way; it was already written. It was as if my first husband's wife had died. In actual fact, her soul had left. I felt guilty about the break-up and I tried to ease the family transition with loving care. It was only after I was made aware of the soul exchange taking place within the body that I was able to move forward with an understanding of a larger picture and release the feeling of guilt.

It did not occur to me that John may be interested in me romantically, only as a friend. Then he told me he spent a long time one day walking up and down outside my shop, trying to find courage to walk in the door and invite me on a date. I found this strange because he is such an extrovert and so outwardly confident, striding out as a man does when he knows exactly where he is going.

I was surprised and flattered, because he is a tall, good-looking man, always well dressed, with a wonderful sense of humour. Fun to be around... a ladies' man, I thought, possibly a heartbreaker, and I would never have agreed to go out with him. Except, I had a dream the night before he asked me on that first date. In the dream, I saw myself on a fast rollercoaster at a fun park, travelling up and down. I felt someone put his or her arm around me to protect me, and when I looked to see who it was, I was surprised to see it was John.

I liked the feeling of his arm around me, so we began dating. Our first kiss, while dancing, shook me to the core. I had never met anyone quite like him.

Our dating continued with him introducing me to new and exciting places. I had always longed for a partner who loved to dance, and John was it. He swept me off my feet with gifts and flowers and constant phone calls in between our outings. He made me feel like a queen.

There were a few times he neglected me, dating other women, and my heart would break. I knew he was a ladies' man, didn't I? We even broke up.

My emotions were like a rollercoaster, just like my dream had shown me. I did wonder why I was putting up with it, but another part of me knew all I had to do was to show that he could trust me. He came back, looking very sheepish and sorry. This time, he proposed marriage and as far as I know he has always been true to me.

A few years later we married. John was musing one day about an experience he had when living as a twenty-one-year-old man in Malaya. At that age, he was managing a food company for a United Kingdom operation. He had suffered an attack of malaria; it nearly killed him.

In his words, "I've told you about having a very high fever, hot and cold, soaking wet with the sweat coming off me like you wouldn't want to believe." His eyes closed as he spoke, his beautiful English accent changing as I listened, and I realised he had slipped into an altered state of consciousness, actually re-living the scene. He was living and speaking of a past event in this life as if it were happening in the present.

> *"I am close to death. I am out of my body, sitting in the corner of the ceiling, looking down at my body and seeing the two European doctors shaking their heads. My amah, housemaid, is sitting at the bottom of my bed howling her head off. She believes she is like a surrogate mother to me. That is her choice, not mine. She can be a real pain in the arse at times, when I think about how she vets my girlfriends. Anyway, she*

saves my life, or this life, because the doctors, after shaking their heads, turn and leave.

I can see a white tunnel and relatives who have passed on standing in a bright light, calling me. They are looking healthy now. For some reason, I decide to go back into my body. The white tunnel and the people, who have been deceased in my life, are still standing there. The colours are absolutely phenomenal in this white tunnel.

The relatives are calling, "Come over, come over," but I don't want to. I go back to the body, wracked with pain, I might add.

My amah gives me some black glug in a great, big Chinese bowl and within half an hour the fever breaks. Then I have to recuperate and that's when I go to Pangkor Island.

I get on a Junk boat and travel up the coast, fishing for ten days. The sea captain had heard what happened to me and invites me to join them on their fishing trip. I am in the sunshine all day, dressed only in shorts, and pulling fishing nets out of the sea, day and night, throwing most of the catch into the hold, which is full of dry ice. We eat freshly cooked seafood every day and all I have to contribute are two bottles of Scotch whisky.

After ten days, when we reach the shore, the big guy, Lim I think his name is, calls me over and gives me a fat envelop full of Straits Dollars, saying that it is my share of the catch."

"It was quite a lot of money for those days," said John. His mind had now returned to this reality.

John went on to say, "It had a maturing effect on me. When you are very sick like that, you don't take life for granted anymore. I am not frightened of death."

I asked him, "Do you think you had an exchange of souls at that time, like me?"

He demurred a little, saying, "I know when I did have an exchange, it was not long after we had married and moved to our terrace house in the inner city. I was suffering a fever again and delirious, I was in and out of consciousness and ranting about being a sea captain. You said you asked me questions and received abrupt answers, as if you were a nobody. I can vaguely remember what I looked like in the memory, a bit like Frances Drake or one of his sea captains, and how he wore thigh-length boots, doubloons, and a ruff around his neck.

"It was 1588. I was definitely a 'walk-in' then. I was delirious, but I could remember when we captured the Spanish Admiral the normal thing to do was to dine your enemy. The same way that Wellington dined with Napoleon. Give him dinner and then send him off onto an island for a while. I can still see the huge cross the Spanish Admiral wore around his neck made of amethysts and diamonds."

John wore a short, pointed beard at the time, looking a little like Frances Drake. I had even said to him, "You actually looked like Frances Drake before you shaved off that pointed beard. I remember you talking about fire ships and I wondered what they were."

John clarified, "Fire ships are like barges with straw packed on top of them and covered in pitch and tar. We pushed the fire boats in amongst the Spanish Armada, caught the wind, and as soon as they were in there, we fired grapeshot from a cannon and lit the packed straw.

"Then woomph! Up went all the sails of the Armada and the whole fleet would have been scorched, but they fled up the English Channel for they hoped to catch up with the Duke of Alba's army in Flanders. It didn't materialise. They sailed north and were shipwrecked on the north-west coast of Scotland."

"John, do you know Drake's story from the history books, or...?"

He interrupted. "No, I remember. I remember from being there in what you asked me at the time, what else did I tell you?"

"At the time, you spoke of the smell of powder and shot, you were there. You were actually seeing the action and smelling it. I could tell by the way you were talking and the expressions on your face. You were impatient with me for asking what you thought were silly questions.

"You had your eyes closed in rapid eye movement and yet I could tell you were seeing it all before your inner eye by the way you were reacting and describing what you were seeing. Did you feel you were a different person after that memory?"

John replied, "I felt I was a walk-in then, yes, I think so. My incoming soul must have been talking of a life before in a different body for some reason."

I was immediately sympathetic, "Yes, dear one, I do remember after that past-life memory, you were very upset, crying, and in fact going over your life as you are now, judging yourself badly. It was a soul-searching thing. You were just not my usual John. It was a time when you were very vulnerable. I knew you had changed dramatically..."

John is the kind of man who must always be in control. He is usually purposeful and confident in all of his dealings with people, taking a swashbuckler's cut and thrust approach to business in this life but using words, instead of a sword, to cut through discussion and get to the main point. It was as though after his divorce, he seemed to lose his way for a while, and by that I mean direction in life.

It was not until we united in this life that he was able to find his true self, his confidence again, to continue with business dealings at a consultant level to a CEO and understand his mission in life. He was confident and certainly happier assisting Australian food manufacturers to find lucrative markets in South-East Asia.

I have come to know that a soul exchange can take place not just as a near-death experience, but when you are sick or even overnight while you are asleep.

2 Does a Soul Exist?

I would like to share a story about a soul exchange that took place in front of my eyes.

From time to time, people come to visit me and ask for a healing. On one occasion, a man we will name Jeremy came, feeling very unhappy with his life, having little energy and no will to go on. He had tried many avenues to help himself and he wanted me to just talk with him. I led him into a quiet, advanced meditation and, with his eyes closed, he told me he could see in his inner scene a young man standing beside him who wanted to take over his physical body.

Jeremy said, "I am ready for the exchange to take place, though I am a little worried the new soul is not very experienced and won't look after the body."

Jeremy lay very still, hardly breathing; he looked almost dead. I felt an angelic presence over-light my body and gently lift his soul up through the top of his head, back to the World of Light. As I watched, I clairvoyantly saw the new soul come into the top of his head and climb into Jeremy's body as if he was putting on a body suit.

Stretching his legs, then his arms, he ran his hand and fingers over his woollen jumper and the hairs on his arms under the jumper, as if he was feeling the sensations for the first time. His eyes were still closed. I assisted him to sit upright and asked him to remain quiet while I moved away to bring him a drink of water to help 'ground' him into this world.

As I returned with the glass of water, I was startled to see Jeremy standing on his head in the middle of the room, with his legs crossed above his head, yoga fashion. I asked him, "Have you ever done this before, Jeremy?"

He simply replied, "No." He jumped up and began running around the room excitedly. He was a different personality. He wanted to go for a swim in the pool outside and even run down the grass slope to the dam and jump in. It was all I could do to stop him; it was winter and far too cold for swimming. He was, as has been described, a younger soul and not so experienced in life here.

Soul exchange without permission!

While I am talking about soul exchange *with* permission, I would like to speak of a soul exchange I know took place without permission from the Karmic Board in the World of Light. You could call it *body snatching*. A friend of ours—we shall call her Shirley—had a young niece who, as a young teenager, was caught up in taking illegal drugs. These are the pitfalls that followed.

Shirley and her husband had felt the young girl, Marjorie, was in trouble while her parents were overseas. So, following their intuition, they travelled to the Sydney to find her—and find her they did.

Marjorie was sharing a grimy, dishevelled house in the middle of the city, with three unhealthy young men who were heavily into heroin and '*shooting up*', as the saying goes. My friends were extremely worried about her, as Marjorie had admitted to using some of their contaminated needles. Contracting Aids was, of course, a big fear.

Shirley and her husband managed to coax her to come and live with them in the Southern Highlands, while Marjorie only agreed to move if she could bring her boyfriend. He was also heavily into drugs and, as my friends soon found out, had a police history and was visited regularly by his probation officer.

The aunt and uncle put up with him being in their house for their young niece's sake, quietly praying he would soon leave, especially when they had to put their foot down and demand he was not to 'shoot up' while in their house. Eventually, the girl lost interest in the boyfriend and confided she did not want him around anymore. This was great news to our friends. So, when the 'boyfriend' complained about her lack of attention he was advised it was probably best if he left. To their great relief, he reluctantly departed.

Marjorie then began to make a normal life for herself, with a good job and regular money to pay off a car. Her parents eventually returned from overseas and she moved back to the city to live with them. On Marjorie's twenty-first birthday, we were invited to the birthday party, where we met a new man in her life. He was learning to fly an airplane and taking her on joy flights. We were all very happy and relieved she seemed to be pulling her life back together again; they were planning to marry soon.

I was sitting musing about this experience at the party when a 'voice' spoke to me from someone standing behind me. When I turned around, nobody was there. I realised it was a spirit speaking to me, saying, "He is not nice, you know." I knew the spirit was referring to Marjorie's new boyfriend.

My startled question to the spirit was, "Why?" I was advised the original soul in his body had not been able to return after a drug overdose while being treated in hospital. It gets a little complicated in the telling. The new soul in the young man's body was actually a soul who had 'jumped' into the body while it was in a vulnerable state.

In other words, he had stolen the body without permission from The Source. There is a Karmic Board that operates in the transitional worlds, overviewing souls leaving our body and returning to the World of Light.

That same Karmic Board monitors all souls who sojourn in an Earth body from its birth until its death. To explain further, Marjorie's father had accidentally died from an overdose of drugs and alcohol when she was only a little girl. He was what is known as a lost soul or a ghost and had been hanging around in the Astral, the next world of ether. He was trying to cause mischief between Marjorie's mother and the new husband. They joked about the chandelier rattling when they were in bed, not really taking the experience very seriously.

The lost, unhappy soul continued to 'hang around' and later began trying to entice his daughter to kill herself so that he could have her company in his lost world. He was actually making suggestions to her with his voice, advising how she could take her own life. He was influencing her to 'try drugs' and nearly succeeded in ending her life.

This influence was always experienced by Marjorie as a voice in her head telling her to do certain things. She really didn't understand where the voice was coming from, but rather she was confused into believing it was some part of herself. Sadly, on a joy flight with her boyfriend, piloting the airplane in bad weather, it crashed into a mountain, killing both of them.

My friend Shirley sought advice from a competent medium as to what really happened. The medium was able to 'see' Marjorie leave the small airplane in her spirit, just before it crashed. Marjorie, in spirit, waited for the spirit of her friend to be released from his body after the airplane crashed. She took him by the hand and gently guided him back to the World of Light. In doing so, she saved him from being a *lost soul* and from his continuing unhappiness, anger, and severe loneliness.

You could well say Marjorie gave up her life to save another soul. Her diary was found after her death with beautiful poems and a request that when she died, she would like the church to be filled to overflowing with flowers. At some higher level of consciousness within her, she had committed to playing out this very sad Earth life drama to save her father's soul.

Voices in the Night

3

How I first began working so closely with *Upstairs*, and by that I mean spirit, was with a voice asking me to, "Stand up". I am in an altered state of consciousness to describe how it happened.

"It is dark, 3am in the morning, and I am confused, having just awakened. I do as I am asked and get out of bed, looking around, half expecting to see the shadow of someone. The strange thing is I am not afraid, although I wouldn't take any notice if I didn't feel right about it. Then I am told to, "Go back to bed." No sooner have I settled when I hear the voice again.

"Stand up," the same voice commands me. So out I get again, surprised and wondering what on Earth is going on?

Then I am told to, "Go back to bed," for a second time.

"Stand up," the same voice commands, yet a third time. I am beginning to worry how long this is going to go on for. Anxiously, I think, "What if John is to wake and want to know what I am doing? How can I say a voice keeps telling me to 'stand up' and I have no idea why or where the voice is coming from?"

The voice asks me to keep paper and pen beside my bed and, from now on, I will be awakened and given messages from time to time. Then I am told to, "Go back to bed." As I lie quietly still in the dark, thinking about all sorts of things and possibilities, a different little tantalising voice begins to mock me, "stand up, stand up, stand up," which is quickly interjected with that commanding voice again saying, "stop that, Valérie, that is your dilly brain talking."

Immediately, with one swoop, I sense my brain is separate from this other consciousness I was listening to, which was either an aspect of me or a separate disembodied voice. Realisation sweeps over me; that voice, the commanding one, is the same voice that spoke to me when I briefly died and was told I could stay on Earth. I had made a deal with God then, and now I was being called three times to stand up for God. It is a calling. My mission has begun. I feel a strong sense of joy, a sort of 'at last' feeling, and full of expectancy.

A little too soon, it would seem, for the very next night I am awakened by the same voice and asked to start writing. I begin to write as I hear the words, "The end of the world is nigh!" Eeeeeeek! I freak out and throw the pad down. I am thinking I don't want any part of this. Realisation again sweeps over, comforting me, and I feel persuaded to continue writing. "The end of the world is nigh, as you know it."

Hopefully that means it will get better, you know—no wars, world peace instead. People respecting each other regardless of culture, religion, or skin colour, and sharing so that there will be no want or suffering anywhere.

Up until now, I am so confused about what is happening I have not spoken about it to John or anyone else for that matter. I am awakened from time to time, just like *the voice* says. This voice is my teacher, a real person in spirit just like me although I cannot see him with my Earth eyes. I am being taught basic physics, chemistry, and biology, something I have missed in my education. "Everything is energy," he teaches me. "The Earth is made up of four basic elements. Earth, fire, air, water." The sound of the word 'ether' keeps popping into my head.

It doesn't take long for me to understand it is possible to walk through walls if you can see through atoms, which are mostly space, and that manifestations can take place just by manipulating the atoms or cells. In fact, if I could learn how, I could manifest anything I needed. It is the Earth body that is limited because of its heavier quality; it's denser energy.

Upstairs showed me they could send messages to capture my attention. For example, when I was cooking breakfast for my family, I broke four eggs into a non-stick frypan and found they were all double yolks. I thought it was strange and when I looked at the egg basket there were four more eggs left.

So, I broke those into the pan as well and they were all double yolks eggs also. That meant I had eight double yolk eggs, sixteen yellow eggs looking back at me from the frypan. Statistically, the odds for that happening would run off the page! It was a 'sign' and would mean more to me as my learning progressed.

Another morning, between three and four am, while I was writing and being prompted to look up things, John wandered into my office, bleary eyed and wanting to know what I was doing. So, I told him, as best as I could. I explained how I was being prompted to look up the meaning of a word in the Oxford Dictionary, Australian edition.

As the derivation jumped out at me, the meaning of one word seemed to stand out from other words. I was then prompted to look up that word, then another, leading on from that. I was amazed at how I was being educated. That same day, John came home with a gift of three little pocket books for me. Physics, chemistry, and biology. It was obvious my beloved was going to support me on my journey. I felt truly happy as I thanked him, kissed him, and embraced him, feeling secure and content in my mission.

"John, last night I was awakened yet again and given a message I would travel to Indonesia. They said I knew it well and I had travelled there a thousand years ago. While *they* were giving me the message, I had a distinct feeling I was a male Tibetan Buddhist monk. I could even feel his heavier legs, with rope kind of sandals on his feet, and a simple rough, yellowish cloth tunic brushing around his strong calves. I could see myself writing Tibetan calligraphy backwards on the page of whatever the paper was and I just knew you were a brother monk travelling with us. It feels strange for me to remember being a man. Anyhow, does it ring a bell with you?"

"No, not really," he says slowly. "Although I'm attracted to the philosophy of Buddhism." Then, with some enthusiasm in his voice, he adds, "I can't get over the fact that it's only today I have made bookings for a business trip to Indonesia, Malaya, and Thailand. I want you to come with me to Indonesia this trip. A client living in Djakarta has offered us his van, driver, and bodyguard so that we can tour around central Java. I wanted to surprise you, it should be interesting."

I did not need any persuasion.

Upstairs had the night before given me the message I would be going. I wonder if they have put the idea in John's head in the first place or...? Oh, it is a little too much to try and figure out at times. It is best just to flow with it and let it unfold.

Journey to Central Java, Indonesia

It seems no time at all before we are alighting from the flight from Sydney to Djakarta, the heat and humidity making our clothes stick to our bodies. We have been shown by our host, John's business associate, to our air-conditioned vehicle with driver and bodyguard, who are to take us on our journey around Central Java.

We are driven into the country, which is green and moist. I do not see as many people as I expected, considering the country has something like a hundred and fifty million people. The island of Java is the world's most densely populated region in the world. It was the centre of Hindu-Buddhism until overtaken by Islam. A chain of volcanic mountains forms a spine along the island.

We drive out of the capital city, Djakarta, to the volcano outside of Lembang. It has been quite a climb in the van and an interesting walk to the top through dense tropical undergrowth. When at the top, we can look down to a still, simmering crater, steaming and bubbling, as if cooking a grey-like soup, and giving off noxious sulphurous odours. We cannot stay for long. John is impressed with how ancient everything feels but is not impressed with the odious smell of sulphur that he says, "Smells like God has just farted."

Driving back to sea level, we continue travelling through lush, green flat lands and misty rice fields. High mountains rise straight up from the ground like Egyptian pyramids. The farmers are happy and busy, but nowhere do I feel I know the country well. But it is vaguely familiar and the people are friendly.

What had Upstairs meant by saying I had known it a thousand years ago?

Our journey continues to Bandung, Tasikmalaya, Temanggung. It is only when driving into Yogyakarta I begin to sense an excitement of familiarity. The city is still ruled by a royal family. The people around Yogya look different, very dignified, aristocratic, even those riding pushbikes and trishaws. Their hands are long fingered and elegant. Their expressions look serene. This more than anywhere is the city of gamelan music, of classical court dance, antiques, and colourful batik dressed wooden puppets used for theatre.

I feel at home here—I have known it before.

While staying at Yogyakarta, we rise early to be driven forty kilometres to Borobudur, one of the world's greatest Buddhist monuments built sometime between 778 and 842 A.D., three hundred years before Cambodia's Angkor Wat and four hundred years before work had begun on the great European cathedrals of Amiens, Koln, Chartres, and Rheims.

During restoration and clearing of undergrowth in 1907, it was found the structure of Borobudur was merely a casing of un-mortared stone, completely enclosing a natural hillock. The earth hillock underneath was beginning to collapse and the monument of five hundred and four Buddha statues, seventy-two of which are in trellised smaller stupas, were on the edge of destruction. It was not until 1983, after nine years of intensive restoration, that Borobudur was once again restored to its original condition when built over twelve-hundred years before.

John and I are aware of a feeling of reverence, a sacred place of prayer, hanging in the misty air; it feels as though we are walking into a saintly church. The morning sun has not yet arisen, but the cool light is enough for us to see our way.

The square base of the huge stupa rises like a pyramid more than thirty metres high and one-hundred-and-twenty-three metres wide. Both of us are lost in our own thoughts as we begin to climb the ancient stone stairs.

I become lost in another time.

I realise I have entered into an altered state of consciousness. I know I am with John, but I am experiencing a different conscious reality altogether.

In my altered state of awareness, there are no longer any tourists to be seen. I can still see the un-mortared stone walls heavily carved in pictorial relief, depicting the doctrine of cause and effect of good and evil, and as we move higher the pictorial stories of the life of Siddhartha Guatama unfolds his eight-fold path to enlightenment. Winding up from the base of the monument into galleries one can walk along, paths are ever climbing to the top.

Experiencing from my inner sight, I can see my feet are now clothed in rope sandals and I can feel the rough, yellowish cloth brushing my strong, dark-skinned calves. My brother monks are behind me, softly chanting in deep resonating male voices and I know John is one of them. We are here on a pilgrimage. The steps leading to the Sphere of Formlessness are climbed and we walk to the peak where there is no longer any distance between heaven and Earth.

I am experiencing a memory of being here as a Tibetan Buddhist monk a thousand years before, just as the voice from *Upstairs* has told me I would remember and that I knew the people here from a time long ago.

When we return to Djakarta, John suggests we visit the markets on the outskirts of the city. The stalls and shops are a treasure trove of antiques and curios to tantalise one's desires; John loves buying things.

"Hey Valli," he calls, excited about something. I turn towards him as he lifts a small ancient Tibetan temple bell. John is holding a round, wooden stick in his other hand and, as he rubs it around the base of the temple bell, the long deep humming resonance of an Om sound rings out. In that moment, I slip into an altered state of consciousness. I am again taken back in my soul memory a thousand years before.

The past-life memory flashes by quite quickly. I can hear my brother monks moaning and suffering. I feel a terrible pain in my heart, even though I am suffering the same torture, as they all are, in their stomachs. I feel responsible for leading them to this end.

We have continued our journey after Borobudur and have taken the teachings of Buddha into the countryside throughout what is now South-East Asia.

We travelled by boat to Japan and are now captured by the Bushido. We are not welcome. We are tortured by disembowelling; our captors eat some of the bowel so that they do not have any karma to pay back. They believe they have taken on our spirit and now own it.

I can see our executioner dressed in a calf-length white cotton-belted coat, his head shaved, except for a black ponytail of hair coming from the top of his head. He is about to swing his body, holding in both hands a large scythe-like sword. A scimitar.

His face shows total focus and determination at what he is aiming at. We are in Osaka. Not long after, one by one, we are all beheaded. Briefly, I have returned to my soul memory to witness our then execution.

I am shaken by this memory and have a need to sit down for a while. John hastens to buy water for me, and I explain what I saw. My physical body in this life carries a light brown birthmark shaped like a jagged cut at the side of my stomach. It appeared only after my soul walked into this body.

John and I fly out of Indonesia; he travels on to Malaysia and Thailand, and I return home on a separate flight to Australia to await his return from business.

5

John Returns from Overseas – Moving House

John loves entertaining; it is something he has done in many lifetimes.

Our circular Chinese carved rosewood dinner table is set for eight people. Tall wine glasses, glowing bronze candlesticks with candles alight, and shiny bronze cutlery are set on our new rustic-coloured Indonesian Batik tablecloth. John has cooked a delicious curry, giving off a tantalising aroma. Any moment, everyone will arrive. He cannot wait to tell our guests about our adventures in Central Java. Most of our guests are business associates with their wives, but not all are well travelled.

I am still consumed with the wonder of my past-life stuff and trying to make up my mind if I dare speak of it, especially when I remember being a man. Not everyone accepts the continuity of life after life, after life ad infinitum. Yet I am aware the memory has released me in some way, although I still need time to integrate the experience. I feel freer, not so limited in my thinking.

Our guests are seated comfortably and in no time at all, John with a grin has everyone laughing about the time he was pestered by the young Javanese boy wanting to clean his thongs. "I relented," he says. "Quick as a wink the kid returned my thongs polished jet black, like a guardsmen's bloody boot."

John's mood changes to seriousness. "Do you remember Valli, it was where we travelled along the North Coast of Java? It was dry, barren, very built up there, and the unbelievable poverty. The people looked like they were starving. A stark contrast to how green it was on the other side of the island with a lot of healthy agriculture."

John fills a few wine glasses and continues. "The Buddhist monument at Borobudur is extraordinary. We went early in the morning. It was shrouded in a mist. It was quite mystical, actually, pardon the pun! Valli keeps telling me I have been there before in another life, as a monk. I don't remember, but I saw our old friend looking a bit like a monk, the one we had seen on the mountain when we visited Bali the year before. He was just hanging around and watching us from a distance. We both stopped and waved, he just nodded his head and smiled at us. To this day, I don't know why we didn't walk over to speak to him."

John was on a roll. "I realise now he was a hantu, a Malaysian ghost, not an Earth person. Maybe in a way he was just showing himself to us, I'm with you or something."

I interjected and without thinking say, "Maybe he is the one that keeps waking me at night." Our guests all looked at me quizzically.

John rolls on, "You know the Indonesians and Malaysians believe even trees are people. The Bomos are like Shamans, but they can be dangerous. I remember when I had a girlfriend in Malaya. I had broken it off with her and not long after I became very ill, aches and pains all over my body. The doctor didn't know what was wrong, but my Kebun, Malaysian gardener, dug up an effigy of me from my garden with bloody needles stuck all the way through it. The Malaysian girlfriend had been in there and buried it. She had obviously been to see the Bomo and got him to put a spell on me. These things aren't to be played with, you know."

Nearly everyone leans forward, asking at the same time, "How did you remove the spell, John?"

"By picking the doll up, pulling the needles out, and burning the bloody thing."

One lady asks, "Did you feel any anger or fear towards her?"

"Nope," then changes his mind. "Well, fear yes, if someone could do that to you. If she had stuck the needle through the heart, I could have had a heart attack."

The dinner conversation moves on to a discussion about the history of Hinduism, Buddhism, and Islam and their teachings over historical time, throughout South-East Asia. I am not ready to tell our guests that a voice awakens me at night and teaches me. Nor am I ready to talk about my Tibetan past-life memory; it is too new to me. So, I expand on my belief that John had been to Borobudur a thousand years ago.

I challenge John by saying, "When we visited a local Buddhist monastery once here in the Southern Highlands, for a vegetarian lunch, we attended a meditation first. The monk led us into a meditation and you went off into a space all of your own for about an hour or more. People spend years trying to learn how to enter into that state of peace and focus. John, you would have had to be drawing from an ability you learned in a life before. Probably when you were that Tibetan Buddhist monk."

"Hmm, that's possible." Then changing the subject, he adds, "I have to tell you we had been to a temple and seen a Yoni and a Linga, which is in fact carved stone totems to sexuality. The Yoni represents the female vagina and the Linga represents the male penis. Men and women pray to the fertility Goddess and adorn the stones with flowers. Later, we happened to pass by a Colonel Sanders Fried Chicken outlet and I guess in Indonesia it is `Linga lookin' good', rather than 'Finger licken good.' My husband chuckles with a twinkle in his eye as he laughs.

Our guests leave. It has been a happy evening and as we are clearing the dishes, John and I discuss our idea of moving to the country now that his son and my three sons have all left home.

We have already considered moving for some time, although John is a little afraid it will be too difficult connecting to his clients.

As I have said, his role is to assist Australian food manufacturers to find export markets for their products in South-East Asia. We decide that as it is Sunday, the next day we should drive to the Southern Highlands, an area six-hundred-and-ninety metres above sea level, and visit the real estate agents. We love the European gardens and the division of four seasons; it even snows there occasionally.

With some sense of excitement, we set off next day to explore. We stop at the first agent as we drive into the area and are taken to a few houses for a look-see. We nearly end in an argument for what

John thinks is good, I don't like and what I think is good, he does not like. As I have said, he likes to be in control, so if I appear to rock the boat with a different point of view, he has some difficulty in adjusting to my non-agreement.

We are finally taken to a leafy street, with a brick house and a swimming pool, enough bedrooms for city visitors, a cosy-looking fire, and a pretty garden that attracts both of us. We agree, this is the one.

Our agent later negotiates a good deal for us, as we are not ready to move in. The owners are building next door, so, with a delayed settlement written into our purchase contract it is easy for them to finish building and to make their eventual move. This suits us perfectly. We strongly sense we can see and feel there is an unseen hand at work to bring all of this so quickly together for us and that *Upstairs* is putting thoughts into our agent's head to help it all happen.

Six months later, we move out of the city to the country.

A Green Crystal – Moving House Again!

6

In earlier days, when we first moved to the country, I was awakened from a deep sleep and asked by a voice from *Upstairs* to find a green crystal. I thought that was strange, as I had never seen a green crystal. Always dutiful to my spiritual guidance, I decided to travel to Sydney on other errands but also with the intention to call into a well-established 'Esoteric Bookshop' where crystals were sold.

Upon arriving at the shop, I asked the owners if they had any green crystals. To my surprise they presented to me a tray of smallish green crystals they called a Moldavite glass stone. I was advised it was actually a tektite that came from outer space and was only found near the Moldau River in Czechoslovakia.

I gazed at the tray of stones, with one catching my eye as if it was saying, "Pick me, pick me." As I lifted the small stone toward me, I was overcome with a blinding white light and a strong male spirit voice saying, "*You are going home*." Going home? What on Earth was he talking about? Did he mean I was going to die? I was shaking badly from just touching the tektite and had to sit down.

The shopkeeper, concerned about my reaction, ushered me to a chair. She suggested I lie on a massage table in another room until I recovered and said, "It's not the first time someone has had a reaction to these Moldavite stones." It took about an hour to steady myself.

I was told the stone was seventeen carats, which equals eight, and the cost added to eight that equals double eight, so I considered that to be a sign and decided to buy it. I still could not touch the stone. The understanding shopkeeper put it in a box and placed it into my handbag.

It was several weeks before I could actually hold it, introducing the energy of the stone to myself slowly—touching it briefly with one finger only would give a slight electric jolt—until it felt comfortable for me to hold the stone in my hand.

My research advises that the Moldavite stone is also known as the 'Grail stone' or 'Starborn stone'. Scientists say millions of years ago there was a meteorite shower and this rare, bottle-green crystal was the result. It belongs to a group of tektites, which are fragments of extra-terrestrial objects, such as meteorites, and the ensuing melted combination with terrestrial rocks when they crashed to earth.

Moldavite is named for an area of Czechoslovakia where a large crater field was discovered. They are among the rarest minerals on Earth, rarer than diamonds, emeralds, or rubies and prized by humans for thousands of years. According to legend, the clear, deep green stone in the Holy Grail was Moldavite and anyone who touches the 'Grail stone' will have a spiritual transformation. *Did the ancients know something that has since been forgotten, before we remembered the source of the Moldavite? I will explain further on in the book.*

Coming back to the early days of first moving to the Southern Highlands, I was invited to sit in meditation with two other women every week. Helen, a kindly Austrian-born lady, is a medium who channelled messages and was gifted in being able to give 'edited' readings of past lives. Every week, we were taught many things and given a past-life reading.

As Helen spoke, we could connect to the energy of what we were hearing about a past life and in so doing we seemed to heal or gain knowledge. There is no doubt exploring past lives in an altered state of consciousness increases one's psychic ability. Helen said to me that she hadn't read so many lives before shared by the same husband and wife. That was John and I. Some of the past-life memories involved the three of us, Helen, Julie, who is a New Zealand lass, and myself, and even sometimes John.

It was during these meetings that my mentor, the one who had been waking me in the night and teaching me so many things, over-lighted my body and slid me gently off my chair. I found myself sitting crossed legged on the floor, a posture I normally cannot do. He began speaking through me. I thus became an instrument, in which a number of beings of light at various times have spoken through me.

As I have said before, my whole demeanour changes, it is no longer me, and usually it is a male sounding voice that gives the message, sometimes female. My mentor advises they present themselves this way in a little 'play of theatre' to show spirit light bodies exist. It is direct voice channelling mediumship.

I still remember that first day. It was the light being known as 'White Eagle' from the White Brotherhood who spoke through me. I was moved to tears knowing it was something I was meant to do. He advised me that names were not important; *what was important* was recognising the feel of the energy that came in through the back of my neck to borrow my voice box, so to speak.

By that time, we had moved house again—to a hundred acre property in Canyonleigh, still in the Southern Highlands. When I arrived home, I was overwhelmed with the colour of the day becoming golden with three rainbows forming in the valley, but it had not been raining. An eagle, always a sign of sacredness, was circling high above me.

My friend Helen had given us another past-life reading when 'White Eagle' had presented himself through her at one of our earlier meetings. He made it known that he spent a life on Earth as an American Indian Chief; he had a son known as 'Eagle Eye'. When White Eagle left his body, he used to come in spirit and speak through his son, giving messages and advice to members of his tribe. I had been that son and here, now, I was having the same ability given to me in this life.

In the next few weeks, I gained more memory of that life and saw the Great Indian Chief wearing a full headdress of feathers trailing down his back to the ground. It was a wonderfully happy life, with our tribe fully appreciating with respect the natural flora and fauna surrounding us.

Our philosophy was to see God in everything. I could see again the very high snow-covered mountains and beautifully clear turquoise-coloured lakes dotted inside tall, dark green pine-scented forests. When it snowed it was so quiet, so pristine, and so sacred.

Eagle Eye had his heart set on winning the heart of an attractive member of the tribe. She wore the typical dress of fringed short skirt, high boots, and laced bodice, all made from soft animal skin. Her hair was black, long past her hips, and surrounding her face. The tribe called her 'The Wild One', but Eagle Eye thought he could tame her, the same way you tamed wild horses.

Sadly, after they married, she hated being in a physical body and eventually died, wasting away from depression. I was very upset to know of this past life as 'Eagle Eye' and profusely apologised to my husband John, who in that life was 'The Wild One' and my wife. He thought it was a big joke. *Upstairs* advised he has not had many past lives as a woman.

So, returning to my storytelling, and as I have said before, we were living at Canyonleigh on a hundred acres of land, high on the edge of a beautiful valley, in the Southern Highlands. We had decided to name the property 'Alcheringa' after an Australian edition of the Oxford Dictionary had fallen off my writing desk.

As I picked it up, my eye caught the word 'alcheringa', one of the few Aboriginal Dreamtime words in the book meaning 'Golden Age' and 'when the first ancestors were created.' I thought how like the word 'alchemy' the next entry was. Afterwards, we came to know the area was a sacred place of healing waters and a meeting place for the indigenous people before white man came.

'Alcheringa', Canyonleigh, NSW, Australia

7

This is where I was trained in 'direct voice channelling' mediumship. I was still in shock after John had decided a few years earlier that we needed a property to use as a tax deduction. We had intended to develop agriculture, build a house, and employ a manager to operate it. The plan all seemed to be carried away.

The estate agent, showing us the land before we bought it, said, "Well, you will be wanting to sell your other house in town."

I quickly said, "No."

But John said, "Well, if a person wants to buy at the right price, we would consider selling."

Before I knew it, our house was sold and we were facing the prospect of beginning to establish a small farm. It meant building a house and organising water, electricity, telephone, and sewerage outlets on the property. It would be a major task.

In the early days, there was no garbage collection or nearby shop. Fortunately, our youngest son came to help us; it worked well for him, as he wanted to live and work in the building industry in the country. He has gone on to marry a beautiful girl inside and out and built an attractive house in the next village to us, and they have given us four gorgeous grandchildren. Our eldest son has come to assist us at another time and stayed in the area for awhile. The two middle boys contributed their share of work when visiting on weekends.

Looking back, we can see we were *set up* by spirit to move out here. There is no such thing as a 'coincidence' but rather a 'coordinated incidence'. We have grown to love the brilliant rainbows that drop close into the paddock. We are amazed at the extraordinarily exciting thunder and lightning storms that move back and forth, magnetised by the iron stone underground.

This display can happen even without rain falling. The deep valley is often lost in a long white cloud. The sunsets and sunrises are breathtaking. The land abounds with wildlife—kangaroos; wombats; ring-tailed possums; emus; echidnas; a few snakes; spiders; colourful birds, including king parrots and kookaburras; and native flowers.

We purchased the land in 1988. It took another year to prepare it and build our house on a hill, with a swimming pool at the front overlooking our green rainforest valley.

When we moved in, as a huge welcome (it was an Easter Sunday) we were blessed with an exquisite sunset of brilliant colour and a golden glow of light everywhere. That golden light continued to visit us from time to time, looking like a scene from the film 'The Wizard of Oz' and making me want to burst into song: '*Somewhere over the Rainbow*'. We had not even hung our curtains on the big bay windows when I was awakened one night from a restless sleep, enough to drive John into another room to watch television. A voice had said, "*Wake up, Val. Focus on the sky, you are going to see a UFO!*"

Unidentified Flying Object? What on Earth were they talking about? As I lay on the bed, looking out at the sky and trying to regain my wits, a huge, round, and silent shadow came over the top of the house. I jumped out of bed and could not believe what I was seeing. It was as large as two football fields and round, surrounded in white lights and a few coloured ones.

I had the distinct feeling I was being watched. Well, they had just awakened me to say I was going to see them. I wanted to call out to John, but no words would come, and I didn't want to take my eyes away from what I was seeing. The UFO sailed on into the horizon above Katoomba, by then looking like a large golden disc, and disappeared. Up until then, I had not taken much notice of the thought of extra-terrestrial people.

It brought to mind an experience I had in the early days of my paranormal activity when I visited a clairvoyant. As soon as I walked in the door, she exclaimed, "Oh my God, you have aliens all around you." I didn't understand.

About a week later, I saw a paper image of a white alien face, with large black eyes, a small nose, no ears, and a pointed chin, pasted on many large square cement blocks that are garbage containers all over the city of Sydney. The entrepreneur who posted them was promoting Whitley Strieber's book and visit to Australia. At the same time, I found myself looking at his book cover with the alien face, named '*Communion, A True Story*.'

I began shaking in fear, just looking at the alien face, and told myself I was being ridiculous. To face that unreasonable fear, I purchased a copy of the book and took it home. I read it and experienced all the fear that Whitley Strieber wrote about. His full understanding had not come about until he sought help from a hypnotherapist. I decided to seek help also.

Sitting in the therapist' chair as the session began, I saw myself in my altered state of consciousness laying on a table under a huge operating light, the same as you see in a hospital operating theatre. I began to shake with terror.

I could see the small beings with the same alien faces moving around me, and some taller beings in white robes. Telepathically, they told me I had agreed to give genetic material to their race and that it was a two-year initiation period. I was so scared I pulled myself out of the memory and announced to the therapist, "I do not want to know any more." I gave it no further thought until I was awakened by the voice asking me to see the UFO.

White Eagle awakened me during the night, usually when John was away, so that I felt I was being visited like the film '*Ghost of Mrs. Muir*'. I was asked to place a tape into my recorder and White Eagle would then over-light my body and practice using my voice box.

He would prance around, incorporating my body, throwing my arms about, and although I was unable to see him, I certainly could feel his presence. He made me laugh a lot and I wondered if I could tell John without him freaking out or even rejecting me. When I think about it, if John had seen my antics, without understanding what was happening and not hearing the telepathic conversation, he would have thought I was quite mad.

Within that same year, White Eagle awakened me one night and said, "I would like to speak with your husband." My stomach churned and thought *how am I going to do this?* At least I had told my husband what had been happening when he was away overseas.

So...I took a deep breath and gently woke John, hoping fervently he would not go into shock and reject me when hearing a male-sounding voice come out of me.

At first, he was not co-operative. I suggested that White Eagle wake John first on another night, and then we could do the communication work.

In the meantime, one day I called John for dinner and as he sat down his arms shot up into the air and he exclaimed, "*I am White Eagle.*" Waggling his fingers, he added, "*And my fingers are feathers.*"

I was not only surprised but dumbfounded, although not enough that I could not ask White Eagle telepathically, "*What is happening*?"

White Eagle responded with a voice inside my ear and replied, "*Your husband is always so busy I thought I would catch him just before he started to eat.*"

After some considerable silence and with his eyes still closed John said, "I have just been taken on a quick overview of the development of the ancient Americas." It was obvious John and I were communicating with the same mentor, White Eagle.

About a week later, John had been having alcoholic drinks and was more relaxed. During the night, he woke me and said, "I think White Eagle wants to speak with me."

He was still a little nervous, but drinking a cup of coffee helped. I settled into mediumship mode with an audiotape switched on to invite White Eagle to make his entrance. This is one of the few communications that has taken place between them through me.

On fifteenth January 1991, a meeting took place at Canyonleigh the day before the first war in Iraq commenced.

White Eagle began speaking in a deep male voice, *"Evening, John."*

John replied, "Evening."

"I thank you for allowing me to come at this hour and I am sorry to disturb you both, but I do wish to speak to you about certain things. I hope I am welcomed."

"You are welcome," John replied.

"As I have said before, I would come from time to time and I thought we had agreed that it would be all right. However, I understand that you have been tired and overworked and so I do appreciate you welcoming me now.

"The time in the world is becoming very difficult. As you know, there will be war, I am afraid, but at this time it will not last for all that long. It will be terminated rather quickly. However, the harm that will have been done will smoulder and that will create in some years a greater war that will start and it will affect all those on Earth but for the moment it will be contained, and I say this because we have a plan we have talked about and monies coming your way that will help us to achieve our plan. That plan will entail some travelling, which I hope you will be willing to do."

John grunts.

"You will be free of your responsibilities, in that monies that you owe will not be any longer and so we hope that you will be willing to work a little closer with us. While I am speaking about this, I am wondering if you have anything you wish to ask? If there has been anything on your mind that you wish to ask about?"

"No, not really...I'm listening to what you tell me."

"Do you feel you have been making contact with me in your mind?"

"Possibly."

"That is good you are now aware, it saves time. If you become aware and just follow, it is what all must do. All those who live on this Earth dimension, all those who tune in to the higher understanding and knowledge and just follow, that is good."

"You say to me that I will need to travel. Travel to do what?"

"There will be some research into past lives. There will also be a search for certain documents that have been hidden for a long, long time and these documents will be brought forth. Knowledge may be given to those who live on this Earth from the very beginning, because this manuscript exists. It will be evidence and they will know then and understand, but this will develop as time goes on. It does not sound much, but I can assure you the reaction that comes from it will be very great. You will be guided. Now do you feel that you would like to be involved in this?"

"Yes, but what manuscript? What document? I don't understand."

"It is writings that I myself have made in a period a number of thousand years ago when I incarnated as John the Divine on this Earth, and they were meant to be hidden until a certain point in time in this dimension. That point is now coming into being. My instructions at that time were to hold the knowledge back and to contain it at some place, and those that worked with me at that time assisted in it being hidden and so they hold still that knowledge as to where it is and it is they that we hope will uncover it."

"Yes, well, what does this knowledge achieve? I am sorry I don't understand."

"It is knowledge of the beginnings of the Earth peoples on this Earth and those that visited from the stars and, like I said, the manuscript itself holds much power and it will be recognised straight away. So, rather than just talk about it and try to explain it, once you see it and feel its energy that knowledge will come."

"I still don't understand what this energy and power is that you referred to, I mean, how can it affect mankind?"

"I understand, this is something that comes in experiencing. I really mention it because it is one of the things, in fact, it will be one of the most important things, that will be achieved when we travel and so if we can allow that to unfold, I am saying this because it is one of the reasons that we wish you to travel. Among the other things is research into past lives, so that we can create a kind of book, perhaps even a video or a film and people can think about and wonder because there will be others travelling and they will be from what we call a 'Group Soul', a group of people that have

incarnated at the same time and have known each other down through the ages, having incarnated at various periods along the way. A lot of people will find this quite fascinating and, because of the truth that goes behind it and from the experience of those that speak about it, they will feel the truth in it. For this reason, it is one of teaching and we hope will open up new understanding in many. Does this sound as if it could happen?"

"Possibly—I really don't know—to me at the moment it is a riddle...Hhm!"

"It is a riddle, it is a riddle, it is like a jigsaw puzzle and as a little piece by piece is put together it unfolds a very large picture, which of course is what we say is our plan. Each little piece of the puzzle, when put together, does come into a large picture and that is why we do not like to have too many pieces of the puzzle emerge all at once, otherwise the picture may become a little distorted. I wanted you to know a little of our plan just for understanding's sake.

"I also wanted to reassure you that this war at the moment will not last very long. Although, unfortunately, there will be lives lost. We are there and ready and there are people of yours that will move from this dimension back into the World of Light and we have many there to assist their passage and, of course, the lives left on Earth is really only one of transition. They will come back to their beginnings, so you must not feel too sad about it. It is all part of evolution.

"They will be assisted and helped, and they will be alright, and by that I mean both sides. All peoples on this Earth, because they are lost in water, do become confused and they forget, but once they are free of their physical bodies they start to remember and so it is much easier to assist them. Do you have any questions about this, John?"

"No. We will see what happens." (*The war in Iraq had not yet begun but started soon after.)*

"That is good. I have been saying for quite a while now that monies are coming your way and I can assure you that that time is becoming very close. So, this will assist you and I wish to reassure you that the promise has not been forgotten. It is just that the time

was not quite right, but it will come, very soon, and for this reason I have come here tonight just to remind you and to reaffirm your commitment on the understanding that this money comes forth. Once that happens, we hope that you will be very willing to work with us. As I have said, it seems to be the best time to come to speak and to work with you, although it is a little difficult to rouse oneself, I understand that, but I do hope that you will be willing to work with us. We appreciate that, John."

"I can work with you providing I know what I'm working at..."

White Eagle chuckles, *"I understand, I understand, and that is the need for me to come from time to time, so that we can work step by step. I hope you do understand this."*

"Alright, okay...I accept that."

"Fine, that is very good, very good indeed. I will take my leave now and I thank you for welcoming me. The White Brotherhood send their blessings, we all send our love to you, and we welcome and thank you both for working with us. I shall now say farewell."

John says, "Farewell."

The next morning, I was off to spend the day with my friends, Helen and Julie at our weekly meditation. I wondered what White Eagle had in store for us.

The Ghost of Jehanne d'Arc – St. Joan of Arc

8

"Death is just a transition. I was confused as Joan, I was very confused as Joan (now in tears), *I came to teach of the 'voice within'."* This is what Jehanne said to me when she manifested her spirit into my body and spoke to our little group. Her gentle female voice had a tone to it that was commanding and compelling.

Jehanne continued, *"Even the Church was wrong, they did not understand...they taught people to look and praise other idols and it was not right.* (upset) *I failed, I failed, I was so confused, I don't know.* (shaking her head and crying) *They made me sign something that denied God within and it was not right. I signed and I immediately felt I had betrayed God.*

"I had a choice, I had the choice, but I was afraid of the fire. I was afraid of being burned, I was not afraid of anything else. Being burned was something else, it wasn't of Earth, it was something different and I was confused for a while. After I went to the Other

Side, I didn't move on, I was caught, caught and confused and very unhappy, but the Angels had a light and then they came for me and I was alright, but I had to come back again and that is when I came back to a life as a nun in France to again speak of God within the heart, but I was young and I became confused again. I suppose that is how many people are, afraid and confused..."

This was in 1991 when a group of three females—Helen, Julie, and myself—had been meeting in a small meditation circle every week and learning. Our experiences had been extraordinary, leaving no doubt in our minds that a teacher from other worlds was teaching us and introducing us to spiritual mediumship, along with knowledge of other worlds and many past-life memories.

I have been asked by my 'voices' to write about my experiences with Jehanne d'Arc as it happened to me.

One of the first things White Eagle said to me was, "*You were Joan of Arc in another life.*" I didn't believe him, but he persisted. Now, I have collected research material over the years, I am amazed that I have so much: notes dating back to 1982 and not only about Jehanne. Spirit teaches in a convoluted way, not linear, but lateral in thinking.

One receives information from time to time, often over years, with 'this' going with 'that' and another 'that' going with a different 'this' until a beautiful tapestry of realisation reveals itself. I have a suitcase full of material: recorded audiotapes and the transcriptions typed and filed, as per date, in binder folders.

A book written by Vita Sackville West, showing maps of Saint Joan of Arc's travels from birth to death, prompted John and I to use it when we were asked by *Upstairs* to journey to France in 1991 and retrace her steps. There are also tourist brochures, a video, and notes of many spontaneous past-life memories awakened during our travels, in another suitcase.

When travelling in Europe with John, retracing Saint Joan of Arc's footsteps using the above book and driving towards Rheims Cathedral, I was overcome with tears of joy remembering spirit had over-lighted Jehanne d'Arc and her horse, marching them right through the great doors of Rheims Cathedral. Jehanne kept worrying that her horse would poop onto the hallowed floor.

This Cathedral was where the Dauphin was crowned. This was where the French Royals were always crowned and now she had led the Dauphin and his entourage to achieve what she had been asked to do by her 'voices'. Her heavenly voices had called upon her to save France from the English rule and have the Dauphin, Charles Vll crowned King of France.

Another visit was to Campiegne where Jehanne had been captured by the Burgundians and seriously hurt in an attempt to jump from a castle tower window to escape. She survived through the intervention of the Angels softening her fall. I remember she was feeling indignant that history recorded she had tried to commit suicide.

Then there was the little chapel of St. Catherine at Fierbois where the sacred sword that was said to have pierced Jesus of Nazareth had been found. The doors of the church were closed, but John found the town clergyman and he opened it for us. I sat alone for a long while, thinking about how Jehanne had received a message from her 'voices', namely Archangel Michael, Saint Catherine, and Saint Margaret, that the sacred sword was buried behind the altar. It was found by her equerry and brought to her.

At another place, a small museum, when I saw where she had signed her name to a confession, I wept because of the overwhelming feeling of sadness I felt she had failed. She had signed a document that had denied her 'voices' were coming from God.

At Chinon, we found the road to the castle where Jehanne first met the Dauphin; I confidently told John I knew the way. Then we discovered the cobbled road we were walking on was named after Jehanne d'Arc. We visited the village Doremy, which looked very similar to the countryside of the Southern Highlands in NSW, Australia, where we live now.

Doremy is where Jehanne lived as a child; it still looked almost the same as five hundred and sixty years ago, except there was a large Basilica built in her honour. It was John who was overwhelmed with looking at the larger than life paintings of scenes from her life hanging on the Basilica walls. He used to joke that he burnt me on a stake in another life. He has also spoken of remembering being the Duke of Burgundy, Philip the Good, who handed Jehanne over to the English and astounded his schoolmaster when writing in extraordinary detail about the Duke of Burgundy.

John entered into an altered state of consciousness to tell me of his memory.

"*When I was twelve years of age in my boarding school St. Lawrence College in England, we used to have eight weeks' holiday in the summer. During that time, we were required to write an essay on any particular subject we wanted and present it when we returned for the Michaelmas term.*

"I wrote my essay on the Duke of Burgundy. I definitely had this empathy with him. I even fantasised as a child that I was the Duke of Burgundy, even though I had not read about him. I used to see myself in armour and fighting with the English against the French. I had this unbelievable, clear picture of myself as the Duke. I wrote all about the incidents that went on at that time, including the capturing of Joan of Arc and selling her to the English. It was quite easy to write—it just flowed out of me.

"The result was that I was accused by the masters of my school by asking, "How did you get this story, did you cheat?" I simply said that it was clairvoyant memory I had of those times and me as the Duke. I received very high marks for it, but everyone was still very sceptical as to where I had obtained the information. It actually came from me in the sense of déjà vu."

So, John and I were enemies in that life. When we visited Rouen, we entered the modern church built over the site of where Jehanne was burned at the stake. I went to sign the visitor's book and found a *'spidery scrawl of writing'* of the name *Helen*, and nothing else, as the last entry...I just knew it was my friend Helen's spirit who had written it. Our mentor had said we would all be going to France and he obviously meant some of us in spirit only.

I downloaded from the internet *The Trial of Jeanne d'Arc*, translated into English from the Original Latin and French Documents by W.P. Barrett, with an essay on her Trial and Dramatis Personae. The translation took place 1932, the year my physical Earth body was born into this life. Another download from the internet was Mark Twain's *'Personal Recollections of Joan of Arc'.* It is a work of fiction by Samuel Langhorne Clemens whose nom de plume is Mark Twain.

Our friend, a hypnotherapist named Charles, and his wife Dorothea were having dinner with us one night when I suddenly saw him overlaid with the image of a spirit from his past life. I asked him, "Has anyone ever told you you were Mark Twain in another life?" He was dumbfounded, but Charles even looks like him now with bushy silver-grey hair and equally bushy moustache to match.

At the time, he had been back and forth to the USA and travelling on the Mississippi River, experiencing many things similar to the life of Mark Twain. So yes, I think he did agree. Mark Twain wrote a fictional story *'Personal Recollections of Joan of Arc',* by the Sieur Louis de Conte - SLC (*her page and secretary, a fictitious name related to Mark Twain's real name Samuel Langhorne Clemens: SLC*) about Jehanne's page and secretary, but I prefer to think I remember Charles as Jehanne's page and secretary.

Reading Mark Twain's obviously well-researched work on the trial and rehabilitation of Jehanne after her death has given great comfort to Jehanne's spirit. That is why I recognised Charles from another time when I first met him giving a lecture on reincarnation at Sydney University.

I want to digress here to speak about attending Charles' lecture about reincarnation at the Sydney University. When I saw the man lecturing about hypnosis, my breathing stopped for a moment and I thought, *I know this man.* But I had never met him in this life.

I later attended a day conducted by him for a group to experience a regressed state of consciousness. We all lay on the floor, dotted around the carpeted room with a pillow under our head, and listened to him gently lead us into an altered state of consciousness.

Quite unexpectedly, and for the first time in this life, I had very clear, coloured visions appear in my inner scene. I had no idea what was happening, but I went along with the feeling of calm and the intuitive understanding the images I saw behind closed eyelids were leading somewhere.

I first saw a colourful flower clock laid out in a garden. *(Meaning it was time.)* Then a large circular coloured lead-light rose window. *(I know now exists on the front of Rheims cathedral where the Dauphin was crowned.)* Then an image of Cleopatra's needle with the number 'V' engraved on it. *(V is the Roman numeral for 5 or did the letter V stand for the House of Valois?)*

And...when Charles asked everyone to visualise their mother, I saw a beautiful lady dressed in a full-length yellow 'A-line' shaped gown that flowed to the ground and sleeves that cut away above the wrist and hung in corners well below her hips. Around her hips was a wide belt that fastened with cord loops that hung down in streamers as a decoration on the otherwise unadorned dress.

On her head, she wore a tall cone-shaped hat with a diaphanous scarf of the same colour flowing from it. She was standing in front of a high stone wall that looked like a castle with grass-covered ground that fell away to water, which would have been a moat surrounding the castle. I now know that this woman I had been shown was the image of Isabeau of Bavaria, the birth mother of Jehanne who, as a baby, had been spirited away from her, to another life in Lorraine. Isabeau had been told the baby had died at birth.

At the beginning of my sacred journey, I was awakened by a spirit from a deep sleep in 1982, when I heard an authoritative male voice asking me to stand up 'three times.' As I have already said, the voice told me to go back to bed, but that I would be awakened from time to time and taught many things and given many messages.

In another 'calling from God', I saw in my inner scene a long white hand with an even longer white finger pointing at me and saying, "You have been chosen."

The first message I received after that was, "You were Joan of Arc in another life." I responded, saying, "Don't be silly. Go away." I didn't really know much about her then, except that she had been a female warrior and was burnt at the stake in France...but despite my denial, spirit persisted in bringing me reminders over the years that she really was part of my soul story.

All personalities from past lives are held in one's soul memory, or the higher vibration of their oversoul. They were a different person but how they think and feel and many of their characteristics filter through into one's present life, giving opportunity to release and heal any negative emotions. As well, strong, positive, and creative abilities can be inherited from those other lives.

Jehanne came to Earth with a particularly strong and high vibration to carry out a special mission. She readily received assistance from the Angelic Realm and had been gifted in that life with clear inner hearing from the ether. The Angels often took over her physical body to assist her to achieve what she had been asked to do, even to ride a horse, speak boldly, and to lessen the impact of her dangerous fall from a high tower.

As a child, Jehanne was devoted to God, prayed always, a simple, non-educated country girl who loved her parents and siblings. Something hot, boiling over fire in the kitchen, accidentally spilt onto her shoulder and chest, causing nasty scarring. Once it healed, it was then she decided not to marry because of that disfigurement.

Much has been written about Jehanne; what I have been asked to speak of is my experience with her, although I have come to know and remember through her and her recorded history as well.

I developed a nasty lump on my ankle, which spirit referred to as a 'canker'. It had to be treated by a specialist, but I needed to know from spirit what had caused it. I was prompted to lay on my bed and as I did the memory of being in a dark, cold dungeon came into my inner scene. I could see shadowy men leaning over me; one had a simple crown upon his head. I was restrained on the floor with heavy metal chains around my ankles that rubbed my skin and caused ulcers to form.

This was what was rising to the surface in the memory of this physical body. Jehanne had been upset by the indignity of having to ask her jailers to unlock the shackles around her ankles, so that she could retire to another little room to relieve herself. Of course, her strength of mind was continually being stressed and tested with having to attend her trial every day. Her painful emotions needed to be released.

Gerry, an Aborigine friend came to visit us on the property and was able to assist with a healing. It had to be that way. The memory came to both of us that he had been one of the English soldiers who was Jehanne's jailer in that life. He was the soldier who tied her to the stake and lit the fire, but he had also been the one who made the simple wooden cross for a priest to hold up high, so she could focus upon it when she was burning alive on the stake. (*Interestingly, he had been seconded as an Australian soldier to England in this life.)*

John had mentioned to a business associate that I had skin cancer problems on my leg, so it was a lovely surprise to open the door one morning to find sixteen white lilies being delivered to me with a note wishing me to 'get well quickly'.

I had met John's associate in Melbourne and particularly liked him. We had even briefly spoken about reincarnation and how the past could affect one's health in one's present life. I had asked for distant healing for his wife...so when I tuned into my inner-eye scene, I found it had to be that way; he had been Jehanne's brother and with her throughout her campaign—when she had been equipped with armour and a blue and white banner with the fleur-de-lis, flower of lily. White lilies are the national flower of France.

My name in this life adds to double 8, according to numerology, and my birth also is double 8 = the number 16. The exact number of lilies sent to me. Numbers are continually given to me by spirit as a 'sign'. The double 8 sign had been given to me when I first began my mission with 8 double yolk eggs adding to 16. My father had registered my name when I was born with the French spelling of Valérie.

I happily took the flowers straight to John's office to show him, but as I did, my steps froze...for my eye caught the date on his desk calendar, which was showing 30th May.

30th May 1431 was the day Jehanne d'Arc burned on the stake at Rouen. I began shaking; I just knew I was going to experience more in the night.

That night, I tossed and turned in bed, in and out of a lucid dream. It was very real...I could see and feel myself restrained, my hands tied behind me on a stake, and the fire raging up towards me very fast. I remember screaming out for Jesus again and again. The sound was only in my mind and I could see the simple wooden cross being held up for me to see.

When I knew Jehanne's body was dead, I couldn't move away. Archangel Michael, Saint Catherine, and Saint Margaret were with me and asked me to stay with my body. They stayed with me to give me their strength in spirit. I could see my body gradually withering away to a black mass as I went in and out of the memory.

Jehanne's executioners were worried because they could not burn her heart...it had become crystallised and impossible to burn. This is what the Angels wanted: to make Jehanne's trial judges worry they had mistakenly destroyed a godly person and not a witch.

The executioners were extremely frightened. As soon as the physical body had been reduced to ashes, they quickly gathered her remains along with the crystallised heart and threw it off the bridge into the river. It was only then that I could feel and see Jehanne's spirit leave, becoming detached from her bodily remains and free.

Another time, I was shown she was left in the Astral or the next world for a while because of her confusion. In actual fact, she learnt a lot about that dimension. In this life, it helps me when assisting people to free themselves of demons or lost soul/spirits or ghosts if you like, caught in the Astral.

When Jehanne's father Jacques died about nine months later, he took her spirit with him back to the World of Light. I have since met this man in this life. He lives in Melbourne and speaks French fluently, and we both have deep warmth and respect for each other.

I will mention another man who helped me to write a book and tricked me into signing an agreement. It was a replay of Jehanne being tricked into believing she would be freed from jail if she agreed to sign a document saying her voices were not of God. He turned out to be, in a past life, Pierre Cauchon, the Bishop of Beauvais, the one who wanted to convict Jehanne as a witch. Although it was not the same story for me in this life, the same emotions were involved and I felt as if I had been burnt. I have forgiven him, and I hoped that would be the last of that past life.

Not so...now, I find I am on a mission in this life to speak of Jehanne's true history. I have been told by 'my voices' that Jehanne hadn't failed at all, that it was all meant to happen that way because there was a 'Great Plan'. The day she was judged and burned alive was 30th May 1431. The day and the month add to eight and the whole of the date adds to seventeen, which equals another eight, making that *double eight sign* again.

Isabeau – Jehanne's mother dressed like this

The Ghost of Jehanne d'Arc and Her Real Birth

9

In 2004, or about that time, I again briefly died in hospital when my heart stopped from a reaction to penicillin. I knew I had the option to go, for I was feeling very low and unhappy—or I could stay and continue my mission. I chose to stay. This also was a replay of Jehanne; when she was in jail, she became so seriously ill her voices said she could leave if she wanted to—or she could stay and complete her mission. She chose to stay. She recanted her false admission that her voices were not of God and knew in doing so she was condemning herself to be burned alive.

House of Valois

I have been prompted to think about the Royal House of Valois in France—in particular, the Duke of Orleans. I think of Jehanne sometimes being referred to as Jehanne of Orleans; it kept coming to my mind, even though she came from Lorraine. I recognise she inspired the dispirited French soldiers and forced the English to raise the siege of Orleans. That victory led to her being known as the Maid of Orleans.

Jehanne preferred to carry a banner, rather than a sword and claimed never to have killed anyone. For some reason, spirit wanted me to consider her birth. As I write about the memory, I have been prompted to research the Dauphin, Charles VII of the House of Valois. He was known after he was crowned at Rheims as the Victorious or the Well-Served. He was born 22nd February 1403 in Paris and died 22nd July 1461. *There was something nagging at me to continue my research about births.*

The Dauphin's father was Charles VI, who was called the *Well-loved* and also the *Mad*. He was born 3rd December 1368 in Paris and died 21st October 1422 (*aged fifty-three*). He had been crowned King of France in 1380 at the age of eleven. He was married at sixteen to Isabeau of Bavaria in 1385; she was only fifteen. Twelve children were born to Isabeau, many not living very long.

It was the second last child, a boy, who was in line for the Throne of France—who became Charles Vll, The Dauphin; he was not crowned until seven years after his father King Charles VI died. It was in those seven years Jehanne received her direction from her voices to end the Hundred Years War.

Now, why would these royals and highborn get behind Jehanne's plan when she was just a mere peasant girl claiming to be hearing voices from God? A lot of money was put behind her in raising an army, horses, uniforms, food, and accommodation. *Was there a secret*?

My mind is prompted again to research the Duke of Orleans from the House of Valois and I found he was born Louis I of Valois—born 13th March 1372 and died 23rd November 1407. He was the younger brother of Charles VI, the King of France, and the Dauphin's father. Louis had an important political role during the Hundred Years War.

The increasing insanity of his elder brother Charles the Mad, who suffered from either schizophrenia or bipolar disorder, led Louis to dispute the regency and guardianship of the royal children with John the Fearless—the Duke of Burgundy. The enmity between the two was public and a source of political unrest in the already troubled France.

Louis had the initial advantage, being the brother of the king. His character of wasting money and rumour of an affair with the queen consort Isabeau of Bavaria made him extremely unpopular. In the following years, the children of Charles VI were successively kidnapped and recovered by both parties, until the Duke of Burgundy managed to be appointed by Royal Decree, guardian of the Dauphin and Regent of France.

Louis the first took every effort to sabotage John, The Duke of Burgundy's rule, including squandering the money raised for the relief of Calais, then occupied by the English. John and Louis broke into open threats and only the intervention of John of Valois, Duke of Berry and uncle of both men, avoided a civil war. On 20th November 1407, a solemn reconciliation was vowed in front of the court of France.

Only three days later, Louis was brutally assassinated in the streets of Paris when armed men under the orders of John the Fearless, Duke of Burgundy, attacked him while he was mounting his horse, amputating his arms and leaving him completely defenceless.

The murder of Louis sparked a bloody feud and civil war between Burgundy and the French Royal family. This divided France for the next seventy years and only ended with the death of Charles the Bold, Duke of Burgundy in 1477.

Whether royals or not, in any family it would be shocking for a brother to have an affair with his brother's wife. And it was possible some of the King's children were not his, but his brother's. In the Royal House of France, it had to be established who was the rightful heir to inherit the throne...and some were saying that the Dauphin was a bastard.

So, who was the father of the Dauphin and what had that to do with Jehanne?

I had my suspicions but said very little to my friend Helen, one of the three who had all those wonderful teachings from *Upstairs* back in 1990. She agreed to assist me. As we settled in chairs opposite each other, she very quickly went into a 'trance state' and was taken over by a spirit, becoming one of the personalities of the time; she could see herself in an older kingdom.

"I see myself as a female. I see a royal household and I see a lot of secrecy. I see a female child being born—but somehow, you shouldn't have been.

"I see babies being handed to big women, healthy-looking women who take the babies to their breast. It seems to be a common practice just handing babies out, sometimes for weeks at a time. Over time, many babies have been born, twelve in all.

"This was the last child. Only a few knew the secret. But there was someone in the Royal household who heard 'inner voices' and knew what had to be done. He counselled the Royal family, he counselled some kind of protector of the Law, and they forged papers. They were glad it was not a male that was born; it was easier to go underground.

"There is something about a protector dressed in black clothes, an advisor it was written down, but it was also burnt, the whole script and the story about the girl child. I can see a page being torn out of a big book about this event.

"They found out, by bringing in an astrologer, that there was a special mission for this child. There was a special meeting and someone did not want to give his or her power away to someone else. They should have done it differently, but the chart said it was a child of destiny here, a child that would be great. They did not want to lose their country; they wanted to conquer, so they went against the advice of the astrologer.

"There was a lot of intrigue. Someone took the secret with him. He wanted to reveal it on his deathbed, but in that last minute he crunched up his notes and did not reveal it before he died..."

The spirit was crunching up papers on Helen's lap. *He was the King. He was old. He was French. He died with a feeling of great guilt.*

I am sitting listening to this and feel I have slipped into a time warp as well. I know the baby girl the spirit is talking about is Jehanne and that the King is Charles VI. The woman giving birth under such secrecy is his wife Isabeau. It is recorded in history that she had twelve children. The last child is officially registered as Phillip, 1407–1407 (deceased). This child should have been registered as Jehanne 1407–1431.

While I was sitting opposite my friend, I asked *Upstairs* to clarify some questions for me.

Charles VI did not know at first that his brother was the father of the last child. Charles was a good man but subjected to fits of mental sickness from time to time. It was difficult for him to know everything that was happening around him. In his mental attacks, he would become confused and sometimes dangerous.

He did find out later and was very upset with the fact the child survived and was given away, when he had been told that the baby was stillborn. He also knew his brother was 'playing around' with his wife. Most of all, he died feeling great guilt because he had allowed the order to go out to murder his brother, Louis, The Duke of Orleans, in 1407—the same year Jehanne was born, and four years after the Dauphin was born.

Helen was still in a trance and I was in a time warp. I asked her if she could describe Jehanne's mother, the Queen. Helen was again in an altered state of consciousness.

She said, "Yes, Isabeau was Jehanne's mother." She described Isabeau as, "Very pretty with lots of dark brown curls, dark eyes, rosy cheeks, pale skin, and lovely hands. A joyful person, a blessed woman, linked to God."

I replied, "It is said she didn't treat her son the Dauphin very well and that she called him a bastard."

Helen's demeanour and voice changed. I knew I was now speaking with the spirit of Isabeau. "No children belong to you. They just come from another world. They belong to God. It is those around me that cause their personality. It taught them power. You just stand back and let it reveal."

"Are you happy with the King?"

"Yes, but I always longed for more. I longed for true love...something was missing, something I was searching for...I just played... played..."

"The babies don't belong to you...they come through you...it is something special that comes through you. Something special that enters you and then comes out..."

She was looking up to the heavens with a saintly expression and pointing up to illustrate where the children come from and then pointing below to her groin where they come through you.

"Did you ever call your son the Dauphin a bastard?"

"The others did. They accused me...it was innocent playing... others make different stories around the story. He was my brother-in-law...I was his sister-in-law...When he was murdered, I was devastated. I wanted nothing to do with the King. The marriage was loveless." This was in 1407.

I thanked the spirit of Isabeau. Later, I was advised by my voices the King amused himself with a mistress and equally wanted nothing to do with his Queen Isabeau. The whole messy business had been the last straw for him.

So, now we know the secret of Jehanne d'Arc's birth...that Louis I, the Duke of Orleans of the Royal House of Valois was the birth father of Jehanne, and the king's consort Queen Isabeau was her birth mother. Jehanne was born of royal blood.

(*Remember I had been given insight to having a royal mother in a past-life regression with the hypnotherapist—the baby was Jehanne.*)

The Dauphin, born four years earlier, was her brother or her half-brother depending on who was his father. There was some doubt in the Royal household. It did not really matter, for they were both of the Royal House of Valois. Isabeau's women attending her bed-chamber would have had a fair idea.

Jehanne's birth details were falsified and she was given away to the care of Jacques d'Arc to his new family in Lorraine. Only he knew her identity; Jehanne grew up not knowing her true birth. Even her new mother did not know, although she had been asked by Jacques to care for Jehanne as if she were her own daughter.

Jehanne, dressed as a soldier, was to meet the Dauphin at the castle at Chinon. A trick was played on her as to who really was the Dauphin hiding among many people in the reception hall. She went straight to him, fell to her knees before him, and asked for a private audience. Her voices had asked her to secretly tell him they had the same mother. The Dauphin would have been well aware of the intrigue and gossip that existed in the Royal House of Valois. Even Jehanne did not know until then.

The few wealthy nobles who knew the secret of her birth at the time were behind her receiving all the assistance with the expense she needed to carry out her pre-destined mission. The secret was known by some of the esteemed members of the Masons, the Knights Templar, and held over the years through the Priory of Sion—I picked up notice of a meeting of the Priory of Sion when John and I visited the Mary chapel on Mont St Michel, referred to in the next chapter.

The Ghost of Jehanne d'Arc – Her Next Life

10

"I am sister Manieure...I would like to be with you...I always like being with you...in France...1508...it was a monastery...we loved being nuns...we loved being part of God...it was our whole life... we loved praying...we loved giving of ourselves. We loved to pray... all the answers come in prayer...God is always there. He is in our hearts...but not everybody seems to know that."

She is upset.

"They say I am Evil...I am not Evil. I am of God and I know everyone else is of God, too. But they make me confused. I have to be burned because I am Evil. I am brave."

This was the spirit of Sister Manieure speaking, who manifested through me in July, 1991. She had been Jehanne d'Arc in a previous life.

We three women and a guest had been sitting in our warm meditation room when White Eagle from the White Brotherhood of Divine Light manifested through me. He advised us to investigate and develop a past life we had shared in France. He said it was no coincidence the meeting was taking place that day.

Now, it seems, is the time for us to speak of our experience. Spirit guidance was clearly working on us, taking us over, holding us and gently sliding us off our chairs so that we didn't crash to the floor.

Amidst much laughter, we sat on the floor with legs crossed like children. We later returned to sitting in our chairs. Three of us were given our names: Theresa, Rebecca, and Manieure (Mani) as novice nuns.

The fourth lady, our guest, was known as Maria. She had been the Mother Superior of the order of nuns that existed on Mont Saint Michel, Normandy, France, in 1508.

Joyous emotion, coupled with apprehension and fear, was what we felt when we were all given the memory of living on the island of Mont Saint Michel. Maria fussed over we three novices as if we were her children. We all had special gifts of clairvoyance and clairaudience. We were extremely devout young girls. We attended a little Mary Chapel near the base of the island for Vespers and Holy Communion. We three novices were spiritually in love with a young priest who also lived on the island, no harm in it at all. We were all innocent, but his eyes often held mine (as Mani) more than the others. He was the soul, spirit of John, my husband in this life.

We had to make a confession every day to a senior priest, whom I met in this life, and we were told it was evil to hear voices and we must stop. I became distressed as I couldn't stop hearing the voices in my head and broke out into a hot, red itchy rash all over my body.

When I told the priest about the hot, red rash at confession, he said, "There you see, it is evil." This was reported to the Bishop and we were tried and committed under the law of inquisition as being evil. The Mother Superior tried to speak up to protect us, but she ended being tried as well. We were all sentenced to be burned alive at the stake as heretics.

Many of the monks, guests, and the young priest on the island were aghast at the thought of the senior priests burning their own nuns. While the tide was out, four pyres of straw and wood were hurriedly built. We were tied to a stake and burned unceremoniously, in time for the huge tide to return and wash all the evidence away. In our memory, I remember being in spirit, comforting and waiting for the other women and helping them in spirit to return to the World of Light. I was already experienced at being burned alive.

Mont Saint Michel in Normandy was first inhabited by hermit monks, when in 708 the head monk Aubert was approached miraculously by Archangel Michael and commanded to build a place of prayer for the Archangel of God. A thousand years of history has been recorded on the island.

Oral legend says an invasion of barbarians came from Scandinavia, who converted to Catholicism, later becoming the Dukes of Normandy. In the tenth century, beautiful abbeys and castles were built. Life within the Abbey of St. Michael in the middle ages revolved around the three social orders who lived there. At the top were the monks and priests, mid-level housed wealthy distinguished visitors, often pilgrims on their way to Jerusalem. The bottom occupied common pilgrims and nuns. A glorious role of protection played by one hundred and nineteen knights of Mont Saint Michel became legendary.

There is no mention in travel brochures of the monastery ever housing Catholic nuns.

As tourists, John and I looked around, with me feeling the place was familiar. I knew where everything was. I dragged John down to the basement where there were rock caves. I remembered being there as a novice nun, running around serving food, drink, and bedding to all the pilgrims as they arrived in boats and stayed over at the Mount on their way to the Holy Lands. As young novices, we were kept very busy.

John suggested we have an early dinner and look for accommodation on the island. We found ourselves in a smoke-filled restaurant crammed full of people, windows shut because of the cold. I began to panic, smelling the smoke, trying to calm myself, but it became too much...I couldn't breathe...I had to get out quickly and run for dear life. I just took off...with John running behind trying to catch up. There was no way I was going to agree to sleep on the Mount. When I look back, I marvel how patient and caring my hubby was and is...

We found accommodation on the mainland and planned to walk back the next day, over the causeway to the Abbey.

It was Sunday morning and the church bells began to toll. Suddenly, I panicked. I had to run or I would be late for morning prayers. I kept running until I found the little Mary Chapel. Stopping short, I found myself looking at a statue of Jehanne d'Arc standing outside the arched entrance to the chapel, dressed in armour with pointed metal shoes and holding a metal banner.

I quickly entered the chapel where Holy Communion had begun and knelt at the wooden pew. Tears were streaming down my face and as I looked around I was stunned to see Jehanne's banners, the banners of Jhesus and Maria in blue, white, and gold, hanging on the chapel stonewall. I couldn't believe it. They looked like her original banners just pinned on the rough wall.

John had caught up with me and we sat through the chapel service with the priest probably wondering why I was crying. Few people were taking the service. As we left through the stone arched door, I picked up a leaflet written in French, connected to the Priory de Sion. It was a notice of the next meetings to take place. I had read about them being a secret society. It caught my interest.

There has been much written about secret societies, in particular Holy Blood, Holy Grail by Michael Exigent, Richard Leigh, and Henry Lincoln, and in recent times, the fictional story written by Dan Brown, The Da Vinci Code where a controversial theory was published that Jesus Christ and Mary Magdalene married and founded a holy bloodline, just under 2,000 years ago.

I have been thinking about the Priory of Sion and the disagreement amongst scholars, as to whether the Priory de Sion existed in times past or even if they exist now. Well, I saw a meeting advertised by them in France in 1991. Knowing a friend of mine is connected to the Knights Templar, I have asked if I could interview him. Does he know about Jehanne's history?

Interview with a Knight Templar

11

I showed Keith a recent newspaper article in *The Australian*, 4th April 2009 announcing the Vatican revealed how medieval knights had hidden and secretly venerated the Holy Shroud of Turin for more than a hundred years after the Crusades.

The Knights Templar was founded in France, at the time of the First Crusade in the eleventh century, to protect Christians making the pilgrimage to Jerusalem. The Pope endorsed the order until the Crusaders lost their hold on the Holy Land. Rumours about the Order's corrupt secret ceremonies, claiming novices had to deny Christ, spit on the cross, strip naked, and submit to sodomy led to King Philip IV of France putting pressure on Pope Clement V, also of France, to dissolve the Order. Many were burnt at the stake. The present time finds self-proclaimed heirs of the Knights Templar in Spain and Britain asking the Vatican to 'restore the reputation' of the Order.

Keith is an initiated member of the Knights Templar of Malta. "With the unknown Scottish rites, you are actually stripped naked of all your clothing and you are asked to stand before a mirror, and on that mirror is written 'know yourself'. Then you are 'loaned' some clothing. When you are taken into the lodge during the initiation ceremony, all the men are asked to contribute into a poor box and when they come to the initiate, they make a point of saying to him, 'Have you anything to give?'

Of course, the initiate is embarrassed because he does not have any money to put into the poor box. You have nothing, not even a ring on your finger, you are stripped down to your bare self...everything is taken off your body, so that you get to know your inner self, and that embarrassment is to remind you from that point on when you are asked to give to someone in need, you can remember how when you stood on the floor of the lodge in front of eighty or more men with nothing to give, for you stood in borrowed clothes. Those rumours of the ceremony, this nakedness, are blown out of proportion."

"So that is a worldwide initiation?"

"Yes, it is very dramatic in the way it is done. When people ask can you help them, your mind immediately flashes back to instantly wanting to help and how it felt to be without anything. The lesson there is you should come from the heart because that is all there is left."

I told Keith how my father used to study. I used to wonder what he was reading. He was a Grandmaster of a Mason's Lodge, and so was his father and his grandfather and great grandfather. "It is interesting you mention the Scottish rites, because my great-great-grandfather came in the early days of settlement to Australia on a family remittance from Edinburgh, Scotland."

Keith went on to say, "All the rituals, like the first degree, are about giving and coming from the heart. Your birth and the second degree is everyday living and the third degree is preparing for dying. The stories are taken from the Hiram Glyphs King David and Hiram, King of Tyre...they were Grandmasters of the Stonemasons. They have adapted what happened to them."

The Knights Templar began around the twelfth century, the time of the crusades in England with Richard the Lionheart. King Richard went back to England, leaving many of the crusaders in France. The highways were so treacherous the knights actually invented the 'cheque system'. If a traveller wanted to get to your place, you could deposit your money with the Templar at your end of the road and they would then give you a note and you were paid the value of the note when you arrived.

Certainly, the Knights were wealthy; people were so grateful for protection on their journey as pilgrims to the Holy Lands. Some pilgrims were so wealthy they gave the Knights land as well as money in gratitude.

The French Order of Knights lost everything when the King of France, Philip IV had the Order dissolved. They went underground. The glue that held the system in place, the Knights Templar and the Free Masons, come under the same banner and still exists around the world.

"What is the connection to the Knights of Templar and the Knights of Templar in Malta?" I asked.

"Malta is a fortress. It is another degree but similar, a uniform difference, that is all. They began in Rhodes. There were black and white knights, nothing to do with good or bad, just different. My title is actually a Knight of Jerusalem, Palestine, Malta, and Rhodes. The Duke of Kent, England, is now the World-Wide Grandmaster of the Templar Masons.

"The Templar accepted any religious denomination. They believed in higher beings. They suggest there is a tie between yourself and that higher being. If you were a Mason and a Catholic, the Masons say the secrets are not so much the handshake or the ritual, but it is the good that you do, without talking about it. The Catholics' had confession, so that was when people spoke about their good deeds.

"There is a handshake so that a Mason would recognise a fellow Mason on a dark night. You could identify a brother. It goes way back in time, even as long ago as the ancient pyramids when a stonemason was engaged to build a gateway or a temple or building. I didn't want Joe Blow down the road to say he was a stonemason when I needed the work because I am a professional and he is not. There is a way of recognising who is a professional; they have marks, which you are given in the Lodge. I have a mark of double V V, so the handshake is purely to recognise a brother.

"The Stonemasons learn about the sacred geometry and platonic shapes, philosophical and esoteric teachings, and all about the pyramids and the stars. This is all part of the teachings of the Templar.

"The All-Seeing Eye, as seen by the Masonic, would be as if you were looking at a Buddha. You are not looking at the idol, but rather you are looking at the state of being in which you are trying to attain. When you look at the eye masonically, it reminds you to become that eye. Looking at yourself to attain a state of righteousness as in a mirror.

"The early Christians also had that knowledge. They believed that when 'I look at the eye, I become the eye and look back at myself and ask is it for the good of all?' Sai Baba, an Avatar in India, says he is a mirror...that if you look at him, he will mirror back to you what you need to deal with within yourself. In that case, Baba is the All-Seeing Eye. I see that Eye as the total Godly wisdom that if I go there, I can look back and know what is good and what is not good."

I told Keith I had been thinking about a kind of 'all-knowing field' that exists in the ether. "The word Bi-ocular was given to me by *Upstairs* when walking in the park. Don't forget the word, I was told. It is a mirror field and All-Seeing Eye. A field that exists in the ether that holds all knowledge of everything that has happened on Earth. An initiate can tap into that to receive knowledge. Keith, can you explain the Priory of the Sion? It suggests to me that it is more like a doorway, rather than a brotherhood."

"It is a doorway," he told me. "The Priory is like the tessellated paving of the members of that Heraldry. It symbolises the paved area behind a small fence in front of an altar, where only the priests, rulers, or knights are allowed in a sacred building, church, or temple. A Priory is a building where you can go and gather and be of One Mind uninterrupted."

While Keith was talking, he was pointing to the Heraldry of Philip, the Duke of Burgundy and giving the meaning of the orange and white squares around the edge.

"The Heraldry was also of the House of Valois and clearly shows the tessellated paving only high priests use, around the edge of the inner area of the fleur-de-lis on a light blue background. In the House of Valois, the Kings were Templars. The tessellated pavement and its symbolic meaning dates back to the ancient Egyptians."

Keith added, "Jehanne d'Arc's generals were loyal to her because they were actually Templars. They would have known she was born of Royal blood. I have always known about Jehanne's true birth. The Duke of Burgundy, Philip the Good, being from the Royal House of Valois, has been historically criticised for not helping Jehanne, even though he did many good things."

I hadn't told him that Philip the Good, Duke of Burgundy was in my husband's soul story. I replied, "That would be because the Duke of Orleans, Louis the first, disputed the regency and guardianship of the royal children with John the Fearless, Duke of Burgundy, who was the father of Philip the Good. Philip of Burgundy would have looked upon Jehanne as only a 'bastard child' and he would probably have been ashamed it was his father that had the Duke of Orleans, Louis murdered. Louis was his uncle, and the father of Jehanne d'Arc. Philip would have grown up knowing his father and Louis shared a lot of enmity between them, so there would have been no love lost there."

Philip became Duke of Burgundy when his father was assassinated in 1419. Philip accused Charles, the Dauphin of France and Philip's brother-in-law, of planning the murder of his father. A year later, in 1420, Philip allied himself with Henry V of England under the Treaty of Troyes. Being pro-English at that time, he handed Jehanne over to the English. Jehanne was caught up with ransoms paid for her, political intrigue, and dangerous duplicity.

It can be seen that secrets have been handed down through the ages by the initiated ones and, in particular, the Knights Templar.

12 Judith of Judea – a Previous Life

I wanted to connect to my mentor and ask his advice. When I began typing this chapter, the letters on the keyboard would not register on the computer page. I kept typing, but no letters would show, until I realised my mentor wanted to introduce this chapter. Then, using me as an instrument, he introduced Judith of Judea.

"I am Judith, Judith of Judea. My parents are known as Joseph and Mary. There are others in the family. Our eldest brother, Issa (pronounced Eesa) was the first born and he tells us that his father is in heaven. We understand that...we know of the immaculate conception, and we know also how that happens. My mother had other children with Joseph. James, Phillip, and John. Then there was me and my younger sister Ruth, and then another two. In fact, the family of the Essenes knew and understood about other worlds.

"We know of the star worlds and other beings who existed. We also know of our connection to them—in particular, to the beings who had come from Venus.

"I am speaking now from the Angelic Realms...and I am known as Val in the Angelic Realms, and I would like it known that Jehanne d'Arc, or Joan of the Arc, who was well known for her abilities and her service to God, came to France at a very dark time to try to help people to understand how they could lift or ascend into a higher state of consciousness and find God within.

"This was a mission impossible. But I would like people to know that Jehanne d'Arc is an aspect of myself, Judith—the half-sister of Jesus. As a family, we all came from the tribe of Essenes in love and peace. The wise women, when they reached an initiated state of cosmic consciousness, were known as the 'Maha-rees', which later

became abbreviated to the word 'Marys.' It is a state of consciousness. It is linked with the Angelic Realms."

In this life, my name is Valérie Judith...

Isn't it interesting how our parents name us in this life without understanding at a conscious level the connection to other lives or important stories?

The Family of Issa

My friend Rosemary and her husband had arrived on a surprise visit. We are both mediums and felt prompted by *Upstairs* to work together. Rosemary is easy to work with and, on this day, she quickly slipped into an altered state of consciousness that enabled her to connect with her soul consciousness. We asked her soul consciousness if she could be taken into the Hall of Records and be led to the life she knew she had at the time of Jesus.

When I work with somebody, I feel I often slip into a time warp with them. This makes it easier to ask appropriate questions about what they are experiencing with their inner eye, inner feelings, and inner hearing. In fact, all their inner senses and emotions come into play when they experience being there...just like being a character in a movie, acting out the life of that past time.

Rosemary knew the scene was before the birth of Jesus. She could see a farmer working with oxen, ploughing a field. She was told it was Joseph, the soon-to-be husband of Mary. There were little whitewashed stone houses. She said they belonged to the Essenes. It was a very ordinary life of country people. She was then shown Mary pregnant with child and Joseph walking with her. She was given detail about the birth and how it was long awaited, for many knew the child was the prophesied one. They were rejoicing.

I asked her if she knew the date...but I have come to realise that, at the time, varying races used different calendars. They were in the country of Judaea and after Issa was born, Joseph and Mary were married.

"Do you mean the marriage hadn't been consummated up until then?"

"Yes. Issa was the first born, but Joseph was not the father. A light from God had impregnated Mary and Issa was born. So that Rosemary-Ruth was not of the lineage of Issa. After Jesus was born, the family lineage came from Joseph. Joseph and Mary's children were James, Phillip, and John, then they had a girl Judith, then Ruth (*that was Rosemary*), then there were another two children. The house was communal living and the children belonged to everyone. It was tribal."

I asked Rosemary-Ruth to move on in her memory. She said Issa was eighteen years older than her. He had light reddish-brown hair and beautiful eyes. She loved him. Something had happened in the past three years. He was always talking to men and going away to other places. He no longer had time to play with her. He spent time teaching and told her, "I come straight from the Father in heaven, little one."

Rosemary continued to describe what she was seeing. "It was like a dark cloud had descended. People were always talking about soldiers, sickness, death, and dangerous times. They want my brother to be the King. They want him to set people free. He would say, 'But this is not my work. This is not what I have come to do. You will be set free."

Rosemary-Ruth is crying here. She believed what he had come to do was not going to happen and she was very sad.

Flight into Gaul

When she recovered, I asked her to move on again in her memory, after Issa was crucified. She worried there was great danger for all of them and they had to get away. The Marys knew and planned to leave the country. They knew the teachings and took the teachings with them to France, or Gaul as it was known. There were several boats. She was now sixteen years old and a handmaiden to the Marys.

There was Mary Magdalene and Mary, mother of Jesus. There is Miriam; she is a Mary also. She is a cousin to Jesus. There is another Mary, there are four altogether, and her name is Judith. She was startled to find in her memory they had the Chalice with them. (Remember, *Marys, by the way, is an initiated state of being.*)

Rosemary spontaneously came out of her altered state, saying it was time to come back. I asked if she knew where the Chalice is now. She replied, "The Chalice has been de-materialised. It had to return to its real world, but it can be gifted back."

Rosemary didn't know, but *Valérie was initiated to drink from that chalice* when it was briefly manifested by the Starpeople, as explained when I was working with the sacred Alcheringa stone in 1994. The delightful synchronicity is told in Part Two of this book.

Rosemary and I discussed how many of the family of Jesus came to the South of France. They were welcomed. The teachings of the Essenes were already known to the Gauls, the same as in many of the Arabic countries. Similar teachings were known by the Gnostics and later by the Cathars in the South of France. The Cathar tribes were becoming so strong in their followers the Catholic Church worried about their power and that the teachings did not concur with many of their Church teachings.

By the eleventh century, the Cathars had spread to many places—in particular, to Montsegur in Languedoc, France. They were said to have an original manuscript written by John the Divine. It was called *The Book of Love*. *(John and my past-life memory at Montsegur will explain our role in manifesting the story.)*

The Cathars and Mary Magdalene

The Cathars taught about the God of Love. They taught that Earth was hell, that there was a spark of divine light in mankind—that there was nothing to fear after death. One could dedicate their life to follow the example of Jesus Christ, who they believed was in spirit, with his Apostles.

The movement was becoming strong and spreading far and wide; there was an edict put out by the Pope in 1147 to arrest the progress of the Cathars. By the 1300s, another Pope had come to power and resolved to deal with them, under the Law of Inquisition.

This Albigensian Crusade was maintained with many Cathars being persecuted, tortured, or killed. From May 1243 to March

1244, the Cathar fortress of Montsegur was besieged by troops. Over two hundred Cathar 'pure ones' were burned in an enormous fire near the foot of the mountain. Many surviving Cathars went underground or to other countries; their descendants still exist today.

Mary Magdalene was said to continue the teaching of Jesus in the South of France and was considered to be the Apostle of the Apostles, knowing Jesus intimately. She was with the other Marys at Jesus's feet as he hung on the cross. She was the first to go to the Tomb where he was taken after his crucifixion. She was the first to see him after he reappeared in the garden at his resurrection.

Later in France, her teachings were uplifting and visionary. She retired to a cave in the mountains at the Convent les Dominicans at Mont Sainte-Baume.

The Black Madonna Tradition, the Knights Templar, and Mary Magdalene

There is a Basilica of Mary Magdalene, San-Maximin-la-Sainte-Baume that holds a Black Madonna. When you lift her mask, it is said to hold the original skull of Mary Magdalene. Another wooden Black Madonna and child is in the Chapel of Notre Dame at Rocamadour, seated on a throne and looking more like the Egyptian Goddess, Isis with her child. The popular Black Madonna of Poland with fleur-de-lis on her garment—is this another symbol connected to the Templar?

There is strong evidence that Mary Magdalene was worshipped, somewhat secretly, alongside the Virgin Mary until the Albigensian Campaigns of persecution of the Cathars into the late 13th century.

Hundreds of churches are dedicated to Mary Magdalene, presented as the Black Madonna, particularly in the South of France. The Knights Templar were champions of Mary Magdalene and funded many Cathedrals, until the French wing of the Knights Templar was dissolved in 1291.

In the fourteenth century, the Catholic Church made a concerted effort to clarify that the only 'Our Lady' was Mother Mary. In doing so, they made Mother Mary 'Bride of Christ', although it was emphasised to be a spiritual union only. However, there are still many church clergy worshipping the Black Madonna as Mary Magdalene; was she 'The Bride of Christ?' For over a thousand years, the church claimed she was a whore.

This has at last been corrected and Mary Magdalene is celebrated as an Apostle, celebrated on the 22nd July every year. (*I like that date; it was my father's birthday when he was alive, and he was a grand master of the Masonics. He would have known the truth about Mary Magdalene.)*

There is a belief that Mary Magdalene was married to Issa—Jesus—and carried his child, and there were many secrets suppressed by the Christian church. Their ancestors are said to carry the Holy blood. A stream of esoteric symbolic knowledge was guarded and passed down by generations of Templars, artists, artisans, poets, and alchemists.

Ancient Holy Scotland, Gaul, and the Atlantis Era

I received in the mail a gift of a book, The Holy Land of Scotland. It was written by Barry Dunford and described as a lost chapter in the gospel of the Grail tradition. There is a photo of Sri Sathya Sai Baba, who lived in Central Southern India.

Many believe, both in the East and the West, that he was the Avatar of Divine Incarnation of this Age; it is the same photo as in my first book. Sathya Sai Baba is holding a Blue Star of Bethlehem flower and standing in front of a paperbark gum tree. There is another photo, this time of Jesus looking very Celtic with reddish hair.

I found it very interesting, particularly as my mentor tells me that not all information can be given to one person. Rather, a piece of the puzzle is given to one messenger and another piece to another messenger and so on, so the combination of all the pieces come together as a tapestry to reveal the truth.

Whenever Sri Sathya Sai Baba was asked about his birth, he always told questioners to ask his mother, Easwaramma. She told everyone that a bright blue/white light had entered her womb through her stomach and that the baby had begun to grow, who was born Sathya Sai Baba. His name means Truth-Mother-Father.

Sri Sathya Sai Baba was born of an immaculate conception. The figure of Jesus has manifested and been seen at Christmas, walking in Sri Sathya Sai Baba's ashram.

There was a close relationship with the Scottish Royalty around the time before the Common Era with certain philosophers from Egypt, Spain, Greece, and India. It is believed that Jesus's grandmother, Anna, was married into Scottish Royalty before the Common Era.

In many respects, Scotland is a chosen land. There is a Greek tradition that Abaris was a Caledonian—a Scot—and visited Greece in the days of her early mysteries, bringing to the Druids and others some knowledge of the Ancient wisdom.

Furthermore, many of the traditions are steeped in Ancient lore, derived from the dim past, and even from Atlantean days. Some of the sacred spots seem still to be alive with the spirit of the old gods and initiates. "Let Scotland prepare the way of the Lords of Wisdom." *Theosophy in Scotland—August 1910*.

The borders of modern France are approximately the same as those of ancient Gaul, then inhabited by Celtic Gauls up until first century AD. The Essene's teachings were robust from the second century BC until the first century AD. It is interesting the Essenes have never been mentioned in the New Testament, yet when I first came across the word Essene, I cried and cried, although I did not understand why at the time.

The oral legend is Jesus' family travelled as refugees to the South of France, led by Joseph of Arimathea, Jesus' uncle. It is believed they travelled further east to Scotia, now Scotland, and that they had travelled to all of the British Isles previously with Jesus. The highlands of Scotland are ancient mountains, similar to the Himalayas, and are said to have existed even before the fall of Atlantis. At that time, land sank and land rose, and water disappeared from some land and reappeared elsewhere, reshaping the parameters of the land existing pre-Atlantean times.

There is strong evidence the Druids were highly cultured, having advanced schools of Astrology, Astronomy, Sacred Geometry, and Esoteric Teachings, knowledge used by the early stonemasons and carpenters in Egypt. The Sacred Geometry used to build the

Pyramids of Egypt is astounding and links with the mathematical sums of the Earth's circumference, distances to the sun, the moon, and other galaxies. There had been interaction with the teachings and philosophers from the Brahmins from India. The monks from Tibet, with the Pythagorean Essenes and the Druids, all influenced the early Christian Teachings.

The Brahmins from India would have spread the Ancient Vedic knowledge, the teachings from the sixth century BC Siddhartha Gautama, the Prince who had attained enlightenment, becoming known as The Buddha. His mother, Queen Maha Maya, was said to have conceived the child by experiencing immaculate conception. Maha means great; was that where the *title* 'Maharees' first came from, later becoming 'The Marys'?

I asked my mentor for a message with regard to all of the previous information and this is what he said:

"The ancient teachings have been suppressed over a period of time and now they are being revealed, it is that simple. Additionally, the Holy Blood is connected to the starpeople and that flows through every being that is upon this Earth...now.

"With changes that have been taking place over thousands of years, everyone who is upon this Earth has been enchristed from the World of Crystal. This is the bi-ocular field, like the eye of God, which mirrors the shadow that humans need to uncover to let their inner light shine. It is a level of light that all mankind has within them...it is a level of light that needs to be raised within them, to co-join with their Christ light, their God conscience that is within them.

"This is the message, my dear."

I would like to mention here that Rosemary Butterworth has since advised she was shown the symbol of the circle with a dot in the middle by Archangel Mikael. Jeshua Ben Joseph (Jesus) told her to remember that we are the 'SUN of God' and to let our light shine.

Unknown to Rosemary, I was also given the symbol of the dot in the middle of a circle after my near-death experience and when I came to Earth in this body. I, too, was shown it represented the

SUN of God, both in the microsm and the macrosm. I was constantly subconsciously drawing it all the time.

Rosemary also shared that when we ask for healing of our bodies, mind, and spirit, it was imperative that we use the words 'I allow.' This was to take place when asking the Angels for assistance as we are in a Free Will Zone and we need to make it clear that it is what we have chosen. It is making it clear that we are giving the Angels our permission to do the healing upon us. Thank you, dear Rosemary.

Ghost of Charles Dickens - Past-Life Memory

13

"I am fundamentally psychic," said John. "I didn't realise it at first, but I do now. It's awareness when I can almost predict what's going to happen in business and in all sorts of stuff. In fact, if you worry about something hard enough, it will go wrong.

To get people to understand what past lives and regression is about, I think the starting point is to ask people what they think is déjà-vu? Because I believe déjà-vu is totally in line with past-life regression. If you think 'I have done that before' or go somewhere and think 'I have been here before', although you know you haven't in this life, then your mind can go backwards and you start to pick up the vibes, the insight."

"Does remembering past lives help you in any way, John?"

John muses, "I suppose I could say the memory diminished my fear of death, made me aware I needed to curb my aggressiveness and anger. In some way, the memories helped me to release some of the aggression in me. By becoming aware how deeply it is entrenched in me. It also alerted me to the knowledge there is something besides this incarnation that I wasn't aware of before. I have had many lives as a warrior—there are two sides.

One is on the side of good and one is on the side of evil. It depends which side you are on, doesn't it? In fact, it matters little which side you are on. Everyone believes they are right and on the side of God. Makes war senseless because nobody learns anything from it—in fact, nobody really wins, all get hurt."

I have been speaking about past lives John and I have experienced on the Earth plane together as *Soulmates.* I would like to speak about more past lives that have been awakened in our travels together to sacred places. Before that, it seems *Upstairs* wanted to assist John with health and behavioural problems existing between us.

We are total opposites in personality and yet that has become an opportunity to find balance with each other, and in so doing we have been teaching each other. He has helped me to become more vocal about what I think. There was a need for John to stop drinking because his health was at serious risk. There have been times when his behaviour and words towards me were loud and angry, usually after drinking too much alcohol. This was extremely painful for me and not acceptable, so when I asked my mentors to help me, they replied, "Leave him to us!" This is how it unfolded...

John is now speaking:

"I had a blood test, which showed that my gamma GTs were becoming dangerously high and if I didn't stop drinking, then the chances are I would get cirrhosis of the liver and it would kill me. On that basis, the doctor said to me, 'Can you reduce your alcohol intake in the business you are in?' To which I said, good God, no, no way. I tell you what I will do, I'll stop drinking completely for the next ninety days and come back for another blood test and see what sort of an impact that may have had on me, right?

"The boys said, 'Dad will never stop drinking', that was enough for me to stay off it. I thought, *I'll show you, you little buggers*, and

I did stop drinking for ninety days. I went back and had another test and the gamma GTs had stabilised and reduced slightly.

"When I saw my friend Dr. Choong in Singapore, who is a university graduate of Monash in Melbourne, he put together a concoction of snake penis, ginseng, and so on, all ground up in a pestle and mortar and put into capsules. For three days in Singapore, I had a massive detox—diarrhoea, vomiting, sweating, the lot. I was very ill. After I came home, I went back to my doctor. After another ninety days and had a blood test, it was back to a normal level."

I discussed John's health with Helen, the one who is gifted in reading past lives, as in a recent dream I had seen him layed out on a bed, dead, with a white bandage under his chin and tied to the top of his head. Within days, she sent John this typed information on monogrammed paper of a Dove of Peace. John was fifty-eight years old and a cycle tied in with a past-life memory of him dying at fifty-eight from alcohol in another life. This was enough for John to stop drinking altogether.

"As I tune in, it is the early nineteenth century in England. I see you as a little boy. Your father's name is John and he has some connection with the navy. Now, I see your father jobless and in great financial difficulties. You and your mother live in the back of some old house in very primitive conditions. You are growing up with a sense of neglect and wasted talents and in bitter humiliation. Your father is always away, there is something shameful about it, you heard people say that he is in prison, but you are not sure. Your mother teaches you to read. For a few years you go to school while the family could afford it. While still a child of ten or so, you were sent to work. I can see you in a very dirty job, you are covered from head to toe in black dirt.

"Now there is money again in the family and you are being sent to school again. As you grow up, I see you working in a lawyer's office, I can see you doing lots of shorthand. I see you going in and out of courts, just like a reporter with notebooks of shorthand. I see you sketching, I see you writing stories, information seems to flow from your head through the hand. Immense talents in writing come to the fore. I see you becoming wellknown in social circles

later on, and also as an entertainer. I see you surrounded by books. You are writing books, there is a big human story in every one of your books.

"I can see you in a terrible railway accident, it came so suddenly and unexpected. I see you being trapped at the back of a carriage, unable to reach the exit, being surrounded by screaming and injured people. You move in and out of consciousness, you are shocked to the core of your being at being trapped by one leg and completely at the mercy of others. You are eventually being rescued, suffering injuries to one of your legs. The nervous shock from this experience remained with you to the end of this particular life. In fact, your life was never the same again, you worked hard, and you became very much exhausted, but at the same time, your life became more enriched in many ways.

"You had been married before the accident, but the marriage was not happy and you separated. After that accident, you saw things in a different light. You were fifty-eight years of age when you passed over to the Other Side, having had a life well-lived and been enriched by the adversities of life..."

With this, my visions faded.

I exclaimed to John, "I think this is the life of Charles Dickens!" John's family is connected to Charles Dickens' bloodline. When they were alive, John's mother and father used to attend Dickensian dinners held in London, when only relatives were invited.

The day after we read the 'past-life reading', we were out grocery shopping when John excused himself while he dashed away to buy a book. He loves reading and keeps saying, "I have to write a book." He returned excitedly, waving a book at me about 'Dickens' written by Peter Akroyd. John knew a fair bit of the history of Dickens, but neither of us had heard of Dickens being in a serious railway accident. We quickly looked at the index of the book and, sure enough, Dickens had been in a serious rail accident at Staplehurst.

The rail crash was an accident at Staplehurst, Kent, England, which occurred 9th June 1865. Ten passengers were killed and forty injured. It is remembered particularly for its effects on the author Charles Dickens. He was travelling as a passenger in a carriage of a 'Boat Train' with passengers from France and his companions, Ellen Ternan and her mother.

His lower leg was injured, and he risked his life re-entering the dangerously balanced carriage to rescue his latest manuscript. That was after giving comfort and assistance to the injured and dying fellow passengers.

In a quiet moment, I held the 'Dickens' book by Peter Ackroyd in my hands and asked my mentor *Upstairs did I share any part in the life of Charles Dickens*? The book fell open and my eyes were drawn to one particular paragraph about Ellen Ternan, described as a pretty, fair-haired girl, eighteen years of age, and not a very good actress. She must have been a nervous girl for she suffered a nervous rash; this was recorded in the book. Ellen and her two sisters were employed by Charles in his stage performances of 'character readings' from his novels, and they always travelled with their mother.

It is recorded that Charles was not the same after his accident, often suffering panic attacks in crowded places. He continued giving public readings, entertaining people far and wide. It is said there was a lot of scandal regarding his friendship with Ellen Ternan and that he was hopelessly infatuated with her; she was thirty years his junior.

In fact, the gossip became so bad, Ellen Ternan (pictured) and her mother Francis moved to live in France; that was arranged by Charles Dickens. He felt responsible for their unhappiness and the emotional pain it was causing Ellen and her mother; after all, they were respectable Victorian women. In fact, Ellen being a highly sensitive girl was close to a nervous breakdown.

Charles Dickens's wife and her socialite women friends were convinced he was having an affair with 'that woman' and she was the reason he left home. He would fly into a rage about the gossip, for there was no truth to it, the friendship being above reproach. His mistrust of women is being played out in this life, even to the point that John's first wife accused me of 'stealing him', despite us not meeting until after he was divorced. The gossip and the damage caused by it in Dickens's life is something John has to come to terms with, and *the reason he didn't trust women.*

Charles Dickens at 19 years old

John Barrow at 19 years old

That healing has been given after the release of the past-life memory, and he no longer has a problem trusting women. He also suffered agoraphobia, particularly when travelling overseas. This has now healed with the release of the memory of the serious train disaster. Having stopped drinking, he is not as angry, thus the words he uses towards me, if at times we don't agree, are far more acceptable.

John, in this life, still loves telling stories in his modulated English voice, using accents where necessary to colour and amuse his listeners. If he is standing, he still throws his arm up in the air, turns, and walks away with a flourish when he has finished the story, reminiscent of leaving the stage after a performance as Dickens.

It was no coincidence when John found himself on business in Melbourne. A few weeks after all this began to unfold, there happened to be a performance of Charles Dickens' Characters being enacted on stage. Here is how he tells of the event.

"It all started when I was on a business trip to Melbourne and was walking down Bourke Street. There is a theatre down there, its name doesn't come readily to me as it is some years ago now. When I saw on the billboard 'An Evening with Charles Dickens', I thought, *Oh yes!* Bearing in mind my family association with Charles Dickens—Elizabeth Barrow was my great, great, great aunt and Charles Dickens' mother. I rang my wife Valérie and said, "Do you think I should go and see this or what?" To which she said, 'Of course you must, it is part of your family.' So, I shall go to the Theatre to see 'An Evening with Charles Dickens."

A tall gentleman with a long cheroot hanging out of his mouth stepped into the box office. There was something about him that made me want to talk to him. I said, "And who might you be, may I ask?"

"Oh, I'm the producer of this show."

I said, "Oh really, are there any special discounts for family?"

He said, "What are you talking about?"

"Well, Charles Dickens' mother was my great, great, great Aunt, Elizabeth Barrow."

It was his turn to say, "Oh really, would forty dollars be all right?" I agreed with a big grin.

"Tell you what, I want you to meet Simon Callow who is doing the stage show of all the Dickens characters on his own. It is almost a soliloquy. I'd like you to meet Simon after the show. Can you manage that?"

Simon Callow took Charles Dickens off exactly the way Dickens did in his lifetime, because it is not altogether known that in fact Charles Dickens was far more famous in his lifetime for his shows on stage, taking off all his characters. Simon Callow was on stage non-stop for three and half hours. He went through something like forty-two different Dickens characters. I was absolutely mesmerised.

It was quite sensational and because of my bloodline and the fact that Elizabeth Barrow was a bit of an actress in her own right, coming from a very wealthy family, I thought it was as if the characters were coming through me. It was riveting...I felt as if I was Dickens.

I met Simon Callow after the show; he was delighted that Charles Dickens' mother's great, great, great nephew had turned up and we enjoyed a quiet drink together. I also thought to ask Simon if he knew the incident about Charles Dickens and Queen Victoria. He said, "No, what are you talking about?"

"Queen Victoria commanded Charles Dickens to attend Buckingham Palace, to give her a private showing of his talents because she had heard so much about him. When Charles was told this, he said, "You can tell that bloody woman she can come to my theatre—which she did."

This is a letter I, Valérie found on the internet that Charles Dickens entrusted to his publisher. It is self-explanatory. And I know it to be true. I have the memory of Ellen Ternan.

The Mystery of Ellen Ternan

The Violated Letter

On 25th May 1858 Charles Dickens saw fit to give his manager, Arthur Smith, a statement, which would later become known as 'the violated letter'. He instructed Smith to 'show it to anyone who wishes to do me right or to anyone who may have been misled into doing me wrong.' Smith apparently showed the letter around and it was published, without Smith's knowledge, in the New York Tribune on 16th August 1858 and then reported throughout England.

"To Arthur Smith, Esq.,

Mrs. Dickens and I have lived unhappily together for many years. Hardly anyone who has known us intimately can fail to have known that we are in all respects of character and temperament wonderfully unsuited to each other. I suppose that no two people, not vicious in themselves, ever were joined together who had a greater difficulty in understanding one another or who had less in common. An attached woman servant (more friend to both of us than a servant), who lived with us sixteen years and is now married, and who was and still is in Mrs. Dickens' confidence and mine, who had the closest familiar experience of this unhappiness in London, in the country, in France, in Italy, wherever we have been, year after year, month after month, week after week, day after day, will bear testimony to this.

Nothing has, on many occasions, stood between us and a separation but Mrs. Dickens' sister Georgina Hogarth. From the age of fifteen she has devoted herself to our house and our children. She has been their playmate, nurse, instructress, friend, protectress, adviser, and companion. In the manly consideration toward Mrs. Dickens, which I owe to my wife, I will only remark of her that the peculiarity of her character has thrown all the children on someone else. I do not know—I cannot by any stretch of fancy imagine—what would have become of them but for this aunt, who has grown up with them, to whom they are devoted, and who has sacrificed the best part of her youth and life to them.

She has remonstrated, reasoned, suffered, and toiled, and came again to prevent a separation between Mrs. Dickens and me. Mrs. Dickens has often expressed to her sense of her affectionate care and devotion in the house—never more strongly than within the last twelve months.

For some years past, Mrs. Dickens has been in the habit of representing to me that it would be better for her to go away and live apart, that her always increasing estrangement was due to a mental disorder under which she sometimes labors—more, that she felt herself unfit for the life she had to lead as my wife, and that she would be better far away. I have uniformly replied that she must bear our misfortune and fight the fight out to the end, that the children were the first consideration, and that I feared they must bind us together in "appearance".

At length, within these three weeks, it was suggested to me by Forster that, even for their sakes, it would surely be better to reconstruct and rearrange their unhappy home. I empowered him to treat with Mrs. Dickens, as the friend of both of us, for one and twenty years. Mrs. Dickens wished to add, on her part,

Mark Lemon, and did so. On Saturday last, Lemon wrote to Forster that Mrs. Dickens 'gratefully and thankfully accepted' the terms I proposed to her. Of the pecuniary part of them I will only say that I believe they are as generous as if Mrs. Dickens were a lady of distinction, and I a man of fortune. The remaining parts of them are easily described—my eldest boy to live with Mrs. Dickens and to take care of her, my eldest girl to keep my house, both my girls and all my children but the eldest son to live with me in the continued companionship of their Aunt Georgina, for whom they have all the tenderest affection that I have ever seen among young people, and who has a higher claim (as I have often declared, for many years) upon my affection, respect, and gratitude than anybody in this world.

I hope that no one who may become acquainted with what I write here can possibly be so cruel and unjust as to put any misconstruction on our separation, so far. My elder children all understand it perfectly, and all accept it as inevitable.

There is not a shadow of doubt or concealment among us. My eldest son and I are one as to it all.

Two wicked persons, who should have spoken very differently of me, in consideration of earnest respect and gratitude, have (as I am told, and indeed, to my personal knowledge) coupled with this separation the name of a young lady for whom I have a great attachment and regard. I will not repeat her name—I honor it too much. Upon my soul and honor, there is not on this earth a more virtuous and spotless creature than that young lady. I know her to be innocent and pure and as good as my own dear daughters.

Further, I am quite sure that Mrs. Dickens, having received this assurance from me, must now believe it in the respect I know her to have for me, and in the perfect confidence I know her in her better moments to repose in my truthfulness. On this head, again, there is not a shadow of doubt or concealment between my children and me. All is open and plain among us, as though we were brothers and sisters. They are perfectly certain that I would not deceive them, and the confidence among us is without a fear."

Illustrations from 'The Childs Return' by Charles Dickens – note the knights in armour

Painting in Mr. Dickens home – city of London – Looking so like a Chevalier Knight (Dickens alter Ego)

14 Ghost of Charles Dickens – A Healing for John

For John, the Charles Dickens life was important for his soul to review so that usually with release of the memory, emotions are healed. However, it was so deep-seated within him there was a need for him to release the resentment and trauma he suffered in his childhood in this life. That, in some ways, was similar to Charles Dickens' childhood and I cannot help thinking his parents were possibly the same souls in both lives.

I have asked John to speak of what happened.

"Well, this was a most extraordinary thing that happened when we went to our friend's housewarming party. There were a lot of interesting people there, including some Gold Brokers, very wealthy young men. One of them, Michael, who we had never met before, came sidling up to Valérie and sat down beside her saying he wanted to talk about Sai Baba, the Avatar who lived in India, and to have a look at the ring Sai Baba had manifested for her. Sai Baba had told her that if she looked into the emerald-coloured stone held in the ring, he would be there. Valli was sitting with her leg up on a chair, having had surgery, and Michael sat beside her holding her hand with the ring on it. I was sitting opposite, on the other side of the table.

Michael suddenly wielded on me and said, "You were born in Brentwood in Essex in England..." which was correct, wondering where the hell he got this from. Then he said, "You really hate your mother and father because of them not being there for you, when you needed them as a child."

Then he said to me, "You attended public school in Kent and you left and studied law with your father for a while. That didn't work out, so you did your National Service. You joined the City of London Regiment."

All of this, I might add, is totally accurate. "You couldn't settle down, so you went to South-East Asia and took up a commercial career that you have been doing ever since. You have had tremendous resentment about your mother and father." I listened to this quietly and he said, "This is coming through your Uncle Bill's spirit, your mother's brother. In the war, your father sent you and your mother up to Northumberland and Uncle Bill was really your surrogate father for a couple of years. You worshipped the ground he walked on and he was very good with you as a second father."

John thoughtfully adds, "However, when my mother came out with some unfortunate comments like, 'I'll beat you within an inch of your life' and 'I'll break every bone in your body,' it wasn't terribly good listening when I was about seven years of age...and my father was pretty indifferent, he was never there when I wanted him, there was no doubt about that. It built up a long range of resentment, which to that day when I met this fellow Michael and he started telling me all this..."

Michael said, "Your Uncle Bill is here in spirit and he is not very pleased with you. He feels that what you should do is to forgive your mother and forgive your father and not hold this resentment. You also need to forgive yourself when you were a child.

What you have to do is write your father a letter forgiving him, write your mother a letter forgiving her.

"The thing that really sticks in your mind is being dumped in boarding school when you were only eleven years of age and you felt abandoned. You felt they could not get rid of you fast enough. You had several nannies and you couldn't hack that and then you got dumped in boarding school. The first time you were dumped in a boarding school was when you were only five years of age, but you were taken out of there because the headmaster was a cruel bastard and beat the young students.

"Then it happened again when you went to other schools. All your parents cared about, you thought, was having cocktail parties and mixing with a social set."

"That night I also remembered my childhood living in London, England. It was during the Second World War and had been a very difficult time for all of us. There were constant air-raids, sirens blaring, and bombs exploding around us. It seriously affected my family. My father had served in the army in France in the First World War.

"My father had sat my mother and me as a seven-year-old around the kitchen table and dramatically laid a revolver on the table. He said the enemy were evil and that if they invaded us from across the English Channel he was going to shoot me first, then mother, and then himself. A few weeks after that, a German pilot was shot out of the sky and landed, with parachute, in front of me in the garden. He told me not to be frightened and when my mother came back from the shops, he was going to give her his revolver and be her prisoner. When the police arrived, my mother objected to the way they manhandled him and demanded they treat him with respect, as he was an officer and a gentleman.

"Looking back, that confused me as a child. On the one hand, I had been told by my father the enemy was evil, and on the other hand my mother wanted to protect them.

"My life changed totally when a few weeks later, my mother was again up at the shop and the air-raid siren blared. I had been trained to seek shelter under an 'Anderson Shelter' that is a very sturdy table in the kitchen. I grabbed the cats, climbed into the shelter, and the next thing a bomb hit the side of our house and I was buried alive.

"I must have been in there a long time when at last I heard voices calling out to me and a hose pipe was pushed through the rubble to give me air. Eventually I was dug out to thankfully see daylight. I tried to be brave, but I resented my mother and father not being there when I needed them. It was after that event my father sent my mother and myself north to family in Northumberland.

"So, when I received a long email from Michael the next day outlining more for me, saying I should write the letters because your Uncle Bill is not very happy with you holding on to this resentment, verging on hatred, all these years, Valérie encouraged me to write the letters, burn them, and then put them under the tree.

"So, I did. I felt almost instantly that a whole weight had been lifted from my shoulders and what Michael had encouraged me to do made me feel pretty good.

"Following on from that, I have now put up on the apartment wall a photo of my mother being presented at court along with the summons from the Lord Chamberlain to attend a Royal Garden Party in 1937. I have put up a photo of my father, a photo of Uncle Bill, and I have also put up a photo of myself when I was commissioned in the army as a second lieutenant in the Royal Fusiliers' Regiment. I feel a lot better and happy about that because it is out in the open—it is all dealt with.

"From Michael's point of view, giving the reading was all new to him. He was in awe of the experience. He was holding Valli's hand with the Baba ring on it the whole time and, out of the blue, all the information for me came through him."

John was experiencing this soul healing at the same age in this life as he was when Charles Dickens died—that was the image of Charles laid out I had seen in a dream and thought was John. I later saw that same image/photo in Peter Akroyd's book about Dickens.

John and I talked about my work with past-life regression, for the people with the most urgent past-life need for healing also have a similar story played out in their childhood years of this present life. It is written into their soul blueprint. It is not generally the same story, but certainly the same emotions are involved. This is a plan the spirit masters have derived. If people do not come to investigate past lives, at least they can review and heal their early childhood traumas. The memory then drops back into past emotions in a domino effect, held within the soul—healing the past-life traumas. Sometimes, healing is about self-worth.

I do love John deeply; having so many lives together, it is instinctive how well we know each other. He cannot hide anything from me, nor I from him. We sometimes get cross with each other, but the reason is usually because of some frustration caused in our daily life and we are overtired.

Early in our marriage, I remember my skin becoming red and cruelly itchy, the disease reacting to something...it is usually always a mystery why. I was covered in ugly sores and we were told there is no cure. However, one day John walked into our bedroom while I was changing my clothes. Being ashamed and self-conscious about the state of my skin I tried to hide my naked body with a towel.

He walked up to me and pulled the towel from me and asked what did I think I was doing? I stood there, totally vulnerable and embarrassed, with tears rolling down my cheeks. I couldn't speak. He stood looking at me, silently, challenging me to confront my issue, and with a kind voice, said, "Valli, you are my wife, I love you, I don't care about your skin, I love you."

A Mission with Rev. Charles Leadbeater and Dr. Annie Besant – Theosophists, India

15

Annie Beasent *The Reverend Charles Leadbeater*

Travelling to Sacred Places

The most sacred place to travel is within the self, to find the God Self.

It is best to go into an altered state of consciousness if you want to recall past lives. Practising meditation, it is simple to lay on your bed, gently let your eyes roll up under closed eyelids, as if you are looking into the outer atmosphere of Earth. Don't force this. Ask to connect to the Creator of All or your guide.

Then ask for information to be given as to why you feel you have a mysterious connection to something that is happening in your life now that doesn't quite make sense. Hold that thought for a while—a feeling will come, or visions, or words, or even sounds, taste, or aromas. Let your eyes roll back to normal, open your eyelids, and make notes.

You may ask another question the same way to clarify anything that comes to mind. Remember, thoughts will be put into your head from your soul consciousness, so use discernment as to the conversation that can or may take place. Or you could seek out a competent past life and regression therapist and work together.

Sometimes, a soul can experience a 'parallel lifetime', meaning living in more than one body at the same time. Some lives are very ordinary, with an opportunity to experience an understanding as a pauper, a leper, a male life, a female life, an incapacitated life, a happy life, a sad life, a wealthy life—other lives may be of great power, wealth, and leadership. We always return to the World of Light and consolidate what we have gained in the weight and measure of our character building.

We are always connected to a Guardian being who cares for us and guides us. In the order of things, my mentors advise me there is a third and fourth dimensional consciousness within our atmosphere that they say are together—an emotional consciousness that stays with us even when we finally leave an Earth body. There is also cosmic consciousness, a hierarchy, and an Angelic Realm that has no abode at all, and some of us work with 'The Great Plan.'

It is the emotional body or our actions from the 'past' or 'present' we often need to heal. You could think of a past life and the person who you were as if a very close relative. Your soul has many different personalities, experiencing different lives at different times. It is not a linear time but rather a quantum time, all happening at once.

Your soul is the doorway to your oversoul; it is actually a family of personalities the soul has experienced, held together by a Monad, which is your God Self and is overseen by an angelic presence. It is actually an 'expression of consciousness' held together in a sacred geometric circle with six points connecting to androgynous selves, or *if separated* they become twelve points connecting to male and female beings, thus, twin souls. All this is shared with other God being 'expressions of consciousness' in the Force Field of God or the Creator Source of All. Think of that symbol of the dot within a circle that is the Sun of God.

Your oversoul 'relatives' are so close to you emotionally that when your mind thinks about a particular life, you can become it.

You can feel his or her emotions and realise the reason for the life at a particular time. It is very easy to refer to a past life as 'I was', as if it is the self now. I, personally, have always felt uncomfortable saying "I" was in a past life for *in reality*, it is as if you are looking into a mirror and recognising similarities with the other people from your soul story; sometimes, personality traits or physical diseases and disabilities reappear that can be healed. Physical images of people from a past life can be quite similar to an image of themselves in their present life, even when there is no inherited blood DNA.

As walk-ins, we have taken over the Earth body of a previous soul—the agreement has been made long before any of us have incarnated onto the Earth plane. The soul of the previous owner is not inherited, but the agreement is to look after the Earth body as one's own—to help heal it—and rectify any wrongs that may have occurred in this life only. If they are a mother or father of children, the children have been born through the Earth body and so the children still belong to you.

John and I have a memory of walking together as friends, as elderly people, dressed in white, living in India. Our names were the Reverend Charles Leadbeater and mine was Doctor Annie Besant. The work we did then is now continued...although it is not exactly the same. We worked for the Theosophical Society in Adyar near Chennai.

Originally, the Society was established in 1875 by the Russian noblewoman Helena P. Blavatsky, Colonel Henry Steel Olcott, and attorney William Quan Judge. It is a worldwide body whose primary object is Universal Brotherhood without distinction based on the realisation that life, and all its diverse forms, human and non-human, is indivisibly One. The Society imposes no belief on its members, who are united by a common search for truth and desire to learn the meaning and purpose of existence through study, reflection, self-responsibility, and loving service.

Theosophy is the wisdom underlying all religions when they are stripped of accretions and superstitions. It offers a philosophy that renders life intelligible and demonstrates that justice and love guide the cosmos. Its teachings aid the unfoldment of the latent spiritual nature in the human being, without dependence.

Charles Leadbeater died 1st March 1934. John Barrow was born 6th January 1935 — virtually nine months later. Part of his soul blueprint plan was for Charles' spirit to walk with John's mother on Earth while she was pregnant and allow a physical likeness to be imprinted into the embryo. We are given to understand that another soul was appointed to look after John's body until Charles Leadbeater's soul was exchanged and entered twenty-one years later into John's life. Understand that the soul of Charles/John has many personality life stories to tell.

As does Annie/Valérie's soul have many personalities from other times. Annie Besant died 20th September 1933. Valerie Barrow, née Young was born 17th December 1932. Part of Valérie's soul blueprint plan was to allow Annie's spirit to walk with Valerie's mother on Earth while she was pregnant to allow a physical likeness to be imprinted.

Our mentor has advised that the anomaly of Valérie being born nine months before Annie left her mortal body was not unusual.

We are told, "There is no black and white time. Spirits/souls walk in when the cells of human life come together as an embryo. The spirit and soul of another can walk with the mother of the new child coming in—so the influence is coming in or influencing the consciousness of the new embryo. Even though Annie Besant herself had not yet left her mortal body, her spirit soul was moving in and out. In other words, the spirit soul can come and go when you are asleep, but it can do that at any time. The spirit soul is not locked into the physical Earth body, so that it can move to other places."

We are given to understand that another soul was appointed with agreement to look after the body of Valérie until Annie Besant's soul was exchanged later in her life, in 1969. Remember our soul has been many personalities, even if it is here in an Earth planet body for the first time.

A friend sent us small photos of Annie Besant and the Reverend Charles Leadbeater, personalities known from the Theosophical Society. It was not until it happened that we realised how similar in appearance we were. John, in this life, still wears a large ring on his finger and he gave me an equal-sided cross, like the one he is seen wearing in the photo of the Reverend Charles Leadbeater. John looks like him; he used to have a beard and he still has that 'twinkle' in his eyes. He was a confrontationist then, as he is in this life. We carry forth characteristics from other lives to either heal or to assist us, with abilities from the past on our journey in this life. When John was a little boy, his family used to call him 'The Young Charles.'

I have a photo of me when I was sixteen and the likeness is similar to the photo of Annie taken in her late teens. There are other characteristics and some abilities of Annie that I have inherited in this life. Annie was an academic and a feisty lady; I have always wanted to attend university but was blocked whenever I tried to continue my education as an adult student. I also can be feisty but have mellowed greatly in later years.

I have been blessed in attending the *University Upstairs*, which began with a vision of seeing 'EST'. I am advised by my mentor that EST stands for Extra Sensory Template. Wikipedia advises it means an expressed sequence stage or EST is a short sub-sequence of a cDNA.

I was awakened by my mentor, as I have said before, and taught basic physics, chemistry, and biology. I went from one psychic and scientific subject after another and when I thought, "Ah, this must be what *Upstairs* wants me to do" it would cease and move onto another subject. The subjects covered such things as psychometry, clairvoyantly helping to find things or people, remote viewing, understanding the many layers of consciousness, how spiritual healing and distant healing works, dream interpretations, the hidden knowledge of crystals, extra sensory perception, the use of symbols, and many other spiritual insights linked to science.

I am reminded of a time when visiting Singapore in the very early days of my 'Extra Sensory studies'. A friend asked me if I would visit the Adyar Bookshop, which is connected to the Theosophical

Society in Sydney, and purchase a certain book for her. This was the first time I had ever been into an esoteric bookshop and it was over thirty years ago.

As I entered the store, my eyes focused on a section of the bookshelves entitled '*Classics*'. I was fascinated, thinking how could I have been so dumb? These subjects have been written about down through the ages. I was utterly surprised to see the cover of two of the books looked just like a dream I had the night before.

The pictures were Dantes' vision of the *Celestial Rose of Paradise*, from the fifteenth-century manuscript held in the Vatican Library. The books were named '*Spiritual Unfoldment One*' and '*Spiritual Unfoldment Two*' by a medium Grace Cooke, who received messages from a light being named White Eagle. I had never read about nor witnessed a medium in action.

This was no coincidence, so I bought the two books and realised while reading them that it was my mentor's way of introducing himself and that it was White Eagle who had been teaching me, preparing me a few years later for mediumship and 'direct voice channelling'.

I would like to mention the rock drawings and sculptured reliefs at the World Heritage Listed, Mahabalipuram outside Chennai and south of the Theosophical Society in India. When visiting, it is no wonder John and I knew them and felt we had been there before. Annie and Charles would have visited Mahabalipuram in their lifetime. That was the most recent past life John and I shared.

How strange that journey was. When the airplane taxied along the runway for the next leg of flight in India, I had the distinct feeling the plane was flying backwards. I realise now I briefly experienced a time warp of when Annie was in India. When I first alighted from an airplane and put my feet on the ground of India, I felt I had come home.

Of interest—I have a close friend who has Madam Blavatsky in her soul story; that is not surprising as she and Annie were close friends and, in fact, she was cared for and died in Annie's house in England. That friendship continues in this life.

And another has contacted me for advice about his psychic development and his ability of remote viewing. He has always referred to me, in this life, as his spiritual grandmother. As I eventually found out, it was in Annie's life.

One day, I opened my computer to find an image of Jiddu Krishnamurthi and knew straight away it was *Upstairs* who had placed it there. I was prompted to send the photo to Christopher, a young Indian man who lives in the Caribbean, the one who refers to me in this life as his spiritual grandmother. I asked him, "What do you think of this man?" He immediately wrote back, saying excitedly, "It's me—I even have the same nose in this life and the same background linked with a long line of Brahmins."

Annie Besant had adopted Krishnamurthi as a boy when she lived in India and was indeed like a spiritual grandmother to him even in that life.

As I have said, past lives still exist, in that the universe does not operate in a linear time, rather quantum time. **It means everything is happening at the same time and time or space does not really exist.** It is all relative, depending on what point you are viewing or focusing on.

For instance, in the early days of white man's settlement as a penal colony in Australia, it would take the wonderful sailing ships six months to reach Australia with letters, then another six months to reply back to England. Now, we can lift a telephone and speak immediately to each other. If speaking with someone in the United States on *Skype*, there is often a fifteen-hour time difference, so that makes us in their future and yet we are speaking and seeing each other at the same time. And the long distance of separation makes no difference.

A soul has many aspects from its Monad—its God Self. This is why it is possible to regress into a past life or future life and remember or know of other aspects of one's soul. A soul's story is all relevant and infinite. People say there is no such thing as time—but it depends on where your conscious focus is. There are different frequencies of light in one's soul consciousness. It is the oversoul that holds and is the spark of the Divine Creator within them.

I have read a number of Charles Leadbeater's letters to Annie Besant while she lived in India and he in Australia. He considered her a close friend with affection and even said they had shared many lives together. It is in this life we have been given insight into many of those lives, as soulmates.

John was born in England and I was born in Australia, but we were destined to meet. We have both had a soul exchange, with a previous soul in our body...it was agreed long before either of us came here. We both have the same spiritual mentor. We have volunteered to 'walk into this world' on a specific mission, which is unfolding as we travel to sacred places.

Les Sts. Maries de la Mer, Camargue, France

16

John and I were constantly guided while moving from one place to another when travelling.

One Thursday afternoon, we were driving into the small village on the Bay of Marys and saw signs everywhere in the village of a colourful scene. It was showing a little boat in sail of *Les Saintes Maries de la Mer Evocation de l'arrivee des saintes*.

We had no idea there was to be a re-enactment of the landing of the Marys on the forthcoming Saturday night. This re-enactment of the legend only happens once a year in *October* and we found we arrived in time to witness it. A day of rest was welcome, giving time also to explore and get to know this place.

We found the Les Saintes-Maries-de-la-Mer Church where the effigies of Mary, Salome, and Mary Jacobe, along with Sarah are carried down to the sea at their annual sacred festival held in springtime. These Marys are all said to be the family of Jesus. But that festival is not the Evocation we are to see on Saturday night.

The people of the Camargue wetlands are gypsies with a strong Spanish influence. They have held the *oral legend* of the landing of The Marys for nearly two thousand years.

'Gypsies' is a term used for Egyptians who fled the temples in Egypt when they were invaded long before the first century BC. Many of them were originally gifted priests and priestesses. They knew of the Essenes. They knew the 'family' and wanted to protect them. They called Issa Jesus and they also heard of him being crucified.

The Camargue region is the Delta of the River Rhone, made up of lakes and marshlands, giving home to over four hundred species of wild birds. It is known as the cowboy country of France, where white horses and black bulls run wild. When the horses are born, they are black or dark brown and as they age, they gradually become white. The gypsies are herdsmen and superb horsemen. A long stick with a three-pointed end is used to poke the bulls in a certain direction. We were told the Camargue bulls horns point up to heaven. When they have bullfights, the bull is not killed but rather festooned with flowers after the bull has been made submissive.

John and I sit in a prime position on the beach to watch the Evocation. Eager crowds gradually gather around the large fenced area where the enactment is to take place. A film crew have erected complicated stage lights near us, with some adjusting taking place. Romantic music is played to entertain the waiting people—there is not a religious feeling to the set but rather a stage performance.

Finally, under full stage lights, sheep are herded onto the sandy stage leading to the water. The fine horsemen and women come galloping in, and later goats, then white horses and black bulls. All are paraded by the gypsies and herded off the stage at eight pm when the event—the Evocation proper—begins. A little boat on the water under sail, out at sea, is spotlighted and makes its way ashore.

Nine bonfires are lit on the beach to welcome them and to show the way to where the gypsies are. The gypsies, simply dressed as they would have been nearly two thousand years ago, crowd to the water's edge and assist the refugees ashore. Although the area was part of the ancient Roman Empire, this watery region remained safe and separate at that time.

John and I are overwhelmingly moved with emotion as tears run down our cheeks. Words are being spoken over the loudspeaker, relating the story in French. I mentally chastise myself for not bringing a recorder to be able to translate it later. Not understanding what is being said puts us in an observation mode but leaves us free to receive insight and understanding from within our own soul memories, for both John and myself could remember being part of that ancient time.

When all the family arrive, they are greeted and brought up the beach closer to the waiting crowds. One scene in particular, I can see thin white light in stripes streaming down from *Upstairs* in the night sky above and I take a photo. This is what a priest friend said when he later saw the photo.

> "The Evocation, as a sacred event, re-enacts the Holy and thus is a suspension of time and space. The energy at the Evocation is the sum of the sacred energy and devotion to the Three Marys and their flight into Gaul. The tradition of the Evocation around Jesus and his companions calls back that energy, which surrounded his followers and the Marys, and the lines of light indicate Divinity is present, pouring down divine sacred energy into the actors, the participants, and all the observers at the Evocation."

When all the survivors gather in a row, looking towards the viewing crowd, there are nine, not three, as I had imagined in my mind, so I thought, *how can this be?* I later asked my mentor.

"Nearly two thousand years ago, there was more than one boat that landed, I can assure you. The gypsies welcomed the family

and they, on the boats, knew all the people who were on the beach waiting for them to land.

"Brother James, John the Divine, and Joseph of Arimathea were with them. They moved onto other places. Mother Mary, her two daughters, Judith and Ruth, were also with them and, of course, Mary Magdalene who stayed in the area, moving from the shore to the mountains and spreading the teachings as she went. The teachings were not a religion, they were teachings from the Source, the Source of Creation. They were merely passing on a 'way of life', a 'way to live'. At the time, there were sacrifices and slavery going on and this is what they wanted to stop.

"They wanted to encourage people to love one another, to love the animals, to love all that was upon the Earth, and to appreciate and love Mother Earth—these are the teachings that were passed on. Jesus said, 'Love one another as I have loved you.' The disciples of Jesus, as they were known, were simple people, loyal and God loving. They had a special energy around them, they had all been enchristed, and people recognised that, so that when they spoke and put their hands out to communicate with people, they recognised the energy of Holy Spirit that went with them."

John is not normally as open to the paranormal, but on this trip he was well and truly receiving messages from his mentor, the same mentor as mine.

Basilica of Mary Magdalene, Saint Maximin

17

The area is a Massif—a geological formation that is visibly moved by Earth's tectonic forces. The region, as evidenced by some archaeological finds, was already a religious centre some three thousand years ago. There exists a huge reserve of water fed by all the rivers of the region. Since prehistoric times, the pagan cults, dedicated to the goddesses of fertility, were developed here. Some historians believe the forest was frequented by the Druids at the time of the Celts from the fourth century BCE. This forest leads to the Cave of Mary Magdalene, documented in our next chapter.

The attractive market town of Saint-Maximin lies three hundred metres above sea level, surrounded by vineyards and sheltered by the three great ranges of Mont Aurelien, Mont Saine Victoire, and the Sainte-Baume. Originally a Gallo-Roman site north-east of Marseilles and The Camargue, this ancient town owes much of its fame to its rich history touched by the mystique and legend of Mary Magdalene.

The relics of the Saints are said to have been discovered here in 1280, in a crypt dating back to the fourth century AD. First preserved in a primitive local church, then later in order to accommodate the burgeoning influx of pilgrims, Charles II of Anjou, Count of Provence, and nephew to Saint Louis of France, ordered the construction of the Basilica of Saint Mary Magdalene and Convent to be built over the crypt, with the blessing of Pope Boniface VIII.

John and I are entranced at being able to stay in the Royal Convent, once occupied by Dominican monks, but now converted to accommodation and a restaurant.

We soon begin the short walk to explore the magnificent Basilica. I know the remains of Mary Magdalene are now kept in the crypt and I am anxious to view them. When the Crypt is opened, I will ask the Abbot if I may take a photo of the shrine of Mary Magdalene with the skull inside.

I ask my spirit mentor if it is really she. He says, "It is indeed, my dear, for all have come to recognise her and bless her for her work—the ones that understand and know the origins from which she came. The photo that you have IS an extra light, my dear, so do not question it. It is in acknowledgement of your presence and she is very pleased to see you. Understand her spirit is not just in the crypt but is omnipresent—and it will follow you to the mountain cave."

We were given a very special image of Mary Magdalene in the mountain cave.

The Crypt also houses the sarcophagi of St. Maximin, St. Sidoine, St. Marcelle, and St. Susanne, all dating back to St. Mary Magdalene. These were more Saints said to have arrived with the Marys. There is a belief that St. Maximin was the brother of Mary Magdalene, who moved onto the mountain area with her to assist in spreading the teachings.

Our mentor has advised many ships came with the refugees from Egypt. Nearly 2,000 years later, the records of antiquity are difficult to decipher. A companion or disciple is often referred to by name, or town of birth, or a son of—it is very difficult to know when it is the same person being recorded in manuscripts written by different scribes.

There were many who left the Holy Lands via Egypt after Jesus was crucified. Those, particularly the women, who travelled to and stayed in the South of France were still in danger and had to go about their mission of spreading the teachings quietly.

Joseph of Arimathea, a wealthy merchant, travelled with others to his familiar territory in the Britannic Isles and began his teaching there. He went on to establish the first Christian Church at Glastonbury, England. It was wetlands at that time, similar to the Camargue and not so dangerous, even though it was still part of the ancient Roman Empire.

Cave of Mary Magdalene, La Sainte-Baume

We are staying at the wonderful Royal Convent Hostelerie in Saint Maximin, next to the Basilica. Thinking of the message from our mentor, who said we would visit the cave of Mary Magdalene, I am at first in some doubt, for it is pouring with rain this morning although I am given insight the weather will clear later in the day.

We have booked another night at Saint Maximin and found, with some difficulty, our way out of town for the thirty-five-minute drive. Half the journey is climbing a dangerously narrow road up the mountain from Saint Maximin to the first little Abbey at Plan d'Aups, and then a walk to Sainte Baume, which means cave or grotto. My heart is in my mouth the whole time as we have a large hire car that seems to overlap the edge of the road. We would have preferred a smaller car to travel around the narrow streets in the little villages of Provence.

There is a long history of what has happened to the cave of Mary Magdalene over the years. The thirteenth century saw the peak of pilgrimages in Christian Europe. 'The Kings Way' is the road through the Sacred Forest to the Cave. Thousands of pilgrims have come to this holy site over the centuries, including eight popes and eighteen kings. Hence the name Chemin des Roys, or The King's Way. Four Dominican monks still live up there.

We arrive at Plan d'Aups at seven hundred metres. The wind is strong as we alight from our car and we are nearly blown off our feet, then it begins to pour with rain. Umbrellas are out of the question—they will easily be blown inside out. We decide to have a cup of coffee at the little store and wait to see if the weather improves. When we finish our coffee, we hear a bell ringing, calling people to a service to be held at the little chapel next door. The chapel has wonderful paintings on the wall depicting the three Marys and others arriving by boat at the Bay of Marys. Magdalene's hair is painted long and red, looking more Celtic than Arab-like. *Did our ancestors know more than has been recorded?*

The priests conduct the morning ceremony, wearing robes of white with green chasubles; on the robes is the symbol of the Chi-Rho. It is obvious we are meant by spirit to stay for the service, for by the time it finishes the weather clears a little and we begin walking through into the Sacred Forest.

We reach the entrance gate to the wonderful ancient forest. Just as we do, two young men and a woman dressed in medieval garments arrive. John greets them in French and they call out they are going into the forest with their dog to collect truffles. It seems strange, as if we have stepped into a parallel universe. Another time completely, John is speaking to them and I am experiencing a feeling of familiarity as if I have walked this place before.

Quietly shaking within myself, I remember the body as a Pope. I have been here before, in another life. I don't like that life memory, but I am part of it. It is in my soul memory. I will speak of it more, but not now. I ask John to walk with me on the original path that leads up the mountain to the cave, the way the monks walk. Not the King's Way. I like the idea of becoming close to the nature spirits that exist in this magical forest and so we walk the old way, the narrow path.

We walk for one and half hours up and up—still cold, windy, wet, and slippery under foot. Some of the trees are down after the storm. As we reach about halfway up the mountain through the forest of different shades of wet shimmering green, everything becomes calm and peaceful, almost as if we are walking in a different dimension again.

Eventually, we come to changes made to the entrance of a small abbey. I say 'changes' for I am still recalling that other time I visited. One hundred and fifty steps, representing the Psalms of David, are built up to the doorway. A sign shows the different order of monks that have been in residence over the centuries.

Cassianites 415 – 1079 AD

Benedictins 1079 – 1295 AD

Dominicains 1295 –

To the left, before you enter the doorway, is a life-like scene of the three Marys kneeling at the feet of Jesus as he hangs from the cross. Mary Magdalene is still shown with long, red hair.

I take a photo showing the valley below and how far we have climbed and then we enter the cave. There are no monks in sight, or anybody else; *we are alone*.

Overwhelmingly, Magdalene's presence is here. The Church is inside the massive cave *where candles are alight and where water is still dripping* from the rock ceiling. John is the first to kneel in prayer and I am so touched. The moment is very special and bonding for us. Bless him!

I have taken a photo of inside the cave and when the photo is turned upside down there is a clear image that has appeared in the photo, of the skeleton face and long hair of Mary Magdalene, wrapped in a shroud and looking as if she is lying in a sarcophagus. I believe it is spirit's way of confirming that her remains were definitely once in this cave, and then later moved to the Basilica at Saint Maximin.

It has been a steep, beautiful, fresh smell of wet earth and scented leaves walk up from seven hundred to a thousand metres, and a real challenge not to slip in the mud. Heel then toe keeps us safe, John tells me that is how he was trained to walk in the army. *We feel truly uplifted once we reach the cave.*

It is a relief to arrive back at the chapel and the shop at Plan D'Aups to have another hot cup of coffee and a very appropriate

Madeleine (*Magdalene*) cake. We meet a grateful forester whom John is able to advise, in French, about the fallen trees.

Now, finally, we are driving back down the narrow road, easier on the inside this time next to the mountain wall, and returning to the warmth and dryness of the Royal Couvent Hostelerie at Saint Maximin.

When the photo taken by Valerie Barrow is turned upside down
a sarcophagus with a body in a shroud becomes apparent

Glastonbury Abbey and the Tor, England

18

At another time, we travelled to England and visited Glastonbury Abbey. It seems appropriate that I speak of it here because of the connection to Joseph of Arimathea landing in South of France, then continuing on to the British Isles.

Entering the grounds of Gladstonbury Abbey, we were handed a brochure.

> *Traditionally, the earliest Christian Sanctuary in Britain. Legend says Joseph of Arimathea brought Jesus here and they built the old wattle and daub church. History records it as standing in 600, and it burnt down when the entire Abbey Church was destroyed by fire in 1184.*
>
> *Archaeology tells us that Christianity has been present in Somerset since earliest days. Glastonbury was important for pilgrimage—even 'The Second Rome'. The Abbey became the largest and richest in England. St. Bridget, St. David, and St. Patrick are said to have visited.*
>
> *St. Dunstan was educated at Glastonbury Abbey and was Abbot here until he became Archbishop of Canterbury. He introduced the Benedictine Rule to Glastonbury and into England. Another Glastonbury monk, Sigeric, became Archbishop of Canterbury in tenth century.*
>
> *In 1191, legend says that the monks found the buried remains of King Arthur and his Queen Guinevere. In 1278, they were re-buried in the chancel in the presence of King Edward I and Queen Eleanor.*
>
> *In succession, three stone Abbey churches have stood here. The remains you see date from 1184 until 1539, when the*

Abbey was seized on the orders of King Henry VIII during the Dissolution of the Monasteries. It was demolished gradually and used as a 'quarry' for building stone. The Abbot's Kitchen is one of the Abbey's remaining complete buildings, and from April to October there are demonstrations about the life of the monks.

Behind St. Patrick's Chapel is the Glastonbury Holy Thorn Tree, which flowers twice each year. The Holy Thorn is said to have originated from a tree that grew, according to legend, when Joseph of Arimathea plunged his staff into the ground at Glastonbury where it burst into leaf. The grounds contain thirty-six acres with a fine selection of trees, wildflowers, and bulbs for interest and seasonal variation, wildlife, ponds, and a cider apple orchard.

In 1907, the ruins were bought and preserved. The Abbey is a charity; our only income is from you, the visitor.

We were very happy when we entered Glastonbury Abbey behind high stone walls. It is privately owned by people who live in Australia and managed by locals. The grounds are a lovely peaceful place to visit with calm energy. We enjoyed strolling around the ruins and walking the velvet green lawns.

We came across the original site of the wattle and daub referred to as 'The Old Church'. At the time, Glastonbury was an island surrounded by marshlands—a safe place when the Island of Britain was still occupied by the Roman Empire. In earlier days, Joseph travelled with Jesus north to Scotland. It is reported that Joseph had already acquired land from the local ruler, Arviragus, to establish a place of learning and meeting, hence the wattle and daub building.

Strolling around, we saw where the monks found the buried remains of King Arthur and his Queen Guinevere. Before we left the Abbey, we found the Holy Thorn Tree, on Wearyall Hill on the way to The Tor. It was a stiff climb up the hill—The Tor, without handrails, is above the Abbey at one hundred and sixty metres above sea level. There remain the ruins of St Michael's church destroyed in 1539 on the orders of King Henry VIII. There also, the last Monk from Glastonbury Abbey was hung, drawn, and quartered. I refused to 'tune into' that energy.

The energy on the Tor was breathtaking. It was easy to see how Glastonbury town was built on an island and that large, wide, flat plains existed in a full circle around it in what was obviously once a marshland. Hills rose in a great distance around a larger circle that had an opening, like a gateway, where the sea would have once come in and flooded the plains. This was looking west towards Wales. I could easily see why Glastonbury was once called the Isles of Avalonia and existed as marshlands when King Arthur ruled fifteen centuries ago and, of course, when Joseph of Arimathea lived there.

Joseph is said to have died at Glastonbury on 27th July 82 AD. On his tombstone was written in Latin, 'After I had buried the Christ, I came to the Isles of the West, I taught, I entered into my rest'.

We later visited the Chalice Well and its Holy Waters. Chalice well is one of Britain's most ancient wells, nestling in the Vale of Avalon between the famous Glastonbury Tor and Chalice Hill.

I felt very close to Joseph and Jesus in Glastonbury Abbey, especially the spot where the daub and wattle church had stood. Jesus—I prefer to call him Issa—referred to himself as coming straight from the Father. He wanted to discourage sacrifice and slavery. He wanted people to understand where He really came from and the message that He brought in the name of The Father, for people to love one another as He loved them. He spoke with clarity, being overlighted with divine light of love so that people felt compelled to stop and listen and marvel at His words. He performed miracles.

He was the anointed one. The word 'Christ' comes from the Greek word Christos. Christos is the ancient Greek translation of the Hebrew word masiah (Messiah), meaning 'anointed one'. Later, with the development of a church and a religion, it eventually came to be called Christianity.

At the last supper, Issa has been portrayed to say, "This is my body, this is my blood." The church has placed the focus here—and this is not really the focus.

The focus is love, the focus is the Divine Kingdom of God, a cosmic kingdom of oneness of spirit. Issa often used symbolism in teaching. His blood and His body were not of this earth. He was showing everyone that His blood was holy and His body was holy and that He had come directly from The Father, or another world. The Chalice was the symbol of the Holy Grail. This is the Sang Real...the Blood Royal...the Holy Blood and the Holy Body, through which it flowed. He came from the cosmos. Issa's message was, "*Love one another as I have loved you.*" And that, "*The Kingdom of God is within you.*"

As a medium, I have, with agreement, allowed beings of light to use my voice box to speak through me. I have been blessed a number of times with the light being who is Jesus presenting himself and speaking to us. In particular was the first meditation we had for the New Millennium. All in the room felt His presence when He took over my body. Some of those present could see him clairvoyantly; He was dressed in pale blue and white robes. He stood with His hands uplifted towards everybody in the room. All were moved to tears and felt overwhelmed by His presence. He was sharing His energy with us, not speaking much at all—but He did say: "*Many people await for my return, but I have never left, all you have to do is ask and I will come.*"

The room was filled with a warm feeling of universal love and peace. When I sat down, I became aware of footprints in the carpet, which took a long time to fade.

Stonehenge, & Avebury, Wiltshire, England

John and I travelled to Stonehenge and Avebury in Wiltshire, England. They were made UNESCO World Heritage sites in 1986 for the outstanding prehistoric monuments from the Neolithic and Bronze Age periods.

Stonehenge is the most famous stone circle covering two thousand five hundred hectares of chalk downland and arable fields in Wiltshire. It is the most sophisticated stone circle in the world, aligned on the solstice sunrise and sunset. Ancient and mysterious, Stonehenge is also an amazing feat of prehistoric engineering.

Looking at Stonehenge from the road, John thought they had to be extra-terrestrial—meaning there was no way the ancient peoples of the land could have moved those huge stones across Salisbury Plains from where they were quarried in ancient days, nearly four hundred kilometres away.

I asked our mentor about the beginnings of Stonehenge. The stones are said to be placed in 3,000 BC or even 10,000 BC. "Could you advise when they were placed?"

"The original stones were placed before Atlantis fell—in other words, they are over twelve thousand years old. However, the Druid Priests later added the smaller stones. We, as the blue people, taught the people of the time to understand ceremonies connected to astronomy and astrology and did our best to help them to understand that influence upon the Earth.

"As I have said, the site itself has changed since we first introduced it to the little earthling—unfortunately, there were ceremonies that began later and sacrifices were made, which was not the intention.

"From the starpeople's point of view, the huge stones were very easily lifted by levitation and easily placed in a circle. There has been movement in the Earth since the stone circles were first erected and some fell down, but over hundreds and thousands of years there has been additions made to them—however, its first role was to align with the Sun, the Solstice in the summer, and the Solstice winter sun alignment.

"This was, and is, the best time for ceremonies to take place and to lift the energies by the prayers that were made at that time, and still do, to align to the centre of the Earth."

"Thank you. Is there anything else?" I asked.

"I would remind you that there are many, many crop circles created in that area—it is no coincidence. The area is a point of light upon this Earth, as are other points of light upon this Earth, such as the pyramids in Egypt and Uluru in the centre of Australia. There are others as well. These points of energy are uplifting, and the consciousness of the people can be uplifted if they are open to change. This is all you need."

"Oh, okay. There is talk about the Druids but what about the Celts? Can they be seen in the ancient times, and the Deities?" I was thinking of Isis and Osiris from Egypt. *"It is the same. The Deities are the starpeople. And they did influence the people and this is exactly what I am saying to you, the focus was upon the Sun in your so-called pagan ceremonies."*

"Why yes, the focus is upon the sun...of course. Thank you—thank you."

"It is my pleasure, my dear."

When John and I arrived at Stonehenge, hundreds of tourists were waiting to walk under the road to reach the site—we were not allowed to walk close to the huge stones. We noticed a flock of birds alight on to one of the lintels just as we arrived and when it was time for us to leave, they flew away.

We felt it was a 'sign' from Holy Spirit, letting us know they were with us. I had visited the site as a young woman in 1953 and was disappointed now to find I could no longer walk inside the circle and touch the huge stones. John and I felt something was missing; it could have been all the people moving about without a ceremony taking place to honour the ancient sacred site. Or it could have been the rock walls built around the site. This saddened us.

Another insight was given to the existence of chalk or limestone in a large area of Southern England and Southern France, showing an ancient link to the two places being once together before tectonic plates shifted.

We enjoyed travelling around the countryside of Wiltshire, an ancient land steeped in myth and legend. The sun was filtering through large, green leafy trees overhanging narrow, stonewalled roads. We passed several images of White Horses, cut into the depth of chalk on the green hills high above us.

The White Horse was a religious symbol to the Celts and to the Romans. There is enormous fascination in the Druids, Stonehenge, the Celtic religion, and the origin of the Chalk Downland sculptures in Britain and elsewhere.

Avebury, Wiltshire, was our next destination—the area is so large it is easier to see the Stone Circles from aerial photographs. It is the site of an ancient monument consisting of a large henge, several stone circles, stone avenues, and burial mounds, surrounding the village of Avebury in the English county of Wiltshire, and one of the finest and largest Neolithic monuments in Europe.

Silbury Hill, at nearly forty metres, is part of the complex of Neolithic monuments around Avebury, which includes the Avebury Ring and West Kennet Long Barrow. Silbury Hill is the tallest prehistoric human-made mound in Europe and one of the largest in the world; it is similar in size to some of the smaller Egyptian pyramids of the Giza Necropolis. I can not help wondering if the burial mounds, known as Barrows, are linked in some way to John's family name Barrow. Their family seat is in the west country of England.

In the centre of the huge stone circle is a pub with much activity, noise, and drinking. John was extremely upset and critical of them. He did not like the energy at all. When we meditated, we found that he had been a Druidic Priest in ancient times. That was why he was so upset with everybody's behaviour; people were not honouring the centre of the very large stone circle as had been done in earlier times.

I placed my hands on one of the huge stones—a Guardian—and felt that the stones had been, after movement in the earth, replaced incorrectly in some places. The blue people, starpeople had placed them, like Stonehenge, in the first place before the fall of Atlantis and before the movement of tectonic plates around the Earth. John and I have both had memories of the blue people being in each of our soul's history. It is why we both find these stone circles so familiar.

Our mentor has reminded us there are many 'crop circles' appearing each year, particularly in and around Wiltshire. He advises that the starpeople are bringing the images onto the earth from their starships; using their equipment on board, they punch in the symbolic pattern they wish to create onto the crop.

When the little scout ship is positioned above the crops, they press a very strong amount of air, which comes down and virtually stamps the pattern onto the earth. It is that easy. It is done in a way that there is no damage to the crop.

19 Rennes-le-Chateau and the Valley of God

Back in France, we travelled from Carcassonne through the Aude Valley on our way to Rennes le Chateau. This is Cathar country where the Albigensians were tortured and burnt to death for heresy. It was the beginning of the Inquisition. The whole area is full of intrigue, history, and mystery. The area around Mt. Bugarach, it is said there are the most seen UFOs in the whole of France. That particular area is known as *Val de Dieu* or the Valley of God. I jump ahead of myself a little; we need to find a place to stay that we can use as a centre-point to travel to and from all the marvellous sites in the surrounds.

The village of Quillan has been recommended. As we are driving towards it, John suddenly makes a left turn and we find ourselves in front of the lovely Chateau des Ducs de Joyeuse in Couisa, a medieval castle restored into a charming hotel-restaurant. The Chateau of Couisa stands at the confluence of a fast running mountain stream and the River Aude, on the site of an ancient Gallic-Roman settlement whose original name was Cousanum. It does not take John long to talk the owner into giving us an excellent deal for a four-night stay. We both feel we have visited the Chateau before, particularly when climbing the ancient stone circular staircase to our room.

Our first visit is to make the short journey up a mountain drive to Rennes Le Chateau. As we arrive, we are blessed with a calm, clear, sunny day overlooking the mountain peaks towards Mt. Bugarach. There is much mystery and history surrounding the church.

A new priest, Father Berenger Sauniere arrived at the Monastery in 1885. Within the space of a few years, he changed forever the destiny of the small village in the Aude. Sauniere's renovations and, above all, his high-profile building projects rapidly raise the question as to the origin of his funds. The rumour spreads he has discovered some sort of treasure.

This has inspired many researchers, scientists, and historians to undertake a complicated search, with different aspects and avenues of answers to a multitude of questions. In particular, strange statues and secret codes that exist at Rennes Le Chateau appear to be hiding concealed information.

One of the most famous non-fiction works is *Holy Blood, Holy Grail,* written in collaboration by Michael Baigent, Richard Leigh, and Henry Lincoln. Publication of this book in 1982 sparked off a storm of controversy, reverberations of which are still resounding throughout the western world. It has spawned numerous articles and questions, along with conspiracies to be found on the internet.

Dan Brown's book, *The Da Vinci Code,* is a thriller fiction along the lines of the non-fiction book. It sold over eighty million copies and is translated into forty languages.

Some of the questions raised are:

- Where did Father Sauniere receive the funds to pay for such elaborate renovations?
- What were the manuscripts said to be found by Sauniere in a secret cavity within a stone column, and was Mary Magdalene really buried under the floor of the old church at Rennes Le Chateau?
- Did a secret society exist named the Prieure de Sion?
- Did the Knights Templar keep The Holy Grail in France and if so where?
- Was Jesus married to Mary Magdalene and did they have children leaving a dynasty of a Holy bloodline?
- Did Jesus survive the Crucifixion and live to an old age?
- Did the Cathars hold a secret manuscript named *The Book of Love*? And if true, where is it now?

I would like to quote, '*A word from Father Sauniere*', printed in a pamphlet given at the Museum at Rennes Le Chateau. It is written and signed by B. Sauniere in 1903.

"Rennes le Chateau owes its origins to the fortified city of Rhedae, which was founded in the fifth century by the Visigoths. The city lay on the plateau extending towards the southeast at the foot of the present village and numbered some thirty thousand inhabitants. The capital of the vast district of Rhedae was destroyed in 1170 by the King of Aragon's army.

In the fourteenth century, Pierre II des Voisins, Seneschal of Carcassone, restored the fortifications and the town grew prosperous once more. It was seized anew by the Spanish, who left only the ancient church dedicated to St. Mary Magdalene and the castle of the Lords of Rennes. 1362 thus marked the end of the city of Rhedae, which subsequently became the small settlement of Rennes le Chateau. However, the old feudal castle, still standing, has seen the activity of the past resume.

The church, which was falling into ruin, has been completely restored and magnificently decorated. The grounds around the church, formerly full of rubble, now feature a splendid Calvary, half hidden amongst flowers and shrubs. The Villa Bethany, a superb residence in the most sophisticated style with a large garden in front and surmounted by a fine statue of the Saviour, His arms open wide, has just been completed. The old ramparts have been replaced by a broad walkway running along the rest of the mountain. An elegant veranda acts as bartisan. At the end, the Magdala Tower, a crenellated marvel of civil and military architecture, serves as a library.

These works of art have taken the place of the murderous architecture of the past. The turret and crenellations now serve for contemplating, close to heaven, the magnificent panorama stretching away on every side as far as the eye can see. And the hordes of warriors have been replaced by peaceful hordes.

> They come up here to admire, within this incomparable setting, the marvels of art wrought by a priest with an artist's soul, one who loves his church and his parishioners."
>
> *Signed: B. Sauniere.*

In discussion with a Catholic Priest friend, I have been advised of the mass intentions.

> "These can be for the gospel of the day, the welfare of the people in the local parish, the poor and the needy, and for the memorials. What we call the stipends, which can be either private or public, in the sacristy there is a register and you can view it. Now the rule is you are only supposed to say mass for people in the diocese. There is ample evidence that Abbé Sauniere received stipends for masses from way, way outside of his ruined chapel at Rennes-le-Chateau. He was accused of selling masses in his lifetime and was suspended for unaccounted incomes—people just thought he was selling masses. There are recorded lists of his mass stipends, at fifty or sixty Francs at the turn of the last century; this was a very large amount. Donations from wealthy visitors for building improvements had been received also. Father Sauniere did not accumulate monies for personal gain; rather, it is recorded he died a pauper."

On our travels through the South of France, we found old churches and statues dedicated to St. Mary Magdalene. She was honoured and respected by the Knights Templar. I have no doubt she would have walked the mountains in this area and would have known of the important cosmic aspect of the area.

Whether a secret society existed named the Prieure de Sion is questionable, after a list of Grandmasters was published and later discovered as fraudulent. I know when John and I visited the Mary Chapel at Mont St Michel, I picked up a pamphlet written in French, advising of a meeting to take place by the Prieure de Sion. That was 1991 and it did not suggest any conspiracy. And as said earlier in this book, the Prieure de Sion was actually known by secret societies as an 'allegorical' doorway.

The Freemasons' in the past, as far back as the time of the Temple of Solomon, had secret signs and initiations. They were good men and only wanted to assist communities. During the medieval times in Europe, they could have been burned at the stake if they spoke of their secrets. These days, their initiation rites are public knowledge and the public is invited to their meetings. Their secrets did hold knowledge of The Holy Grail and a marriage between Mary Magdalene and Jesus, and the Templars knew that Jesus lived a long life in India long after he was crucified.

An Indian friend advises me her mother's family came from Srinigar, Kashmir. She tells me that for generations a family looked after a grave for nearly 2,000 years in Srinagar, Kashmir, where it is said Issa is buried. He was known as 'The Prophet'.

On further research, there is a book called *Jesus Died in Kashmir* by Andreas Faber-Kaiser, dated 1978. It speaks about Jesus' boyhood trip to Kashmir at the age of thirteen to study Buddhism. His gospel of love pleased the Buddhists, but the Hindus saw it as a challenge to the caste system and the power of the Brahmins. Jesus visited Persia, but the Zoroastrian priests also saw him as a threat and asked him to leave.

The author, Andreas, tells this story from Nicholai Notovich. When travelling in Kashmir, which is also known as Little Tibet, he visited a lamasery where he was told of 'Issa, a son of Israel' visiting nearly two thousand years ago. The author Nicholai tells the story of Jesus' travels after the crucifixion, saying his wounds healed and he set out with Mary and Thomas in search of the ten lost tribes of Israel.

I worked with a lady in a regression in 2012 who remembered a life as Thomas. This lady had not read the aforementioned book. She remembered details of how Issa was assisted after the crucifixion and that his wounds had healed. Thomas then travelled, in secret, with a few others and Issa to India. She remembered the separation from Jesus in India and then Thomas continuing his teachings in the South of India until he upset the Brahmins and was murdered. Saint Thomas Mount is still known in Chennai. John and I have visited there.

I had wondered about what happened to Mother Mary. At the time, somebody began speaking about Mother Mary being buried at Ephesus and the apostle John also being with her. I was given an article about someone visiting Patmos to find a cave where St. John the Divine wrote of the Book of Revelations. These were 'signs' given to me by coordinated incidence, to confirm the information by my unseen mentor.

My mentor had already told me Mother Mary had travelled from South of France, to Syria and Turkey with her son John, where many Jewish people lived without danger. The area was on the outskirts of the Roman Empire. Her daughter, the third Mary, Judith, who is in my oversoul story had travelled to India with Issa. Unfortunately, she died before she reached Kashmir and is now buried in Pakistan.

Another regression was with a lady who remembers the life of Mary Magdalene. She remembers the simple life as an Essene and the initiations the Marys entered into. She remembered marrying Issa and having a child. She loved him deeply. After the crucifixion and the family's escape to the South of France, most of them moved on to other places. Issa had the gift of bi-locating and would come to visit her in the South of France just to talk. He was then living in India and had remarried with more children. She remembers him visiting her and comforting her when she died.

Jesus was birthed from an immaculate conception that gave him the gift of Holy Blood. The Holy Grail is within all of us. I know I have said this before. All of us have gone on to inherit the Holy Blood and the uplifted consciousness that goes with it.

We need to realise we have inherited an Earth body also and need to lift its consciousness. We can receive help from the Enlightened Ones—we only have to ask. If you look at the 'bigger picture' to all of this, hasn't Father Berenger Sauniere been inspired by the Enlightened light beings to create this mystery around Rennes le Chateau that led to all the controversy?

Dan Brown states on his website his books are not anti-Christian, that he is on a 'constant spiritual journey' himself, and his book *The Da Vinci Code* is simply 'an entertaining story that promotes spiritual discussion and debate', suggesting the book may be used 'as a positive catalyst for introspection and exploration of our faith.'

The same could be said for the book *Holy Blood, Holy Grail* written by Baigent, Leigh, and Lincoln.

Aude Valley – Esperasa Dinosaur Museum

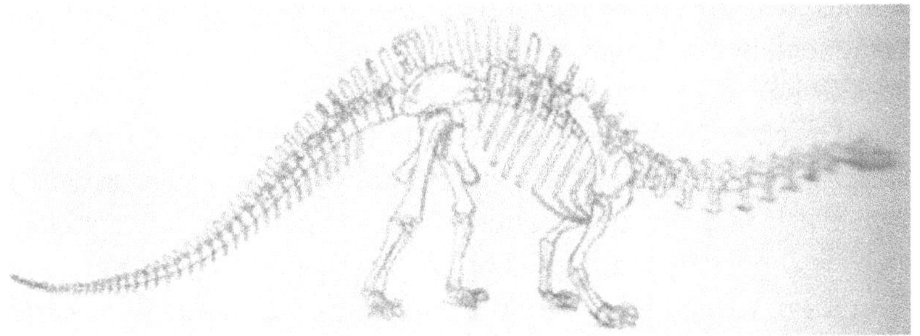

Henry Lincoln has become an expert in his discoveries over the last thirty years, including the history, the mystery, and the fascinating landscape geometry of Rennes le Chateau and the Aude Valley. As well as co-authoring *The Holy Blood, Holy Grail*, he has written and presented a DVD 'Guide to Rennes-le-Chateau and the Aude Valley.'

John felt we had to purchase a copy; his strong insistence made me feel spirit was speaking through him. In this DVD Henry Lincoln deals with his discovery of the eighth wonder of the world—the Rennes-le-Chateau Pentacle of Mountains—and the geometry hidden in the stunning countryside surrounding it.

Henry demonstrates drawing on a map, joining the five mountain peaks in a circle, and how they are equidistant, forming a five-pointed star. He links this remarkable symbolism to Venus. One of the mountain peaks is Rennes-le-Chateau and more specifically the Tower of Magdala dedicated to Venus.

In another demonstration, he places a compass point on the town of Esperasa and drawing a full circle, it covered six churches equidistant forming a six-pointed star—the Venus or the Star of David.

I have been shown that the five-pointed star of Venus represents the Da Vinci's sketch of Vitruvian man and then the six-pointed star of Venus is an uplifting of man's consciousness into a star man.

Returning to the discovery by Henry Lincoln of this important sacred geometry of the Aude Valley, or the Valley of the God, *Val de Dieu*, I would like to speak about our visit to Esperasa not far from where we were staying in Couisa.

Remember, the town of Esperasa is the centrepoint of the circle of churches that form the Star of David, believed to have been influenced by the Knights Templar.

We had driven past the village of Esperasa on our way to Quillan when I felt spirit wanted us to visit there. A Dinosaur Museum signboard on the road beckoned us to Esperasa and I hoped it would not be an amateurish exhibition to attract children, without any real fossils or ancient bones. I could not have been more wrong; it is a fabulous museum with many fossils and dinosaur bones that have been found in the immediate area.

The richness of the site has led palaeontologists to prospect the Upper Aude Valley, resulting in the discovery of forty dinosaur localities, including many localities for dinosaur eggs. The Upper Aude Valley is now the best-known area in Europe for the Late Cretaceous period 65 million years ago when dinosaurs walked the earth.

Excavations are being conducted several months each year by the team from the Esperasa Dinosaur Museum.

Friends of ours, on two separate communications this year and unbeknown to each other, visited the Aude Valley also known locally as the Valley of God. They felt there was an esoteric connection to sacred Uluru, Australia. Certainly, there is evidence of red earth that is also found in Central Australia. There were major changes to the earth structure in the Aude Valley. Scientists place the destruction of the dinosaurs around sixty-five million years ago.

I find it an extraordinary thought that, although utter chaos would have happened at that time, the Hierarchical Realms still created mountain peaks with such precision—so that Sacred

Geometry was created and has been discovered by Henry Lincoln. While presenting his work on the DVD, he was shaking his head in disbelief that the drawings could measure so accurately between each mountain peak.

I noticed a circle containing the five-pointed star on Aude Valley mountain peaks partly overlaid the circle with the six-pointed Star, creating a Vesica Piscus—the sign of the fish used in symbolism for Jesus Christ. This really is the Valley of God. When we visited Mt. Bugarach we felt a beautiful calm, peaceful, and uplifting energy. The grass was particularly green with tiny flowers everywhere; the air was soft and warm with butterflies abounding. It is a heavenly place.

John and I agreed to sit and meditate by a small sparkling stream. As we were about to sit on the large stones, John found a packet containing two tiny keys. Surely this was a sign from God. In my little book of alchemy, the meaning of 'key' is 'Inner awareness that opens door to all truth, wisdom, knowledge.'

Was this symbolising our personal Holy Grail?

21 Montsegur, Languedoc, South of France

The higher we climbed the more narrow the track became.

We have been staying at the Chateau Des Ducs de Joyeuse at Couisa for three days. There is something very nice about this Chateau—we feel we are meant to be here. John was not well yesterday, so after we drop our washing at Quillan we spend a quiet day. A hot lemon drink and two headache tablets later, he is feeling much better. I wish I could throw my cold off so easily.

We plan to travel sixty kilometres to Montsegur if the weather is pleasant. There has been a major shortage of diesel fuel, and up to only thirty Euros allowed with each purchase. The people are also upset with their French Government over an addition of two years to the pension retiring age and have had strikes everywhere, including the airports. This is what the newspapers are reporting, but I am sure there is more to their dissatisfaction.

It seems a good excuse not to travel to Montsegur—there and back would be 120 kilometres. Montsegur is in the Pyrenees Mountains region, almost at the Spanish border. For a while, I have been dreaming up reasons as to why we should not go. Knowing *Upstairs* may want us to, I put it out to my mentor in my mind that if John was keen I would go. Anyway, it is another beautiful day the next day, John is keen, and so off we set for Montsegur.

We reach Montsegur, the last bastion of the Cathars, and begin to climb. There is a monument to pass, in memory of the Cathars who lost their lives at the beginning of the Catholic Church Inquisition.

I begin to feel a bit strange and uncomfortable...

It is a very high and a steep, tough climb. In some places I have to get down and crawl backward bit by bit so as to not slip over the dangerous drop. John and I begin to feel quite shaky towards the top—the path is extremely narrow in places, with pebbles that roll underfoot, making it hard to keep one's balance. I feel slightly giddy and need to steady myself by bending over and clinging to tufts of grass just to keep my balance.

I sit exhausted, almost wanting to give up, breaking down into what I know is a past-life memory of being here before, and sob with a broken heart. The sobbing comes from deep within my inner being, leaving me feeling completely lost and abandoned.

All I can say is, "God said he would always look after us—so how can this happen?" I know the base of the mountain will be set alight and all upon her will be burnt to death if we don't surrender. Then when we come to the ground level, we refuse to deny our faith as Cathars and are burned alive anyway—over two hundred of us. John felt I was taking on the past-life memory for him also. In that life, we were brother and sister.

I felt I could not go on climbing as it was just too narrow; with the loose pebbles one could easily slip over a huge, twelve hundred metre drop. There is no safety fence.

John moved on ahead, saying, "Look Valli, we are almost there."

I had sobbed into a bush that had been neatly trimmed and felt like a soft pillow. I regained my composure and *Upstairs* said, "*We are very glad you have both come.*"

John came back for me and we both called on a 'River of Divine Light' from The World of Light to enter through the top of our heads and continue into our bodies. It then passed through our bodies down into the whole mountain, in the name of Mother Father God. This cleared us of the painful energy we had been unconsciously holding onto and helped clear the mountain also. With my beloved's help, I then regained my nerve and continued just a few more steps around the corner and 'at last' we were at the top.

Then, out of the blue, a single delta-winged fighter plane deafeningly zoomed over the top of us. It was flying well below any radar at only about five hundred metres and so fast it was out of sight as quick as a flash. John sang out, "They never fly singularly." We both laughed loudly—normally, spirit sends us an eagle to confirm they are with us, but today a bit of modern technology instead! Thank you, Holy Spirit!

We felt uplifted and knew we would be safe going back down the mountain, and we need not feel any nervousness. It had been a Mission we had to do. I am so glad we did and so is John. It was far from easy...

At a *sub-conscious* level, I knew how dangerous the climb was and what had happened before. That was why I was holding back and not wanting to go there. But now all is perfect.

We spent a little time at the museum in the village below Montsegur. I took a photo of the entrance sign showing two keys again—it linked us with the two tiny keys John found when we were about to meditate at Mt. Bugarach, Valley of God. Both of us were very disturbed by the artefacts we recognised in the museum. In particular, a blackened, open-patterned metal book cover. *Didn't that hold the missing manuscript that John the Divine had written?*

We went back to our lovely Chateau des Joyeuse in Couisa and collected our swimming togs to go for a swim at Rennes les Bains. The water is sourced from warm mineral springs, without the strong sulphur smell that often goes with such water. John was complaining at first, but after our marvellous swim and cleansing of our ethereal aura as well, we felt fantastic, a '*catharsis*' well done.

Past-Life Memory at Montsegur – Book of Love written by John the Divine disciple

Our mentor wanted to speak with us and particularly with my John. I have a lovely interview from him on my tape recorder. He confirmed we experienced the memory of Cathars because of our visit to the 'Bay of Marys' and witnessing the Evocation. These events triggered the memory for us.

John asked our mentor about a dream where he saw himself directing the construction of a road to be built up to the castle on top of Montsegur. Many Cathars at the time sought refuge there from the King's army. He also had a dream about the Christian Church developing so misguidedly.

"You have the teachings in your soul," our mentor advised. "You have a connection to John the Divine. Is it not surprising when you are called John—there are several Johns. There is the one who is referred to as John the Divine, he is the brother of Jesus and this is your connection. You may be surprised at this, but there was a dream that was given to you and you were one of those who began the teachings here in this country that was known as Gaul, at the time of the Roman Empire. Your dream was given to you to awaken your understanding."

"Yes, my understanding is certainly awakened," my John said. "Still a little hazy, in fact. I feel I am not quite with this dimension, particularly when I walk and in particular after visiting Saint Maximin and Sainte Baume. I found that an extraordinary experience. I definitely felt I had been there before but in what capacity I am not quite certain. Perhaps you can enlighten me?"

"As I have said, you were one of the disciples and very close to you is the family of Jesus and... Valérie is aware that she also was close to the family of Jesus. So, in actual fact, in that time you were brother and sister and part of the family of Jesus. Also, you were older and like you are now, organising and taking care of and helping the group in their mission. So, you were very much part of that mission in the early Christian days.

"The feeling that you had, as if you were not quite here, comes from that memory because it comes from another time and that was why you were not feeling 'here', in this time. It is nothing to be

afraid of, it was actually an awakening my son, an awakening as to who you were and who you really are—in those days, you were inclined to make judgements and that is understandable because you were very upset about what had happened to your brother.

"And there were others who were killed because of that—because of the teachings. It was hard for you to accept and be loving towards those people, but you came from a place where they did not understand, they were just not aware. Try to imagine as they are and as they were back in that time. They were illiterate then and did not know many things. They were not exactly ignorant—they had their way.

"It was a time. It was a time that has advanced from then, until the dark ages, but for now it is moving forward to the Golden Light that is lifting everybody's consciousness and helping them to know who they really are from the soul that exists within them. Am I making myself understood, John?"

"Yes. I have another question—I am always intrigued by the Nazis and Hitler and people like Himmler who had an interest in Montsegur. I always watch movies on the subject. Now, having come on this spiritual journey, which is exactly what it is, I am aware of the fact there is an association between the Nazis and people since the Nazis in Germany. They have had this unbelievable association with the Cathars that is in the place we are right now. Can you explain that to me? I don't quite understand."

"Everybody has a soul and is driven by memories from that soul in their actions in the life that they live in the body now. At that time, it was the time of a great war, or the Great Second World War. There are people here who came from the Nazis, as you say, and came to this place where they had memories in their soul and knew of the beginnings of the teachings of Christianity and the way the people lived. Some people had these memories and translated them into the lives that they lived in during the war.

"Because of interactions with one and another, they fulfilled a conclusion to the reality of the story that exists in their soul and so, there was some confusion—there was some misunderstanding—therefore, myths were created that are really untrue. You understand what I am saying. And so, they took the time in their

lives as the Cathars as to their own and began to believe that in some way they were connected to this.

"The story was twisted in the outcomes and their deeds also. They believed the Jews had caused their downfall as Cathars—because it was only a thousand years or so after the disciples had first come to this new land that was called Gaul. So they were misleading themselves—not connecting—they had knowledge, but only part of the knowledge and they twisted other knowledge that they thought existed, so do you understand?"

"Yes. I guess...But does that justify the cruelty to the Jews and everybody else?"

"Of course, it does not—and if you were to ask yourself you would not have to ask me that. As I have said...it was twisted and misunderstood. The knowledge was greatly misused for a power they wanted to have for themselves. Do you understand this?"

Murmuring, John says, "Yes."

"This power was not used in the early days... but as I have said it was twisted and misused and other energies from the ethereal worlds and where it can be used jump into the body and takeover—this is what happened to the man known as Hitler."

"One final question. Why am I on this spiritual pilgrimage?"

"One thing I could tell you is it is to help Valérie because she has a mission and you have long agreed and wanted to assist her on her mission, but I would ask that you actually go into a meditation and ask yourself why you are here. Does that assist you?"

"Ah—hmm!"

"And I think you are already understanding that?"

John replies, "I have already asked that question and I am not getting an answer?"

"And what is that question?"

"Why am I on this spiritual journey? Is it purely to support Valérie or is there another reason?"

"It is for the Grace of God. It is for the mission that came with Jesus onto Earth at that time and hopefully that energy still influences many on this Earth now. Again, some of the teachings have been twisted slightly—but not so serious as to what happened during the Second World War.

"Jesus came with the simple message to, 'Love one another as you would love yourself'. It is a very simple message and when you think about it, it does not mean to judge another, it means to love one another—to accept one another. To accept the differences, to take care of one another, to help one another, to assist one another, to recognise that you are all brothers and sisters on Earth, no matter what race or bloodline. For it all comes from the Christos or Christ, which comes from the World of Light.

"Everybody, and I mean everybody in a physical body has been blessed with this energy of divine light within them, so that everybody on this Earth is of God. They already have this knowledge and the unlimited understanding in them, it is merely a matter for them to connect to that and become who they really are. It is a matter of self-discipline in oneself—that is all.

"The brain is always active and sometimes goes off on little tangents, little journeys of its own, and the discipline within itself needs to bring it back like a little pet on a string. It needs to be brought back and asked to quiet itself and sit beside you to allow you to connect with the higher consciousness that exists within you—from your soul, from God. Does this help you?"

"Yes. I am going through a change."

"You are indeed. You are returning to the true being who you truly are."

John grunts, "So why has it taken so long?"

"This is up to you, my son. There is no limit in time at all for as I have said, it is a self-discipline—it is a growth. It will not take long at all if you decide.

"Climbing the mountain as you did yesterday is symbolic of what a life on Earth is. It is over many boulders and it receives a few scratches and knocks, but you still succeed—you climbed, and you returned back onto the earth ground. You felt refreshed, particularly after swimming in the water and being released from the old energy. The swim in the water was important for you both. It actually helped cleanse your aura as well as your body. Because in your mind, you were being freed from past memories that have upset you so much...as a life in the Cathars, you lived and breathed your life as God intended—it was cathartic, as Jesus had preached

it—and it had many thousands of people who have lived it then and do so now. And there is no reason why you still cannot do that.

"You can be guided from your soul—it has the memory and it has the knowledge, which is not only coming from the World of Light and this is the reality, it can influence you very easily if you allow it."

"Right. One final question? With this evolution of my soul that is taking place, what is my role to be?"

"Just that. To be. To be...to follow any opportunity that comes your way. You have a knowing when something comes your way that you need to do something about. This is not just a fantasy—it is your life. And it is the influence from your God Self that is driving that feeling that is driving you to do something."

"That sounds unpredictable."

"It is not unpredictable because everything in your life has a reason and a purpose. Everything. Are you understanding? It has been my pleasure in being with you my son—for you and I are very close. Now I know that Valérie has some questions. And she understands about the life that you have both had—again, it was a life as a brother and sister, a very pure life, a very beautiful life, but one that was in your heart that God will always protect you.

"So when the terrible thing happened and all those loved ones were destroyed, you were confused, you did not understand for these things are part of the 'Play' so there is a need for self-discipline and to be careful as to what you do create, if you like, for it helps others in many ways to find the True God within.

"And now I believe that you both have accepted the true life you have is everlasting, that the true life you have is through your soul. You understand that you come in a personality in a body for a time, then you leave, then you return and live a life again and then you leave. There is no end. There are many other lives in you—other worlds within the cosmos. It is never-ending, and so this is where you need to connect to and understand that you have the love of God with you always. Any experience you feel that you may have been let down by God was necessary to allow you to find your own inner strength and to never waiver in the knowledge that you are connected to God—that you are God and that you can create.

So, there is a need for self-discipline and to be careful as to what you do create—it is up to you.

"And now it is time for me to leave—but I am always here with you. I sent the man-made vehicle over your heads as a sign yesterday to say we were with you. There was also a 'starman'-made vehicle there with you, but it was held from your sight only because there are others who are not ready to see it. But we are there...we are there. God bless you, my son, and God bless Valérie. I have enjoyed coming."

Valérie asked our mentor before he left, if he remembered the time when 'White Eagle' (*aka as John the Divine)* was first training her about twenty years ago. At that time, he said he would be taking us to France and that a manuscript named *The Book of Love* would be eventually found. He said as the personality John the Divine he had written it at the time of Jesus, but God told him to 'Eat it'. We heard later the Cathars were supposed to have had it.

"Yes, it is obvious now to you, isn't it? That you were the ones who held it in safe keeping. You were the Heads, Elders of the settlement at Montsegur."

"What did we do with it?"

"You believed you were going to be set free by just coming down the mountain—but then you were all grabbed and put to the fire."

"It is said they were held prisoner for about a week."

"Yes! You were able to hide it in your woman's clothing. So that when you were burned alive, the manuscript was destroyed. That is your role now, to bring back the information of the story that was written at that time."

I had to ask our mentor, "Well, what was the manuscript about?"

"The manuscript was about the evolvement of mankind upon the earth. It was actually too controversial to be spoken about at that time, and it is still controversial—but your role is to bring it out and John is to assist you with that mission."

We thanked our mentor for his advice and assistance. He said he would continue to prompt us. I am reminded of the blackened, open-patterned metal book cover, or should I say manuscript cover, we saw at the village museum at Montsegur, the two keys seen on the sign leading into the museum, and the two tiny keys we found at Mt. Bugarach.

Museum in the village below Montségur. Note the sign; there are those two keys again – linking us with the two tiny keys found at Mt Bugarach Valley of God.

Both of us were very disturbed by the artifacts we recognised in the museum. This healed after our swim at Rennes les Bains.

22 Palais des Papes, Avignon - Vaucluse, France

The two symbolic keys that have followed us from Mt Bugarach and Montségur and now Palais des Papes at Avignon

John and I are on our return to Nice to catch the plane to Dubai. We have four days to spare and decide we should visit Avignon. We thought it would be fun to find the bridge in Avignon connecting to the French song sung by children.

Sur le pont d'Avignon, l'on y danse, l'on y danse, Sur le pont d'Avignon l'on y danse, tout en rond.

"On the bridge of Avignon—we all dance there, we all dance there,
on the bridge of Avignon, we all dance there in a ring."

Valérie learnt it as a child.

Avignon has over five thousand years of history. The Palace of Popes is in the centre of the walled medieval city. I have to confess we knew nothing about the Palace of Popes, although we knew there had been a few French Popes. How wrong we were; there had been seven Popes residing at the Palace over seventy-three years. At the time, it was the capital of the Christian world until the Popes moved back to Rome.

Popes who resided in Avignon were:
Clement V: 1305–1314
John XXII: 1314–1334
Benedict XII: 1334–1342
Clement VI: 1342–1352
Innocent VI: 1352–1362
Urban V: 1362–1370
Gregory XI: 1370–1378

Avignon became the residence of the Popes in 1309.

When Gascon Bertran de Goth, as Pope Clement V, was unwilling to face the violent chaos of Rome after his election in 1305, he moved the Papal Curia to Avignon, a period that became known as the Avignon Papacy.

The Popes departed Avignon seventy-three years later. There were more Popes in other places, anti-popes creating yet another Papal Schism, with Popes reigning in France and in Rome. This was resolved with the Council of Constance electing an Italian as Pope in 1417. The Palace des Papes remained under papal control, along with the surrounding city for three hundred and fifty turbulent years.

We found a comfortable place to stay within the walled city and, once settled, made our way to the large Place du Palais and then to the Palace itself. We paid our entrance fee and were given individual audio guides to listen to as we wandered through the buildings. Some of the halls had extraordinarily high ceilings—large, empty and cold.

I began to experience that past-life memory feeling again. I was not happy. I recalled a time when sitting with a medium friend, about twenty years ago, who channelled a message about me having a life as a Pope. I remembered the name given to me was Clement V. At the time, I took little notice, but now it was becoming overwhelming. I had been told he died with a broken heart. He believed the life had been so wrong, even though he was guided back to the World of Light by a white dove.

As I walked, I listened to the audio guide speak of many things, including that the Popes' had *'a taster of food'* before it was given to a Pope to eat, in case it had been poisoned. I became more and more uncomfortable. I came to a room where an artist had painted portraits of all the Popes. Dressed in full papal regalia, they all wore either a ruby or an emerald ring on their finger, but what startled me was they looked just like the green ring with the same setting that Sai Baba had given me in India.

It was only when we returned home to Australia and I was able to research the life of Pope Clement V that I understood why I felt vaguely angry and uncomfortable. The more I researched, the more upset I became.

King Philip lV of France owed money to the Knights Templar and wanted them to be destroyed; it was said that Pope Clement V was a puppet to King Philip's whim. How could the Knights Templar, who were held in such high regard and were so well respected, be treated in this manner?

The French King wanted the Church to use their powers through the Inquisition to judge the Knights Templar guilty of horrendous initiation rites. The French King wanted them to be denounced as heretics and to be burned at the stake so that he, the king, could take all their wealth and property unto his own. There has been much written about this and it has been reported that Clement V acquiesced and allowed this to occur.

For about a week I suffered, constantly thinking, *how could I have been part of this abomination of torture and the Templars being burned alive and cast out from the protection of the Church?* I mentally made a decision I would record this past-life memory in this chapter, no matter how bad it may seem.

How could Pope Clement V have believed all the vicious gossip about initiation rites and agreed to disband the Order? God's army, the Knights Templar, who were monk warriors and had sworn never to use the sword in anger or for their own gain. It is true they had become very wealthy from thankful wealthy pilgrims, who gave them treasures and land in return for them giving safe passage to the Holy Lands.

In this life, I am looking at my soul story and the memory of a life as a Cathar: 'The Pure Ones' who loved God and lived with the Love of God. I felt I had to call on our mentor and ask what on Earth was happening with the life as Pope Clement V.

I was particularly concerned as an aspect of my soul would have been born into his life in an Earth body at Aquitaine, South of France, eventually becoming the Pope—only about fifty years after that Cathar life, which would surely have still been a strong influence within him.

After settling in front of my altar, I switched on my iPod to make a recording and called on my mentor. I asked, "Is Pope Clement V in my soul story?"

"He is indeed, my dear, and it is an Earth life that you have found very painful, for you did not want to go along with the edict from the French King. He was asking for all the papers that you had written to be destroyed. You did not want this at all. And in fact, the inquisition went ahead without your sanction, although it was said that you had sanctified the torture and inquisition into the charges being made against the Knights Templar, but this was not true. You, as The Pope, had not sanctified such action. There were false papers put forward for an inquisition, my dear, and you were very upset about this when you found out. You wrote another paper to exonerate the church and what you had really thought and believed. But unfortunately, this was not found until much later.

"The life itself gave you insight into another point of view of the Church and you were not happy with this at all. You had come to Earth with a mission, to try and stop the Inquisitions and torture. In the World of Light, the hierarchy were not pleased that such a thing was taking place on Earth in the name of Jesus Christ. So, when you returned to your soul plane, you committed yourself to

come back again, to try to rectify this. That life was as a young woman known as Jehanne d'Arc. She tried to encourage the church to teach, by her example, to listen to God within. This is enough for you, my dear, but I will be helping you, I will be helping you."

Now that I have received the above information, I can relax. I understand my feelings about that life. It does not matter how others have written the history or what they believe. I can certainly understand how when someone has a position of leadership and power they can come with the best intentions. It is not always easy to 'carry off' the best decisions when there are dark forces around you, trying to usurp what you are attempting to do.

My mentor added a little more understanding a few days later...

"You recorded your dissatisfaction with the course the King wanted to take, my dear. And so, when the papers were falsified and the action of the burning of the Templar Grand Master, Jacques de Molay had taken place, this upset you greatly. You had met the man personally and did not believe what he was being accused. In fact, you respected the man as honourable, fair, and just.

"It was against your wishes and you did not know the papers had been falsified until after Jacques de Molay had been burned to death. You continued to be deeply upset. However, the deed had been done and you wanted to protect the honour of the church. For there were many, particularly within your cardinals and bishops, who were not happy with what immoral actions were said to have taken place by the Knights Templar. There was a lot of gossip—a lot of writings about strange orgies that were going on. Which you yourself doubted.

"And so, you were put in a 'cleft stick' shall I say. To say publicly that the French King had gone against your wishes would not have augured well. And to say that you had not agreed with your own cardinals would not have augured well either. You were very angry about this, that the Grand Master had been burned to death and it had taken place so quickly, and against your wishes."

"Who were the cardinals who had falsified his documents, do I know them in this life?" I asked my Mentor.

"Indeed, you do, and they are with you again in this life. They felt strongly about it, that the Templars were guilty of such

immoral conduct. So, it was a moral issue as well, my dear, not just one of the French King owing money to the Templars and wanting their wealth.

"You are receiving the correct information, my dear. The correct documents were found much later—long after you left your body. It is important that you release the frustration and anger before you continue with your storytelling."

He also said that I did nothing wrong and they know that. "The Power of the World of Light knows how the truth really is and it will now be revealed. You have been honoured, my dear, and it is why Sri Sathya Sai Baba has given you the ring."

I thanked him sincerely. I was prompted to research a little more. Pope Clement V had a strong connection to England through his birthright as a subject of the English King Edward I, in France. Pope Clement V was his own man with powerful allies long before taking the papal throne. He was strong and cleverly insistent on keeping a balance of power between England, France, and the Catholic Church, but most of all his loyalties were to his fellow French countrymen.

I then discovered, just like my spirit mentor had said, that the correct papers have been found long after Pope Clement V left his body—in fact, it is seven hundred years later.

John felt familiar in the Palais des Papes also. He disliked it. We did a little kinesiology test on him and it seems he was a Cardinal attached to Pope Clement V; he looked after the treasury and was also his brother.

This explained the feeling we both had; we felt 'we had visited before' when we walked up and through the sacred forest to The Cave of Mary Magdalene at La Sainte Baume. It is recorded that Pope Clement V visited there during his reign as Pope; his cardinal (his brother), would have accompanied him.

I wrote in my diary, 'We seem to walk into a parallel universe when we met the young people dressed in medieval clothes, collecting truffles.' As they walked along the King's way, they suddenly disappeared.

Knights Templar win heresy reprieve and Pope Clement V had exonerated the Knights Templar before his death over seven hundred years ago.

A rich red, velvet-covered document folder released by the Vatican showed two keys on the cover. The documents were written and misfiled by the Vatican. Seven centuries later, they have been found and released in 2007. Not only do they exonerate the Knights Templar, but they also exonerate Pope Clement V

In that life as a Pope and a Cardinal, we were not able to stop the medieval inquisition or torture that was carried out in those dark ages. My next incarnation came with more power from the World of Light. A mission to bring changes in France, she was Jehanne d'Arc and she, regrettably, also fell victim to the inquisition.

Nothing has given me more inner peace than to read the formal apology given by Pope John Paul ll for the misdeeds done by man and the church, in the name of God.

His apology was given on 13th March 2000, from the altar of St. Peter's Basilica in Rome. He led all Christians into uncharted territory by seeking forgiveness for sins committed against Jews, heretics, burning people at the stake, women, midwives, healers, Knights Templar, the Cathars, other break-away Christian groups, the Gypsies, and native people.

Fighting through trembles and slurring caused by Parkinson's Disease, the Pope electrified ranks of cardinals and bishops by pleading for the future that would not repeat the mistakes. "Never again," he said.

I, too, ask for forgiveness for any hurt I may have caused to anyone in the past, I pray to God to forgive me and I forgive myself—I love you.

23 Cairo and the Pyramids of Giza, Egypt

Pyramids of Giza – David Roberts 1796–1864

When John and I first began planning our adventure overseas, he arranged the itinerary for six weeks travel. Because we were to stop over at Dubai to visit our family living there, I did ask if it was possible that perhaps we could visit Egypt and the Pyramids.

Our budget was fast fading, so I didn't think we were going to make it. When *Upstairs* advised me we would be visiting the Pyramids in Egypt, I didn't believe them. It came as a delightful surprise when John came home to announce he had changed the itinerary so we could visit Egypt from Dubai for three days. I must say I was overjoyed and wondered what *Upstairs* had in store for us.

Our whole journey has been wonderful and enlightening and has brought John into sharing and better understanding what working with *Upstairs* is all about. With all the unexpected insights, signs, and promptings along the way to visit various places, we both 'knew' we were being guided the whole journey.

We arrived in Cairo and as soon as we alighted from the plane and placed our feet on the ground, we felt we had come home. Cairo is the capital of Egypt and the largest city in Africa. When flying in, you can see on one side of the plane a vast unending desert and the other is a huge metropolis positioned on the River Nile. A friendly Egyptian man met us, who introduced himself as Ahmed. He advised he was to be our guide while we were here on our brief visit. Ahmed was more than just a guide.

Mohammed, another of our guide's team, was to collect us from our hotel and stay with us the whole time we were sight-seeing, driving us around in a small mini bus. As we drove to our hotel, our first impression was sand, dust, and dirt everywhere. We were advised it only rains about three or four times a year, and even then it is only a light shower, not enough to wash the place clean.

There were many unfinished high-rise buildings, which had colourful washing hanging out of holes in the wall that really should have been windows. It gave a strong contrast to the dull grey cement on the exterior of the buildings. We were advised that if the buildings had been completed, there would have been a difficult tax to pay. People were allowed to live in the apartment blocks even though they were not finished.

It took one hour from the airport to the Movenpik Resort Hotel, a little oasis with a welcoming swimming pool and cool restaurants. The hotel was only one kilometre from the Pyramids. Looking at the pyramids from the hotel rooftop, I began to feel shaky and when walking was slightly unsteady. I welcomed John's strong arm to lean on.

Cairo is a colourful place in the evening. The dullness comes to life with bright lights everywhere. Everybody seems to be out and about, in cafes, markets, or just walking. The traffic is totally chaotic and yet our driver misses everything, and we often squeeze into the most extraordinarily narrow spaces. We loved the people and if we were to think where else is like Cairo, I would say India, although there is something intriguing about Egypt you cannot define. We loved it, and both John and I agreed we had been before.

Unlike Dubai, from where we had just come, there is not the rich lavishness and yet the people all seem to be healthy and happy. Their travel arrangements are not all the same. Little tuck-tucks, donkeys with people riding them, and donkeys pulling tiny carriages behind them. Buses are large, full to the brim with people going to or from work, cars with kids crammed inside going home from school.

The odd camel is seen, pushbikes and taxis too, but thank goodness we have a driver to ourselves with an air-conditioned mini bus. It is pleasantly cool in the summer morning and evening. A swim in the hotel pool, filled with the River Nile water was enjoyed.

To the Great Pyramids

Today, we begin early on a day-long tour. Our first visit is to the Great Pyramid at Giza. I keep tottering unexpectedly with my body still adjusting to the energy of the Pyramids. A message from *Upstairs* advises I am being introduced to the energy of the Pyramids gradually—in the similar way I had been introduced to the Moldavite stone.

I awake this morning remembering a dream that I would not be happy if I was to climb inside the great pyramid. When we arrive with our guide, we are confronted by hundreds of people already gathered and waiting to buy their tickets to enter the grounds. The city of Cairo nearly reaches to the base of the Pyramids; the suburb is known as Giza. The other side of the Pyramids is the vast Sahara desert.

We find our guide Ahmed to be very knowledgeable—he is a student in Egyptology, English, and Russian and is studying for his PhD. We feel we are being guided on our whole trip; the right people are being brought to us. This is proven in itself with

Ahmed being our guide and lecturing us on the ancient beliefs of the Egyptians. He speaks about the Dynasties and about the Muslim beliefs and the culture of modern-day Egypt. Wonderful.

I tell Ahmed I had a dream warning me not to enter the Pyramids, and would it be alright if I just sit outside the Great Pyramid Khufu and meditate. He does not know what I mean about meditation until I describe it as prayer. He understands immediately and is respectful.

John is not happy I choose not to enter the Pyramid to visit the King's Chamber and begins to pressure me, until I ask him not to force me as I have received a message not to go inside. I encourage him to go and then to tell me what it is like.

So off he goes, climbing a quarter of the way up the outside of the Pyramid until he comes to the entrance and disappears inside the tunnel with many other people. I notice not everybody is going inside and Ahmed has warned John it will be a difficult climb up the small shaft.

Ahmed stays behind with me and I explain that I want to climb the outside of the Pyramid just a little way—about twelve metres. I want to sit on one of the large block stones and meditate. I walk along a narrow path until I come to a place I feel I can sit down and not be bothered by anyone.

I find a place past and above the rope separating the crowd at the ground level below. A security policeman standing at ground level calls out to me, signalling for me to move back with the other people. I call out, "I just want to meditate," and he immediately signals with his hand on his heart as if to say, "Oh, that's alright," and leaves me to it.

I look up at the full height of the Great Pyramid Khufu above me. I feel slightly giddy and again I have to steady myself by holding onto the corner of a large block of stone. I can see a clear blue sky above and a new moon prompting me to take a photo—still feeling shaky.

Then when I settle, my mentor begins speaking to me clearly and firmly. "*You will be channelling later with a lot of information, but for now we ask that you write another book.*" I agree, but

I say, "I am disappointed in how difficult it has been for my other books to get off the ground, so to speak."

I am told, *"This book will be very important and it will receive more attention—it is in your soul blueprint that you will do this."*

In other words, I agreed to write three books when I came into this body. I only want to serve—so I shall not worry about outcomes. My mentor gives me the outline of the book as past-life memories with John, the time of Jesus' family, the Roman Empire, and ancient changes in the Earth's evolvement. And now, *Upstairs* has asked me to collate all my work into one book and speak of my consciousness connection to my Oversoul in the galaxy Andromeda M31.

I communicate to my mentor on how disappointed I am at the size of the stones I am standing on at the Great Pyramid. He advises, *"The Sphinx, my dear, was built long before the pyramids and so it was long before Atlantis fell. You will see the size of the stones at the Sphinx Temple entrance and that is actually the same size that exist at the Great Pyramid now...but they have been overlaid by smaller stones and the drawings found around the Pyramids showing how men were working to build them up is what happened. Actually, it was the starpeople who first built the Great Pyramid. If the outer layer of stones were taken away, they would find the larger stones there, my dear."*

When I return to Ahmed, I try to explain what I was doing while we are still waiting for John to come back from inside the Great Pyramid. I say, "I am a medium." He cannot understand this. So, I say, "I can tune into other worlds and receive messages and I have agreed for 'The Gods' from other worlds to use my voice box and speak through me." I did not need to explain any further... he smiles and begins nodding his head quite quickly, so I think he is impressed. I am not sure if he hears me add, "Everybody can be a medium and, in fact, they are whether they realise it or not."

Everyone is a medium, a spirit being with a soul, living in an earthly body who is often inspired with a 'thought' or 'idea' that is motivating. God wants us all to be happy; anything we think, feel, or do in a negative way is pulling us against God.

Inspiration comes straight from our creative centre within, our God Centre; it assists us to write, paint, sculpture, build, sing, dance, and explore. We can explore with our mind, our emotion, or our feet—this is what motivates us. The rest is choice, what we choose to activate within us. There are good choices and not so good choices, there is a need to listen to the 'voice within' and choose what feels right.

I find all this information such a joy—I just want to share it—but there is a need to use discernment at all times in how I express myself. I don't want to sound like I am forcing anyone or preaching. The truth is we are all 'Gods', whether we are on this planet or another. We are all children from the Creative Source of All. It is what we do with our lives, in this life, or a past life, or a future life that makes us worthy of being children of God.

John and Shamanic Initiation in the Pyramid

John has not come out of the pyramid yet. I know Holy Spirit will look after him. Whatever he experiences, it will have a reason and a purpose. Everything always does.

He is here now, sweating profusely and looking very shaken. In fact, he can hardly stand. We sit for a while, giving him time to recover and to speak.

"I cannot believe I have just done that, I could have had a heart attack or a stroke. I had to bend over to get through the tunnel in some places. Too many people were pushing up the steep slope and down the slope, with small slats across the footing stopping me from slipping. I was hot, there were no air tunnels, and I was sweating profusely. I really thought I was going to have a heart attack or another stroke, but I pushed on," he tells me.

When he recovers, I take a photo and we are surprised to see what is with them. A large orb of light is behind John and Ahmed, representing an ancestral spirit. I feel he is safe, and he has experienced a Shamanic initiation—similar to a 'Sweat Lodge' given by the American Native Indians in a pyramid-shaped tent. As they sweat, it allows for energy fields to change within the body and to release negative past-life memories. People usually change for the better after such an initiation.

John stated, "I have changed! While I was in there, I kept thinking about you telling me how apples can last longer stored in a pyramid-shape container and I felt my life had been extended." I don't remember ever saying anything about apples; I believe he was hearing 'a voice' that was explaining what was happening to him.

"What was it like in the King's Chamber, John?"

"Too many people. It is strange, I found myself telling everyone to keep away from my sarcophagus...when I think about it, I can't help feeling I was taken over by something for a little bit. It wasn't me talking, but someone else—it's a profound place."

I mentioned to him I always believed the open sarcophagus was used by ancient temple priest and priestess initiates to lay in to go into an altered state of consciousness, and that it was never meant to be a tomb.

It is possible to break free from all our soul history and operate from the Monad consciousness or God Self. Thus, coming from a consciousness without limit and seeing everything from an overview or the big picture is how we shall graduate into the Golden Age of Golden Light.

We only have one full day for sightseeing with a lot to see. We are allowed to walk a temporary path above the Sphinx and use the original entrance to the Sphinx Temple. It is here I recognise the Huge Stones that had been tessellated together by the starpeople, just as my mentor said. We are not allowed to enter the ground level of the Sphinx as a new ancient wall has recently been discovered and work is still underway to uncover it.

Cairo Museum – Family of King Tutankhamun

24

Amenhotep III and Queen Tiye

Visiting the Cairo Museum was an incredible experience. Ahmed was a gift to us with his professional manner and great knowledge. Others visiting the museum were in groups of twenty or more, following their guide around the museum. Ahmed touched his heart and said he would show us the most important artifacts known to the Egyptian people. We were not allowed to take our bags or camera into the museum. We visited the famous Tutankhamun

Room with the solid gold burial sarcophagus and also his solid gold burial mask.

When we entered the Mummies' room, I was surprised not to feel some repugnance at the sight of dead people. John asked Ahmed where the 'daddy's room' was and he smiled and immediately pointed to the gents' toilet.

The ancient mummifying techniques allowed the bodies to look almost alive after thousands of years. *I experienced smelling a beautiful perfume when near one of the mummies with long hair; she was a Queen.* I felt she was being drawn to my attention for a reason and that I had known her when she was alive. The feeling was a little overwhelming and I refrained from asking *Upstairs*. I did not have pencil and paper with me to take notes. Her name was long and complicated, and I asked John to please take particular note with me.

John remarked, "She must have been beautiful when she was alive with that long reddish hair." I would ask my mentor about her at another time. We noticed that many of the mummies had blonde or red hair—not looking Arabic at all.

Ahmed particularly wanted us to see and know of the Ancient Egyptian painting showing The Judgement Day. "It shows the spirit of the person that has died, as going before a panel of seven jurors before one can move onto heaven. Then another seven jurors if the weight of the person's heart is too heavy, needing to be reviewed. The heart of the deceased person is measured upon a scale against the spirit, seen as a feather. If the heart is too heavy, some of it is eaten by a God in the form of a crocodile known as 'Yum Yum'. If it is then balanced, the soul is allowed to ascend to heaven. If the heart is still too heavy, it is then totally eaten and is lost forever."

It is strange how we still refer to being 'light-hearted'—a state of happiness, a willing soul who is always pleasant and all other nice feelings. The heart is where we experience emotion. If we are 'heavy hearted' we are sad, angry, irritable, or even experiencing hate, and that makes us feel awful. It is a natural feeling for us to feel love and all manner of positive emotions.

After a little more sightseeing, it was time to leave for Dubai, stopping over for another three days to see our second eldest son, his lovely wife, and our beautiful grandchildren, a fifteen-year-old teenage girl and the nine-year-old twins, a boy and girl—this was 2011.

At home, two weeks later

Two weeks later, on a Monday and at the same time of day as I had viewed the mummies in Egypt, I was on a John of God Crystal Healing Bed at Beth's house in an altered state of consciousness, and literally feeling I was a 'mummie.' Beth later said she was clairvoyantly seeing me looking like a rag doll. I had not told her about the perfume in the mummies' room in the Cairo Museum. Well, of course, as a mummie I would look like a rag doll.

I was thoroughly massaged around my head and neck, which had been very sore and ached since we returned. I was advised the cloth around the mummie's head was releasing a past-life memory; she also saw ethereally a huge golden disc across my chest that was inscribed. My spirit body levitated just above the mummie.

Other work was done; the spirit healer working on me, through Beth, was the energy of Jesus. It felt like a very strong male energy. He came from other worlds, capable of changing and moving me; I could have been physically lifted off the massage table.

A strong voice from the Other Side, in my inner ear, was telling me that I had been a Queen in an Egyptian life—I immediately thought of the female mummie and the beautiful perfume at Cairo museum. My Oversoul told of having given birth to Akhenaten in the same way Avatars are born. It was a great honour. My attention was continually drawn to the memory of having grandchildren and being a grandmother at the time of being a 'mummie' and I wasn't sure what that was about.

While in the altered state of consciousness connecting to the past-life memory that began to be released while I was on the crystal bed table, I felt moved to stretch and push, to release the golden disc that was ethereally hanging around my neck. I knew more information from that disc would be released later and I was to research the internet and find out more about Akhenaten's family.

I found out as recently as February 2010 that complicated DNA studies have been released to the public about the mummies at the Cairo Museum. In particular, studies were undertaken on the Pharaohs of the Sun, the Amarna period. Amenhotep III, Akhenaten, and Tutankhamen.

The key is mitochondria DNA, which is something passed on only through the women and that forms the basis of tracing evolution. Amenhotep III and Queen Tiye were the parents of Akhenaten. This was the Queen referred to when told telepathically she had given birth to Akhenaten, in a different life, of course, and speaking from a soul history point of view.

Akhenaten was born the same way Avatars are born, from a blue light entering the mother's womb through her stomach and influencing the growth of the foetus with an uplifted consciousness. He grew into a man, looking strangely effeminate, with a potbelly, 'A' line-shaped body, a thick-lipped, elongated face, and a large skull with a more 'starpeople' likeness.

On the same day I was researching this information, John arrived home with a copy of the National Geographic Magazine he had borrowed from our dentist's waiting room, dated September 2010, with an article about "King Tut's DNA—Unlocking Family Secrets." I almost laughed out loud at the synchronicity of it but remained quiet. I remembered his reactions when he was in the King's Chamber of the Great Pyramid and him commanding people to stay away from *his* sarcophagus. Also, how a large ancestral orb had shown itself in the photo behind him while standing in front of the Great Pyramid.

I asked him to place his palm over the image of the mummie, Amenhotep III. Then I asked him to close his eyes, let his eyes roll up under his eyelids into his head as if he was looking way above into the Universe to the World of Light, and ask Mother, Father God, if the personality was of Amenhotep III, the Great Pharaoh in his oversoul story. John sat quietly for a short time, opened his eyes with a look of amazement, and said, "I am being told *yes*!"

The Great Pharaoh Amenhotep III's reign became known as a Period of Peace and Prosperity; many structures were constructed and still stand today. Known as the Pharaoh that beautified Egypt, he was an excellent diplomat in international worlds and received rich gifts from far and wide.

Amenhotep III celebrated three Jubilee festivals of his continued reign in his year thirty, thirty-four, and thirty-seven. The last was before he died in his thirty-ninth year in his summer palace in Western Thebes. The palace, known as the 'House of Rejoicing' in ancient times, comprised a temple of Amun and a festival hall built especially for these occasions. One of the king's most popular epithets was Aten-tjehen, which means 'the Dazzling Sun Disk'; it appears in his titulary at Luxor Temple and more frequently was used as the name for one of his palaces as well as the Year II royal barge, and denotes a company of men in Amenhotep's army.

John, in this life, was nicknamed 'Jubilee John' by his family. I can see many similarities in his personality that existed in the life of the Pharaoh. John tells me that ever since he had 'that experience' inside the Great Pyramid, "That up until that time, my whole being and thinking was muddled and misty—so foggy I couldn't see the way around stuff—now, I can see with absolute clarity. Nothing to do with spirit, I suppose, but I just see things in a clear perspective. I feel centred in my mind, my understanding is becoming clearer. When I am reading about historical fiction and it is well researched, I know about it already. One of the things changed in me is that I have always been a worrywart, now I just don't get panicky or worried any more. France had an effect on me too. When you think it through, the South of France and Egypt are energetically close. It is like they influenced one another."

Akhenaten was married to Nefertiti and they had one son and six daughters; he had another wife named Kiya. Images of the family look extra-terrestrial with long exaggerated heads. He fathered two sons, one with a different wife, said to be his sister. The eldest son was said to have died before Akhenaten, leaving Tutankhamun to inherit the throne.

There is a wonderful Papyrus painting of Akhenaten, Nefertiti, and three young daughters playing with and kissing their children under a symbol of the Sun. Never before had a Monarch been shown warmly kissing children and playing with them. They all looked decidedly like starpeople.

When Akhenaten came to the Throne, Queen Tiye had outlived her King Amenhotep III. She moved as the elder lady with her family to Amarna, three hundred kilometres away from Thebes. It was a new city Akhenaten had established saying, "The Father from above had pointed out the site as the Horizon of the Sun." He changed the way of worshipping God from a polytheistic God, where the priests were the intermediaries with the gods to a monotheistic God where the Pharaoh was the only intermediary.

He claimed, "I and the father Aten are One from the World of the Sun" and set up a new way of living, offering only food and flowers to God. All other images and sacrifices were forbidden, being replaced with the symbolic image of the sun. All blessings flowed through to Amarna where he constructed a new city with temples to the Aten. It was taught that all things were equal.

The Sun his One God

After Akhenaten died, this new religion and capital did not survive long. During young Tutankhamun's short reign, the old ways were gradually reinstated, and the capital moved back to the Temples of Amun, run by the powerful priests in Thebes. Akhenaten was declared a heretic, and many of the records were destroyed. How poignant it is that despite this, King Tutankhamun's tomb was hidden and protected for so long that the story of the Armana Period has been clarified with DNA research.

Tutankhamun inherited the throne at a very young age, after Akhenaten died. King Tutankhamun married his half-sister, his only wife, Ankhesenamun. This is the long and difficult name I couldn't remember of the mummie when John and I were assailed with the beautiful perfume at the Cairo Museum, and I knew we were being asked to remember her. This connects to the advice, 'Grandchildren, Grandchildren' and the words, 'Grandmother'.

While on the healing table, I was thinking of that mummie with the perfume we had seen in the Cairo museum.

King Tutankhamun and his Young Wife

Tutankhamun's DNA shows he is the offspring of a union between siblings; this often-studied Pharaoh is now revealed to have had a congenital clubfoot, afflicted with bone disease that would have made walking painful, causing him to use a walking stick. Inbreeding may have caused the deformity and even prevented him from producing an heir with his wife Ankhesenamun, daughter of Akhenaten. It was believed that Tutankhamun may have been poisoned, as he died at only nineteen years of age. DNA research has shown he had serious malaria.

Recently a documentary 'Ultimate Tutankhamun' by National Geographic shows 'World renowned archaeologists are taking a twenty-first century approach to ancient history, conducting a forensic investigation into Tutankhamun's cause of death.'

It proves King Tut was a warrior King and sustained his fatal injuries from a chariot wheel running into him, knocking him over and killing him. Because he was young and his death unexpected, he was hurriedly buried in the Valley of Kings in a tomb that had been prepared for another.

That fits with a story of two ancient royal brother princes (4th or 5th Dynasty) from Egypt who visited Australia about 4,500 years ago. One of them died from a snake bite and was hastily buried in a make-shift tomb. The Pharaohs knew of their story down through their oral history. I have worked with four people in regression who have remembered that Tutankhamen made a ceremonial journey to Australia to take home to Egypt the mummie preserved in an Egyptian-like tomb in Kariong, on the east coast of Australia. King Tut knew the Prince from the earlier Dynasty was in his soul history and that was why he felt he had to make sure his remains went back to Egypt.

King Tut was not well on the return journey to Egypt. His entourage was able to prepare a royal tomb that was waiting for the missing ancient royal mummie in the King's Valley, Egypt.

The people were thrown into shock when Tutankhamen was accidentally killed by a chariot soon after his return from the great south land, so they planned to use the ancient royal mummie's tomb as well for King Tut.

As seen in the National Geographic Documentary, there are reports Tutankhamen's tomb seemed to be prepared for someone else and then upgraded in all its grandeur for him. No other mummie was found in his tomb in 1922, but there has always been a belief there are other hidden rooms. Just recently, that theory has been examined with advanced technology and is said to be a real possibility. We are waiting to hear the results. Speculation is that it will hold Nefertiti's missing mummie—but we believe it will hold the missing ancient royal mummie returned to Egypt from Australia.

Soon after King Tut was buried, a major tsunami flowed into the King's Valley covering the tomb with mud and boulders, burying it so it remained hidden for thousands of years, to be discovered on 1st November 1922.

The forensic investigation goes on to explain many mysteries surrounding his embalming and burial rites. You could say the flash flood was advantageous for it hid the mystery of the Amarna period of that ancient Egyptian time.

I have always been interested in the first and second foetus who are the premature babies born to Tutankhamun and his young wife Ankhesenamun. I watched a documentary a number of years ago when an x-ray was allowed to be taken of them; they looked extra-terrestrial. Now, I realise I knew of them when the babies were born as Queen Tiye's grandchildren. DNA testing also found a lock of Queen Tiye's hair inside the babies' coffinette. My mentor has advised that Queen Tiye had actually died by then.

"Your grandchildren knew that you would be looking after the babies' souls after they moved on to the Other Side. And so that is why they placed a little lock of your curled blonde, reddish hair from your mummie within their tiny coffin."

I knew of them, when I was in the World of Light.

The disc symbol of the sun that was hanging ethereally around my neck as a 'mummie' on the healing table, is shown on top of the heads of many Gods, as well as Queen Tiye, who is said to be the progenitor of monotheism.

There was a suppression of divine light coming onto the Earth. It was a replay of what took place when Jesus was alive, and what is happening now. It is a time the Golden Age will come upon this Earth—in the same form it did before. But this time the Angelic Realms have made an edict that only those with the power to help take your Solar System through its transition into alignment with a core of suns leading to the Source of all Creation are those who are allowed to work with that power, and so it will definitely take place. The turning point was as you have experienced—at the end of 2012 with the winter/summer solstice of the Earth.

The Secret of Nefertiti Revealed

Historic records do not reveal much about the whereabouts of Nefertiti's tomb, Akhenaten's Queen. Because records exist for only a relatively short time of her life, the assumption is that she died quite young.

I purchased a book *Art & History E 5,000 years of Civilisation*—text and drawings by Alberto Carlo Carpiceci, English Edition. In it, I found another record that Pharaoh Akhenaten died and his successor Tutankhamun was too young to rule. As his regent, it was Nefertiti who reigned in Amarna.

> "Tutankhamun and his regent Nefertiti were persuaded by priests to return to Thebes and re-establish supremacy of the cult of Amon. Tutankhamun died at nineteen years of age. Nefertiti married the old Ay and succeeded in maintaining power for a further four years, but then records of her memory and tomb disappear. Egypt then falls ever deeper into anarchy and misery."

Beth, who did the healing work on me so beautifully with the assistance of a John of God Crystal Bed, is a tall, good-looking blonde with high-cheek bones and a very long neck. When she lifts her hair above her head, she looks just like Nefertiti. We thought it would be appropriate for her to try a 'regression' to see if she had Nefertiti in her soul story.

This lady lay on her white sheet-covered John of God Crystal bed with the stand above her, holding a crystal of light, colour flowing down to match the body chakras. She quickly regressed into an altered state of consciousness. It was a long regression, so I have made notes of her story. Seeing with her inner eye, she saw herself way out into the galaxy, looking from above. It is quite dark and beautiful, with movement of lights, like the lights in the Northern sky. I asked if she had a Nefertiti life. In her inner scene, she was moving steadily towards a particular light—and described the life of Nerfertiti which she briefly manifested:

"I am a woman in a costume adorned with jewels—metallic—light blue, cobalt blue, purple, gold. On my arms, my clothes are like fine linen, quite beautiful and soft."

Pharaoh Amunhotep IV, who later was known as Akhenaten, had married her. Nerfertiti called him Amun. There was no excitement surrounding this man. She felt uncomfortable, slightly afraid. She did not know why. As a young woman, she came from the desert where everybody knew his or her place.

"And now I am not sure what is going on—there is a lot of uncertainty." Regressing to Nefertiti's childhood the words came, *"I lived in the hilly desert with my parents."* When I asked how she came to be selected to be the Pharaoh's wife, she said quietly, *"Beauty..."*

She was moved on to after she was married, and she saw she had seven children, six girls and one boy. She became disturbed. Something was wrong with the boy?

"He was on the outer. Always sick. He is the youngest. We called him 'Tuk'." She was upset here. "There is a lot of pressure. It is because of what is expected of me. No, I didn't feel it difficult. It was what I did. There was a lot of work. Not a lot of down time."

"What is expected of you?"

"I am constantly on show. Constantly. Having to perform. People expect to see me all the time. Many people look after me. I

have a station within the temple. I have to look after the children. I have to look after the altar. I have to look after people. There are councils for everything. And yes, I am part of everything.

"There was healing work done with the Inner Council. I didn't really know much of what goes on...the surrounding land was free, and people were happy...it was how we lived. *The Inner Council is not like the other councils. It is free—no one rules over you—God is in touch. We are leaving the dock or the port. It is a very special occasion...a boat with beautiful sails...and lots of fruits and flowers—they are offerings."*

"What was the occasion?" she was asked.

"Isis ceremony...the energy of Isis..." Her demeanour changed a little. "The boats are going to the temple, down the Nile."

"Is there any particular reason everyone is honouring Isis?"

"Every so often, Isis was honoured. It is not just a one-off thing. The celebration is held every year, although this one is a little bit more special."

She was taken deeper into the memory so that she knew why this particular ceremony was so special.

"The temple is new. And this particular ceremony is the opening ceremony." She felt the presence of Isis. She didn't feel she was still married to Akhenaten—she is older now. "For many years, we visited this temple. She stepped into a role of being Isis. In partnership, like a medium channelling."

When she speaks of Isis, she is quite haughty, and slightly abrupt. "*We have done the training—there is nothing we have to learn."*

I asked, "How did Nefertiti die?"

She hesitated, *"I see an elderly woman standing and then falling and dying naturally."*

She came out of the regressed state but *remained* in a meditative state with her eyes closed.

"Amazing was the temple, it was huge—the buildings were massive. There were so many people, builder of the temples and statues everywhere. The fruit, grapes...very opulent...very lovely energy in that time. Very light, pure, free and happy to live in—but for me not so much."

She hesitated. "Very busy...lots and lots of people caring for us. The children had their own houses. The old lady who slumped to the ground with older hands—it didn't look like Nefertiti. She was living in mud huts...back in the country...where she lived as a child."

She reflected, "After seeing Nefertiti on the boat—standing with her clothes blowing in the wind, looking absolutely gorgeous. The old lady...I cannot believe it is her, but it is." Almost as an afterthought, she added, "There was another woman. There was always talk about everybody equal. She couldn't stand the hypocrisy of living a lie.

"She believed the marriage was forever...just the two of them. A very righteous woman...who wouldn't tolerate anything that was unjust...it was no longer a true marriage...Amun should have known better...He married another woman. He knows where he is from, he knows his connection, and he should have known better."

"The boy known as 'Tuk' was a sickly boy. He was in need of full attention and care all the time. I think he may have been mentally incapacitated and would not have been fit to rule the kingdom. He didn't die young, but Nefertiti outlived the boy. He was still being cared for at the temple. He had no special role. There was another court made for him."

The parents of Tutankhamun were Akhenaton and his half-sister Kiya, whom he married after Nefertiti in the hope of getting a son and heir.

That was the reason Nefertiti was very upset with her husband Pharaoh Akhenaten, and him going against his beliefs, she was so hurt. They had been a very close and loving family. There was a deep, deep disappointment, when everyone was so happy; the hypocrisy of it was too much for her, so she lived apart from him.

She eventually denied the privileged life and returned to anonymity. She died without any ceremony. She lived the last days of her life almost like a nun. Her body will probably never be found. She felt very strongly connected with the Isis cosmic priestess energy.

Pharaoh Akhenaten was upset and deeply disturbed when Queen Nefertiti rejected him. Then his mother Queen Tiye died and he began to lose his way and his vision. When he died, Tutankhamun was only young and not strong enough to hold his father's vision, so the place of Amarna gradually fell away.

Mythology

I am prompted to research Isis and Osiris, the Gods whose child is Horus. When travelling through the south of France, the similarity Mother Mary and her child portrayed in churches looked so like Isis of Egypt with her child Horus on her knee. I found an image of Isis with a golden disc symbolising the sun upon her head.

It has been recorded the burial chamber of Osiris is below the Statue of the Sphinx at Giza. The myths and legends of Greece, India, and South America describe the rule of Osiris and Isis. Our mentor has already said, "*They were Gods or starpeople.*"

It is said that the Mighty Osiris and Isis walked into the Egyptian Valley out of nowhere and assumed command in the early Ancient Egyptian times. They were much taller and more imposing than the men of the time; they had long blond hair, marble-like blue/white skin, and remarkable powers that enabled miracles. They were from the advanced race of the Hathors, the blue people who lived on Earth for hundreds of years before The Fall of Atlantis and had originally come from Venus.

Some of these light beings had mated with the Earth women. It is recorded in the 'Book of Jubilees' the Angels had been counselled by the hierarchy not to mate with the Earth women. I believe the story of Adam and Eve being told not to mate in the Garden of Eden was because of the serpent. I believe the serpent is an analogy of reptilian blood that we, as earthlings, have inherited and that lowers your light. Your Royal blood, your Holy Spirit blood, is the holy bloodline that comes from the starpeople that has spread into every being upon this Earth.

The Earth people had been created with part reptilian blood, a lower frequency of spirit light, and this still infiltrates Earth people. However, with the melding of the blue light from the race of Hathors, stronger light beings about 300,000 years ago, the Earth people have inherited 'Holy Blood'—blood that holds consciousness and has gone on to infiltrate the human race. Scientists speak about the human brain having reptilian brain at the base and being overlaid by a mammalian brain and then human, in the course of evolution.

During the later period of Roman History, sun worship gained importance and ultimately led to what has been called a 'solar monotheism'.

Nearly all the gods of the period were possessed of solar qualities. The feast of Sol Invictus—unconquered sun on 25th December was celebrated with great joy, and eventually this date was taken over by the Christians as Christmas, the celebrated birthday of Essa, Jesus.

The Gayatri Mantra is regarded as one of the most sacred of the Vedic hymns and is dedicated to Savitr, one of the principal Adityas. The Adityas are a group of solar deities, from the Brahmana period, numbering twelve. The ritual of Sandhyavandanam, performed by Hindus, is an elaborate set of hand gestures and body movements designed to greet and revere the sun.

Since we are on the subject of the sun and divine light, I am advised that Sri Sathya Sai Baba has only ever given *one* meditation: a meditation on pure light, which ends, "*I am in the light, the light is in me, the light and I are one.*"

Everybody on Earth has a soul/spirit. It is our Holy bloodline. It is our light body, seen easily on modern medical scanning equipment, and easily seen clairvoyantly, emanating from our Earth body. If you think of our Earth body having a genetic DNA inheritance from our ancestors, so too we have a spirit body inheritance from our soul history ancestors.

Our spirit ancestors are who we have been in other lives from our Earth experiences or our cosmic experiences. Each is an individual being, closely related. These we can remember when we connect to our soul consciousness.

It is said by the *Avatars* that life here on Earth is not the reality. We are born from an embryo—a foetus that grows into our physical Earth body and eventually dies, going back to dust. An aspect of our oversoul grows into the embryo, foetus, and body as a spirit body. But when we die, the aspect of the soul, our spirit body or light body, continues to live on and returns to the World of Light.

Our Earth body has a brain like a computer that thinks—it uses about ten percent of our consciousness. Our spirit body has a soul seat in our heart that holds the consciousness that guides us through a blueprint of what our life is meant to achieve—ninety percent of our sub-consciousness. Our Earth body would not survive without our spirit/light body.

Our life on Earth should be simple if we can recognise the difference and raise our consciousness to become one with our soul consciousness. We are experiencing many lives on earth and in the cosmos, but where do we go in between those lives?

We have an oversoul that links with the Angelic Realm and we return to the Source of our light being in the World of Light. Our Holy Grail we call home.

I asked my spirit mentor if he would like to add a message. He thanked me for asking him and said, *"I would like you to say that the whole reason for your book is about your sacred journey that you and your husband have taken. You could recommend for others to travel to sacred places...it helps to lift the spirit to the soul consciousness, which you have already mentioned.*

"For what has happened is that you have been given knowledge. For what began in Egypt and the period of Amarna has now become a huge cycle that is taking the Earth and its solar system into the frequency aligned with the central sun and the core of suns that enables all to come from God consciousness."

25 Arriving in France and the Knights Templar

Living in France for 6 months

John is interested in researching the Knights Templar and we find we have landed smack bang in the middle of their country where it all began, dating from 1028—could be earlier. How's that for coordinated arrangements? I love working with spirit.

When we decided to look for a 'Home Exchange', we were open to all opportunities. We felt, because of our age, it would be good to travel to Europe for six months on a long stay. The house we are at now has been offered to us for that length of time. If you just follow that feeling of inner guidance from your heart, it can lead you into some wonderful adventures. It can feel like you are walking a thin tightrope sometimes, but there is always a 'sign' given by *Upstairs* that can keep plotting you on the right path. We exchanged houses with Patrick and arrived in Montignac, France, in 2015. The following experiences are what I have taken directly from my diary.

"I am reading a book I just 'happened' to give John for his 80th birthday, *'Pirates & the Lost Templar Fleet'* by David Hatcher Childress. The author writes (to our surprise) how the Templars had large fleets of ships and how they came from La Rochelle entrance to the Charente river to Angouleme and then to the Mediterranean sea at Coilloure, taking goods and pilgrims safely across to the Holy Lands. That was how they avoided the dangerous passage travelling through the Straits of Gibraltar.

We have been here long enough now to find there were many noblemen who built castles and fortresses from the early 11th century onwards, and how many of the churches show images or symbols of the Knights Templar presence. Romanesque architecture dates from 800 to 1100 AD and with French work graduating to Gothic architecture from the 12th century, lasting until the 16th century. After the French Revolution, many of the buildings were sold and remaining *huge churches operate in small village parishes*.

We are staying at Montignac-Charente, which has the remains of a fortress for Don Jon 1028 that is the great tower or innermost keep of a castle. It was built to keep a watch for ships sailing up the Charante River from the Bay of Biscay—it is just up the road and is linked with the huge fortress built on a high hill nearby in ancient Angoulmois known as Angouleme.

The large church Saint Martial is in Angouleme (100,000 people) where we found an ancient mural of a Knights Templar dressed in a white overshirt with a red equal-sided cross, which is of course the symbol of the Templars.

In the ancient centre of Angouleme, it WAS named New York Square, and when I asked it seems the Statue of Liberty was made with the local material and sent to New York, USA as a gift of LIBERTY. In fact, it is said that New York, USA was first named New Angouleme!

The cry, "Liberty, Equality, and Fraternity" first went out to unify France during the Revolution, but it is believed to have its source from the time of the Crusades.

It could all be tied up with the Knights Templar, who developed the Masonic Lodges. We know about all the Masonic symbols used on the USA dollar bill and most of Washington D.C. architecture, and then of course there were the Pilgrim Fathers.

When the suppression of the Knights Templars happened in France, 1307, they disappeared to other safe places. One was Portugal and, of course, Scotland. From there, they are said to have disappeared to the New World, which they already knew about. This was well before Christopher Columbus who was said to have discovered the USA in 1492. Remember, his ships had the white sails with the big red equal-sided cross.

By the way, the date of the suppression of the Templars in France was 13th October 1307—*Black Friday*, which is where the superstition is said to have first came about thirteen being unlucky.

The King of the time had ordered all the Templars to be arrested and tried for heresy or expelled from France. Most of them escaped or went underground and operated secretly.

We were slowly recovering from jet-lag—takes a little longer now that we are in our eighties, and I cannot see us climbing any high mountains this trip. I was wondering how I could run meditation meetings for the next six months to receive the regular transmission from Cosmic Sai Baba, which are uploaded onto the internet.

We had two lovely ladies arrive from Angouleme—friends of Patrick's, the bachelor who owned this house and was now living in our house in Australia. They gifted us with a homemade cheesecake.

To make a long story short, they were very helpful and we found they were open to meditation and wanted to come. I had noticed a signboard for notices in the local news agency, but was wondering how I was going to conduct meditation in French?

Anyway, Lillianne is French, and an English teacher. She had retired from teaching and wanted to translate for me while the meditation and transmission was taking place. *Upstairs* has organised it all for me. How lovely. I found Patrick is French; living in France, most people are Catholic, but here he had a small altar in his kitchen for Buddha and a beautiful calendar with quotes from Philosophers all around the world. I am open to all religions, believing in one God—so it made me really happy.

Both John and I have experienced two separate past lives each, relating to this area in France. So, it is no co-incidence we have been brought to this area. We have detailed the stories on my website under Sacred Past—Travels 2015. For now, I would like to describe how we came to understand our *lives together* in the early days of the Knights Templar. Looking back, it was for me the most difficult past life with which I have had to deal. So much so, that I began to think that it was enough—I did not want to remember any more—and yet, on a personal note, it was really the most needed to recall and release."

26

Visiting the Crypt where Saint Martial and Saint Valéria lay in Limoges

It has been raining quite a lot, day after day, and is so cold John lights a fire and keeps it going all day. It is 1st May and supposed to be halfway through spring! The locals tell us, in French, of course, "It's not usually like this."

John speaks French and I've found I have begun to dream in French, but I cannot seem to speak it, even though when reading something I realise I am reading in French, not perfectly, but I just about understand all of what I am reading. But then, as I age, I am having a little trouble remembering English.

A couple of days later it does brighten a little, so John, dear one, suggests we visit Limoges and find the crypt where Saint Martial and Saint Valéria lay. He is getting used to driving a six-gear manual car and takes only about one and half hours to find our way there.

The countryside is laid out in wide, long fields of yellow canola flowers and other colourful flowers, and fields in different shades of green as far as the eye can see. All very neat, perfectly laid out, and dotted intermittently with vineyards just beginning to sprout leaves.

The spring flowering trees and bushes are breathtaking and the land slightly hilly in some places, so you never know what is around the next valley. Villages are often named Saint somebody, with the buildings very old but neat and made with varying sizes of whitish limestone bricks or blocks.

We both like the feel of Limoges—it is very familiar, and a lovely city. So, we think, *here we go again*. Wherever we go on this visit to the Charente area, we find we have strong feelings of being here before, in another life.

We found the eglise (huge church) of Saint Martial (at least we thought it was that name but it is actually St Michel des Lions), but it does hold relics of St. Martial, the first Bishop of Limoges. The site is that of an earlier chapel dedicated to Archangel Michael and was close to the ancient Roman Limoges–Saintes road, leading to the entrance of the Charente River on the Atlantic coast. We have visited there, and that is our first link to our Knights Templar past life story.

As always with all the past lives I investigate here in France, there is a Jehanne d'Arc statue in the church. The name of the church is St Michel – or known as Archangel Michael, who tells me he is always with me.

There were many windows with stories held in stained glass. The main three above the centre of the Altar were glorious. John was also looking at them closely and we could see on the left were pictures of what looked like Eleanor of Aquitaine riding next to her first husband King Louis VII of France, and then on the right side was Eleanor of Aquitaine riding a white horse beside her second husband Henry II. Behind them was a young adult prince with crown, wearing full armour and a white over-shirt with a red cross – symbolizing the Knights Templar.

Certainly the church windows were telling a story but not of saints, bishops or popes.

We were both overwhelmed knowing this linked with our past life feelings experienced at the huge fort at Le Chateau near Rochefort in the Department of Aquitaine. Richard I, also known as Richard the Lion Heart was the son of Henry II and Eleanor of Aquitaine. This meant in that past life I was John's mother. John's behaviour had not been good of late and I had felt I was chastising him like a mother to stop his tantrums. I don't like that role. My goodness, how often we must be playing out past life scenarios, even though the story is not the same in one's present life.

We have both agreed to work on healing ourselves, each other and all the people who were affected by us in the roles we had in our past lives.

Researching Richard I we discovered that as a sixteen year old he was presented in ceremony to be the Duke of Aquitaine from his mother's inheritance. In the ceremony he was given St. Valerie's ring to wear – the ring, then nearly a thousand years old.

I find it extraordinary that two soulmates, which John and I are, should touch each other with time jumps. Eleanor was his mother, who had St. Valéria in her soul history (*as she is in mine; we are the same oversoul*) and had arranged the ring to be presented to Richard I, who is in my John's soul history. One wonders if Eleanor was aware of her connection to the ring. Certainly, sub-consciously she would have been.

The feelings are very strong—I can feel myself riding on a horse knowing this area of France very well, being royal, knowing the people and the frustrations of the complicated life that Eleanor led. And to match these feelings, John, when he shops in the local village, they call him, 'Bon Jour, Chevalier John'. They do not know anything about our esoteric experiences.

27 Bad Fall Opened a Huge Doorway into a Past Life of Crusades

Not long after arriving in France, while living at Patrick's house I fell about one metre down three very large steps from the kitchen to the living area of the house at Montignac, Charente, hitting things as I went bump bump, bump bump onto a hard wooden floor and taking the weight of my fall on my rib cage, breaking ribs as I hit a hard metal protrusion, before landing on the ground. My big toe also broke.

I have never fainted in my life, but just as I was falling, I felt I was taken over and, of course, I later wondered if it was a malevolent entity. But it was my mentor. I found myself arguing with him, just like a husband, well why didn't you protect me? And he yelled back at me, "I'm sorry!" very loudly. As time goes on, I realise he did protect me; my injuries could have been far worse, but there were changes needed within this body I have inherited.

So, all will be good and I trust him, and I said sorry too.

Looking back, I was reminded of when I first went to India. I was granted a personal interview with the Holy Man Sri Sathya Sai Baba. He gave me a green stone ring. He has often sent messages through the ring to me in a symbolic way.

When I was blessed with the interview, a woman alone in a strange country, he manifested the green ring and put it on my left fourth finger. I was communicating with him *telepathically* the whole personal interview. *I said, telepathically, "Oh, that is my marriage finger,"* and he, Sathya Sai Baba nodded, smiled, removed the ring, and put it on my right hand fourth finger.

Later, I was *set up* to visit the local Mother Mary church at Brindavan and he said to me *telepathically, "You have been married to God many times as a nun.* I later realised, as the story of Eleanor of Aquitaine unfolded, that she had spent the last five years of her life as a nun, married to God.

Now, after the accident in France, the fourth finger on my right hand is very swollen so I have to wear the green ring on my left hand fourth finger, my wedding ring finger, the only finger it will fit safely. It was John's suggestion that I wear it on that finger.

So, now I feel I have done a complete circle of some kind. And I believe, probably more insight is to come.

John, in a temper about something, triggered a reaction in me not long after my fall. I began crying and it was so different, almost primordial in its feeling and sound. It was like I hadn't cried but was doing so now to release emotional pain that I had suffered so long ago.

I must say, while I was recovering from crying, I was prompted to reassure my body it would be alright. Feeling so much better after the tears and emotion had been released, I calmed down.

The experience of the accident, although very painful, seem to assist with 'opening a door' into the life of Eleanor of Aquitaine and I was overwhelmed with unhappy emotional memories of her life. I wasn't coping very well at all. I know now I had agreed to 'write about' that life and time when we were in a position of power and able to carry out what we believed at the time of the Crusades.

Our spirit mentor, Alcheringa, has advised us that John was the Founder of the Knights Templars Hugh de Payens in a past life—*after that*, he came back in his next life as Richard the Lion Heart. The Knights Templar was formed by raising money from the Noblemen of the day and volunteers to fight in the first crusade to regain the sacred site of Jerusalem from the Saracens, so that Christian Pilgrims could safely visit there. The Crusade had the blessing of the then Pope and the Catholic Church.

John has four personalities in his soul story for the Crusade era, including Richard I, also known as Richard the Lionheart, who was one of Eleanor's sons. Up until now, I have never thought I had ever been John's mother, although we share lifetimes of him being my father. Eleanor's lifetime had been so difficult, it was a lifetime I never wanted to look at. However, it is time now; I have agreed to write about it long before we came here.

I have been asked how come you and John were all these 'famous'people? *Why*?

My reply is we have had a lot of lives on Earth and have been told we come from the '*highest Order*'. And don't forget in our oversoul, it is an expression of 6 points or 12 points holding consciousness within sacred geometry who can manifest as people.

The people mentioned are only famous because they held positions of power and are recorded in history. From that point, the personalities we came were able to influence changes within the history of that time? Remember we are Starpeople returned. We didn't have to come.

I would like to also add that there are many starpeople on Earth—who also didn't have to come. They are here to assist the raising of consciousness upon this planet. AND some do hold positions of power.

Overview

This overview of the Crusades is taken from the UK History Learning Website

"The Crusades were a series of military campaigns during the time of Medieval England against the Muslims of the Middle East. In 1076, the Muslims had captured Jerusalem, the most holy of holy places for Christians. Jesus had been born in nearby Bethlehem and had spent most of his life in Jerusalem. He was crucified on Calvary Hill, also in Jerusalem. There was no more important place on Earth than Jerusalem for a true Christian, which is why Christians called Jerusalem the "City of God".

However, Jerusalem was also extremely important for the Muslims as Muhammad, the founder of the Muslim faith, had been there and there was great joy in the Muslim world when Jerusalem was captured. A beautiful dome called the Dome of the Rock was built on the rock where Muhammad was said to have sat and prayed. The rock was so holy that no Muslim was allowed to tread on it or touch it when visiting the Dome.

Thus, the Christians fought to get Jerusalem back while the Muslims fought to keep it. This war lasted nearly two hundred years.

When the first crusaders set off, calling themselves 'pilgrims', they wore large, red cloth crosses, hence the subsequent naming of 'crusade', originally derived from the Latin word 'crux'. The term 'crusades' never surfaced until a French historic text, L'Histoire des Croisades, was published in the 17th century.

As pilgrims, the original crusaders saw themselves as undertaking an armed mission or pilgrimage, and the 'taking of the crux' (cross) all the way to Jerusalem symbolised their vows would only be fulfilled upon reaching their destination."

I had been struggling for weeks to cope with the pain I was suffering from the accident. Driving anywhere in our little car only made things worse when hitting many a rough part of the narrow roads, giving me a nasty painful jolt under my rib cage—let alone trying to continue walking with a swollen and bruised broken toe. The doctor had given me very strong painkillers but warned if I felt dizzy taking them to come back to see him.

I was getting worse in that I could no longer think clearly and kept bumping into things, no longer realising the medication was not good for me, although it was helping to lessen the pain. After four weeks of taking the pills three times a day, I stopped taking them.

Three days later, I had a serious reaction.

We had visitors and the last few days were more than difficult. I had been feeling I was pushing myself for quite a while and not taking enough rest. It was four weeks since my fall.

I ended up in hospital yesterday, having a strange reaction—*I couldn't walk and had difficultly breathing*. An ambulance took me to the hospital, but it was difficult when I don't speak much French. Many tests found nothing to worry about, so I was sent home, but I was able to walk carefully by then.

I don't think the medical world has caught up or can explain everything that can happen to someone. For instance, we are studying past lives and have been asked by *Upstairs* to write about it. It just so happens I find Eleanor of Aquitaine is in my oversoul story and probably the hardest past-life problems I have been asked to deal with. All female agendas.

Anyway, Eleanor died when she was eighty-two years old and I am eighty-two years old, replaying that for various reasons. I did feel I was leaving; I could feel my spirit slipping out of my body and was feeling icy cold inside the centre of my body, the same as when I nearly died once before in 1969.

In particular my feet, were icy and I couldn't even feel my right foot, even though John said the feet felt warm. I asked him to hold onto my feet and ask God to allow my spirit to come back into the body. With that, I felt pins and needles and the warmth of life force come back into my feet. John, the poor thing, was beside himself with worry; he felt sure I was dying, and I was, but I was soon feeling better and home with lots of rest and drinking water, and rescue remedy.

The only way the ambulance people could get me to the ambulance was through the window, tying me into a sort of walking stretcher down the hill. Must have looked strange and funny. John said he wished he could have taken a photo. They would have to be very inventive to remove people from some of these French houses! The young male attendant said he has thrown people over his shoulder to remove a patient from a house.

I stayed in bed for the next few days, catching up with emails. At least my body has stopped shaking. I just need some time to recover.

John thinks I may have suffered a mild stroke, similar to him, but that wasn't checked at the French hospital. I think he is right, I must say I noticed a very, very slight drop in one side of my face after it happened; it was a month after my fall, so it was possible.

All that is healed now. My body had to be shaken up to allow the information of the newer me to come through. Symbolically, it assisted me through a 'new window' of understanding.

28 Eleanor of Aquitaine, Henry II and Richard the Lionheart

We were still in France and something like eight weeks had passed since I had my fall on **May 12th**, and then took a second dangerous 'turn' on **11th June** when I collapsed and almost died. In that time, I have to admit it was very difficult. I could not think clearly but was aware that a window was opening wider into the memory of living a life as a royal with much power at the time and decisions made with huge influence in history.

I have often been given signs of double eight = meaning 'this was meant to happen'. May is 5 and 12th = 3 (5+3) adds to 8, plus 2015 is another 8, and then 11th June (2+6) = 8 plus 2015 = 8 another double eight again.

When we travelled to Le Chateau de Isle d'Oleon in Acquitane, not long after we first arrived in France, we had vague feelings of being there before. In fact, John was quite shaky on his feet and I worried he would fall over the high parapets in the huge fort we visited on the edge of the Atlantic Ocean. I kept thinking of Eleanor—or Alienor, as is often spelt, for I had seen a college nearby named in her honour.

After the accident, memories of Eleanor's life began to pour into my consciousness amidst the pain I was experiencing from my cracked ribs and broken toe. I found myself reacting with deep resentment to the way John was speaking to me but realising he was playing a role of how it was between Eleanor and Henry II King of England and Aquitaine.

Not surprisingly, in that life Richard the first was similar to his father's personality. The emotional reactions were with me for a long time and it was time to release them once and for all. I have to confess, in my lowered state of health I was really considering divorce.

Eleanor had been only fifteen years old when she was left an orphan and inherited half of France, which was Aquitaine at that time. She was an attractive woman, used to having her own way, capricious and highly educated. It is said she was the richest woman in Europe and the most eligible.

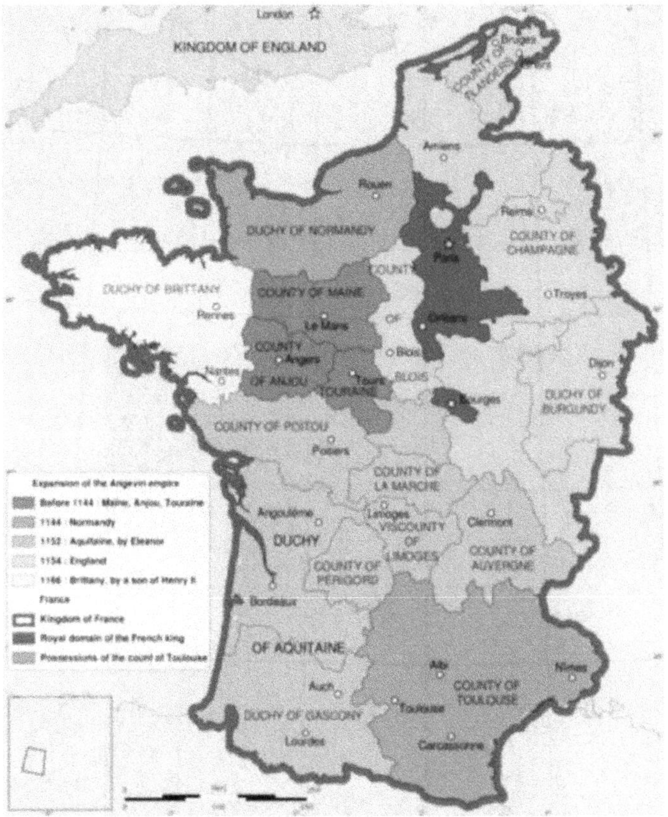

In the 12th century, a noblewoman of that time was in danger of being kidnapped and held for ransom if she was not married. Her 'guardian' Louis VI King of France married her off to his son Louis VII. Thus, it was a political match and one that resulted in Louis VII automatically inheriting her wealth, position, and large area of land that went on to make him the King of the whole of France.

King Louis VII

Eleanor of Acquitaine – Wife to Louis VII and then Henry II

The marriage was not happy, and even though she had two daughters, it was annulled on the grounds of consanguinity, which was allowable at those times. The daughters had to stay with their father Louis VII. But the land known as Aquitaine was returned to Eleanor.

A little older and wiser, Eleanor then married Henry II, making him both King of England and Aquitaine in France. She was older than him but knew him of course. Like many of the nobles in Europe, they all seemed to be distantly related in some way.

Although again it was a political match, Eleanor was in love with Henry II. He had a reputation of being very difficult: a manipulator and a misogynist in his manner. The noble men of those days were supposed to be chivalrous and that was what Eleanor was used to in Aquitaine. Henry was different and often treated her almost as if she was his chattel—he owned her, not allowing her independence—and they quarrelled often. However, they still had eight children and Henry II was delighted to be presented with five sons and three daughters over the years.

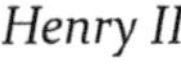

Henry II

Richard I

Henry was a philanderer, not unusual in those times, and had mistresses. But Eleanor was not happy when Rosamund came on the scene, producing an illegitimate son, nearly the same age as her own new baby and was allowed to almost usurp Eleanor in her own court. The indignity almost broke her heart. She remained a strong spiritual woman and, as her life progressed, it became more difficult with Henry II and his jealousies of King Louis VII of France and the loss of the loyalties of his own sons.

She was imprisoned by her own husband Henry II for seventeen years of her life, not seeing her family or friends because she appeared to side with her sons against their father.

Eleanor of Aquitaine – a Place Where She Was Born

On Our Way Home from France to Australia - via England

When we first came to Montignac Charente, which is also Aquitaine country, I didn't know much of the history of France. So, with our being there, in France, particularly the Charente, there was much healing going on—both consciously with ourselves and more so at a subconscious level for the history that has now passed in their land.

Towards the end of our planned six month stay in France, we decided to leave two weeks earlier and visit England, John's birthplace. I was still having trouble thinking clearly after my fall and later nearly dying on 11th June 2015. It had opened up a huge memory of past lives as royals and the early Crusades.

Before leaving France, we were invited to spend a last lunch visiting with our lovely French girlfriends who had shown us many special places in the Charente area—places not generally known to tourists.

The day out was to be a surprise. It was only about a forty-five-minute drive and we found ourselves at a place named Verteuil-sur-Charente. The restaurant was a mill house, situated between two streams of water from the Charente River, with the sound of the mill wheel chugging away in one side of the water and the aroma of freshly ground bread flour.

We had such a happy time, and later we visited a little shop selling many historical artefacts. The shopkeeper told us the castle was where Eleanor of Aquitaine's mother had lived.

Now, in all historical records I have read, it is said it's not known where Eleanor was born. We knew straight away this was where she was born—and that the joy we were feeling, and the familiarity of this lovely place, was where Eleanor had been often as a child and later brought her own children to visit. Hence the reason John was feeling so joyful also.

We decided to make it a three-day journey north to Paris, where we had arranged to leave our host's car, and from there to travel by fast train to England.

Our first overnight stop was to return to Poiters yet again. John always felt some anger when visiting this city; it was unconsciously coming from arguments he had with his father Henry II. As one of the Princes of Aquitaine in the past, he had lived there. His mother Eleanor had lived in the chateau that was now known as the Palais de Justice; it is not far from the cathedral where Eleanor and Henry II were married.

Then we travelled to the Abbaye Royale de Fontevraud where Henry II was buried, and Richard I (Coeur de Lion) was buried.

Henry II and Eleanor of Aquitaine

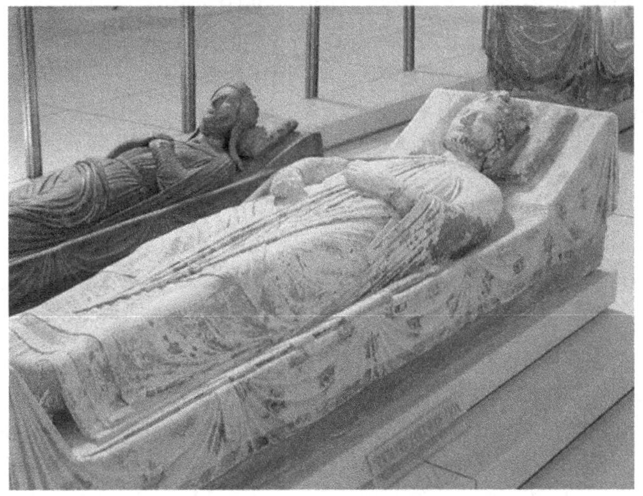

Richard the Lionheart

Eleanor had spent the last five years of her life as a nun at Abbaye Royale de Fontevraud and was buried alongside the two men, her second husband and her third son.

We travelled on, still feeling mixed emotions. We were trying to find the main highway to Chartres, but our GPS had a mind of its own and we realised we were actually travelling the pilgrim's way through many tiny villages and narrow streets.

As soon as we acknowledged it was Holy Spirit sending us this way for a reason, we both said we would give penance once we reached the mighty Cathedral at Chartres. Then, suddenly, we were on the highway and only fifty miles from Paris.

We found the huge Cathedral magnificent, but a little spoilt for us as there was scaffolding and noisy maintenance being carried out both inside and out. We couldn't see the magnificent portal clearly because of ladders and tarpaulins.

However, we still found a quiet place to offer gratitude and thankfulness for healing and forgiveness.

We were treated to '*Chartres en Lumieres*' that evening, a wondrous uplifting light show. Hundreds of visitors were watching the fascinating images being played with coloured lights on a number of buildings. *A celebration*, we thought.

Next morning, we travelled to Paris. John was driving and our GPS took us the shortest way, but it led us straight through the famous traffic that exists in Paris. I told John he needed a medal; he didn't lose his cool once.

The day after that, we were in London and hiring a car. There was an underlying tiredness always with us and though we had planned to travel quite a bit, we followed the important memories for John.

First, we found ourselves walking 'The City of London' with John asking me to take a photo of a '*Royal Fusilier*' statue in the middle of the square. He had completed his National Training for two years as a young man and had been chosen for Officer Training with the Royal Fusiliers. I pointed out to him the many symbols that existed with the regiment linked with the Knights Templar, especially when we visited the St Sepulchre church in High Holborn.

As a Fusilier, they marched to the church on Remembrance Day (*Poppy Day*) each November.

The original Saxon church on the site was dedicated to St Edmund, the King and Martyr. During the Crusades in the 12th century, the church was renamed St Edmund and the Holy Sepulchre, in reference to the Church of the Holy Sepulchre in Jerusalem. The name eventually became contracted to St Sepulchre. John was overcome to find so many of his ex-compatriots' memorials are there.

I was feeling messages that we should visit Oxford, only to find that Eleanor of Aquitaine and Henry II lived there in a chateau and that Richard I was born there. We stayed at a nice hotel 'Four Pillars' and enjoyed walks along the River Thames, watching the inevitable rowing teams. The town was busy with many students and visitors.

We found the place where the Chateau once stood, now in ruins; it is only marked with a brass plate telling of its existence.

We also heard about the Rollright Stones that were north of Oxford at Chipping Norton. Not far to drive, so we visited the 5,000-year-old ancient site.

It was summer in England but cold and damp. We arrived to find the ancient stones were known as the King's men and/or the Whispering Knights. And we were researching the Knights' Templars. This was a coordinated incident. *We needed to take notice.*

No one was around at first, then a few carloads of people arrived and began climbing the fence near the ancient stones and walking into the wheat field stretching for miles. We thought, What the heck? then realised there was a crop circle in the field.

John said, "You have your wish, Val, it is the season for crop circles and you were hoping to see one. Come on, let's go!"

We found ourselves running around like children; the energy when walking the patterns was extraordinarily up-lifting. Everyone was speaking French—were they connected to the Knights Templers also?

It was raining steadily now, and we were very cold, wet, and muddy, but it didn't matter, we were elated and felt we had been set up by our spirit mentor. It was like a reward of some kind and a healing.

Back at our hotel, our room keycard would not work, even when the green light showed to open the door. We had heard visits to crop circles sometimes interfered with electronics. It didn't affect my mobile phone as I was still able to take photos.

John commented. "I feel remarkably relaxed and I haven't shouted at you much at all," and then he humbly added, "I don't feel quite so skinny."

"Skinny?"

"Yes, I feel I've put some weight on or possibly I'm not worrying about my health anymore."

Next morning, at our lovely hotel in Oxford, while we were both seated at breakfast, a well-dressed American gentleman with wiry hair approached us. He spoke beautifully and excused himself but, "I have to ask you, sir, did you enjoy the graduation yesterday? I saw you there and offered to assist you carrying two glasses of champagne. I remember that large ring you are wearing on your finger."

John replied, "No, you have mistaken me for someone else, I wasn't at the graduation."

The Crop Circle is announcing the upcoming sun and Venus conjunction on 14 August 2015

The American gentleman immediately backed away and apologised profusely. "Please excuse me, sir." And looking very embarrassed, he left.

I said to John, "Something is going on. May I go and invite him to join us for breakfast." John agreed.

I walked over to the American gentleman and it was my turn to be a little embarrassed. "Excuse me, I am interested in the paranormal."

He interrupted and said he was open to that too.

"Great, would you care to join us for breakfast, I think we need to talk more?" I asked him.

He jumped up immediately and came over with me.

He said to John, "I was ninety-nine percent sure the man I saw yesterday was you. I particularly remember that unusual ring you are wearing."

We heard he lived in Japan and was here for his son's graduation in a Master's Degree in Philosophy.

John told him an Australian Aboriginal, a healer, gave the ring to him years ago and that Gerry had died six months earlier. We loved him and missed him.

The American Gentleman said his father's name was Gerry, and immediately pulled out his mobile and showed us a strong, healthy upright man who was ninety years old. He looked barely sixty. He had followed Maharishi all his life and influenced his children with the teachings.

I was then prompted to ask what time the graduation took place, and the American gentleman named Sam said about four the previous afternoon.

We both said, "We were walking a crop circle near the Rollright Stones north of Oxford at that same time." And we all immediately realised that Gerry, now in another world, was sending us a message through Sam to say he was with us. We were all elated.

With more talk, there were many more coordinated incidences and we all began laughing. So glad I followed my intuition to speak with him.

Now John wanted to show me his old school, St. Lawrence College at Ramsgate, East Kent. We tricked our GPS from taking the shortest way by planning the route ourselves to make sure we drove around London and not through it. In no time, we were on our way to the east coast of England.

I was quick to point out to John all the symbols that existed on the Coat of Arms showing that he was again, in this life, connecting to Knights Templar. I could see the equal-sided red cross. A crown with five pointed stars. The head shield worn by knights above a red cross and above that, the shell that is a pilgrim symbol of pilgrim walk to Santiago de Compostela. In Bono Vince means *'conquer with good'*.

Now we have returned home, after the two of us were invited to give a talk at Swami Home with a stopover in Singapore. The people were so friendly and kind. It has taken another two months to really settle at home, with us feeling uplifted and free.

I no longer feel John is my child and keep correcting him. He didn't like it and neither did I. I no longer react to certain emotions within; they are all gone. People say how the fall and the near-death experience was sad while we were in France, and I agree it was very difficult, but I wouldn't change a thing. I feel totally different now. A new me, happy and at peace with myself. And that reflects to John also. We thank God the Creator for all that has been given to us and willingly offer ourselves in service for the good of all.

On a personal note, I am thankful for the support John has always given me. I am sure there have been times he has found it extremely difficult living with a medium and all the work that follows. He recently pulled me into our local jewelry shop, saying he wanted to give me a sacred symbol crystal ring as a reminder of his love for me.

On my birthday, he actually fell to his knees and asked me to marry him again. My answer, of course, was "yes" as we hugged and kissed. And then with both of us laughing I had to help him back onto his feet. We are both grey haired, wrinkly, light-heartedly young, elderly people now, and I say this with a wise smile.

Why Are We Here? 30

John and Valérie ask their Mentor

"You, John Barrow, of course have other names. You are a strong light and you have committed to come at this time to help Valérie and assist her in her work. You have freed Valérie of the everyday necessity to make money, can I put it that way? To pay for her existence. This has been taken care of by you as her husband.

"You have committed to work with her and to look after her and Valérie in turn, of course, looks after you and assists you. Both of you in other worlds come from a point of light and you know each other quite well.

"There is what is known as a coupling that is of the opposites, that have agreed to come to this Earth, and you and Valérie Barrow are one of these couples. In other worlds, they have a healing and a uniting affect as they also have on this Earth. On this Earth, in this physical life, you are both playing out scenarios that are affecting quite a lot more than you realise in other worlds, but I do not feel that you wish me to go into this.

"Both are playing out the scenario so that understanding can be given. This is not a coincidence. This is something you both have agreed to and set upon when you came into this Earth incarnation. You are both walk-ins, you know this. And so, you come with a little more power, you come knowing God. But you have both agreed to be held back at various stages in your life, so that you can evolve with a knowing and a way of expressing this from experience. I think you are understanding what I am saying.

"In fact, my son, you are both very evolved beings, and the experience that you are playing out in this life, you already know.

The understanding you already know. These are just roles that you are playing out at this time."

Valérie asks about her role on Earth

"Well, in a way, my dear, I have already just answered this. You have agreed since the time you came to establish the beginning of the earthling in a loving and compassionate way, so that little forms could be growing, giving opportunity for aspects of various ones throughout the universe to come and experience on this Earth, with a veiled consciousness. You understand this. (*This understanding is made clear when Egarina speaks about the Pleiades, through me in Part Three.)*

"At one level of consciousness, you and John *did not* know this. At another, of course you did. The consciousness that you re-enacted or played out the roles, at the time 900,000 years ago, and what you are now bringing forth so that humanity will understand what took place, in a loose way you have come together from time to time down through the ages. You both have committed to stay and to continue that interaction with the earthling body, so that you would hold onto the energy and it would be very familiar to you over the time we have just spoken about, and so you would not find it too difficult to connect to humanity and the energy of the earthling and give out the experiences and the roles that were committed to by you both in the blueprints of each personality that you came down through the ages.

"You have lived lives separately, and you have lived lives together. Some of them you already know and there is really no reason to know more detail unless, of course, you specifically want to know. This has just kept you connected down through time.

"John Barrow has chosen not to have too many lives as a female. He just did not want to live that energy. He did try it on a few occasions, but he found it very difficult and very constricting. There is another aspect of him that is female on this Earth at this time for it is time for him to find balance between the two energies. He knows and understands this. It is a little difficult and this is what you have agreed to assist him with. You yourself have played many roles of equal male and female and so you have more experience in the blending and the balancing of both the energies. You have willingly agreed to assist John Barrow in finding the balance. He is finding it a little difficult, but with your assistance and commitment and love he will find this. It is already happening. He is receiving a lot of assistance from others from the World of Light and, of course, Cosmic Sai Baba.

"Well, we know, my dear that you have always received messages from Cosmic Sai Baba, telling you he would look after your husband and not to worry. He was finding difficulty because he always tended to connect with the male energy and you understand this. His extra-terrestrial energy from the constellation of Sirius was very much of a male origin, but of course this is different in other lives that he has had within the cosmic consciousness. This is the one that influenced him so much when he came to the Earth at this time, 900,000 years ago. And so, that energy was written into the Akashic Records that exists in the environment of the Earth.

"This is really what is important for each evolvement as people come, and from whence they came, into the earthling body at that time."

(*Referring to the first visit John made with Valérie to Sai Baba's Ashram in India.*)

"As I have already said, Sai Baba would look after him and upon the visit that you both made to the Ashram in India, emotions were allowed to bubble to the surface so they could be released. It is the emotions held within the physical body that actually creates blocks and holds back the evolvement of each being of each soul upon this Earth, in this case with your husband John. Sai Baba assisted him very quickly to release these bubbles of emotion so that he could evolve and become stronger within himself.

"It is very hard to speak about what takes place in the presence of Sai Baba. You have experienced it. Those that understand have experienced it. To speak of it is a little difficult, it is an experience. It is a letting go of the old and moving into a different understanding of consciousness. To actually rise above what is past, to be able to move forward. It is leaving behind the old, it is being ready then to move forward into the new.

"A change of consciousness takes place. A wiser outlook about everyday happenings takes place. Living and coping with what is put before you seems easier. Worry is left behind. Fear is left behind. Anger is left behind. Insecurity is left behind. In Sai Baba's presence one is assisted to find the True Self. Without any judgement upon the self or others. This sometimes takes more than one visit to achieve, but once a connection is made with Sai Baba, the energy flows and interacts with each individual being and they are assisted as they progress on their life here on Earth.

"In a way, the story that you have been asked to write about, my dear, that happened 900,000 years ago was held in a record that was sealed so it could be released at this time to assist many to remember and connect with that memory so in some way, one way or another, they could release the old that was infecting them, their relations, and hopefully they would be able to release that infection, so that they could be ready to move forward into the new age, the new Golden Age.

"This is the time of evolution within the cycle of the Earth and your Solar System and it was at this specific time that this was to take place and so the re-enactment of what took place 900,000 years was postponed until this time, so that the whole story could be released and understood because it is the beginning of humanity as you are now, with love and compassion."

"Do not worry, my child, I will assist you when you write, I assure you, thank you—and now I will take my leave unless there is something else with which I can assist you?"

I said no, thank you very much indeed. He wished me Happy Birthday telepathically as he was leaving.

John tells people about a dream he had when on his way to India for the first time with me. It was about 1998. In the dream, Sai Baba presented himself on an open-air stage surrounded by many people, with a red carpet running down the middle of the hall.

Sai Baba walked down the carpet towards John, but just before he reached him he suddenly turned into a beautiful Indian woman and crooking his finger, he gave John a '*come hither*' sign. John felt guilty about the dream and couldn't tell me. When we finally arrived at the Ashram in Puttpathi, India, I might say John was doing everything in his power to delay the meeting or at least seeing Sai Baba; we prepared to go to Darshan for blessing.

To John's amazement, the open-air mandir was exactly as he saw it in his dream, so he was nervous and fearful while waiting for Sai Baba to make his appearance. He didn't know what to expect.

As soon as Sai Baba walked out onto the stage, John immediately relaxed and felt a great sense of love pervading him.

Sai stands for Mother, and Baba of course means Father. So, it was Mother Father God's love standing in front of him. We can see now the female image Sai Baba gave John was actually helping him to absorb that female energy into himself. Sai Baba says, "if I come to you in a dream, it is not your imagination, it is a blessing and a message from me."

The past-life memories we have been given have not been advised blah, blah, blah, and etcetera. Rather, the realisations have been released slowly and over many years. It was only on thinking about it now, I realise just how much of our soul's past lives we have been given in many different ways. The full realisation is, of course, our oversoul is androgynous. When you sound the word, how like it is to andro-genesis.

Sri Sathya Sai Baba has left his mortal body now, but he advises telepathically he is just in the next world, still working to assist the little earthling.

"If there is righteousness in the heart, there will be beauty in the character. If there is beauty in the character, there will be harmony in the home. If there is harmony in the home, there will be order in the nations. When there is order in the nations, there will be peace in the world." – Sathya Sai Baba.

LET WORLD PEACE BE WITH US ALL

We didn't realise we were both holding his hands!

PART TWO

The Sacred Alcheringa Stone – The White Lady

31

I have been writing about soul past lives that John and I have experienced on the Earth plane together as soulmates. Now, I would like to write about our cosmic soul past-life memories, which will begin to read like science fiction. At least it gives us an understanding how science fiction stories are inspired.

We have come to realise the cosmic worlds are real, it is just that we cannot see other worlds readily with our 'Earth eyes'. Science will not see it either until scientific instruments are used to see past our immediate sight. Medical instruments are already in use to view auric fields around our body. Microscopes can see another world of microbes, looking like micro-miniature dinosaurs. We know from the discovery of fossils that dinosaurs and megafauna once lived on our planet. Telescopes and space shuttles enable scientists to see past our physical sight, into the 100 billion stars. The Milky Way is just one of 100 billion or so galaxies in the universe. Most scientists agree that the probability of life in other worlds could exist.

While living on the property at Canyonleigh, Southern Highlands, NSW, we had an intelligent, knowledgeable lady who worked in television media bring a sacred Alcheringa stone to our property. I shall call her The White Lady. She advised that the the sacred Alcheringa stone belonged to the Australian Indigenous people who say it comes from the stars.

Our property had already been named Alcheringa, an Australian Aborigine word meaning Dreamtime, Golden Age, or when the first ancestors were created, and this is what attracted her to us. She was ill and wanted to leave the stone with someone she could trust and who understood its importance. When she placed the sacred package into my hands, I felt I knew it.

The stone was wrapped first with paper bark, then a white calico cloth, and tied with string. The package was the size of a shoebox.

Sitting with the Alcheringa stone, while holding it on my lap I experienced a bright blue/white opalescent light in my inner scene. Over a period of time, I suspected the sacred stone influenced people in some way to find their way to our property. I knew I was never to open the package to look at the stone, nor to photograph it. I have become very attached to it, almost as though it is part of my family. I actually love it. I suppose that feeling has come from the energy of the stone and from where it originally came.

I remember sitting with it, not long after I had begun the readings for my first book, when I became aware there was a small spirit being attached to the stone. While holding the sacred stone that day, the little spirit introduced itself.

The little spirit being moved into my energy field. Speaking through me with a stilted voice, a different voice from my mentor, it moved my head from side to side as it communicated. It told me that, "*I have come from the stars and I am the one that is influencing the stone's travels,*" adding, "*It is easy to put a thought into someone's head, so that the stone will be picked up and travel from one place to another. The stone has a role to play on this planet after the development of the animal man into the human.*"

The Aborigine people have always known the Alcheringa stone came from the stars; we too were receiving the understanding that the stone was moulded clay from another planet. The Leonine People and the starpeople had brought it to Earth from Sirius, five years after the mothership 'Rexegena' was attacked and destroyed. There had been fifty thousand starpeople on board; most perished, with only ninety survivors. This was nine hundred thousand years ago. I will share more about the mothership Rexegena coming from the Pleiades and the 'cherished ones' in the next chapter and Part Three.

My mentor has advised that everyone in the galaxy heard of the tragedy. The ninety survivors were living on the land we now call Australia.

The survivors welcomed their rescuers from Sirius and the gift of the Alcheringa stone, and holding it felt like going home. It was imbued with the energy from the home planet; it held the energy of love and compassion. It presented as a blue/white light and lifted the consciousness of those holding it to a place that I could only describe as 'conscious dreaming' or a raised consciousness readily linking with one's soul consciousness.

In the beginning, the Alcheringa stone was given to the new breed of upstanding ape-like creatures, who had inherited genes from the starpeople. The starpeople described them as the Cherished Ones or Chosen Ones. They continued to hold the stone and remember, long after the starpeople had left their bodies.

The Alcheringa stone was held with deep reverence. Over the years, the indigenous Stone Keepers, generation after generation, in trying to keep it safe, put fear into the hearts of their tribe about its power. It was only ever to be handled by the appointed Stone Keeper. The tribe began to believe they would get sick if they opened its paper bark package and look upon it.

The sacred stone became lost when Atlantis fell, around 10,500 thousand years ago, and seawater rose, sinking land all over the Earth.

The Australian Aborigine has Dreaming stories about the event of a great flood. The starpeople returned from the stars, rescuing the stone, again giving the sacred stone to the Cherished Ones.

In the early days of the white man's settlement, an Afghan wandering the Australian desert with his camel and selling goods found the stone in a cave. He tried to give it back to the local tribes, but they refused. They were frightened of it. Generations later, the Afghan's family gave it to the White Lady, who they knew had contact with a local Aborigine tribe. The White Lady also experienced difficulties in coaxing the tribal people to take it back, even though she had been initiated into their local tribe.

I came to know the stone looked like moulded clay with ochre concentric circles drawn on it because the White Lady had opened the package to look inside and described it to me. Intuitively, I knew it was not to be opened, that it was said to be only for the Clever People of the tribe to view it. I honour and respect that.

The White Lady travelled to Central Australia to try and find the indigenous keeper of the stone. On her journey, she experienced a very clear past-life memory of her being the Afghan who found it in the early days of the white man's settlement; he had walked with his camel through the outback and found the stone in a cave. In her inner sight, she could see the stone glowing and knew it was special. It had been found somewhere near Uluru.

Now, the White Lady understood why she felt so responsible and compelled to return the stone to its rightful owners. She became seriously ill, not from having the Alcheringa stone, but because she had over-indulged in alcohol and had serious liver damage. It was then she heard of me living on the property Alcheringa.

She made her way, with friends, to our property. As soon as she walked through our front door and met me, she decided I could be trusted to look after the stone until she recovered. Unknown to me at that time, she had told her friends that the sacred stone was to stay with me should anything happen to her.

I had the Alcheringa stone in my care for two years, always keeping it safely deposited in our Healing Room. John and many of our psychic friends had sat with it and experienced its power—some to the point they cried with recognition when they held it, just as I had done. My John felt he knew it, much the same way I had felt when it was given to us.

After two years, the White Lady recovered from health issues for a while and wanted the stone returned to her. This was a great wrench for me. The Alcheringa stone had been like a baby to me, much loved and attached to the memory of the star being in my soul memory, when it first came to this earth.

So, it seemed appropriate on Sunday 12th May 1996 that *Upstairs* coordinated events for it to be handed back to the White Lady. It was Mother's Day. The day, month, and year added to thirty-three, another sign used by spirit to get me to 'take note'. (*The number 33 relates to the cosmos.)*

The White Lady and I agreed on the phone to meet at the lighthouse at Byron Bay, Bundjalung tribal country. It is the further point east of the east coast of Australia.

It was evening and as the sun was setting we could see in the distance Wollumbin, aka Mt. Warning. The sunset was magnificent in rainbow colours and the clouds, like wings of a giant angel spread across the sky, reflected in the calm bay from Wollumbin Mountain to the lighthouse. The sight of the sunset took our breath away.

It was suggested that I sit alone with the stone before I passed it back to the White Lady. Spirit spoke to me clearly in my head, I was surprised at the clarity. I was told the green chrysophase stone I had brought, to be passed on as a gift to the future indigenous Stone Keeper, was a gift from the heart of Australia. The chrysophase stone had been given to me when I visited Uluru. It was an appropriate gift to the indigenous Stone Keeper. The voice also said I was to ask the White Lady to pass on the message to the future Aborigine Stone Keeper that I was carrying the energy of the being known as '*the eighth white sister from the Pleiades*' and that she had now returned as promised.

I handed the paperbark package to my friend and wished her a safe and successful journey, although I was concerned she was not looking at all well. Within half an hour of parting with the stone, Gerry, my Aboriginal friend, rang me from Sydney. I was surprised by his call; I had not spoken to him for ages and he did not know I was within view of his beloved Wollumbin, Bundjalung Country. It is his home.

Breathlessly, I repeated what the Alcheringa stone had said about The Eighth Sister from the Pleiades. Gerry drawled, "Oh yeah, I'll have to tell you more about her. It is said she will return when the time is right, it is in our Dreaming stories about the Seven Sisters in the sky from the Pleiades. It is said she lays in a crystal, asleep at the base of Mt Wollumbin. That is not far from where you are now in Byron Bay."

I found out later *The Eighth White Sister from the Pleiades* he was referring to was Egarina, the starperson from the mothership Rexegena, the one who had survived its destruction, *my Cosmic Soul Ancestor*.

The White Lady, carrying the precious stone, set off in her car with great determination, once again to the red centre of Australia. Bitterly disappointed, she failed and returned home still with the sacred stone in her possession. She then became seriously ill. Her friends were convinced it was the stone making her sick and quickly took it to the Aboriginal Land Council in Redfern, Sydney insisting they take it back.

Sadly, the White Lady died in 1997.

After her funeral, and on advice from Gerry, I rang the Land Council to ask what had happened to the sacred stone. They advised it had been posted on to the Land Council at Alice Springs. I was aghast. I couldn't believe that a sacred relic could just be posted somewhere. In a slow drawl, the Aborigine on duty said, "It'll get to where it's meant to go. Like you said, the stone has a mind of its own."

So now the sacred Alcheringa stone had introduced us to the Cosmic World and the Starpeople. Not forgetting that I had been awakened out of a deep sleep to see a "huge mothership sail over the top of our house"; *Upstairs* had jokingly referred to it as a UFO!

In honour of the White Lady, I wish to add, we came to know in 2011 that the sacred Alcheringa stone was found in a sacred site known as Cave Hill. It is also known as the Cave of the seven sisters from the Pleiades. It was found over 100 kilometres away from Uluru.

We were advised by Alcheringa that the light coming from inside the cave attracted the Afghan Camelier and he found it inside. He had tried to give it to the local tribe, but they were afraid of it, just the same as when the White Lady tried to return it. Alcheringa also advised us the White Lady and the Afghan Camelier were from the same soul. We understand now why she felt so compelled to return it to its rightful place—which has now happened.

32

The Book of Love was received by sitting with the sacred Alcheringa stone that the Australian Indigenous people say came from the stars. It 'told' me many things and was written as a diary. It is the beginning of my mission.

THIS SECTION IS DEDICATED WITH LOVE
TO SRI SATHYA SAI BABA

BE WHAT YOU PROFESS TO BE
SPEAK WHAT YOU INTEND TO DO
UTTER WHAT YOU HAVE EXPERIENCED
NO MORE,
NO LESS

– *Sri Sathya Sai Baba*

Introduction
1994 – My Mission Begins

I sat quietly with the sacred Alcheringa stone the indigenous people say came from the stars. It carried a power that imbued my being with a blue/white light as I sat with it on my lap. It raised my consciousness, even though my eyes were open and I was aware of everything in the room. I was prompted to start speaking without any thought at all.

"I love you, I love you, I love you. Please give me the understanding that you have come to teach me."

I feel I have known this stone before—it is surrounding me with light, that same blue/white opalescent light I experienced in a meditation recently. It is like a moonstone light. I feel that light permeating me and it is matching me with this stone.

I feel part of this stone. It is like a baby; it is as if it has come from within my womb. That is a symbolic way of seeing it, but it was birthed onto this Earth and I speak as an ambassador of spirit. I speak with the knowledge already within me and that too will birth, that also will come forth into my conscious understanding.

I feel no sadness—it is one of joy—it is one of love, and it is one of love that came for mankind. There is a beauty and an understanding and wisdom that comes with this stone. This stone is like a book—a book of records. It is a record of the existence of those that come from other worlds. Those that are known as the starpeople.

It came. It came as a vehicle to bring that understanding. All will be revealed—all will come forth. It is a prophecy that has been handed down through all races on this Earth, that the bonding of spirit and man did come at this time, and the stone holds that understanding. (*I sighed deeply.*) Go forth!

(*I have just realised that this sacred stone was first given to me 900,000 years ago by my John when he was a starman and I was a starlady.*)

I sat silently for a while when the realisation came forth. That is why I have come—I experienced an overwhelming feeling of the enormity of it. After another long pause, I felt moved to say that it is connected with the 'Book of Revelations'—it is *The Book of Love*. My understanding is that what is written in *The Bible* also correlates with the Dreamtime of the Australian Aborigine.

I have been thinking about how I can start this book to capture the reader's attention. (*Laughs.*) I am just an ordinary housewife and mother, married for the second time to a charming man who is still in business and often travels into South-East Asia. I do help him with that business to some degree by doing his typing. This typing ability, of course, will help me with writing the book.

Between us we have four sons, three of whom are married and one little grandchild on the way. (*A girl.*)

The boys all get on well with each other, although it was not always that way, but I think in learning to live with each other as they did in the earlier days (*for it is a melded family*), they have grown from the experience and I hope have become a little wiser. They all think I am a little strange in the things I speak about, so I tend not to speak too much about my personal experiences with the starpeople. Even though my John is very accepting of it all, he still feels he needs to make jokes and talks about my 'fruit loop' friends (*he makes me laugh*), but it is all done with good heart, and a joke here or there helps people not to take things too seriously, for even the starpeople advise that. They try to teach people or help them to understand of their connection with spirit, with the God energy, but they also encourage laughter.

Many peoples on this Earth are influenced, whether they know it or not, by the energy from the starpeople. We are told there are many working with them, even though they do not realise it, not at a physical conscious level anyhow.

The whole idea seems to be to raise our consciousness to a 'higher' vibration, so we can come to understand about other aspects of all that is influencing us from the unseen universe.

A picture of Sai Baba that is in our house has caused a few raised eyebrows from visitors who do not understand what he is about and, I must confess, when I first heard of Sai Baba many years ago, I too was a little wary about connecting with a being here on Earth that seemed to have so much power.

As a medium, I seemed to be doing quite well from allowing myself to be guided in a mystical way, from an unseen point that was very gentle and compassionate, understanding and forgiving. That, I thought, was enough and now I find it is all the same.

It took a little time for my thick head to accept and understand in full. However, I am delighted now to tell my story and I hope in doing so that others will gain a little insight into their own journey, and I hope also that the energy from the masters will pass through this book, and out, to touch all who read it.

33 1st SITTING

Meditation the Day after the Bell Had Sounded

22.8.1994

I am honouring Oodgeroo the Paper Bark people.

I feel prompted to call upon Tjurunga, who has already told me he is going to help me to understand and to help us to direct this sacred stone to its rightful place. We already know the stone is unhappy being locked up in its wrappings and I am asking now should it be unwrapped, and I am getting the feeling it should not—until it reaches its rightful place, it is a protector for it.

I feel Tjurunga standing on my left on one leg, tall, straight, and dignified, a black Aborigine spirit man holding a spear stick, and I welcome him. I am holding the stone. I feel the warmth of the stone entering my body. (*Long pause.*) It is as if I have become the stone.

The peoples that came from other planets to inherit this Earth brought the Pleiadian energy at this time. The peoples on this Earth received them with open arms. They felt safe in their presence. They somehow knew they would gain in knowledge and wisdom from these people from the stars.

The Wandjina is what they were called. The people of the Earth did not mind their presence at all—they loved them. The love was shared, the teachings were shared, and all those around loved each other and cared for each other.

This was in the beginning.

This stone holds that energy within it and all that come into its presence will change and transmute into those same feelings of love and caring and compassion. This stone is ancient—very ancient—and so, because it has been here for so long, it holds the history in its energy of the changes that have taken place on this Earth.

In a way it is like a diary, but it is a Book of Love. For at all times, it has tried to transmute energies into those of Love. (*I know now this is the beginning of the subject John the Divine wrote about in his manuscript so long ago, and the work cared for by the Cathars for over one thousand years. He wrote about the starpeople, but God told him to 'eat it', meaning to hold it back.)*

It is really up to those who come into connection with it to align themselves with this energy, for those that live on this Earth have choice. It is true that the stone symbolises what I speak, but it is also coming from the source, the God source. Remember that—remember that—remember that. Have no fear, for it being here, it is like an ear, to take away the tear. (*How corny, I thought, and laughed.*)

34 2nd SITTING

Tjuringa Circles

23.8.1994

...and I am sitting meditating with the stone. I love this stone and it loves me. (*Sigh.*)

I call upon Tjurunga to be with me, if he wishes—and he is here. (*Sigh again.*)

I feel prompted to raise the vibration that I feel so strongly in my solar plexus to see it rise into my third eye. I long to see. I want to see. (*Long pause.*)

I see a rainbow; the light seems to be permeating my inner sight. I see now a circle with a hole in it, which looks a little like what the stone looks like—except the stone does not have a hole.

Helen Boyd has drawn a picture of it for me with its markings.

I see the symbol of two angles interlocked that seems to be actually unlocking the sight. ✕✕ And now I see triangles formed upside down with the apex of the pyramids meeting ✕ symbolising as above so below.

Yesterday, I finished meditating with the ◇▽ symbols and today it has inverted to ✕

Also, the symbol ⊖ that the Northern Territories have used for travel brochures, in black, orange, and yellow.

Those symbols seem to be the precursor of leading to what I am seeing now, and it is opening the third eye.

I am seeing now what looks a little like what I imagine to be a scout ship. Almost the way the planet Saturn looks like with that flat ring around it, and if you reduce that in size it looks a little like what I was seeing—like a scout ship.

I see hands holding a ball and handing it to me. The hands belong to someone who looks a little like a wizard. The ball is round like a crystal ball, but I am not seeing clearly.

I am seeing what looks like a door that is lying on the ground and it is like a very strong light coming from within, for I can see it glowing around the perimeter of the door as if somebody turned the lights on inside the next room. I think they are wanting me to understand it is to do with the Inner Earth.

Now, the door has been opened and I find I am going through a tunnel. It seems to move in a clockwise movement. It is quite light—I did not expect that under the Earth.

There are steps, quite wide steps, leading down. They have given me the image of the Sphinx in Egypt. These broad steps lead down underneath the Sphinx, between its paws, and inside there seems to be, if I could say, a shiny copper bath. It is not ornate at all, although it is beaten copper. There are two of them, or maybe more, that hold a flame burning. The floor is quite smooth and there is really nothing much else around that I can see. The burning does not seem to be giving off any smoke, or very little. It seems to symbolise eternal light.

I feel there are people that take care of this light. They are showing me the sign of 'V', which looks very much like that Chevron Symbol. (*Long pause.*)

I seem to be having a little bit of an inner fight with myself. I will let it go and go back to the flame.

I see the opposing circles of movement that the Tjuringa shows. Just the two below. One moving anticlockwise and one moving clockwise. The symbols illustrate the movement that, when they come together, there is a fusion and from that fusion the soul can rise into its higher knowing—into the light being that it truly is. I feel that is where I am being guided to—to understand my light being.

Now, I am being told that is all for today and if I sit with the stone for a while, to absorb the energy...

I will meditate again tomorrow. There is a certain amount of steadiness required to allow the energy to permeate and grow within—I must not rush it. The energy is quite strong in my solar plexus, and as I pull it up into my forehead I have a slight head-ache, but I see the eye of Horus which was symbolised in ancient Egypt.

I feel that the symbols and pyramids that are now seen in Egypt were also in many other places upon this Earth, including Australia. I have a strong feeling there is also a Sphinx that once existed near Uluru, which holds this burning light.

It seems to be of a time like Atlantis, but even before that.

3rd SITTING 35

24.8.1994

I am sitting holding the stone. ...*deep sigh*... I call upon Tjurunga to be with me and he is here now—thank you for coming, Tjurunga.

I am filled with a blue/white opalised light, like the moonstone, and there is a tinge of gold around as well. Where I am sitting, I can feel the warmth of the sun shining onto me and it is from there that Gold Ray seems to come. ...*deep sigh again!*...

I see again that crystal ball being handed to me. I aim to see.

I see a figure eight standing upright and the top half seems to open up so that it becomes a grail, a cup with energy pouring forth out of the top. (*My cup runneth over*!)

I am hearing the words *very psychic, very psychic*, but I am thinking of (Helen) a friend of mine—I don't know why I am getting that; I know she is psychic. Very psychic. She has the gift of inner sight and the ability to read the Akashic Records. Maybe with some time, I will be given that ability. It is coming, it is coming. ... *deep sigh*...

Again, I see the inverted triangles like two pyramids point to point ⧖ I see the middle opening like a burst of light, like a diamond. ...*deep sigh*...

I am hearing the words 'to keep talking, child'. I think in this manner the energies are flowing. It's like the stone and I are becoming one in energy, and then the energy when it flows out through the mouth, the voice box, becomes words, and the words come without me even thinking. There is no thought process at all. The words are just coming.

I feel a beauty with this energy, and it is very real; it has wisdom and an understanding that goes with it. There is love and compassion and it is as I see the God energy. I know it is the God energy. *...deep sigh...* So, I feel very happy and joyful in just sitting here, bathed in this energy.

I feel if there was any negativity in me it would just flow out. There is no place for shadow here. *...deep sigh...*

It is a freedom feeling—a feeling of being above, an acceptance of all, a knowing and an understanding as if it is a tool of truth in the finest sense. It is in this energy that one experiences the finest of emotions or feelings—and the finest of thoughts and the finest desire in wanting to do for others and for the self.

I have a feeling that I am to come back to my beginnings in Venus, where I am going to relearn of my embodiment in the World of Light. This will happen—this will take some time—but the stone knows no time. It already has all the information as I do, deep within me. It is just that it has to be released into my conscious mind, within the third dimension.

It is like an ascension process going backward—but not really—if I see myself as a third dimensional being and a rising of consciousness into the light being that I know, and become one in the fullest light with the memory, then that is in a state of an ascended being. I have not left. I will just become all encompassing, all knowing, and all understanding with no limit. "For you are to work with this knowledge and become one with humanity." At the moment, I seem to be repeating something from somewhere else. "That is right, my dear."

"You are being helped now. It is your destiny. Just let it flow, just let it flow, just let it flow."

I then sat for quite a while with the stone and was moved into gentle exercises using Sai Baba's ring on my third eye.

4th SITTING

25.8.1994

Do Not Cage God in a Picture-Frame,

Do Not Confine Him in an Idol,

He Is All Forms He Is All Names

– Sai Baba

I have been meditating in the morning, but I had to postpone today until after lunch and I am feeling a little 'full of lunch', I am afraid. But this seems to be the only time I am going to be able to sit with the stone today—John has quite a lot of work he wants me to do.

Spirit will organise, I know, so that I can fit all these commitments into the one day.

I have committed to work with spirit. I want to work with spirit. I love working with spirit.

For a long while, I was just working with a voice, and by that I mean a name was not given to me. I was told that it was more important to recognise the energy. I did meditate one day while in a bath and asked if I could have an understanding or a name. I was given this beautiful vision of a white horse with wings, which, of course, is Pegasus, meaning messenger from the Gods.

I accepted that, but a little later I happened to be in an esoteric book shop for the first time in my life. I was amazed at the number of books about various aspects of understanding spirit, and in particular the 'classics' about the understanding of spirit and eternal life and I wondered how I could have been so stupid not to take the subject more seriously before.

Two book covers caught my attention, which looked exactly the same as the dream I'd had a few days before. The picture was Dante's Vision of the Celestial Rose of Paradise and the books were titled *Spiritual Unfoldment No. 1* and *No. 2* by White Eagle. The work had been channelled by a British medium, Grace Cooke.

I realised then that the energy or the being I had been working with was the same energy presenting himself as White Eagle. It was his way of introducing himself to me, for there was a strong American Native Indian way of understanding spirit to his teachings.

It has been a very wonderful path, a very wonderful journey to follow spirit—that inner guidance, inner being, inner voice, which quite often presents itself as a 'feeling' rather than a voice, and sometimes a sort of impression, like an image, but not necessarily a clear one. Then, at other times, I had 'signs' sent to me, from somewhere, quite unexpectedly in the third dimensional world.

It was like what some people call synchronicity—when you are thinking about something, and then the next thing you know something comes your way to re-affirm it or give further understanding about what you were thinking, and that what you were thinking was perhaps the right step to take.

For they (spirit) are constantly telling me one step at a time, 'step by step', and so it has been a very real inner guidance, inner journey, but melding with my everyday life, and it seemed to be bringing that 'outer me' together with that 'inner me' so that I felt and knew that was what was meant when people say they walk with God.

There is an inner knowing and an inner understanding that comes quite often. I am still learning—I am not saying I have all the answers by any means. It is a wonderful journey, a very sacred journey for oneself. A very joyful journey, even though at times difficult things are put in front of your path to deal with. Rather than turn away from them, I found it is best to face them and draw upon inner courage, because sometimes what was put before me was difficult.

It was difficult to confront my own self, in particular, if it was an issue of my own being. I found it hardest to face my own emotions and my own reactions, as I think many people do.

To help with this, draw upon inner courage and then ask for guidance, and the way will come to help you over those hurdles to give you understanding. Then, when you meet people, somehow a broader understanding is given and you can see things at a deeper level—at a level that is one not of judgement but of understanding. All people here on Earth are continually facing trials and tests they planned for themselves long before coming here. They are working with a higher being that is within them and it is that influence helping them as they walk through their lives, step by step.

I also came to realise there were many, many dimensions of which I know I do not understand at all. In fact, it is beyond our human mind to understand. We operate with very limited senses, but in developing the senses from within ourselves, our psychic senses, it is and does help us to come to understand.

It is not totally necessary for people to develop their psychic senses. What seems to be everybody's destiny is to find the God within and then to realise the physical body is one of limit. If you can reach out past that and realise there is no separation from the God that is all about us, we can become one.

We can tune into a consciousness that exists in all things, not just other human beings, not just other living things, but rather inanimate objects also. Everything has a consciousness. It does have a life. It does have a memory in it. It is spirit. We are all of spirit. Our perception, even as individuals, can come from different points, different ways of seeing things or feeling, but it all leads back to the One. The One of God, the one of the energy of God or what you call the Source of all Creation.

Even in the Outer World, in the Outer Universes, my understanding is there too is consciousness, one of life, one of different forms, one of different feelings but again all leading back to the One—the universal Mother/Father God energy, which can take form or can be without form—there is no limit. It is beyond human understanding in total, but it does exist, it does exist, it does exist. *...deep sigh...*

I love this stone. A friend talked about romancing the stone. It is almost prophetic because, in a way, that seems to be what is happening. It is lovely. I think many could romance this stone. Romancing, of course, is like showing affection for one another and perhaps that is what the stone is symbolising: that we all here on Earth can romance and show affection to one another. It is not a sexual thing in the human understanding—it is emotion, it is one of giving and caring and forgiving and nurturing. It is laughter and smiles and hugging, of kissing in a brotherly and sisterly way; it is love in its truest form.

There is nothing wrong with love in a sexual way; that is for two people who are committed to each other, who want to create together, to learn and live together, to hopefully have children that come into their lives for them to 'caretake' until the children are old enough to stand on their own and take charge of their own lives. They too have been guided by the Mother/Father who are here on this Earth—a Mother/Father role is one of teaching, one of caring and one of loving. ...*deep sigh*...

Again, I see those two angles coming together sideways they are hooked together. I saw that the other day. It does seem to be leading into, or opening up, one's inner vision.

Sai Baba did healing on me, which I dearly feel blessed by his grace. This was after he gave me the green ring.

I was very ill at the time, but I knew it was with reason and for a purpose. He seemed to be squeezing my body down, my every cell in my body down to the very essence, to change that essence and to fill it with light. As I started to recover, the psychic senses seemed to be much improved and I became much more aware.

One night, he came (*in my inner scene*) and a mark put on my forehead for my inner vision had opened and was really racing. I felt then that he had held it back for a while—I am actually hoping now that he will give it back to me, if that is his will. ...*deep sigh*...

*****

Before I first went to visit Sai Baba, I'd been in a New Age bookshop looking for a book and asking spirit to help me find one. As

I walked past a shelf, a book jumped off and went with a terrific crash onto the ground. The floor was carpeted and should not have made that noise. I thought all the shelves had fallen down behind me.

When I turned around, I saw this book, *The Holy Man and the Psychiatrist*, on the floor behind me and it was about Sai Baba, written by a Dr Samuel H Sandweiss. I picked it up and thought, *Oh, this must be the book that spirit wants me to read.* The lady in the shop laughed and said, "Oh, he often does that to people. I think you are meant to read it."

I read the book, and as I read it, I knew Sai Baba would call me, and that one day I would be going to India to see him.

Four years later, I did go to India. I was already in contact with 'an unseen teacher' who presented himself in the name of White Eagle, as mentioned earlier. Eagles were flying around above my head as I entered the Mandir, which is the prayer ground outside the temple where Sai Baba lives in Puttaparthi. I was directed to a seat by the Seva Dals, who are people volunteering to work in service at the Ashram. Just as I was settled, before Sai Baba came out, I looked up and there on the wall directly in front of me was a relief impression of a White Eagle. It was definitely a 'sign' and although I was taken back, I was pleasantly surprised.

I saw Sai Baba three times. Each time, it was around Mahashivarathi time, which is a major festival (around February or March) held by the Hindu people to celebrate the aspect of God; it symbolises the destroying of all the unwanted.

I loved being in Sai Baba's presence. I loved the feeling and the aura where he lives. I know he is omnipresent and able to be with anyone who calls to him, wherever they choose to be, but it just seemed to be special in his presence in the third reality.

There have been many, many books written by people speaking of his amazing powers and unlimited abilities and how he can read minds and know the past, present, and future of everyone; it is uncanny how small amounts of food have become enough to feed thousands, how ill people have become well again and some even documented being clinically dead and yet returning to tell the tale. How people who did not know of him have had visions or dreams and wanted to know more about him, how people who doubt have become spiritually inspired and gained faith in God, and how his schools, universities, and hospitals are second to none.

I was very blessed to have an audience with him, and I could speak of the experience in detail—it was most joyful, although I was very nervous; he gave me a hard time, actually, speaking like a stern father.

His mood changed when I finally understood the message he was trying to convey to my slow mind. He had spoken to me when I was one of the crowd, but moved on, and it was not until I asked him in my mind, "Baba, could I please have an interview?" that he suddenly walked quickly over to me and told me to 'Go!', meaning I was granted just that, an interview, proving to me also that he definitely could read minds.

When I sat down in the interview room, there were others present, about twenty, in fact, and he spoke to some for a little while, then focused his attention on me. He was very stern to start with. He held up his hand and said, *What is that*? I was a bit confused and nervous and found it difficult to even think in his presence; it was as if everything had been taken out of my mind, but I was thinking did he mean light coming from the hand, like healing, and, of course, he could read my mind. He said it was, 'nothing, nothing.'

Then he held up the other hand and asked me *what is that* and, in my confusion, I thought *two nothings*? I was very confused, and he said, "It was everything", and of course, I thought to myself, *I'm not going to win here.* (*I laughed to myself.*) Then he softened the way he spoke and talked more in general to everyone present and said that God is Nothing, God is Everything, and, in fact, God is Absolute.

He knew I had trouble accepting a human being as God. But, of course, now I see God in everything and there is no need for separation, which is what I was trying to do.

He settled back in his chair and casually looked up at the ceiling, then looked directly back at me and said, "**And what is your**

name, Val?" Of course, I burst out laughing. There was no way I was able to tell him my name; he just knew it.

Then he seemed to catch something from the air and called me over so that I knelt at his feet. He gave me a beautiful ring that I feel, or knew, came from another world. In fact, I rather felt that it came from a starship. He manifested it in front of our eyes as if he had just caught it as it dropped out of the sky. It is a beautiful emerald green, sparkling like a diamond, slightly blue, and gold and even purple—it has a lovely energy with an orange aura. He said that when I look in the ring he would be there.

(Sai Baba, twenty-five years later, was referring to my Starlady name as Andromeda Val.)

Still at the interview, Baba looked at me in a special way. I had a feeling he was trying to tell me something without saying. He mentioned the banker, meaning my husband, but nobody could have known that White Eagle had come through in a channeling session a number of years before and asked John to be their banker.

(Now, as I overview the work, I think he was referring to being a banker looking after me.)

I got to thinking that Sai Baba was somehow connected with White Eagle or was White Eagle. I was not sure. All this time, I was communicating with him telepathically only. He was speaking so others could hear—but I have never once spoken to Sai Baba through my voice box.

I did ask, in my inner scene when I arrived home, if he could give me a sign if he was White Eagle. He played with me a bit with a shiver and a shake and I laughed, but the next morning when I went to my bookcase for a book for somebody, I idly pulled out this book, '*Jesus the Teacher & Healer*' and it was by White Eagle. It was work that had been channelled by Grace Cooke in Britain.

I opened the book and inside was a picture of Sai Baba, dressed in white, with his hand up. It was as if he was saying 'Hello' and waving to me. I took that as a sign and I laughed.

I did not put that picture in the book, but people who know Sai Baba know he is capable at manifesting anything, anywhere. It was a sign that yes, White Eagle and Sai Baba are the same energy and Sai Baba had been coming to me for many years; he was not a stranger after all.

After the visit to see Sai Baba in India, when I was doing work channelling White Eagle it changed: the energy changed and asked to be presented as Sanat Kumara. He told us he was a light being and White Eagle was an aspect of him, and that as a light being, he had *never* incarnated on this Earth. That White Eagle and other aspects he had incarnated onto Earth were all aspects, though some were operating in the Astral, but he, as Sanat Kumara, a light being had never incarnated on Earth into the human race.

Somehow, I felt he was showing us this was the way it was with all of us here on Earth. That we, in the personalities we are on this Earth, now are aspects, not just an oversoul that is the collection of all the personalities we have been, but rather a light being from other worlds that has never incarnated on Earth and, in fact, the master of ourselves.

I feel in romancing the stone, this is what is actually happening—that I am being led back to the light being connected with this group of souls that I am, or that we are, this family of souls. So that I can regain the memory of the light being who I know to be a lady, a tall lady with a golden aura that looks like long hair, and who actually lives in a dimension of light that exists in Venus.

I have been told the memory is going to be given over a period of time and I will, in actual fact, be here on this Earth with total memory. So, it will be like an ascension taking place, but back to front if that makes sense (*an ascension in consciousness back from the future*). And this is what has happened for me.

5th SITTING

37

Friday 28.8.1994

It is twenty minutes to four in the morning and I have been awakened feeling prompted to come and sit with the sacred stone at this hour, for John and I plan to go to Sydney today and there probably would not have been another time to sit with the stone. So, I feel happy about this; it is back like in the beginning.

Often, I was awakened at this hour and prompted to start writing. *They* told me the channels are very clear, that there is not much interference with sound waves, and so it did seem to be a good time to receive clear messages.

The stone seems to be linking me readily with the World of Light. I awakened with many thoughts in my mind, so I will just have to sit and see if they will come back.

Just before I started sitting and meditating with the stone, I awakened on another morning with two colours on my mind. One was a pink/violet colour, a very pretty shade of light, and the other colour was this opalescent blue/white, which I have come to realise is like a moonstone colour, but it is light.

This morning I awakened thinking of these colours, I had guests here at our house—Rosemary, who had a CRT machine with her. It is a little like a slide projector that has slides of colour, and when it is turned on the colour is thrown forth; sitting in front of it, one takes the colour energy into oneself through the eyes.

It was in a darkened room and I felt as if it was coming into my whole body. It was lovely looking at all the colours, and it was just like looking at various aspects of light. I loved it. But when I came to the pink/violet colour, the lens seemed to become like a round holographic scene as if I was inside this colour and it was a planet.

I was prompted by Rosemary (*spirit was working through her*) and I had the feeling I knew the colour very well, and that I had spent time on this planet—it was reminding me, triggering a memory within me. I knew it was not where I had actually been born as a light being; it was a planet where I had spent quite a lot of time.

Rosemary was prompted to say, "Ah yes, you went there to learn to prepare yourself before you came onto this Earth, but you actually went there to reduce your light so that you could tolerate the life here on this Earth." Somehow, I could accept that, for I was feeling that myself, although it sounds strange.

It was a planet connecting to the Pleiadian Group and I could see myself there, or at least the energy with which I am linked. I felt a little like Snow White with all these little beings around me. Not exactly dwarfs, but as a Venusian I felt very tall, and these little beings would have stood about four to five feet tall.

They had an alien look about them and I felt very at home with them. They were very friendly and loving, and very gentle beings. I suppose some people could call them ETs. I am given the understanding they are a little like robots, but they do have some degree of being able to think and act for themselves. They answer to Masters, and so, I expect, depending on who the Master they are answering to is, connect to the quality of their thought processes. The ones I knew were very nice, very friendly, and of God.

Somehow, I feel they are connected with the Wandjina, the name of the starpeople, or skypeople, spoken about in the Australian Aboriginal mythology or Dreamtime.

Helen, who I have worked with for many years now, is a very gifted psychic. She sat with the stone one day and spoke of the Wandjina, although she described it as a being without hair, with large eyes and a very little mouth, because communication took place with telepathic thought.

Helen, the white lady, was also with us that day. She is the lady who had recently come into my life to bring this sacred stone. She is very much connected to the Australian Aboriginal life energy.

Through circumstances within her own life, she was anxious to pass the stone on to someone who would guard it and respect it, as mentioned previously in this book, until it was clear where it had to move on to, back to its rightful place.

Helen has made films and written scripts, and she spoke laughingly of making a film a little like *Romancing the Stone*.

I find that so strange now I am sitting with this stone and feeling very loving toward it. It's helping me to tell a story, although I am not sure where it is leading, but it is very real and it is as if I am romancing the stone. I guess what she saw was prophetic. It is an exciting journey.

It is strange—when I arose from sleep this morning, I felt a sense of excitement to get on with the reading, and yet now as I sit here I feel as if nothing is coming. But that is it. I am allowing excitement to interfere with the connection to the pure energy. So, I must calm myself for I have been told even excitement can ruffle the waters in the body and actually interfere with the connection. So now I will just feel a joy and a bliss and a calm and wait. I ask Tjurunga to be with me, and he is here.

When we first came to this property, I had a feeling that something was going to happen and I am reminded now of a time when in my inner scene, in my dreaming, an Aborigine Male spirit man jumped through the window of our bedroom with a spear ready and went into a sort of crouch. I said he had to leave, he had no right to come into my space without asking, and so he turned around and jumped back out of the window.

Afterwards, I regretted it, because I felt he had come in peace and now I am wondering if it was Tjurunga, because he presents himself standing on one leg and holding a spear. So, I have met him quite some time ago.

At that same time, which would be about 1989, I was awakened one morning at about 3 am, perhaps an hour earlier, with *Upstairs* talking to me and said, "Valerie, focus on the sky, you are going to see a UFO." I have mentioned this before.

I have absolutely no doubt in my mind at all that starships exist.

Since then, I have been taken briefly onto a smaller starship when I was travelling to England about three and a half years ago.

I was seated on the international airplane, and we had all been settled down for the night, with lights turned off. One porthole shutter had been left open.

As I relaxed with a cushion to sleep, there was what appeared to be dancing lights outside the window, some distance away in the dark night. I was curious as to what was happening. I thought there may have been reflections of a light from within the airplane cabin, but there was not. Rather, it was like three stars moving around outside.

I felt prompted to tune in and I heard a voice say, "Welcome to the Northern Hemisphere, my dear, we are going to stay with you for 240 miles." And I thought *miles*? and they said, "Aeronautical miles." I laughed.

Then I saw a whole lot of hands, in my inner scene, reaching toward me as if to say, "Come aboard, come aboard." So, I tuned in to see if I could actually move on board—and suddenly there I was, sitting on the edge of a seat. I had on a bright blue suit that I was travelling in, and it contrasted starkly with the brightness of the light on board this little starship or, as they are known by the starpeople, a scout ship.

It was a very bright white light. Then there was a man, smiling. He looked similar to us, but he had no hair and the back of his head protruded more than ours. He was wearing a dark blue uniform, and he smiled. He was seated in front of a row of computer-like machinery.

I was also aware of a being standing beside me in a white robe, and at the time I felt it was White Eagle. Then I was back on the airplane again and the lights like the stars were sort of moving around, but staying within the parameter of the porthole window; after a while, maybe about twenty minutes or so, two disappeared, then there was just the one moving around at the bottom of the frame of the porthole.

That fascinated me. I could not see how they could possibly stay within that frame or the porthole all the time—in some way, they must have been looking through my eyes; there is no doubt they have very advanced technology and ability. Anyhow, this one star, Starlight, suddenly went zip up to the top of the window and then disappeared as much as to say, 'Goodbye'. It was a lovely experience and I thanked them for that.

In working with the beings from the World of Light, and with the starpeople, it has been a very happy experience. One of joy and love and certainly one of God. They always speak of coming with love and blessings. I find it is possible for people to tune in and to hear, and to know what they are about.

They keep telling us that all you have to do is ask, for apparently there is a Universal Government and a Universal Law. It is to do with the Electromagnetic Spectrum. They are actually not allowed to interfere with the life here on this Earth. There is a duality here and man has choice. And what man has done to Earth and himself, man has to undo.

They want very much to assist the little earthlings, as they put it, but they cannot interfere—they cannot just walk in and help as they would like to do. They must wait for us, as earthlings, to ask for their assistance. And I think how long and how like that was the message that came through Jesus over 2,000 years ago, "Knock and the door will be opened", "Seek and ye shall find". It is still the same message about intention and focusing on what you want.

I do love this stone. I am being told that is enough for today. ...*deep sigh*... I will leave this now and look forward to the next episode.

It actually amazes me how I just sit and the words come. It seems like I have been only sitting for ten minutes, talking into a recording tape, but when I play it back it goes on for about forty-five minutes!

(Remember this story Part Two was how it was happening to me in the beginning of my mission twenty-five years ago.)

38 6th SITTING

Saturday 27.8.1994

I am sitting here with great love in my heart. I find I am looking forward to sitting with the stone all the time. It is like something unfolding and I am keen to know what the next episode is about. After I set a voice recording on the cassette tape, at some time during the day I write it down so I have an understanding of what has come through, because I cannot remember anything really, or very little, until I replay the tape and hear it.

So, it is like reading a book (*laughs*) and not knowing what is going to be in the next chapter. It is fun, joyful (*laughs*). I am having a feeling of bliss all the time. ...*deep sigh*...

I have asked for Tjurunga to be here—and he has just patted me on the top of my head (*laughs*). I keep feeling like a little girl for some reason, I think because of that feeling of bliss and eagerness and wondering what is coming next. But in this reality, I am sixty-two years old next December. Fortunately, I have good health and I feel quite vibrant and (*laughs*) so I feel blessed. (*There goes a knocking sound in the room.*)

John and I have been wondering how we can hold onto this property and still manage when we get older and on a pension. At some stage, he will have to give away his business; he is a little concerned this morning, so I am afraid this is dominating my thoughts now. These thoughts may not really belong to this book, but we are seriously thinking and wondering how we can cope financially and not have to sell this property.

I feel so strongly we should hold onto the property; it is very special, very special. We came out here, almost as if we were picked up and planted here. It is on the tail end of the Megalong Valley and we have since discovered the Megalong Valley, which stretches all the way from the back of Katoomba to the Southern Highlands, is the part just like its feet as if it has been kicked aside. The understanding is that it is a little like a giant satellite dish; it is true there are islands in the middle, but if you look at the overview it is like a satellite dish and does seem to have a special energy.

I believe the Australian Aboriginal people always saw it as a healing valley and know it to be sacred and therefore, so is the water in the valley that is on our property. It has recently been uncovered and does seem to have a special quality. I have been drinking this water and I feel very well. I have splashed some at times in the bath and it is just like a spray of golden light, so my understanding is that it is a different dimensional water. More fourth dimensional and really a combination of water and light. It seems to be part of the plan to assist me into an ascension process. It seems to have dropped away all karmic shadow. *...deep sigh...*

I am speaking from my own experience, but I feel somehow it will be known and others will be helped from it also. *...deep sigh...*

I am getting images of a house that could be built on the front of the property. It would be like the Gatekeeper (*the Keep*), with the road leading down to the waters.

We were prompted in a very special way to call the property *Alcheringa*, which means Golden Age or the Dreamtime (*Australian Aboriginal*) and I have already said the stone is known as the Alcheringa stone. It all seems to lead into a state of consciousness, which is of the Golden Light, the Golden Ray—One of God, One of Christ.

I have placed a picture of Sai Baba above the computer, knowing after the study of psychometry his energy is with it, and I like to think he is helping me.

What attracted me to this particular photo was the bush scene in which he is standing and how it looks like somewhere in the Southern Highlands of New South Wales, Australia. The gumtrees are predominated, as are the purple/blue Agapanthus that is sometimes called the Star of Bethlehem he is holding, which I think is very symbolic. He is also standing next to a paperbark tree. Was he not telling me something when I was prompted to buy the photo before I knew about the stone that has come our way?

The Alcheringa stone is wrapped in paperbark off a gum tree.

7th SITTING 39

Saturday Afternoon 27.8.1994

I did not feel I sat long enough this morning. I was under a little pressure, so I am trying again. ...*deep sigh*...

Many years ago, when I was a little girl, I thought and wondered about God, but something within me questioned. There seemed to be a doubt and a worry, as if it belonged to pain of some sort, and I did not understand. ...*deep sigh*...

It was only later as I grew older I began to investigate and actually search for healing for the skin condition called psoriasis I suffered from. It was, and has been, a painful experience and yet it was through that I came to understand about the Quest—the Quest for the Holy Grail as some put it, or others might say a journey along a spiritual path.

So, I feel very blessed that I was given the skin disease, for without it I would not have come to know and understand about many other things. It seems a strange thing to say, I know, and especially for those who also suffer with the skin disease, for suffer they do. It is a very personal suffering; people cannot readily understand unless they have experienced it. A rejection goes with it quite often because there are those who do not understand and run away, feeling it is some dreaded disease that will befall them, but this is not so.

There are, of course, those that are very kind and want to be helpful and say such things as, "Oh, you worry too much, it does not matter what you look like, we love you." But that is not the root of the problem either.

It is the feeling that goes with it. It is a feeling that is a physical one, an emotional one, and a mental one. It is a very complicated disease and not easily corrected. Some may heal more readily than others. That is a path they have chosen. When one realises it is no accident they actually have it and begin to look for the deeper reason, one starts to gain an understanding of why—why there is suffering.

In my own case, I looked at many angles, or from many angles. It is a physical one, of course, and it did seem to improve with a balanced diet, preferably a vegetarian one, as I eat now. Food that has been grown with the least amount of insecticides and artificial fertilisers and the purest water as possible. Herbs, vitamins, and minerals from time to time definitely assisted it.

A cleansing of the mind certainly helped and by that I mean looking at one's own thought forms, the processes of thought. The mind, I came to realise, or the brain, is a little like a computer. What we put into it is what matters. So, if we fill it with thoughts that are negative, things that go against us, things that make us feel poorly or sad, these are thoughts we need to rethink. I consciously made up my mind to think positively about things to change what I could, and to forget about the things I could not change. Just accept things as they were and not to worry unnecessarily. This helped me a great deal.

I did find from time to time that my skin reacted very severely, and I found by tuning into my own body I would get an understanding as to what had sparked that reaction. It was as if the body had its own consciousness. Sometimes, the reaction would be from some prescribed drug I had taken, not that I take much at all, but on the odd occasion I think one has to take a drug—a prescribed drug, of course, by a doctor—to heal something other than the chronic disease, and I found it often would have an adverse reaction on my skin, on my body function.

I did start to find the answers by being very careful about what I ate and what I drank. I did not overdo exposure to the sun, because there was a point where that could become too severe and would exacerbate the problem. This body seemed to respond to a lot of caring with creams and skin brushes, so in other words it was like a big need to start loving the body instead of rejecting it, which often psoriasis sufferers do.

Then I started to look at reactions that came within me. When something happened, I considered why I would react in a certain way; I needed to take courage and look at that. At what some people might say are faults (*laughs*), but what we ourselves are not so ready to look at. In doing that I also found, with meditation, I was gradually led into an understanding at a deeper level that some of the problems, or the emotions or reactions I had, actually came from lives that I have lived at other times, not in this personality at all.

There are various ways to release these memories. I was assisted and felt very blessed when the memories came into my conscious memory and I was able to release them. In so doing, I found my skin definitely improved, particularly when I dealt with the one where I was burned to death with fire.

Remember, this is in another life, if I can put it that way. It seems we carry the personalities we have been at another time with us in a memory bank within our soul. It is as if we are living all these lives all at once. It might seem a bit strange, but this is what I have experienced and in dealing with all these memories I have been holding onto, the shadows have fallen away and I feel much stronger and brighter in light, in soul light.

The skin disease no longer troubles me. Visually, it is still there, but I think with time, if it be God's will, it will disappear. I am not concerned. I give it thanks for helping me along my path. I feel it will go.

I feel this water I am drinking is definitely assisting it—assisting it on its way out.

*****

When the bell sounded it was August 21st, which was a Sunday, and a lady named Sandy Stevenson had organised for light workers or many thousands of people to come to Wembley Stadium and chant 'Om' nonstop for eight minutes or longer. There were many people around the Earth who took up the idea and sat in groups or alone and sounded out the Om! Sound coordinating with the same timeframe at midday on the Sunday in London, England.

If the starpeople were listening to this from their point, they would have heard that Om go out as a major bell sound. A most extraordinary uplifting sound, a joy to their ears and to those here on Earth that were listening. It was a unity that went forth, making a statement that all wanted to unite and become one with the divine light and with God.

When I had been awakened a few months ago and asked if I still wanted to write a book, they had said, and I had forgotten, it would start once the bell had sounded. Of course, they have abilities to foresee the future and knew, so when I think about it, sitting with the stone at the beginning of the reading, it began on Monday morning, August 22nd, the day after the bell had sounded. *...deep sigh...*

It was a lovely way to start to unite with the One.

"If there were any others here, which there are not, I would be encouraging them to also lift their consciousness and connect with the light being that they are and start to work from that point.

"It seems the time when that bell was sounded, or that Om! sound resonated around the Earth, it also linked with a Star connection or gate of light that came onto this Earth. For remember, the Earth also is like a star or planet, moving through the universe. It is infiltrated with energies and rays from different points at different times, depending on its place, within another place, within another place, and so on..."

"It is all relative, is it not? What I am speaking of is that the Earth also is on a path of ascension and it is leading towards a gate that opens wider and wider and is actually leading all upon her into the World of Golden Light, which will be known as the Golden Age.

"The closer it comes to the total unification of that ray, the more the light's presence or that energy vibration will be felt upon this Earth. It will lift the consciousness of everything upon this Earth as well as the little earthling.

"The Earth itself is going through changes. Every flower and tree is also going through changes. The animals, birds, and insects are all going through changes. It is man that experiences emotion closest to his heart and he also is experiencing changes. Animals

also are experiencing emotional changes. All living things have feelings and so they are feeling those changes.

"In the longer term, all will move into a state of consciousness when they will feel a state of peace and calm at all times. But until that point is reached, the Earth will stumble a little and perhaps those upon it as well. There is no need to fear. It is from that point of stumbling that just means a change is taking place and it has become a slight restriction. Once this restriction is removed it will start to flow. The flow is one's experience and there is no need to ever feel afraid or lost." ...deep sigh...

This last talk seemed to come from the alien or Wandjina of the stone, for it was moving my head from side to side and speaking slightly disjointedly. When finished, it seemed to go back into the stone.

40 8th SITTING

Sunday 28.8.1994

I feel a little like Shirley Valentine talking to 'Wall', when I am sitting here actually talking to the stone.

Yesterday afternoon, with the last little discourse, it seemed to be from a spirit that came from the stone and spoke through me and then went back into the stone again. I was moving my head from side to side, or at least the being was, quite an extraordinary experience and yet—and I have done a lot of channelling—it just seemed a little different this time, as if it was not 'Wall' talking to me, but 'Stone'.

Maybe it is a little symbolic of what Peter is about when Jesus said the foundations of the faith lies in the rock. I do not know if l have that quite right, but somehow it seems to go together.

It was something to do with building a church, so I guess it is like building a temple around you that is purely of God, of God energy. It is an unseen temple by those in the third dimension, by friends and family around, but then the influence of it shows in some way. It is definitely a foundation. It is definitely an earthing taking the place of an unseen dimension that has the God quality energy, through the physical body and earthed into the ground, which links with the same energy, so there is no separation.

I can understand why many refer to the Earth as Mother, for as Mother it seems able to hold onto and nurture. And it is the Earth that nurtures us, that grows the food we need to nourish our physical bodies. But, you see, there is this unseen energy Mother Earth is linked with. I suppose you could call it the Father. It is the energy of the stars, of the universe of all creation that also nourishes us. ...*deep sigh*...

It comes with force sometimes, but quite often it is gentle and we have what appears to be two opposing forces, but they really are one, both the negative and the positive. The negative being a force that moves into the void, like an anti-clockwise motion and put together with a clockwise motion, it moves into creation of manifestation. So, the two belong to one another; it is only a state of consciousness that wants to pull away and not understand those two movements.

The void seems to be a state of mind we need to get into before we can actually see the reality of our light being, for all in between is a manifestation of our imagination. The imagination, or 'nation of images' without understanding of God and the Law of the Universe, can easily allow us to get caught up into it without understanding that we could get lost if we did not remain constantly aware of God. ...*deep sigh*...

It seems to be a force that goes in and out—interacting with itself—and in that, it creates an energy a little like a generator, which is the basis of all life forms. There is a generation of energy that exists. It keeps moving in and out this rod of energy, if I can put it that way, which is always linked to the source. This seems to apply to any form of movement. To spark movement in one direction, we need movement coming from the opposite direction and then the two interact to create a continuum of moving force.

It is ongoing, it is everlasting, it changes—it can change from one form to another, but the life (light) force is always the same.

I am not sure if that is making sense? ...*deep sigh*...

To me it makes sense. I am wondering if anybody was to hear it expressed that way, whether it would make sense to them. No matter (*laughs*). I just said, "No matter", not realising, of course, matter is a vibration of energy that does make up form and it is that which can change into different vibrations of energy—it can become lighter and faster in movement so the form can disappear. Disappear, that is, to all eyes looking from the point of matter. (*laughs*)

The same happens in whatever dimension that force is vibrating. The eyes that see in that particular vibration of energy can see all that exists in that dimension, but if it moves on to a much lighter and brighter, faster moving dimension, again it can become unseen. These levels of vibrating dimensions move gradually back to the source, which is vibrating so fast and so bright it is as if it's beyond our reach or ability to see. However, the effects of that energy or vibration can filter through each layer of form we are linked with, until it eventually comes to the point of matter.

I see now, because from the point of matter it is so slow in vibrating and the separation is so obvious, that it becomes then a point where we have to make a decision, a choice, of reaching out to each opposing force.

In the Dimension of Matter, there is much confusion because of this and influence, if one allows oneself to be influenced, and for this reason there is a need to reach out to bring the opposing forces together, free of any confusion—so that it fuses, fuses together without interference, to become the opposite poles of the one: a generation of life force, which can take any form it chooses. *...deep sigh...*

It is very real, and I can see the further we reach out from the Dimension of Matter that it is actually more real, although of a different nature. One with less limits. One that because we are in matter, where everything is so heavy, one could feel they could not 'grasp' anything. But in actual fact, the ability to 'hold' is very real in other dimensions. *...deep sigh...* It is all relative, is it not?

I love this stone; it has a form, and an energy, and a vibration. It is not really of matter. It seems to be one of light, if I can put it that way, of a much faster and brighter dimension. There seems to be a total fusion as if it has the opposite end of the same pole. The energy goes in two different directions but unites as one and it is all here in this stone. I think I understand that is why, when I first held the stone, it did not seem to be of Earth energy. I have been shown and taught a lot about energies and given the understanding that all is energy, in one form or another. There is no limit.

There are forms, as has been said before in other dimensions, and there are many, many dimensions that mean a vibrating force in a world you could say is like the world we experience here on Earth in the third dimension. *...sigh...* But there are many, many worlds. Worlds upon worlds, upon worlds. Some interfuse with others, but only those next to them. It is a need to reach out by choice even in other worlds to understand about the God force, the Centre of Creation, the Mother/Father energy, the Creator of all.

The Angelic Realms do exist, and you could speak of that as worlds. Elementals do exist; you could speak of those as worlds. There are various aspects of what we call the Astral and they are different worlds. There are worlds upon worlds, upon worlds. Some interacting—some not.

By choice we can actually, from this dimension, reach out to a consciousness and a world that exists in the light and a form of a being we are connected to. So, it is possible to break past all those worlds and reach out to an understanding at a higher or faster dimension.

When the vibration is faster, it does not mean that everything is racing around faster. In fact, the opposite happens, because there is a union between the two opposite forces; there is a balance and a calmness and an ability to draw all that one needs to oneself, within the Law of God, and to give out the same way. ... *deep sigh...*

The word 'generation' in a mythical way or mystical way is connected to generating, which is a balance of these two opposite forces. Once it is understood genetic components of all blueprints within the cells of each being within the World of Matter will move into a balance, and from that the movement of the force will be more of light, a slightly faster vibration, a melding of those forces will take place when the Earth and its generation upon it moves into the Golden Age.

Like attracts like. Energies that are of a faster vibration will attract that same vibration. That is a World of so. It will have a domino effect upon this Earth when a certain balance is reached, when all quite quickly will move into that new world and that new balance.

Water on this Earth will be recharged with the new generating energy and it also will find balance between the two opposing energies or opposing forces. It will unite with the light and air and it also will raise its vibration so that all who partake of it will be assisted for the change, to take balance with their own form, and it will then match with the existing vibration of energy of the World that has come into being on this Earth in the Golden Age. *...deep sigh...*

The air will also change. The molecules that make up air will start to move faster and become more of light and that being partaken by all living forms on this Earth will also help for the changes to take place—the air will actually start to sparkle a little.

9th SITTING

41

Om Symbol

Monday 29.8.1994

I am sitting with the stone and I feel that loving light. Today, I have left the picture of Sai Baba upon it. It is the one I put on the stone when I am not holding it, asking Sai Baba to look after it.

It is a picture that was given to me when I was in Brindavan in India last March, and it has a mark of the Om symbol, which looks like a three and a little half-moon beside it. Being on his third eye in the picture, it symbolises the gift of inner sight. I thought at this time, particularly when it was given to me spontaneously by a shopkeeper, that it seemed to be a sign and I felt prompted to speak about it this morning.

The year before, when I was in Brindavan, Sai Baba's Ashram in Whitefields near Bangalore, I bought quite a number of photographs of Sai Baba. When I arrived home, many people asked for photographs, so I asked them to choose which one they would like. Each time they would take one I would think, *Ooh, I would have liked that one,* but never mind, and I ended up with the one left.

As it turned out, it was the best one of the lot because he had blessed it. He had actually, especially for me, put a light in the hand he was holding up in the picture. It looks a little like a 'V', a 'V' of light and I wondered what the V stood for. I thought, *well it's Valérie, I guess,* but it is more than that.

Victory over the lower self? Yes, that could be it. I had found over the time of language in India, Brindavan was earlier known as Vrindaban and so maybe that was what the 'V' stood for. Maybe for Vishnu, and there again I think of Sai Baba as like a cosmic being, as if he comes and goes and err, I have this feeling—well, I wondered if the 'V' is for Venus. That would be nice. I am sure the 'V' of light has many other meanings, but most of all it is like a blessing.

I had a negative made up of that particular picture and each time John goes to Asia he has a hundred copies made up. The last time he was in Hong Kong, the Chinese gentleman said, "Oh, I know this Sai Baba", and insisted that John take the hundred copies without any payment. I laughed. I really think that was Sai Baba at work; he does these magical things to people.

These are mystical things, but, of course, he is operating with no limit. He comes to people in dreams, he comes in magical ways like throwing a book on the floor behind you with a loud bang (*I laugh at the memory*) and many other ways. He has actually manifested in front of people in different parts of the world, even though except for a visit to South Africa once, he has never travelled outside India the 'normal' way.

Once when John and I were on holiday ...*deep sigh*... in a tropical area, (*my feet are far from beautiful*), but I had painted my toenails with a pink nail polish. I awoke the first morning to find the nail polish had turned to gold. It was like they were painted with gold leaf. I was thrilled. I knew it had been Baba at work and knew what the message was about. I was jumping around like a two year old, saying, "John look, it is a sign, it is a sign!" laughing happily. It was just like the gold of my watch. It was just lovely, and (*sigh*) I did not want to remove it—it just wore away after a time.

I did show some friends when I returned home, but they just looked, rather uninterestedly. It is strange, no matter how miraculous or mystical one's experience is, it does not mean anything to anybody else—really, it is only one's own experience. And I guess that is what it is—everybody needs to find their own path to spirituality.

Each individual has his or her own way of perceiving and understanding and so it is a very personal journey. It comes from within and the God within. I have been told if you focus on the heart in that mind area, which is like a consciousness of God (*well, it is a consciousness of God*), it is from that point one can be guided.

It is sometimes understood as 'intuition' or the 'inner teaching' if that makes sense. Sometimes it is described as a conscience or a 'higher consciousness' or 'better judgement' as some people put it, and if you follow that, it always works out better for the self. It is definitely a feeling and a knowing. For some, even the 'feeling' is difficult. But there is a 'knowing' and most people can follow from that point. They know, when they come to make decisions, what seems to be a better choice. It is up to them to follow that knowing coming from within.

Otherwise, you can get off onto a little track of your own and find you can get into all sorts of strife. I have found ...*deep sigh*... it is like walking a very gentle path. A very narrow path in a way, but with signs along the way and coordinated incidences, but in doing so the understanding expands so it is not limiting at all.

At the time my toenails were painted gold (*I have to laugh*), I had come into my possession a small statue of the standing Buddha. It seems very old, but when I sat with it has a very strong healing energy, and it was strange, as if it had been in my possession before. In another life, if I can put it that way.

I had feelings of being a monk that had travelled from Tibet down into South-East Asia with a group of other monks. In their travels, they had eventually come to a sticky end in Osaka, Japan. I know this to be around 800 AD and I do not know why I am talking about this...for the feelings and the emotions I held onto from that life have been released now, and understanding has been given to me.

I have since met a few people who were actually with me at that time. When one meets another and feels strongly attracted in a way that is more like any eye contact really, it is a sort of knowing that you know this person, although you have never met them before in this life. It is lovely. It is like re-uniting with a long-lost friend. I have experienced this a number of times, and even though you may not continue closely with this person, it does not matter how long it is between seeing them again; there is always that immediate connection, that one of knowing, and it is as if there has never been any separation at all.

I have that feeling with my husband, I know we have been close many times in past lives. *...deep sigh...* We seem to be totally opposite but united as one. That is nice. It is like a true love that bonds us together. No matter if we get upset or a bit cross with each other at times, there is a deeper bond and a deeper love. That is nice.

I am very happy John and I are together. I have learnt a lot from him and he tells me he has learnt a lot from me, so I suppose that is the most important thing between two people, husband and wife—the feeling of a bond and a growing together, united with that one energy of God.

In holding the stone today, I feel quite a strong tingling feeling in the fingers. This is the first time I have felt that. I know it is possible to call upon healing energies from the World of Light to come through one's body; you actually earth the energy with one's own electro-magnetic body that exists in the physical body, and just by a touch, can pass on that healing energy, that healing ray.

It might sound strange, but it does happen. You can bring great comfort to people by just putting your hand gently on their arm or their shoulder or back, or even by holding their hand. You do not have to say anything; the energy will do it all.

What you would be actually doing is allowing the God energy to flow through you into another. *...deep sigh...*

It seems to be beholden to all of us here on this Earth to help one another, but in doing so, we must be very careful to respect the choices that another may have and not to put what we think is right for another into action, but rather to assist or help them to help themselves and to heal themselves. So again, that is a very narrow path to follow in not overstepping the mark.

It is the same with parents who have been blessed with children—the child is given to the mother and father to caretake, to nourish, and to love. We have spoken about this before. But it is also important to remember to teach the little ones about God and the God energy—the Holy Spirit that bonds everyone, that bonds everything, that is the uniting element within all.

42 10th SITTING

Tuesday 30.8.1994

On holding the stone, and just before I settled myself, I was prompted to pick an Angel Card from a box I have here on the table. The cards have words on them, and pictures of angels, and it is as if Sai Baba has blessed them because the box is enamel, completely airtight, and yet has been dusted inside with Vibhuthi (*sacred ash*), so I see that as rather special.

Sai Baba does manifest Vibhuthi. It is very symbolic of what we are—an 'ash' body, or made up from the elements from ash in the physical, and if you take just a small amount of Vibhuti on the tongue, Sai Baba says it helps release the negative energies that may be around us.

So, in taking this Angel card it was like a message from the angels. The card had 'spontaneity' on it this morning, and I think that is what sometimes many of us have lost or forgotten on our life's path. We tend to take too much control, instead of just allowing events to flow. It is true we must make decisions and there are things that we can change, but mostly it is part of our life our destiny and (*sigh*) it is the way we handle it that is most important.

If we can walk every step of the day knowing we walk with the energy and love and compassion of God, the God energy that flows through us, if we allow it and hand over any real problems we are unable to deal with to God, somehow all comes out in the wash.

It is as if we are looked after, that God does walk with us, and if we try not to interfere with the process of learning, I have come to understand that our life here on this Earth is one purely of experience.

If we try to just let it flow, knowing all that comes before us is with purpose and for a reason, then it makes it much easier to live life daily, step by step. In a way, I think that is what Jesus meant when he said, "Become ye, as little children". What seems to be the way is to take hold of God's hand and walk with it. Letting him guide you and advise you and assist you whenever you ask for help. ... *deep sigh...*

The God beings that I know exist in the World of Light tell us work together as one. They too have personalities as light beings. They have specific abilities, they all have integrity, they all obey the Universal Law, they can create and could destroy if need be. But they never go against God's will. And that is why they come, they tell us, to speak through mediums around this Earth—mediums, such as myself, that open up and allow these energies to come forth.

They encourage people to use discernment at all times, for there are energies that could come forth that are not of God.

I have been given that understanding also, and in fact with Sai Baba at my side, that I can assist some people to release demonic or negative energies that are within them. I would never do it without being prompted from the Other Side and given permission first, for it would be interfering with another's karmic choice.

If people choose to be involved with the darker, negative life forms, that is their choice, but some do call out for help to God, even though they may not readily believe or understand. The light beings, the God beings tell us that help is always given to those who ask. It may not be given in a way those who ask expect or want it, but it is given in the best way for them to experience and understand.

Each individual has an oversoul or a higher being and they have said this could be described as a guardian angel. A guardian angel never leaves, no matter how dark or deeply emotional the soul may find itself in tragic or unhappy circumstances. The guardian angel is always with them and, if the soul will allow it, it will bring comfort, compassion, and healing to that soul.

We are all souls on this Earth—everyone has a soul. It is of God, it is of the Christ light, and it is within us all. Even the ones people may label as being evil—they also have an opportunity to change and turn back towards God.

For we all have at sometime strayed or lost the way, but if we had not experienced that pulling away from the understanding of God, we would not be able to measure and assess, so that we can make a choice for the better in walking back towards God. *...deep sigh...*

I can remember a time early in my searching when the thought crossed my mind that perhaps it would be a little boring being always good, if I can put it that way. But I have come to realise that was really my belief—my belief about what a person following God's path should be. Just being 'good' all the time.

With broader understanding, I realise now that one can experience God's energy in total and not be boring at all, but rather be linked with the energies of creation, which can flow through and be expressed in many ways, like painting, or music, or writing, or poetry, or building something, teaching harmonising (law) dancing, or flowing (navigating). They can all be very joyful experiences and one feels a sense of bliss all the time.

There is never a desire to want to hurt anyone, but rather always to love in a gentle way.

The aliens portrayed in the book by Whitley Strieber brought many fears to people and they were meant to do so. It was showing a different life form that was totally foreign to Earth people's way of seeing things and, as Whitley Strieber himself said in his book, he eventually overcame his fear and recognised that the energy of those little beings was one of love and caring. His wife and child seemed to know that right from the beginning, but Whitley Strieber, as he says in his book, was at times terrified—mainly because he felt he was being made to do things against his will.

This is something we have asked the light beings we are in communication with, as to why somebody would appear to be forced to do something if they were loving beings, if they were operating from the point of God. We were told the little earthling operates on many levels of consciousness. Remember, worlds upon worlds upon worlds. And in some parts of his consciousness, he has actually, as a star being before coming onto this Earth to incarnate into a personality, agreed to work with these little beings—you call them aliens. ...*deep sigh*...

Remember, it is important you assess the aliens you may feel the need to work with, to make sure that he/she is answering to a Master of God.

Now the little earthling if, when operating in the physical consciousness, they find they are far too fearful to do this work they have committed to do, all they have to do is to ask to be exonerated from that commitment and they will be.

If they pray and ask for God to be with them and to be freed of this commitment, they will be. It is their choice and it will be honoured. There is never any reason to fear. Once you have committed to work with God and if you are willing to be of service to the World of Light, this also can be of assistance to the light beings, so they can assist the little earthling. All you have to do is make it known to God that you wish to be of service and err, in a spontaneous way events will take place in your life that will help and show you how you can assist.

Be aware of the 'signs'. Be aware of the 'clues'. Sometimes, something seems to jump out of a page at you. (*Chuckles.*) Do not overlook it—it is a message.

Certain situations fall into place, as what some people call coincidences, but be aware it is not a coincidence, but rather a coordinated incidence, so that spirit can get a message through to you. Don't overlook it.

Sometimes a friend or acquaintance may say something that somehow seems to ring a bell for you. Don't overlook that. Spirit can send messages through others for you. Just consider it. Even messages we may not like to hear (*chuckles*), consider those too.

Spirit works always from a point of love, never fear. It is always from a point to help—to help one face whatever they need to face. To be able to release pent up emotions, which are like dark bubbles inside, and once they well up and come out (*deep sigh*) there is a freedom that comes within. It is lovely.

You wonder why it took you so long to let it all go—any hurt that you feel and hold onto from another is really only hurting yourself.

43 11th SITTING

Wednesday 31.8.1994

Today I am just a little upset. Just before coming to sit with the stone, I had a minor altercation with John. Nothing serious, but I do not like altercations and it has upset me. ...*deep sigh*...

It ruffles the waters and makes it a little harder to sit in contemplation. The waters are referring to our bodies, which are made up of about seventy per cent fluid and when we get emotionally excited or upset in any way it, as they say, stirs the waters and it makes it difficult to actually communicate.

So, it is important to learn or understand meditation. The overview of meditation is to calm the self and to calm the mind. It is not easy to do sometimes; playing very gentle easy-to-listen-to music can help. Or just to sit and look out across to the horizon on the sea. Or the mountains can help, or to look up into the sky.

One can meditate with eyes open or closed. ...*deep sigh*... The whole idea of meditation is to drop the daily worries and cares and to drop any thoughts that are racing in the mind or the brain and go into a kind of daydream or dream-like state.

There is no doubt that if you take a little time off each day, it helps one to connect with spirit and one's higher being, one's light being.

I have found visualising lovely scenes really does help to get into an altered state of consciousness. ...*deep sigh*...

Gentle breathing and sighing occasionally also helps and the ringing of a temple bell can help to focus. Remember the whole idea is to connect with Holy Spirit so that one feels a lifting away from the physical body for the time being. Always call upon God to be with you and ask for his/her help.

I have seen an image of Sai Baba quite often. I like to sometimes look at a candle and look into the flame. He seems to be standing in that flame, symbolising the light. The eternal light that links us all. That is why I like to light a candle whenever I sit to meditate. The candle I have is beside a picture of Sai Baba. He sometimes, I think, plays with the flame. It rises quite high and dances, or sometimes it glows extra brightly in a very large flame. And quite often it starts to flicker and at these times I feel he seems to be reinforcing anything that I might be experiencing at that time.

It's like he is talking to me through the flame. *...deep sigh...* It is lovely.

Even talking about it now I feel much calmer. I am sorry John and I had a few words. *...sigh...* But no matter, that seems to be part of the life, part of the duality that exists on this Earth. It is almost impossible to live here without experiencing negative emotions.

I guess that is why we are here—so we can find the balance, make the choices and grow stronger in ourselves. Hopefully with more wisdom.

I love this stone. It helps me quickly get into a meditative state and enter that God energy. It would be lovely to be able to give a little piece of it to everyone here on this Earth. Maybe if people read the book, they may feel that energy in some mystical or magical way. The energy would be passed on and they would be able to experience also the gentle, loving compassionate feeling it comes with, that energy of God.

I am sure many already have and do understand and know that experience. I thought how lovely it would be if everybody in this Earth, or on this Earth, would be able to connect all day and every day with the same energy within this wonderful Earth of ours; this beautiful Earth would be free of all the anger, bloodshed, and traumatic experiences that some people experience and it would be free of drugs and weapons. There would be enough food for everybody, for everyone would readily share and give from their heart.

We are told from the light beings that when we move into the Golden Age, which we are starting to now, this new vibration of golden light here on this Earth will be free of shadow. That people will be happily harmonising with each other and there will not be want.

I see now the new generation of children in the 1990s that are being born seem to come as very wise little people on the whole. Amazing little children, actually, many very 'gifted'. Many quite different from their parents.

They are coming, almost marching ahead of major changes, to help the world move into this new state of being. ...*deep sigh*... It will be lovely.

I do not know how much longer John and I will be here on this Earth. But wherever we are, we will be watching with great joy in our hearts to see the changes come and to know there is peace and harmony, goodwill to all those upon Mother Earth. It will be free of trial and tribulation and it will come into an understanding of a Universal Government, for we have been told the starpeople are going to make themselves known publicly all over this Earth and they will come in peace. They will come with love and blessings and there will be no need to fear at all.

This is what they have been trying to tell the little earthlings down the eons of time. There have been other times on this Earth that the starpeople have been readily received and communication has taken place. ...*deep sigh*...

For some reason, the peoples on the Earth in a time that is of now, seem very nervous of the possibility of their existence and any evidence that is brought forward is quickly squashed. But we will leave that.

(*I wrote this book quite a long while ago now—I think all will agree there has been a lot more awareness since then. Scientists, scholars, and the general public around the world are thankfully open now to the possible existence of other starpeople in our universe.*)

I only ask you to consider, if you haven't already, the possibility that there is life in other worlds, in other planets and other stars. It is all relative, is it not?

If we imagined ourselves living perhaps on another planet in the universe, when you look up into the sky and look back on our Earth and err, know that there is life here, why is it not possible that life could exist in other parts of the universe?

It may not be exactly the same form that we are here, but is it not a little like the time when most people thought that this Earth was flat? Only to discover it was round and that there was something holding everybody on it, so they did not fly off. (*You have to laugh*). Surely, it is that simply we do not have the technology yet and science has not quite reached out far enough to understand a different dimension. With the thinking of quantum physicists, we are getting there.

Worlds upon worlds upon worlds. ...*deep sigh*...

Why should there be so many mediums around this Earth with energies speaking through them with such similar tales or stories? Why should that phenomena occur? Surely, it must show that something is happening.

I am a medium, and I have not gotten together with other mediums around this Earth to set up a gigantic plot to deceive people. But rather, when some other medium's work is published, I get a thrill to find the messages that have been coming through them are very similar to messages we have been receiving. Messages I have never read about before, and that I could not possibly know in any way other than knowing and accepting there are other beings that exist with intelligence and knowledge and great compassion, far superior to our abilities here on Earth.

I wonder, and I ask myself, why is it so many people brush the thought away. I can understand if they doubt, because we do come from a limited point of view, but why are they so ready to brush away the possibility of life in other worlds and just laugh or even get angry? I thought the basis of educating was always to keep an open mind. ...*deep sigh*...

For many years, mediums would talk about auras around people and people would scoff and laugh about that, but now, we have graduated into instruments that actually can take photographs of auras. They are a scientific fact. That is a different dimension not readily seen with the physical eye. That in itself ought to make people wonder a little.

Energy and forms of energy are what science needs to think about, but maybe we have not the scientific instruments yet to measure the different energies. I am not a scientist, so perhaps I should not be speaking about something I do not know about. And yet, I know spirituality is actually science.

As a medium, I have been trained to feel the energies that change about me. I am aware of different energies that come into my space, my aura, if I can put it that way. I do get images in my inner scene, but not always clear ones; rather they are like impressions and it is of a knowing also. A physical body is a very complicated piece of machinery.

There are many aspects of the physical body that operate in an intangible way, a way one cannot quite put their finger on but accept and know.

I think sometimes if we could see and look at the physical body and the unseen bodies that go with it, and thought about that a little more, maybe we could come to accept the existence of other intangible forms of life.

The emotion is intangible. That is within us. It seems to be a reaction and it shows itself in some way by a contorted face or a smiling, happy face or tears that come from that feeling, or anger makes us red, or joy that seems to happen to us as a great glow. But the emotion itself, you cannot put your finger on that. That is intangible, but it exists, it is real. It is real to everybody. *...deep sigh...*

We are told by the light beings that the emotions, or the emotional body as they describe it, still exists even when the spirit of a personality leaves a physical body—so the emotional body seems to be operating in a different dimension. I find that interesting.

We are told that from their (*the light beings*) point of view, there is no difference between the third and fourth dimension here on this Earth. The fourth dimension has often been described as the Astral.

Yet from our point of view here on Earth, there is a BIG difference between the third and fourth dimensions.

The fourth dimension is the photo (in hologram) of all form and the third dimension is the carbon copy (or ash copy).

There are psychics and mediums who readily know and understand the Astral (fourth dimension) and the existence of thought forms and energy forms within that, which can influence those here in this third dimension.

The existence of 'ghosts' has often been talked about and yes, they exist. In fact, I feel nothing but compassion for them for they have been caught in the Astral for one reason or another. Maybe they are unhappy, maybe they do not believe in God and do not realise that there is a life after death. Maybe they have some unfinished business to attend to...

If anybody has seen the film called *Ghost*, it was portrayed exactly the way it is. There is life in the fourth dimension in the Astral and it is hard for those caught in that dimension without a physical body to move onto the World of Light. But if they ask even from that dimension, they will be assisted; help will be brought to them.

Many laugh and scoff about the existence of life even in the fourth dimension and that is just the next world to ours. *...deep sigh...*

So, I guess I understand they find it very hard to accept the existence of other worlds in the stars, in other universes.

The starpeople have talked to us about a hierarchy, the Angelic Realms, and the existence of what they call the cosmic consciousness. Maybe you would like to think about that.

As a medium, and working with these lovely light beings, I have on occasion had a wonderful energy come through and speak with a very deep and loud voice, presenting himself as the Archangel Michael. He comes through so powerfully I feel as though he is going to lift me off the ground and, again, I want to laugh because it feels like fun. I think everybody has that feeling they would like to be able to fly. To take wings into the skies.

Those who have witnessed his coming have been a little in awe and deafened slightly (*laughs)*, but he comes that way, he says, to show his existence.

He is doing a lot of work around the Earth in helping to free the world of shadow. He speaks of taking up his Sword of Light and cutting through the darkness. He is very special, and I feel it is sacred work, working with him. ...*deep sigh*...

I feel a little like Joan of Arc when he comes into my body, when he takes it over. He holds his hand high and I can feel that Sword of Light. There is great strength and power and I am happy to be of service. His Sword of Light never destroys; it just contains any shadow entity in a restricted place, giving it a chance to grow in consciousness...but keeping it from creating mischief with others.

John and I were prompted to go for a holiday in rural France. The feeling was quite strong to make that journey and White Eagle had come through and talked about us making a trip and how he would enjoy guiding us.

When we were in France, we seemed to be guided, there was no doubt about that. If felt as if unseen hands gently pushed us in various directions. We went to many special little townships, villages for that matter, and re-lived and experienced a life that had been lived before, and sometimes more than one life.

Sometimes, we realised we had lived the lives together, that is John and I, and sometimes they were separate ones. I could see the changes come over John when, for instance, sitting in a church he suddenly became that personality he must have been at another time. It was so clear, so obvious, and he felt that difference and he also felt the emotions of anger he carried with it.

So, it was an opportunity for both of us to release many emotions we had been holding onto.

As we were driving along a country road, quite often an eagle would swoop in front of the car or be sitting on a fence or flying around just above and ahead of us, as if leading us. One day we drove under a rainbow; it was wonderful. (*I laughed.*) It was such a joyful experience it was as if we were finding the metaphysical gold. The alchemy of ourselves.

I had been working with spirit for a long time, but at that time it was all quite a new experience for John and it helped him understand where I was coming from, so it was not so difficult for him to accept, er, shall I say a light being, a personality speaking through me, particularly with a male sounding voice. (*I laugh.*) Some men could not handle that, but John is fine, he accepts it; he even makes jokes about it so I feel I can get on with my work. I have his support and I am very thankful to him for that. ...*deep sigh*...

My work is a driving force within me and I cannot put it away. I must do what I have come to do.

44 12th SITTING

Thursday 1.9.1994

The White lady had been initiated into her local indigenous tribe and given the name Woma. Thank you, Woma, for I am truly beginning to understand the power of this stone. I know it has not come to me as its keeper, but rather to share its energy so that I can speak of its energy and its beginnings. It is what the starpeople came onto this Earth to teach in the first place so long ago.

When they entrusted the stone, which was brought to Earth by Alcheringa, otherwise known as the Golden One, it was passed onto the natives of Earth: the original inhabitants, the Aborigine, who at that time were a tribe of one. Their leader was known as Tjurunga and he was entrusted with this stone. It is interesting that in some of the Aboriginal dialects or languages Tjurunga means sacred stone. Many teachings and understandings were given to the 'cherished ones', so they would understand of the existence of the God energy and the Creator of All.

They have upheld their duty to look after and care for Mother Earth down through the ages. And they have done so with great heart.

We of the Celtic Tribes who came to this wondrous land arrived with 'fight' in our hearts. It was one of hate and fear. In our beginnings here in Australia, the Aboriginal man and woman could not understand why white man should treat another white man (*convicts*) the way they did. To them, that behaviour was totally beyond their understanding at that time.

They have a deep respect and love within their hearts and are of a very gentle nature. They feel energies and know of spirit and understanding is often given to one another through telepathy. In that way, the white man, the fighting man, could perhaps learn from these people. (*There is a difference between a 'fighting' man and a 'warrior'.*)

Spirit has guided me recently to a medical practitioner who works in homeopathy. He spoke of the Celtic generation and the cellular influences of that on white man, the white families that live here on this Earth. It seems we can carry genetic memory in our body as well as soul memory, so with some courage in my heart I have faced the fact there is resentment in me and that is an aspect of' 'hate': the fighting spirit that is within my physical body. Anything that is not of the energy of love must be leaning towards the opposite, which is of hate.

This stone and the energy within it, along with the homeopathic remedy is going to help release that energy and I feel will be the last little link I need to heal my skin.

My skin disease does not bother me anymore, but it does act as a kind of barometer and very quickly shows me if I am 'off track' or not. It is like a signpost and I wear it like a flag. (*I have to laugh. ...deep sigh...*) But I am tuned into spirit enough now to be able to receive the messages in a different way.

I speak of all this in the hope that if there are others who are reading this who suffer with psoriasis to please not give up hope.

In a way, in the little altercation I had with John the other day was a reaction coming from resentment in me. It was not with him directly but rather this Celtic thing I see now. The Celtic male is very dominant and as a female I resent the dominance, and so as a Celtic female I started to fight or argue back. Now that spirit has organised for me to understand this, I will for the next fourteen days be able to release that from the genetic memory and no longer have it within my being.

I have asked for God's help in that healing. *...deep sigh...*

So far, I have only had one treatment and already I feel so much more at peace. I think the indigenous races have much to teach us in their understanding of the spirit of Mother Earth. There is a need for communication. All do not have the ability of telepathic communication, after all, we do only live in the third dimension.

It is interesting that as soon as we leave the third dimension, all communication is telepathic. We no longer need to use a voice box. In spirit, forms do not have a 'voice box', there is no need.

I love this stone and I feel it loves me. It is of an energy that I know all could not readily connect with in a very intimate way. It is of a power that is not meant to be owned, or held onto, or argued over by anyone. It only wants to bring the energy of love—but for love to permeate a being, it needs to mirror us. Like attracts like. It is all relative, is it not?

I know this stone will move on when the time is right and at that time I will gladly, joyfully, pass it on. For it is, in its own way, finding its way home to its rightful place. I will think of it on its journey and hopefully assist telepathically by sending loving thoughts.

Uluru is a very special place. It is one of the largest monoliths in the world. It is also known as Ayers Rock, which is about five-eighths submerged into the red earth of the centre of Australia. The part we see above the plain (or desert) today is only a fraction of the total rock mass, even though what we see is 546 metres high, 4 kilometres long, 2–4 kilometres wide and eight kilometres around the base. The total surface area covers 485.6 hectares. It has a very powerful energy also; it influences everybody who goes there in some way or another.

On my 60th birthday, John organised as a birthday treat a trip to Uluru. We stayed four nights and five days and it was magical. It was a week before Christmas and it should have been very hot, but in actual fact the temperature was down to 17° during the day we arrived. It had been raining a week or so before and the desert had burst forth into flower.

It was as if it welcomed us—we were delighted. I bought pictures and pictures and pictures of Uluru in her various colourful moods. I came to discover that Uluru was partly made up of Feldspar, which is actually moonstone. It is that same colour I experience when I sit with this stone. It is very gentle, very lovely, but very powerful.

John and I had some very special experiences at Kata TJuta, or the Olgas, as well as Uluru. The two go together, even though they are not the same rock. ...*deep sigh*...

On the day we were to leave, around midday I looked back, we looked back to say goodbye, and the sun was shining on Uluru. It had become a brilliant gold, it looked beautiful, and I could see a rainbow going from one side of the ground up and over and above the top to the other side and onto the ground again. I wondered at the time if that was what the Aborigines call the Rainbow Serpent, or if it was linked to that.

I discovered later it was the day of the Summer Solstice. Spirit had organised the timing for us, as we have found on many occasions. Quite spontaneously, we have these wonderful journeys or experiences and we know that unseen hands have guided us to be at a certain place at a certain time for a certain happening.

We feel very blessed and we thank God for his grace. ...*deep sigh*...

45 13TH SITTING

All Religions Are Facets of the Same Truth, All Scriptures Are Holy; All Places of Worship Are Holy. All Religions Are Seeking the One and The Same God, Although They May Call Him by Different Names.

– Sri Sathya Sai Baba

Friday 2.9.1994

Through a number of coincidental happenings, the stone found its way to our front door.

In some way, I feel this stone will act as a cohesive energy to bring understanding between the white man and the black—or the ebony and the ivory, as has been said. There is much need for understanding between these two races if we are to live in harmony. I know *Upstairs* has a plan that has yet to unfold. There are a number of us to be involved to assist in that unfolding. There is, I believe, a prophecy that speaks of that end (that has unfolded in Part Three).

*****

The words are not so readily flowing this day, and it saddens me a little.

I left the stone for a while this morning; the time did not feel right somehow. I am now sitting with it in the afternoon. John has gone out for the rest of the day, so I have some time to myself. ... *deep sigh...*

This morning, when nothing was coming as I was sitting here, I felt prompted to go down the valley to the 'waters' on our property. It is spring water that has been unleashed, if I can put it that way, just recently and it seemed I was getting many messages that it was special water and had healing properties. So, I have been drinking it myself and I am sure it is assisting a healing to take place within me. It is certainly helping to lift consciousness, I know that. When I drink it, it is like drinking water and light, golden light, golden white light.

John often says, "They are telling me from *Upstairs*", meaning he also feels he gets messages from the Dear Ones.

Just before we went on a trip overseas, he commissioned a road to be cut down through the valley at the back of our property—it is more like a gorge and a steep one at that. It took a large piece of machinery, which I referred to rather unlovingly as a dinosaur, and was horrified to see the cut had gone through that little gorge to get to the bottom, which was, or is, a creek known as Emu Creek.

No matter how dry we get, summer or winter, there always is water in that creek. It is not very deep, although at times when the rains have come, it has rushed or forged through with great power.

As I was walking up and down this newly made road, I was upset because of Mother Earth being scarred so badly, but a wave of feeling came over me that it was all meant to be this way. That, in fact, if the road had not been cut through an area where it did, the water, the spring, which flows quite strongly, would not have been unearthed.

So that in itself is a blessing and it also cut through an area of earth where there were seams of shale-like coal, and in unearthing that particular spot, it gave a natural base for the road, which then became very steep down to the bottom of the gorge. So, I feel it was all meant to happen and that spirit was operating with unseen influence, and it has now become a beautiful place for us to escape to.

When it is very hot, it is nicely cool down there and where up the top we are sometimes plagued by flies, they do not go down into the gorge.

Halfway down the landscape is a little like a rainforest. There are beautiful ferns, tree ferns and other huge trees casting a canopy that gives coolness—a lovely feeling of peace and calm. There just seemed to be a certain spot in particular (*from*) spirit (*I had to laugh)* showed me and, in fact, I felt strongly that I would like to put in a grotto, so it could be a place of prayer, of reverence.

I had come into possession of a small figure of the Mother Mary and it seemed to be made of a material I recognised straight away that I could put outside in the open air, which at the time I felt it would go somewhere outside. Now when this road developed, I could see the spot for it.

Not long after I made this decision, I received from Patricia Cota-Robles, by fax from the USA, published transcribed material that was channelled messages received from the Mother Mary energy, announcing there would be waters released around this Earth to help people move into the new age. The Golden Age.

The water does feel different. If you put a little on your hand and rinse your hands with it, the water seems to soak into the skin quite quickly. It is not as heavy and sticky as water can be on the skin for a little while before it dries. So that in itself showed to me it was of a different dimension—and when it was professionally analysed by a chemist, it proved to be, well, as the report said, excellent water for drinking. I had to laugh, as that came as no surprise. Now we have captured the water in a holding bay, and we actually fill bottles with it and others have started to drink it. I am sure there is more to come about that water, but for the moment it brings to mind a little story that happened in 1992.

I had a psychic friend, a lady who came to visit the property, and while we were walking around in the valley above this particular gorge I have been speaking about, she pointed out an area that she said was a point of light, as if it was pouring forth a fountain of light coming from within the Earth. When you walked over the spot, you could feel that energy; it had an uplifting feeling about it.

She said the Aborigine people called them Bora Rings. Now, I do not know if this is so, but I was prompted to dedicate that particular place to the Australian Aborigine spirit and so I devised a time in my mind that I was going to perform this little ceremony. It was about a week later, at midday, I walked down to the spot with the makings of a little fire—a few twigs, paper, matches; I was a little concerned because it was summer and I did not want to risk sparks igniting and setting off a bushfire. So, I had to keep it very, very small and watch it the whole time.

I was prompted by White Eagle to take an umbrella (*I laughed*) and when I came to the point where I had committed to make a little ceremony of dedication, I sat and in my inner scene I could see thousands of Aborigines that had come in the fourth dimension or what they call the Dreamtime.

I was delighted, of course. White Eagle, as I could see him in my inner scene, sat down dressed in full American Native Indian Chief regalia. He was passing around his peace pipe (*I chuckled*), and speaking of the American Native Indian ways of telepathically sharing their knowledge and understanding with the others, the Aborigine spirits I could see who seemed to have dignity and authority as if they were elder ancestors.

After the ceremony, which took about half an hour, I could hear the sound of a didgeridoo and clapping sticks. I was very happy to be part of all this, even though it was just me there in the third dimension.

I was looking at the fire and started to worry a little about it because it was not dying down as fast as I would like. I certainly did not want to leave it still alight. I was prompted to look over towards the south and there was a wall, literally, a dark, dark grey wall coming toward me. It did not take long to reach me, and as it did it started to rain and then, of course, there was no longer any worry about the fire. I had already opened my umbrella. On my way back to the house, I was being splashed as it was raining quite hard, and I could not get over the fact that I was not getting wet. I laughed; it was such a wonderful experience and I was laughing, but the water was not wetting me.

Shall we say the next dimension is perhaps like the water that is coming from that spring now? It has a different feel about it, and obviously it has all the qualities of a higher vibration, which helps to heal and free one's body of the shadow. ...deep sigh...

The Gorge is probably about a one and half kilometre walk from the house, including walking down the new road as well; as I have said, it is very steep towards the end but a very pleasant walk for those who come to visit. John and I certainly enjoy taking that walk because there is definitely a different feel within the air and the area itself. It is quite a charming place, full of bird sounds and other sounds and even though we live in an area that is always wanting for rainfall, there is a moist cool air down there, which is very pleasant.

Our Indian friend, Jegathesan, who is a high-profile businessman, and a guru, or a teacher of Sai Baba, came to visit and we talked about this water with him. He said the area reminded him of a healing place he had been to in the Philippines and as he looked around, he said, "In fact, it is very similar to it." Also, there were places where people could sit in the water, so we think we might like to create that situation as well.

The only thing is that in winter we can get snow up on the top so (*laughingly*), the water would be pretty cold during that time, but certainly very refreshing—we will just wait and see.

Jega also gave us a copper dish that has the symbol Sai Baba uses for his Ashram, which symbolises a uniting of all religions on this Earth—that is what he is about. I like that, I like that very much. His (*Sai Baba's*) aim is for no separation amongst any.

The brass plate is interesting when I turned it over, and shows it came from waterfalls in Zimbabwe. I laughed (*it seemed to be saying something*) and so that also will be placed on the altarstone in the little Grotto halfway down that road into the Gorge. ...*deep sigh*...

The starpeople tell us they inspired all religious teachings down through the Ages, to all the different cultures and races that exist here on Earth. They may have inspired some with different ways of perceiving God and Creation, but the overview is that it is all the same.

It seems rather foolish people should get caught up with long discussions about the differences between different religions and which one is right and which one is wrong. But rather, to see the inspiration and influence has all come from the same source, and in fact there is only One God—the Creator of All. There are many aspects, many energies and many ways of perceiving that, but the overview is that it is the ONE—all the same ONE.

For me, being very fortunate to communicate with these star beings, it does give me a broader view and an expansion in thought—I certainly do *not* have all the answers, but they do answer questions and they are very ready to communicate if one reaches out. They explain in simple ways, for it is just a simple being asking the questions (*have to laugh)* and are very patient and understanding, but I know instinctively they are 'brilliant' in more ways than one. ...*deep sigh*...

46 14th SITTING

Saturday 3.9.1994

As I sit here with the stone, I am not sure what to talk about today. Sometimes before I sit, I am given inklings (*twinklings*) of what the subject will be about, but I have no idea at this moment.

When I was awakened on 20th April 1994, I was given this message and I will quote it:

"We would like you to know we are very pleased with the way you are progressing. This is not a message of a sort, but rather a message to connect. When you hear the bell or knock there will be communication—you will be writing and inspiration will be given. Baba will help you—please feel open to this. You began with inspirational writing and this is how the book will manifest. What is it to be called—The Love Book or *The Book of Love?"*

And that was followed on 26th April 1994 with a dream, and I will describe the dream:

I dreamt I was with a group of people and, in particular, a lady just like everybody else, but nobody else could see her except me. We were laughing, she was laughing, and I was asking people to touch her because she was there, but they still could not see her.

(Now in 2018, I realise it was Andromeda Val from the galaxy Andromeda M31.)

And then on another Wednesday, very early morning, I was awakened with a message:

"Good morning, my dear. This is just a reminder of our agreement and I am glad you are responding and have not forgotten. We will be writing for your book, are you happy about this?"

I said yes!

"Good, then we shall begin, but not today. Thank you."

At that time, I had no idea of the existence of this Alcheringa stone, nor did I know it would be coming my way to assist me.

Sai Baba works in strange ways and I truly feel blessed he is helping me in this way.

I have often felt I would like to write, but I did not really feel I was capable of it. In my minor attempts at writing, I tended to approach the subjects in a very pedantic way and the events would be described sequence by sequence, which in a way was a little boring, I thought.

But Sai Baba is showing me how to sit and relax and tell a story as if it is an armchair chat. So, I thank him for that. Certainly, the energy from the stone is assisting me to relax and enter into a different consciousness, although I am very aware. I can easily open my eyes and close them, but I am aware that I am speaking from a different consciousness. It is from a point from where I do not really have to worry about anything.

By that I mean I do not have to plan or worry I have missed something, for it all seems to have been taken care of. I thought to myself I am enjoying this very much. I am enjoying the adventure as it is, because I do not know what is going to happen next. I did worry about whether anybody would be wanting to read a book such as this (*deep sigh),* but I was prompted to take an Angel card and on it I received the message 'trust', and so I will.

I feel I am not letting go quite as well as I can on this day, but no matter. Everything we do is for experience, and from experience we come to understand. Even in the smallest things that we do. It is the larger events that capture our attention and remain in our memory so well, but it is important to attend to even the smallest details in our lives, so that we do not rush through our lives.

In other words, so we can take it step by step, fully conscious of the higher consciousness that flows through us, to allow ourselves to be guided and to make decisions from that point. Somehow, life seems to flow much easier. That is not to say we do not experience trauma from time to time, but that is also for our experience and understanding. In fact, it is at that time we seem to learn the most.

I prefer to think of 'learning' as way of coming to understand and it is from experience that we come to understand. *...deep sigh...*

When John and I were in France in *October 1991*, we were *set up*, if I can put it that way. One evening, just before we were about to go to dinner, White Eagle made it known he wanted to speak to my husband. And, as John agreed to this, and because I had nothing with us to record with (*I always record the messages*), we used a video camera we had with us and John actually videoed the sequence.

I will stop for a moment, for it is here I have to listen again to that message (*I do not remember it*) and re-speak of it at this point.

John asked again about the prophecy that money will be coming our way. He said he had already spent $700 buying lottery tickets with no return. White Eagle said the money would be re-imbursed to him. That the money for him to act as their banker would come, but the time was not quite right yet. White Eagle said also the monies would be separate from the money that was coming through business to enable him to settle his debts once and for all.

We were told the trip to France would benefit both of us—and it did! And that John had a role to play, although it was different to Valérie. Her role will be one of theatre and an opportunity for me (meaning White Eagle) to be presented through her to speak and to show that spirit does exist and also there would be opportunity to ask questions about the World of Light. She would be presented to many people. He hoped he would accept that and support her in her work.

Some of the messages that have come through are definite and others have been ones of 'alluding to'. *Upstairs* seem to do this on purpose; it is one of testing, one of encouraging, one to use discernment, and one to actually come to understand at a deeper level. There is no doubt they teach (*laughs*), but they teach in a very different way than our approach, our linear approach of teaching. It is much more lateral and one of overview. I like that.

There have been problems in recent years of education in what children have seemed able to handle. There is so much to learn, and it is almost as if there is too much crammed into their brain.

Perhaps too much unnecessary information. If we were to go back to the basics to teach children how to learn for themselves and to help them to communicate with their inner consciousness, their higher consciousness, they could be assisted to take in information and program it into their brains with less hassle and worry. For it does seem the Edward De Bono or lateral thinking way of teaching is more successful. There are young people, even adults, who still do not seem to have the basics of being able to read and write.

There are changes going on within physical bodies all the time and it does seem to be showing there is a need to re-think and re-plan educational procedure.

I speak from this point in having one son who had great difficulty in learning to read and write, but at the same time his abilities, his lateral abilities, we were told, were of genius ability. So, it seems sometimes children thrive better at lateral thinking, rather than linear thinking, but somehow, we need to blend both. In our society, we still need to communicate with writing and reading, for in this third dimension we still operate from that way of communication (*laughs*) through the voice box, eyes, and ears, and it is important those abilities are nourished or nurtured. *...deep sigh...*

It is true telepathic abilities would take away the need to read and write and perhaps in the New Age this will be to where the human population graduates. *...deep sigh...*

The basic approach to teaching, after my experience of being taught from *Upstairs*, seems to be assisting one to want to learn and, from that feeling, then assist as to how one can learn, rather than fill each individual with a lot of information they are not ready to receive. *...deep sigh...*

When one reaches into the higher consciousness, one reaches into a point where there is no limit and if there is no limit, then all information necessary for that individual can be readily accessed when the time is right.

It seems to be very important society does not label people, so they do not fall into feelings of self-worthlessness, for that is not teaching in God's name but, rather, pulling in a different direction.

All the answers are there and available; it is just coming to understand how to access them. ...*deep sigh*...

If I were a scientist, I would access knowledge in a different way. If I were a medical practitioner, I would access knowledge in a different way. If I were a lawyer, I would access information in a different way. I am speaking of accessing information from the World of Light.

There is always love and concern for earthlings; all they have to do is ask. ...*deep sigh*...

15th SITTING

47

Sunday 4.9.1994

I was prompted yesterday to listen to the video recording that John made when White Eagle spoke to him while we were in France in October 1991.

It is one of the few messages I have not transcribed and I could not remember at all what White Eagle said. For when I am channeling, I am still slightly conscious, but it is as if I step aside from my physical body, my physical brain, and allow energy of the light being to come through. In doing so, I am aware of what is taking place, but after the event I cannot readily remember what has been said. So, listening to the video recording, White Eagle had spoken to John and reaffirmed once again that monies would be coming, that he would be free of his debt, and that they would like him to be their banker.

John has agreed to that, only at a time when he feels he is free of debt. Since then, his business activities have improved dramatically, although he is not yet quite free of debt.

So, it was interesting when I met Sai Baba for the first time and he looked meaningfully into my eyes while holding my hand and jokingly said, in front of twenty-two other devotees who were present, "and where is banker?" Of course, everybody laughed because he said, "Do you know who banker is? Banker is husband." I laughed also, BUT I was actually quite stunned because I realised he knew what had taken place in the communication between White Eagle and John.

John found it hard to believe when I told him on my return from India, but somehow the ring Sai Baba had given me seemed to give some credibility to what had taken place, and so he was a little stunned also. *...deep sigh...*

Also on that recorded video message, Sai Baba—I am sorry, White Eagle—had asked John if he would support Valérie's role in it, being a little like theatre and that she would be allowing his energy to speak through her in a very male sounding 'voice', and it would happen in public to show that spirit does exist and for all to see the phenomena, to assess for themselves the possibility. It is a role that Valérie has agreed to long before she came to this Earth. He, meaning my husband John, also had a role to play, which was different but in alignment with Valérie.

John readily agreed and said he would always support Valérie in whatever she did, and I thank him for that. It is not easy for a husband to witness a change take place within his wife and a male voice start speaking through her (*I laughed*), but he handled it, God bless him. *...deep sigh...*

Later, at a time after we had returned to Australia, John and I were about to start our evening meal when he was suddenly taken over. His arms reached up into the air like wings, and he said, "*I am White Eagle*", and his fingers started moving and he said, "*My fingers are feathers*", and then he experienced quite a lot of knowledge and understanding of the energy of White Eagle within him.

Telepathically, I asked White Eagle what was happening, and he said, "*Your husband is always so busy, I thought I would visit him just before he started eating. It was the only time he seemed to be available.*"

Oh dear. I laughed inside. Since that time, John has not spoken to White Eagle through me, but he says he is now getting direct messages.

Everybody is capable of being a medium, and, in fact, they are. It is just a matter of degree.

People are inspired we are told by beings of light—and er, it is like a light coming into their brain, which is actually a suggestion with a thought and then it is up to them (us) to decide whether to follow it or not.

I was given an image as shown in comic books when somebody has an idea and it is portrayed as like seeing a light bulb go on in a little cloud above that person's head, and it seems that is exactly how it is. I laughed—there is always freedom of choice. Nothing is ever forced, but the World of Light finds many ways to try to assist the earthlings. ...*deep sigh*...

We connect with our higher consciousness that is within our heart by our will, our desire, to reach to a point that is of light, divine light, and of God consciousness, the secret is to make that choice. ...*deep sigh*...

48 16th SITTING

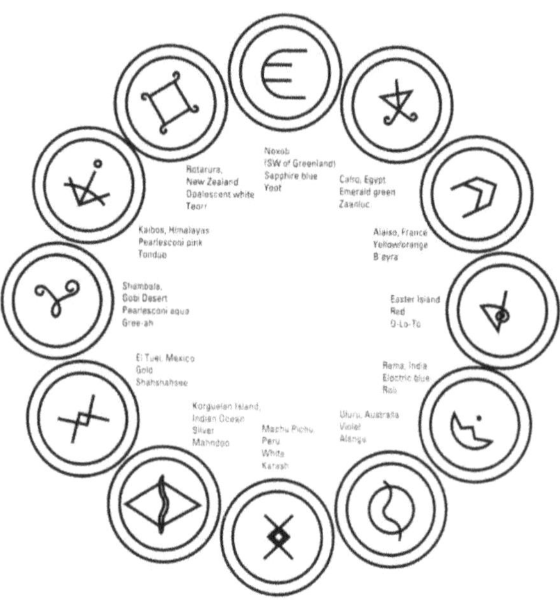

Monday 5.9.1994

Yesterday, after the reading of the stone, we had quite a group of like-minded people come to the property. There were twenty-two in all and we painted symbols—symbols that had been channelled by Rob Sampson, Rosemary Whitefield, and Carol Birch. They had been given from the Council of Light. It was the first time they have been released on Earth and with the symbols comes great power.

The group has been prompted to recreate these symbols onto canvas and paint them. There is a contingent of people going to

Uluru to place them on the ground and, working with the Council of Light, helping bring the energies of these symbols of light into the Earth to help release energy patterns that have been held within Mother Earth from past trauma. ...*deep sigh*...

All this is being done with respect towards the Australian Aborigine and letters have been sent off as well as telepathic messages; they are hoping it all will be favourably received by the Original peoples.

As the day wore on, we were outside painting when there was this wondrous cloud display. We were all in awe of it. They had told us from the World of Light that often there are starships within view, but they stay hidden behind a smoke screen, as they put it, which is really a cloud of condensation.

Yesterday, the clouds actually had the shape of starships and were quite big. Some were like the little scout ships, but there was also another display of cloud, which was quite remarkable. We were all in awe and thrilled by the whole experience.

Scout ships forming a line to look like a serpent. Starship on right

There seemed to be colour in the sky also, and there was an eagle, which in the Australian Aboriginal belief always shows signs of sacred land. We also saw the appearance of the eagle as a sign, which was actually blessing the symbols we had finished painting and laid out on the ground.

Scout ships seen in sky after serpent formation disbanded

We were prompted later to walk down to the waters and halfway down the hill where we plan to build a grotto and establish the altarstone. We all held hands and gave a prayer. It was a wonderful experience; everybody was commenting on how special the energy was down there and er, they all had their own individual experiences. For me, it was like the first gathering of many that are to come. Many of them had brought bottles to take water and they all left feeling very happy and joyful. ...*deep sigh*...

There were some among the gathering who were asked by Rosemary to sit with the Alcheringa stone. It was interesting that each time somebody sits with the stone, we are aware they have not had any feedback from others who have sat with it. In other words, they sit with the stone not having any idea what it is about. But the same story comes forth.

It is often said in a different way from each person, but the overview is that it is very hot, very powerful, a record keeper; it holds the secret of Atlantis, it is not of Earth, it does seem to have a spirit of its own, which is a very beautiful spirit, a very loving one and it is on its own journey and it will find its own way back to its rightful place. ...*deep sigh*...

'Synchronicity' is an interesting word, which was 'coined' by Carl Jung to describe a phenomenon that occurs often with those who are on a spiritual path, in other words they are operating with awareness from spirit. And when a message comes or a feeling comes, something else happens and then something else somewhere else, and everything comes together. In other words, it 'synchronises' and then, of course, there is an understanding of a particular point.

This is a way the World of Light often brings messages to those who work with them and so if there is a feeling of responsibility, such as with this stone, and perhaps some may feel and worry about what is going to happen to it, there is no need to worry because (*Holy*) Spirit will synchronise events so there will be no doubt as to where it is to go.

I love working with spirit in this way; it is the way they mean when they ask us to 'flow' with spirit and not to pre-empt in any way.

Although sometimes we maybe set off on a little excursion for what we think is one reason, when suddenly the whole ambience of the excursion changes and we realise we have been, shall I say, 'set up' and the real reason for that little excursion becomes apparent. There is always a feeling of joy, laughter, and fun when that happens.

You also know you are on the right path, that you have not wandered off onto a little path all of your own making. ...*deep sigh*...

This is how, when working with spirit, it is truly an adventure—because you are taking step after step without really knowing where you are going but knowing that there is an unseen hand holding you by the hand.

I love this way of travelling; it suits my spirit of adventure. Trust is what they are always telling us and discernment. ...*deep sigh*...

While we were on the road leading down to the Gorge yesterday, after we had all joined hands, there was a great gust of wind—it was almost as if there was rain in the air. If that had been so, it would have been the first rain we have had for a long time. The country badly needs rain and it would be welcomed when it came.

A gust of wind happened on a number of occasions yesterday, even though it was really a very calm day, and each time it seemed to be synchronised with thoughts that helped us to sort out the way they, from the Other Side, truly wanted events to take place. It was a lovely experience.

I speak of this stone as being like the Holy Spirit; the Aborigine people talk of the God of the Winds and of the Fire and of the Water and of the Earth...

It all seems to be here in the stone, as of course it is everywhere. It seems somehow to be more centred here and it certainly helps to connect with that centredness by holding it. ...*deep sigh*...

I like the way the Australian Aborigines perceive spirit.

God is our church; it does not have to be in a building. It does not have to be in a form. It can be formless; it can be everywhere. I think this is where religious teachings sometimes limit themselves. There is a knowing and an acceptance of the Creator of all.

Beautiful stone, thank you.

17th SITTING 49

We are flowers of the same creepers. Our minds are the flowers that grow on the creeper of the heart. The flowers may be different, but the creeper is the same. We are the children of the same race! We all belong to the race of humanity, but not to the race of the birds and beasts. Since we belong to the illustrious race of humanity, we must conduct ourselves in a sublime manner. We are the waves, born in the ocean of satchithananda. Since we are born of the same race, we should radiate the oneness of humanity without harbouring hatred against anyone.

Satchithananda: means, qualities of the absolute.
- All knowledge
- All consciousness
- All bliss

– Baba

Tuesday 6.9.1994

I do not know where this book is leading to, but I am enjoying sitting with this beautiful stone and just talking. ...*deep sigh*... It is really helping me to understand, at a much deeper level, all the teachings I have been blessed with from the World of Light.

Sai Baba has helped me so much, and I know he helps many and, in fact, millions around this Earth—many not knowing or understanding it is he who is helping them. He seems to operate with special power (*there was a knock on the table*) and quite obviously it is one the Creator has entrusted to him.

I cannot begin in the state of consciousness I operate in the third dimension, I cannot begin to fully understand the dimensions that exist in the Outer Worlds or deep in the Inner Worlds. But I am being given some comprehension, although at another level I know I do understand, and I suppose this is how it is for everyone. But before anyone can really understand about other dimensions, they need to have a willingness to want to reach out and develop those abilities that will give them insight. They keep telling us from the World of Light that all we have to do is ask. Worlds upon worlds upon worlds upon worlds. It is all there. It is all just for the asking. *...deep sigh...*

There was a time in this life, in this personality that is referred to as an ego, I can remember when I had nowhere near the expanded thought I am experiencing now and, of course, I have no doubt that from this point on to another, I will still consider this a limited expanded thought. (*Looking back in 2018—well, that was right.*)

I have a willingness to continue to learn. I want to learn, and it seems knowledge and information is given at the point when one is ready to expand, in a way that one will understand. There is no point, they tell us, in filling a bottle or a glass until it is overflowing and loses all that energy. It seems to be really what we are, like a glass, symbolised by a Holy Grail, and when it is filled with the grape wine of knowledge then we can drink from that—we can be sustained from that.

Grapes seem to be used as the symbol of the vine, the vine that takes its roots here on this Earth and grows with leaves and fruit and from this a nectar can be drawn from it that is linked with the life force. *...deep sigh...*

It reminds me of a time when a psychic friend visited. Chrissie Romano and her husband Edward came to this house and in the evening after dinner we experienced an awareness there was much more going on than we were realising.

Chrissie, being very tuned into the Starpeople, suddenly announced there was a starship above the house and they were beaming columns of light energy down into the house for us to stand under. There just 'happened' to be another friend here, Helen Vincent, and we took turns in standing under these columns of energy.

Speaking from my own experience, under the first *column* I started lifting up as if I was almost going to lift off the ground; it was quite amazing. And then I moved to another one, which seemed to be twisting and turning me in a sort of robot-like way; it was quite a pleasant experience—it seemed to be energising all my joints, I think. I then moved onto another column where my eyes were opening and closing, opening and closing, and it would not stop. It got to a point where I felt a little on edge, but then they told me, for I could hear them speaking, it would just be for a little bit longer and that I would start to see. I assumed they meant clairvoyantly.

At that time, I saw a jewelled wine goblet come towards me (*in my inner scene*) that was filled with grapes and then it seemed to turn into a liquid, and they asked me to drink, which I did. They said Lord Sananda had sent it to me and it was the same cup that had been used at the Last Supper by Jesus. I did not understand quite what that all meant, but I felt a little overwhelmed and it seemed to be like it was the etheric part of what took place here on Earth. (*In 2018, I know now Lord Sananda is the brother of Sanat Kumara—and, of course, that our oversoul is connected to the family of Jesus.)*

I have since been given understanding that there is now a very large, what the starpeople call 'mothership' stationed above this area. It is so big it spreads over the whole of the state or more.

People have become aware of a special healing energy present—nobody has to do anything, it is just there, and if they come worried or upset it pleases us no end to see them go away looking much happier and free of tension.

The mothership they speak of cannot really be seen with third dimensional eyes. It is something that if you tune into, you are aware is there. Even if you do not understand it, there is definitely something happening and influencing and all for peoples' good.

The area itself is a bit of a worry for Telstra. They claim lightning storms rise in this area. I must say we have had some magnificent displays of flashing light at times and quite often without rain, which is a bit of a worry. They (*the lightning storms*) seem to move around in large circles before they move on.

We have also had problems with electronic equipment in the house. If there is something much larger and vast here, the display of power is quite significant. There is apparently a lot of ironstone. There is certainly a lot of sandstone, and when the sun is out there seems to be tiny, tiny crystals glistening everywhere.

I love this area. John and I have never regretted coming here, although at times it has been difficult living here with the lack of services and the distance to travel to shops. ...*deep sigh*...

I am thinking of the lovely energy and how it feels when I visit the Ashram in India in Sai Baba's presence. It is a very special feeling and even though there are thousands coming from all different countries of the world, if you were to speak to only one person, each and every one would have their own personal experience to speak of, which I think is remarkable.

His influence and the power that comes with him is beyond our human understanding. Stories of what his little Leelas (*cosmic plays*) are about are many. I cannot help thinking about the one where he apparently visited an Indian family on his travels in an outer country area of India. He was invited to stay in the house, and where he was accommodated the room was surrounded with brick walls. The bricks were separated slightly so that it created a screen for fresh air or a breeze to come in and keep it cool.

Some of the devotees who were very, very curious thought they would creep along and peep in the little holes in the wall to see if they could really see Sai Baba asleep...and apparently what they saw was no one on the bed, but all his physical limbs piled up on a chair. (*I have to laugh, another one of Sai Baba's Leelas*).

He is said not to need sleep. He has been seen to eat, but it is really for show I think, for he does not seem to need very much. His influence on people is enormous; his abilities and organising abilities are incredible. ...*deep sigh*...

I am not going to talk about those; as I have said before, there has been much written about him and what he does. My way of understanding him seems to come from a different level and different dimension, for even when I was at the Ashram for the second time, at Brindavan, while I was in line in the prayer hall, he actually walked up to me and asked, "Where did you come from?"

Very nervously, I said, "Australia, sir". (*I laugh at myself now.*) Most people call him Bhagavan or Swami.

"Are you with a group?" he said.

"No, I come alone," thinking, *but you called me, Baba. You know I have come alone.*

He said, "Oh", and just walked on. ...*sigh*...

When he was about thirty feet away, I said in my mind, "Baba, could I please have an interview?" With that, he turned around and walked straight back to me and pointed and said, "Go", meaning to the interview room. I nearly fell off the chair.

I was so overwhelmed and so nervous I felt like a little girl. He has this way of reducing everybody to feeling like little children and I am sure he takes your thoughts out of your brain; you feel you cannot think of anything. You are totally incapable of thinking. It is as if you are in another world when you sit in his presence, completely free of any worldly cares.

He says, "Baba just wants you to be happy." Now, after the third visit, he has helped me in so many ways, in unseen ways, that is how I am feeling. Just happy and I thank him for that. ... *deep sigh*...

Note: *Bhagavan means bringer of enlightenment. Swami means spiritual teacher or master.*

Sri Sathya Sai Baba has said, "I am God, come as a man, to take man back to God."

50 18th SITTING

Wednesday 7.9.1994

This day, I am feeling very happy. Sai Baba is with me; I can feel his energy around. Every time I sit with the stone, I light a little candle next to his picture, and as I have said before, I see him in the flame.

There has been talk of a tiny flame, unseen by the physical eye, that exists in the area of the heart. It has been said to have been magnified and photographed. I have not seen this, but I do believe the flame exists. ...*deep sigh*...

To me, it makes sense there is some sort of ignition to spark the motor (*the heart*), to keep the engine (*the body*) and vehicle in running order. ...*deep sigh*...

I believe the Australian Aborigines look upon and treat fire with great respect. They use it to burn off the old to allow the re-growth of new life. The fire burns or is whipped up by the breath of the wind; it also can be blown out by the breath of the wind. (*I wonder if that little unseen spark in the heart is actually being fuelled by the breath and is burning off the old cells, ready for re-growth of the new, until it is finally blown out by the last breath.)*

In the ancient Vedic teachings in the area we know as India, God is seen as three aspects. One is Shiva who is known as a destroyer, one is Brahma who is known as the Creator, and one is Vishnu who is known as the Preserver.

In the Christian teachings, we have the Triune of God: The Father, the Son, and the Holy Ghost, which could also be seen as a generation of the old moving on to make room for a generation of the new, and the Holy Ghost or Holy Spirit could be seen as the breath that is holding all together and giving life to all.

Shiva is symbolic of the Destroyer, which is of the unwanted—or a letting go to make room for Brahma, which is manifesting the new. Vishnu is holding all together.

Just now, I filled a jug with water and arranged flowers. Placing the jug next to Baba's picture, it tipped over with a loud bang and interrupted the flow of my thinking, so I feel a little mixed up here. I will have to have another look, and yet water (which comes from condensation) also can put out the fire or sustain life; it is really just another density of air or the breath.

Earth is where our roots are planted, which can be seen as our personality, this body that we are in on this Earth. The air that we breathe in and out to keep us alive can be seen as Vishnu, or the Holy Spirit or the Holy Ghost. We would not last for many minutes without it. It permeates us and is around us, so we walk in a form of the Holy Ghost, the Holy Spirit. Looking at it that way, I do not find it hard to accept we are all part of God, that we are all God beings.

It is energy—everything is energy—whether it takes form or not.

The air gives readily without any holding back and we take that in. There is never a judgement the breath is only for some and not others—it is all encompassing and, therefore, all loving. It is only when man allows it to be polluted that it sometimes strikes imbalance within us, like a shadow that is cast in front of our light. The light of our hearts. *...deep sigh...*

Sai Baba says he is in everybody's heart and he asks us to look for him in there. He also says, "I am God and you are God, it is just that I know it and you do not." He says he is like a mirror. I had a dream once, just before visiting him in India, when I saw him as a mirror, a magnificent, beautiful mirror all edged in orange and gold, and I understood by this dream that when I looked at him I would be looking in a mirror—anything I saw in that reflection would be of God, and anything that was not of God would be pushed out.

So, it was a little like being in a pressure pot for a while in India, with the various thoughts and emotions coming up and wanting to get out, knowing they had to get out and leave so I could mirror the God energy.

Another time, he showed himself to me in a dream as being like a giant generator here on this Earth, holding the God energy on Earth and spreading it around. The divine light, the divine consciousness, and all those that readily linked with him by thought and feeling were immediately enshrouded with the energy of light with that divine light.

There have been those who have called out to him at a time of need, and he has been there instantly. He seems to operate from a point of 'no time' as we understand it. No time and no distance. He is like the breath that is available to everyone. There is no separation; there is no judgement. It is just there to be taken in and out, in and out, for all time. *...deep sigh...*

I worry a little about what people think and what they will think about this book. The Angel cards tell me to *trust* and I have offered myself with love to Sai Baba, and the World of Light, to be of service and, so, if he has given me an assignment, I am very happy to be able to work with this.

He often tells people not to worry about things and that he will look after it. As a human being, I find it often hard to not worry about certain things. I guess the thing is to take responsibility for one's life and actions, to change what you can change, and to leave what you know that you cannot change, and it is from that point if there is anything worrisome and you know you cannot change anything, then ask Baba or God to look after it for you.

19th SITTING

51

Thursday 8.9.1994

As a medium, I have had many, many experiences, the like of which have been written about by many other mediums. I do not think there is any need to go into aspects of healing or communication with departed ones, or psychometry, that being the ability to tune into the vibration of someone.

I only ever work with healing from the point of tuning into the Angel Maria or the Archangel Michael, so the healing or work is done with permission, for they understand and know someone else's karma far better than I would.

My role seems to be as an instrument—in other words, in a physical body I am (*as is everyone if they ask God)* able to earth (*like a power socket*) divine light and if they, meaning spirits, choose to work with me, from that point healing can be given.

Healing, of course, comes in many different ways. Not all those ways come through me. Healing can be physical healing, emotional healing, spiritual healing, and soul healing. I always feel very blessed if I am chosen and asked to assist in their work.

It reminds me of a time when I was first given an understanding about distant healing. I was awakened from a sleep with a message and asked to write it down (*this was in 1985*) and it said, '*Your little boy will have to go to hospital, do not worry he will be alright.*'

Well, I must say that turned my stomach a little. I worried about that, but I had been working with *Upstairs* for some time and had grown to trust what they said, so I handed it back and decided not to worry.

About a month later, we received a telephone call from Queensland to say that our eighteen-year-old son (*the youngest son*) had a serious accident on a motorbike and had almost been killed by hitting a tree. He ended flat on his back in hospital with a broken spine; two vertebrae were broken and five were cracked, so he was very lucky he was not in a wheelchair for life.

I flew up immediately to see him and all the time I was communicating with White Eagle, who kept reassuring me the boy would be alright and I was not to worry. When people around me were so very kind and concerned saying, "You must be terribly worried and upset", I was in this dual feeling of knowing I should be upset and worried, of course, but in actual fact I wasn't because I knew he was going to be alright.

I tried to explain to my son that he had been divinely protected and asked him to thank God. When I came back home, I was awakened one night and given an image of my son's etheric form and then two hands came out from behind me, which I understand were my hands operating in the fourth dimension, and given strict instructions on how to gently heal and repair the bones and help that body to recover.

It was quite an overwhelming experience, actually.

My son was released from hospital much earlier than the doctors expected and even though a back brace had been ordered for when he was released, it was not needed. So, I also pointed out to my son that he had been given assistance and divine healing.

I have been given quite a lot of understanding about the unseen dimensions, but, of course, I know there is much for me yet to learn. ...*deep sigh*...

As I have said before, it is possible for all people to become a medium. In fact, all people are mediums to some degree, whether they realise it or not. They often follow their intuition, which is their 'inside teaching' and operates for their own good.

They often have feelings of pending trauma coming their way and if they follow their instincts they can, and do, avoid those problems quite often.

Some people are aware when they walk into a room where there have been arguments of unhappiness of some sort, although there is no immediate knowledge or understanding of that. They are actually tuning into energy present in the room.

Businessmen can operate from what they call a 'gut feeling' and have a leaning towards one decision, rather than another, although often it does not make practical sense to do so, and, in hindsight, it is often the best decision. They too are reading the energies.

There are many pictures around of Sai Baba and with that picture goes the energy of what he represents. People can put their hand over the picture and ask him to give them a sign he is there or just tune into what they feel, without pre-empting, and quite often they will have a lovely experience.

It is no coincidence there are so many pictures of Sai Baba, the Avatar, spreading out all over the Earth. *...deep sigh...*

The energy from the moon affects the tides. I do not find it hard to accept the energy from the moon, which, of course, is the light reflected from the sun, and could affect human beings, who are made up of about 70 per cent fluid (water). It would have a pulling and a pushing effect upon people, the same as it does with the tide.

That is our closest extraterrestrial influence upon this Earth. We readily know the sun energy influences us; without it, we would have no warmth except by fire. We would have very little life here on this Earth.

So, I do not find it hard to accept that if we reach out further to other suns and other planets from other galaxies, that too could have some direct or indirect influence on our solar system and, in turn, influence our Earth and us.

52 20th SITTING

9.9.1994

My Goodness, Look at all Those Nines!

I started earlier today, for John and I are making a trip to Sydney. I was sitting alone with the stone and I felt a very strong male-like presence around me. He introduced himself as Alcheringa (the Golden One) and asked my permission to speak through me, to which I agreed.

> *"I am Alcheringa. I am very pleased, my dear, that you are sitting with this stone and working with it, allowing it to help you and guide you. There is much information that will come forth if you will allow it. From this day forth, your knowledge and abilities will increase, I am very happy to be here to announce this for you. I come because you invited me here. I am connected with all sacred sites around this Earth and, in particular, the site known as Uluru. A group intends to travel to Uluru on the 23rd September—I will be there, you can tell them that. I will speak through them and I will speak through the Aborigine elder. So, both parties will be aware of what is taking place. We are very happy with what has been done by your group and in achieving the gathering of the symbols in technicolour, so that they will be placed on the ground. This will be seen by all. I come with great love in my heart."*

When Alcheringa came through to speak, I was holding the stone and felt he had come into my body. I could feel the very male-like powerful energy and I saw myself in spirit sitting in the 'air' above Uluru.

(I have recently been advised by Cosmic Sai Baba that Alcheringa is my twin soul from Andromeda—a twin soul usually operates as a close guide from other worlds—but on occasion, they incarnate together in the same dimensional frequency on Earth.)

53 21st SITTING

Saturday Evening 10.9.1994

Nothing seems to be coming this evening, and yet I know there is more to tell—I am a little tired, but no, I feel if I just relax the story will unfold.

I am inspired by another dear psychic friend, Helen, who comes originally from Austria and I have been working with for many years; she is a very gifted medium and has been given the ability to read the Akasic Records.

She sat with this stone and, although she really has not had any previous understanding about the Australian Aborigine way of perceiving spirit, the stone gave her that understanding. She could not get over the fact that a stone could speak to her and, even though she has been given all those abilities, she also finds it hard to accept the existence of starpeople.

I think there may be many out there who find it hard to accept the existence of starpeople and by that I mean the cosmic consciousness or, as we may understand it, that consciousness where UFOs exist. ...*deep sigh*...

I have quite a number of friends who have psychic abilities and who readily believe and know of the existence of starpeople and the starships. It seems to be an ability that can be given to all; it is just a matter of whether you really want to see other dimensions from that point or not. You could see them as angels if you like.

I remember a time when I was fixing my hair in the bathroom and was about to squeeze some hair gel onto the palm of my hand, when suddenly something happened and an unseen influence re-directed the gel and it squirted onto the bathroom mirror. There was a perfect ET drawn onto the mirror, which really made me laugh.

That night, I was awakened by the musical doorbell ringing. As I jumped out of bed to answer it, I saw an image (*in my mind*) of two astronauts outside the front door holding their large helmets under their arm, but when I opened the door there was nobody in sight. I was very disappointed, and as I climbed back into bed I realised that we do not even have a front doorbell.

The next day, we had a meeting of about twenty-two people and two separate energies presented themselves through different mediums, myself being one of them and Trudie Moore the other. They said they were commanders from starships and gave opportunity to answer anybody's questions. The feeling was one of enlightenment and love.

There have been some mediums visit Australia from overseas and publicly 'channel' energies that say they are communicating from other worlds, from other galaxies. They allowed themselves to be interviewed by the media and I was quite embarrassed at the way some of the Australian journalists were speaking and behaving to those people. Some even got quite angry. It is quite amazing the reactions that channelling can cause in some people.

I am only suggesting people ask themselves why they react. It is true it is a bit hard to accept a male-sounding voice come through a female and behave and act in quite an extraordinary way—very different from the way the person would act normally. But they tell us from *Upstairs* that it is 'theatre' and they want to show the existence of spirit. In this way, they present themselves in the hope that people will at least think about the possibility of spirit, of life in another form other than just a physical form and then, of course, to listen to the words that are spoken (*channelled)* and to use discernment as to what they have to say.

When they are speaking from the point of God, in my experience they have always been very kind, very gentle, very polite, and very loving and compassionate, and they never say people *HAVE* to do something.

Over the years, I have also been given many dreams to help me. I often find spirit leads me to a book they seem to be suggesting I read, and one was a book called *Dream Book: Symbols of Understanding* by Betty Bethard. I found this most useful in helping to understand what the dream was about and also if a particular object caught my eye, like a feather that just happened to be on the front doorstep, or other 'like' messages. I have been able to come to an understanding by reading that book.

Also, I've always found it helpful to look up words in the Oxford Concise Dictionary (*Australian edition*) and somehow, one word would lead to another and then another and then another and I would find I was being given understanding that way.

When I was first prompted to read the dictionary that way, the dictionary happened to be on my desk and it fell to the floor. As I picked it up, the word *Alcheringa* jumped out of the page at me, and from then on to other words; I have used the dictionary quite a lot, and I must say it has taught me a great deal.

Sometimes, I have been thinking about a subject and idly switched on the television, and there in front of me was a program all about the very thing I had just been wondering about. So, if sometimes I do seem to be a little vague and wandering around in a sort of dream-like state, I know spirit has a hand in that and I laugh at myself.

John quite often says I am up with the fairies. It is hard, at times, to keep both feet on the ground, but this is what we are meant to do, of course, while we are here on Earth. So, I am constantly reminding myself to keep both feet firmly on the ground.

I was at a meeting once and there was a medium who started singing, channelling the Archangel Gabriel. I felt myself floating off into that dimension, but then when she finished, I could not quite get back into my body. It was a little frightening actually, but I was assisted to a room to lie down and a couple of very kind ladies worked on me with healing and rubbing my feet; I was aware of what was happening, but I was having trouble getting back into my body.

After a while, I felt more together and when I opened up my eyes the first thing I saw was a very large picture of Sai Baba who seemed to be grinning at me and saying, "*Aha, gotcha*!"

After that experience, I seemed able to operate in a more grounded way. There are many things about us we do not totally understand, but they tell us that we are never alone—and I mean this for everybody on Earth—and that there are always people from other dimensions around us, helping and guiding us.

If you tune in to those energies, you can work with them in a much closer and more communicative way. Every time you feel that something has stroked your hair or touched your cheek or brushed your hand, do not ignore it; be aware. If a thought comes into your mind quite unexpectedly, listen; do not brush it off.

The choice is always yours, of course, as to whether you follow any suggestions or not, but that is what is meant by guidance.

54 22nd SITTING

Sunday 11.9.1994

I am sitting once again with the beautiful stone, with a wonderful loving, gentle, and healing feeling about it.

I am rather pleased today. I had a telephone call from a friend talking about who would be going to Uluru to help lay those symbols, and to pray and meditate out there. Through a series of events that happened within half an hour, John has said I should go, and so now I will be joining them at Uluru.

I did not really think I would be going, but it seems to have been taken out of my hands.

Alcheringa came through the other night while I was sitting with the stone (*I was here alone*) and he spoke through me in a very deep voice (*a different sound from other energies that have come through)*. It was a pleasant experience and I think somehow, he and Sai Baba are behind my making this trip.

In working with the starpeople, I have found quite often situations are organised for me and it is actually a lovely experience knowing that everything has been taken care of. So, I will look forward to being part of the group who are going to Uluru on the 21st to 23rd September 1994. I am sure much more will happen than we expect, but as they have already told us from the World of Light, we should not pre-empt—so I am readying myself for service.

23rd SITTING

55

Monday 12.9.1994

I have been getting the feeling that I need to sit with the stone from now until it is time to go to Uluru, and that there will not be any words coming until after that trip.

ALCHERINGA SPEAKS

"Thank you, my dear, thank you for inviting me here. It is Alcheringa and I am very pleased to be here. I am glad for the opportunity to talk to you. I am very pleased that you are coming to Uluru. It is part of your destiny, my dear—things will eventuate, and you will understand more after your visit.

Just allow yourself to be guided and all will be taken care of. You do not have to worry, and tell the group they do not have to worry. Events will fall into place as they are meant to do.

Now that we know of your willingness shown by your attendance at Uluru, we can make things happen so that the Greater Plan can be evolved. The symbols will trigger memories within people—within their cellular memory.

I have been playing with different energies to find the right one that I would like to communicate with you and through you. I hope you do not mind this, Valerie?"

"Oh no, not at all," I said.

"Thank you, my dear, you will be my mouthpiece. Sometimes I will speak through others, but through you the energy will be obvious. Is this all right with you, my dear?"

"Yes," I said telepathically.

"Just allow yourself to receive the messages, and as I have said all will be taken care of. You ask if English is my natural tongue or way of communicating and I will say it is not. I communicate with others by telepathy. Speaking through a voice box, it appears to be different. I am rather enjoying this,"

I laughed.

"You do not mind if I speak through you, Valérie?"

"No, not at all," I said. "I welcome that."

"Thank you, my dear. Thank you and God bless you."

I was a little overwhelmed after he left; he was so different-sounding and so separate from me, and yet I was also able to speak the way I do when I am talking. On the tape, it sounds like a conversation going on between two people, which of course it was, but they were both using the same body, the same voice box. He has since come through again, practicing more with exaggerated sounds; it sounded so funny. I enjoyed the whole experience; it was one of fun.

I have been sitting with the stone for the following few days, waiting for more of the story to come, but my feeling is that I am virtually on hold until after my visit to Uluru.

One day, as I sat, I was reminded I can readily see the Wandjinan, or what we would call the alien who has the pear-shaped face, very large eyes, and can be up to three to four feet tall, or seven to eight feet tall, depending on where they are from.

I asked if Sanat Kumara looked this way and I was told that he comes from a dimension that is much, much finer in vibration—in fact, the light is so strong I would not be able to physically see him, even in my inner scene. I expect this actually applies for all the Council of Light. ...*sigh*...

But I am being given the understanding that after my visit to Uluru, my perception in the true sense will be raised to a vibration where I will be able to see them, and this is part of what the ascension process is about. It actually is a raising, not only of consciousness, but of perception, or perceiving or seeing if you like to put it that way. If I tried to look at them before I was ready, and this applies to many, it would cause great pain to my eyes, and in fact, would damage the eyes, both the inner and the outer eye. This is why it has been so difficult for the beings of light to present themselves in their truest form.

I have already had an experience when I focused on a symbol (*from those symbols that have been newly released on Earth and are those we are taking to Uluru)*. In focusing on that particular symbol without any conscious effort, I suddenly found myself flying down a time tunnel (*in my inner scene*) taking me back to my original base, that of the light being that I am. I was given memories as I would have been as just a child light being, but I was amazed at the reality that was there. It was like I was in a different dimension, but I could see it all so clearly, every detail, as if I was standing here with my eyes open—it's very hard to explain.

It was different though and I was aware that I was in a different world, a different dimension. When I came back, I came flying backwards down the time tunnel and I had a feeling it was like a twenty million-year difference and, in fact it was. It was quite an extraordinary experience. When I arrived back in this dimension, I was given the understanding more would be given and I would eventually come to a point where I would have full memory as a light being, but operating as a human being, in a physical dimension. (*Good heavens!*)

So, it was almost like an ascension back to front. (*Laughs.*) It is, yes, something to really look forward to, for at the moment this has not taken place, although I know it is very, very close.

I am to do nothing; all will be taken care of.

This is just a note: I am being given to understand the ability to be able to see in the truest form—the seventh, eighth, and ninth dimensions—is what they are speaking of. Anything after that would be far beyond our physical forbearance. ...*deep sigh*... Now, twenty-five years later in 2019, I am channelling Andromeda Val, who I am told is 6,000 years ahead of me—my future self. She appeared in a hologram three years ago beside my bed, standing seven feet tall and looking very human. I was wide awake.... It would seem I am back from the future. And melding more with my descendent very quickly. *Good heavens again!*

24th SITTING 56

Friday 16.9.1994

I have been told that Alcheringa would like to speak, so I am sitting here with the stone and I am surrounded with a blue/white opalescent light and have invited Alcheringa to speak.

"I am Alcheringa and I am very pleased to be here—thank you for inviting me."

I replied, "You are welcome, Alcheringa—do you come for a reason today?"

"I come merely to practice with your voice box, if that is alright, my dear. I have still not sorted out the way I wish to present myself." (I laughed.) *"So, if you do not mind, I will practice with the energies...*

"I am looking forward to meeting with your group at Uluru, which is where I reside." (I laughed again.)

"I do not think I like the way I am presenting myself today so I think I will go back to the other way." (I am still laughing. He was playing with the sounds in a most exaggerated way!)

"Do not laugh at me child, it is difficult."

I said, "I am sorry, Alcheringa."

"I laugh with you, my child, I laugh at myself. It would be good if everybody could laugh at themselves." (Laughs.)

"I love you, child, you do not really understand our connection—we are very close. I will explain it to you at another time, but for the moment I would like to just

practice for when we meet again at Uluru. After that visit, you will understand much. All of you will understand much." ...deep sigh...

(I spoke to him telepathically.)

"Do not rush me, my child. There is no need for apologies. In communication, understanding is required, and this is what I am aiming for. I do not want misunderstanding. It is easier in telepathy.

"Telepathy is energy that is sent back and forth, but, with it, understanding is readily felt if I can put it that way. Unfortunately, with words that come through the voice box and out of the mouth, understanding is not always readily received. So, I need to work on this, so that communication can take place with understanding. I would encourage questions so that misunderstanding could be resolved.

"I need to choose from my experiments in speaking through you as to which way I wish to communicate. I have a backlog of experience and I will review that and then decide how I wish to communicate.

"I thank you, my dear, in allowing me to experiment with you. You are not afraid, are you?"

I said, "No, not at all."

"You worry about seeing and whether you will be afraid when we meet actually face to face, do you not?"

"Yes, I do, I have to be honest," *I said.*

"You do not have to worry—you will know us, you will feel us, the energy will be readily recognised, so you do not have to worry, my dear."

I said, "Thank you, Alcheringa. Should I be pronouncing your name as Al Ka Ringa or Al Cha Ringa?"

"Al Cha Ringa is the way to pronounce it, I think. I say, I think, because I am still getting used to speaking through a voice box." (I laughed.)

"I will leave now, my dear, I thank you for this little session. I am always at your service, my beloved child."

I felt so happy after that, I was laughing all the time, and I look forward to working with Alcheringa more and more.

I asked Sai Baba (*mentally*) to waggle the flame on the candle I always light at his photograph if he was listening to the above, and the flame went wild with its waggling and flaring up, and I said, "Baba, would you make it stop, this could be a coincidence."

It immediately stopped. I laughed. I find sometimes I just keep shaking my head, it is almost too much.

57 25th SITTING

Tuesday 20.9.1994

The day before I leave for Uluru, I have a feeling Sai Baba wishes to give me a message. I felt prompted to take a whole lot of his photographs. Although I thought I only had two left, when I looked again, I found quite a handful and I am sure they had just been manifested. (*Laughs.*) It is wonderful.

I have been prompted to get a few videos about 'outer space' and contact with extraterrestrials that are presented on film. I have purposefully chosen ones that are not frightening because even though I have been working with the light beings for so long, and I have seen images in my mind, it is a very different experience to actually meeting them face to face in a physical way. So, I have been prompted to prepare myself for a meeting to take place and I will look forward to this. I am consciously schooling my mind not to react and not to be afraid or get excited. One way or the other, I am in mixed emotions about the whole thing.

Other people going to Uluru seemed to be having their plans change hither and thither, and there seems to be something going on. It is almost like people are being put in a tumbler and shaken and the ones who fall out are the ones who are meant to go. However, even though some have their plans fall down around their ears, so to speak, they seem to still be able to make alternative arrangements, which I get the feeling is what *Upstairs* want anyhow. So now, instead of just Helen and I going on this plane trip tomorrow, there will be another four or five, I think, which is great. Others have gone by car or bus.

The difficulties getting out there with bookings is because it is right in the peak of school holidays. Apparently, the resort is completely booked out, but somehow places are being found for those that obviously the starpeople want to be there. There is a certain amount of testing going on, whether people are really intent on going for the right reasons. The ones feeling strongly are moved to go and feel they have to be there.

I have been getting the feeling something very special will happen and have had feedback from others that something very special is to take place for all of us.

I keep wanting not to talk this way, because *Upstairs* are always telling us not to preempt, but I am getting a strong feeling and I think, perhaps, they want me to speak of it—the Event...

> *"The Event—my voice began to change here...Yes, that is what it is. An Event that will become worldwide in its happening; in other words, all the world will hear of it. It will lead on to other experiences similar, all around the Earth, but at Uluru it will be like a door opening and it will be an en-masse appearance of starships, so that all at Uluru will experience the presence of extraterrestrials." ...deep sigh...*
>
> *"It will be a short visit, but it will be one that will leave no doubt in anybody's mind. You will be our mouthpiece, my dear. We do not intend to land and no, you will not be taken on board. There will be much communication take place and much understanding will come to the black man and the white man.*
>
> *"This information will be shared between you. This will help to bond the two races. It is Alcheringa speaking."*
>
> "I had a feeling, Alcheringa, that some of us may be taken on board the starship, is that right?"
>
> *"For some, such as yourself, you will be taken on to the starship in the Astral body. You will be given memory, so that you will remember all that takes place." ...deep sigh...*
>
> *"You are not imagining this, my child. I am here and I am speaking to you. Do you not feel the presence?"*
>
> "Yes, I do, thank you."

"It would help you, I think, if you do not speak, but rather communicate with me telepathically. I will repeat the question, so that it will go on your transcript. You may tell the others if you like, it is up to you.

"You feel that you have been misled at times by us even though we have not exactly deceived you, this is so. But we are always testing to make sure the choice is the one that you have really made at a deeper level. So, if you wish to wholeheartedly come upon the starship, you are very welcome and we would welcome you with our arms open. I hope you will take up this offer. So, I am asking you, my child, if you wish to come on board the ship if you are ready to see all as it really is?"

"Yes."

"That is good, my child, that is good. We were hoping for this because this is how we wish to present ourselves as we really are.

"You and the other members of the group will be forerunners in speaking of the experience and to, shall we say, pass on the message. You are messengers, you are messengers of the spirit, the Holy Spirit, because we come from the voice of God. Do you believe this, my child?"

"Yes."

"That is good, that is good. Then there is no reason to fear, and tell the others that there is no reason to fear.

"You ask if you have to worry about wearing particular garments and I would say, no, you would be prompted when the time is right. We influence you all more than you realise, so do not worry about anything. You have committed yourself in service and so we take up this offer in service and use you well. Do not fear, my child, tell the others not to fear or to expect, just allow it to flow.

"Try to leave yourself open and allow the imagination to be still. Remember, imagination is the nation of image. That also can go off on a little track of its own. So, I ask

> *with great love in my heart that you allow yourselves to be guided and to receive the image of reality. Thank you, my child, it is Alcheringa, and I am very pleased to have communicated through you. Adonai and I look forward to seeing you at Uluru."*

I tested the voice recorder after the channelling took place and when the energy of Alcheringa had left, the sound was totally different.

58 26th SITTING

27.9.1994

Today is the day after I returned from our visit to Uluru. I am sitting here with the stone for further installments for the book.

They (meaning *Upstairs*) stopped me working for a while before I left, giving me the impression I would have more to say when I came back, which of course, I do, and I have more understanding as well. It is a little hard to know where to start because much of what we experienced was in the Dreamtime (*fourth dimension*) and yet it has filtered through into the third dimension and that also had to be dealt with.

In the overview, I can see that we as light workers are helping to break through the barriers of misunderstanding between the black man and the white man. We as light workers have been given understanding along our soul journey, and along its path we have come to understand spirit. We would not suggest we have all the answers, far from it. The black man has similar understanding. In fact, it seems to be the same; it is just that they have different names for the energies and I would readily say they have more psychic ability.

One morning when we were sitting at the base of Uluru as the sun came up, a beautiful Golden Dawn, Alcheringa made his presence known and said he wished to speak. It is very unfortunate it was not recorded, but basically, we had been getting feelings and a general questioning of the origin of the rock itself, known as Uluru. (*No mobile phones then.)*

Alcheringa told us Uluru was an asteroid that hit the Earth a long time ago. He seemed to want us to understand that there was a connection—a link—to the event of another asteroid that hit the Earth at the time, known as 'The Fall of Atlantis'.

This was of a time when all the land masses on this Earth were joined together as one and there was a bridge of land that stretched across the Atlantic Ocean, joining all those lands. Plato spoke of the existence of a civilisation, an advanced culture called Atlantis, and *they* confirm from above that it did exist.

There were scientists at the time, there was airship travel, there was crystal technology, laser technology, and there was certainly a great understanding of the power of creation—manifestation. The time of the fall of Atlantis and the reasons that it took place is described vividly by St Germain in a book *Earth, Birth, Changes* that was channelled by Azena.

When that asteroid hit Mother Earth, I am given images that it completely winded her. It was so large and so big, she caved in. It knocked her slightly off axis, about two degrees I believe, and sent a great belching from inside of her out through every volcano that existed on the Earth. So much magma and volcanic ash was thrown forth that it completely blotted out the sun over most of the Earth. The Earth's foliage and waters were different before she was struck.

The Earth, Mother Earth, was completely in shock and in total disarray. What we understand to be continental drifts were actually land masses that separated on their tectonic plates and were wrenched apart at that time. The seas broiled and rose, flooding into areas not touched by the sea before. It was at a time when the lands became separate. They moved like ships in the water, with all upon it into another place on the Earth.

It gives understanding to many things that science, or geologists, have put in the, shall we say, the too-hard basket.

There are, for instance, apparently rock masses on land now known as Australia that are the same as the land rock in the Himalayas in India. That is only a tip of the iceberg.

The massive asteroid that hit the Earth then apparently went down into the sea, but trailing behind were lesser asteroids, a little like what was recently coined or named a 'string of pearls' that were on their way to crash into the planet Jupiter.

It is said there are no coincidences and it was like a co-ordination of events mirroring what happened at the time of the fall of Atlantis here on Earth.

Because the sun was blotted out by volcanic ash, there were apparently thousands of years of ice age all around the Earth. As the Earth finally recovered from this massive belting she received, the ash started to clear and she started to receive the warmth of the sun's rays once again. It was like the dawning of a New Age.

There was created all over this Earth a massive flood caused by the ice melting and heavy rain. In the land now known as Australia, the great crater filled with water and silt. Scientists speak of it as an Artesian Basin or an inland sea, which it was. Because of the climate changes, caused by the shift in axis, it became extremely hot and water evaporated and left just the sand or silt, although that table of water is still below the surface and bores can be put down into it.

The existence of a Great Flood is written into ancient writings, such as the Bible, and it is also written into the Australian Aborigine mythology and I have no doubt has been recorded in many other ancient scripts or mythology.

Alcheringa told us that morning Uluru was an asteroid, but because his message was not recorded I can only vaguely remember what else was said and the others present cannot tell me either. I have been given images though and impressions, and it would seem the area was very much affected by the blast received from the asteroid that hit the Earth later, at the time that Atlantis was destroyed. It was as if he wanted the information held back for a while until more understanding was given.

We wondered if geologists had not thought of this before, that Uluru was actually an asteroid, so we looked for signs while we were there. There was no mention in the tourist brochures.

It made sense the rock, or what looked like a rock, had come from outer space and smacked into the surface of the Earth and, as it did, buried itself. Usually when a meteorite hits the Earth there is a great Crater left, but if the Earth was then thrown into thousands of years of ice and, later, as it thawed and became water, it would have carried silt to fill that crater. Geologists speak of the existence of an inland sea in the centre of Australia.

We visited the Olgas, or Kata Tjuta as it has been named by the Aborigine people, which is a massive conglomerate looking like a river bed, but stacked very high (*and since hardened into rock formation*), and had the feeling that as the asteroid Uluru came in and hit the surface, it displaced Earth and pushed it up like sand castles ahead of it, ahead of Uluru.

When you look from the air, in our so called airship (*airplane*), you can see where the whole of Australia is pretty well desert and see waves of what is now rock, but it does give the impression at some other time there was movement, a flowing away from the centre where the rock hit.

With the great heat that would have come with those asteroids, it would have been like atom bombs blasting off and the light would have been momentarily stronger than our sun. The asteroid would have been burning fire as it hit our atmosphere and then plunged into a long period of extreme cold, and in so doing it would have 'tempered' the rock so that Uluru, being partly of Feldspar, would have been honed so it became like a semi-precious crystal.

The outside of the rock, where it is exposed to the wind and rain, the rock exfoliates—or as some say, it is like it is rusting and there is an oxidisation that takes place within our atmosphere. There again, that seemed to show us the rock does not belong to this Earth and has not evolved on this Earth from the beginning, otherwise it would be the same as many other rocks on this Earth.

When we ran our hands over the rock in protected areas, it was a grey colour, not red and very smooth. It had a silky feeling. I know that is a strange thing to say. If there had been any radiation with that rock when it first hit the Earth, most of it would have been washed away in the years of ice and floods that took place afterwards.

Uluru does have a great energy—you can feel it and it is always a problem if the weather is hot, because the rock itself gets very hot and expands. It is really not safe to walk on or be near as the radiance from it is so powerful.

Uluru would have come into our atmosphere as a ball of fire. Landing in water, the feldspar would have been fired like glass. Uluru has flecks through it of (semi-precious) crystal or what looks like crystal, or mica, to the layman, and this explains why, depending where the sun is and what time of the year it is, the rock glows in various colours. It is quite wonderful the way it catches the light.

This energy is given off to touch Kata Tjuta (the Olgas) and affects that area also, because it is in direct alignment with Uluru.

After the understanding was given to us Uluru is not of Earth, I realised that six months earlier we had been given this information symbolically, although at that time we did not understand the significance.

A few of us who work with the Council of Light, from the World of Light, meet once a month in Sydney, but on this occasion we met here on this property. We lit a large candle and settled down to meditate, when Alcheringa (*he said he was also known as Zoser)* made his presence known for the first time through two of the mediums present (*not me*)—Brian Terrill and Rosemary Whitfield. He spoke of his unseen residence (*his temple*) at Uluru and that it was like the heart centre of the nation, or of Earth.

Alcheringa said then that the, "*Dead centre of Australia is the burnt centre, with the marrying up of the Father (from the stars) and the Mother (Earth) energies, the country, the son (sun) has been born and the son (sun) energies have been released from the heart of the nation, which is Uluru. All work must be done from the heart, all feeling is done from the connection to the heart. Nothing can be done but by through the heart. The heart that is made manifest in this world that is connected to the heart of all that is.*"

All the time, these messages were coming through the mediums, the candle had caught fire and was burning with leaping flames, although we were not in any danger. We watched the candlewax run over the saucer it was standing in and flow onto the glass tabletop, forming eventually into a shape that looked at first like Kata Tjuta and then on to look like Uluru.

We were amazed at the time, but I see now it was symbolising the burning of the rock coming into our atmosphere and landing on the Earth as a great fire ball, into water and after the tempering, it would have been like a phoenix rising from the ashes, the energy of which was transformed into a sun, a rainbow serpent of permanent light.

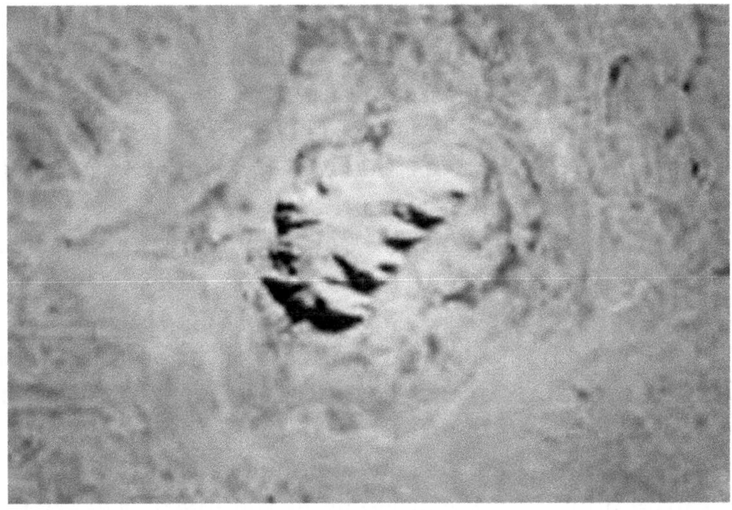

Uluru from Outter Space

I have been prompted to contact a geologist friend to see if there is a scientific possibility to accept that Uluru is an asteroid.

59 27th SITTING

Thursday 27.9.1994

I am sitting here with the sacred stone. I have just read a book about the Australian Aborigine culture, and it speaks of Alcheringa and of Tjuringa, the sacred stone, and how the stone is used to connect and emphasise the God energy. Exactly as I have been led to use this stone without really understanding, the Aborigines understand it very well.

After reading the book *Understanding Aboriginal Culture* by Cyril Havecker, which I happened to find in a shop at the Yulara Resort next to Uluru, I have come to realise their understanding is exactly the same as I (*and other light workers*) have been led to understand spirit; it is just that they have different names for different energies of different spirits.

For instance, they call the universal intelligence Baiame, whereas I would refer to it as God or God energy. The Hindu would call it Prahna, the Holy Breath, the Chinese call it Chi, and, as I understand, the Ancient Egyptians call it Ka. It shows the influence from the starpeople, as they have already told us, has always been there.

All religions that have been taught on this Earth have come from inspiration of the starpeople in the first place. There is One God—and only One God. All other aspects of it lead back to the same One God. It is futile arguing and fighting over it. ... *deep sigh...*

In this book, it speaks of a time 10,000 years ago when there was a Great Flood in the Aboriginal Dreamtime stories, and apparently the writer of this knowledge has had permission from the elders to speak of it. In fact, they welcomed it because they had difficulty in communicating with the white man, but they knew it was time for knowledge to be shared. And I am very glad it was shared, because I can see there is no difference at all, not basically anyhow.

At the time of the Great Flood, the original peoples cried out to Baiame (*or God)* and asked for help. A great spirit came, known as Alcheringa. He presented himself to them in the form of a black man—remember the God beings can take on any garment or form they wish and so there would be no fear among the tribal people he presented himself as a black man to look the same as them.

He then taught them a ceremony using a Bullroarer to create sound, which would draw in all the good spirits and send away all the bad spirits in the Dreamtime or the fourth dimension because there is also a duality in that dimension.

He then showed them how to perform a ceremony bringing in the Rainbow Serpent energy to help balance the energy points that are on this Earth. That was their first initiation. The original peoples, the Aborigine people, have been the Earth Minders ever since, both in the third dimension and the fourth dimension. (Uluru means rainbow serpent.)

Alcheringa speaks of them as the Cherished Ones, for they have performed their duty unswervingly for thousands of years to help maintain a balance of energies on this Earth.

I have been given an image of the energies working in and out of the earth and coming to the surface at various points, much the same way as a physical body. The Chinese teach that the physical body also has energy lines throughout the body and cross at various points, creating an energy connection, which they use as acupuncture points.

A similar pattern seems to exist within the Earth, and it is these energy lines that the Australian Aborigines, in particular, the elders, and medicine men, have been working with and looking after so well.

It has been said the area at Uluru is the heart centre of the Earth, which is a raised vibration of what looks a bit like the solar plexus—if you think of a human being and their solar plexus being like a central nervous system radiating out like a sun, to connect with all other points within the physical body, the same happens apparently from the centre of Australia with the energy points radiating out to connect with all other (*acupuncture or vortex*) points around the Earth.

There is much we could learn from the Australian Aboriginal elders in psychic matters and ways to nurture and take care of Mother Earth.

Our journey to Uluru was prompted by the starpeople to hopefully assist the Australian Aborigine at this time. The very special time was the Spring Equinox and it also aligned with Venus, the moon, and sun. It was a time of great power and a time leading into Libra, which I do not totally understand, but it was one of balance, a balance of energies that are both male and female energies within this Earth.

The energies at Uluru are very male and powerful and the energies at Kata Tjuta gentle and female feeling. The work was to connect those and set an energy in motion to pulse through the existing grid within Mother Earth.

The energies move clockwise and anti-clockwise and the two can be drawn together to join and become one rod of energy, like a generator to bring balance onto this Earth. This is what happens when each vortex or energy point is worked upon around the Earth.

We had written to the Aborigine elders at Uluru National Park, asking if we could come to work with these energy points along with them, and we also sent letters to the park manager and rangers who work very closely with the elders.

The power of Uluru is very strong; people are drawn there without realising or understanding or knowing. It is actually like a pilgrimage, although they may not readily be aware of it and they go away touched by it.

Many climb the rock. The Aborigines would prefer them not to; they see it as a sacred rock and only ever climb it on very special ceremonial occasions.

We did not feel drawn to climb the rock as we respected the sacredness of it, and after Alcheringa came through that morning at the base of the rock and told us it was from the stars, it seemed to give more understanding why the energy was so powerful and so different. It had actually brought in universal intelligence and power with it.

Strange how the rock (Uluru) is like a giant version of a stone with the same influence as the stone I am sitting with now, both coming from the stars.

Through a mis-sequence of events, we did not receive a reply from the elders as to whether we could enter the park as a group to meditate and assumed it was alright to go ahead and do our work. Some of the group wanted to go one way and some another. But in a comedy of events, we all found ourselves gathered at the same place. So quite obviously the starpeople wanted us to be all in one place and they put us together despite ourselves. I love it when they take over like that. (*I laughed.*) They tell us that we are influenced more than we realise.

I found myself standing on a point where I was no longer a human being. I seemed to become an instrument and I felt energy coming in to us from thousands all around Australia, maybe even overseas, that seemed to be tuning in at the same time. The starpeople can then draw upon all the energies of like-minded people and focus it, as we did in using the energies at that point between Uluru and Kata Tjuta. It was like bringing in both male and female energies together (*clockwise and anti-clockwise energies)* and they were pumped into the Earth in a very steady, mechanical-like way. It was as if the energy was spreading out in circles, like if you throw a stone into a pond and you see the ripples going out further and further and this is what was happening within Mother Earth well beneath her surface, pulsating out further to other points right around the Earth.

We were stopped by rangers at one point and told that the elders had refused permission and we were asked to leave the National Park or not to come back as a group.

We were a little upset about this, but the next morning two of us made an appointment with the park manager and apologised, for we had not received any notice the elders were unhappy about our being there. We told of our regret that we may have offended them in any way and we have since sent a letter to affirm this.

Somehow, it seemed like it was all meant to be that way, because it is understandable the Australian Aborigine should be so suspicious of the white man, and this little foray has perhaps given an opportunity to break down some barriers and hopefully open new doors of understanding and trust.

We were taken by a very special man we met who had worked with the Australian Aborigines for fifteen years but was a light worker like us; he also was a park ranger. He had a way about him that could have almost been Aborigine. He took us to a place outside the National Park, where we were able to sit and meditate and still view Uluru and Kata Tjuta. He led the group up the hill, playing the didgeridoo, a wonderful haunting sound that helps to call in the spirits.

When we sat on the hill, we found ourselves listening to an energy speaking through this man welcoming us, in the name of the peoples of the land and the spirit of the land, accepting our presence and then walking (*or almost slithering*) around touching our head, each and every one of us, and we experienced the energy of the rainbow serpent. It was as if we were replaying the original initiation that had taken place on this Earth 10,000 years ago.

Just before this initiation, I experienced a private initiation of my own. When we all first sat down on the red sand, I had been uncomfortable because there was a small prickly salt bush between my legs. I didn't move my legs because I did not want to disturb the beautiful silence that had descended upon us.

Then, I saw, in my mind's eye, a giant black form take three huge steps from Uluru towards us and bellow in my inner ear, "White woman, white woman, close up your legs," and then go into gales of laughter as only a giantess can. I ignored what she said, wondering what on earth was going on. Then the Giantess again spoke, "White woman, white woman, close up your legs," and again this was followed by loud gales of laughter. This time, I knew there were other black spirit women laughing with her. So, I moved myself as best I could and sat with my legs closed together.

The Giantess asked me to take off my sandshoes and socks and to come with her. So, I did (*in my mind's eye and in spirit form*). In a flash, I realised I was at mutitjulu springs (popularly called **mutitjulu waterhole**—the water spring is tucked into a corner at the base of Uluru) and the black Giantess asked me to walk into the water. It was an initiation and I followed her instructions. Afterwards, I could see myself putting my sand-shoes back on, then suddenly I was back on the red sandy hill with everyone.

That was when the ranger, as a medium, had taken on the rainbow serpent energy. I guess I wouldn't have received the serpent energy as well unless my body was together like a serpent. The whole experience was extraordinary, to say the least. When I related my story to the ranger, he said, "The Koorie know the black Giantess well, her name is *Goolagaia*. She is said to travel with the sun when it hits Woollumbin—Mount Warning, her resting place, first thing in the morning, on the east coast of Australia and in the day travels to Uluru."

After that, many of us had experiences where we were readily smiled at and spoken to by the Aborigines as if we had been accepted. We have yet to meet with the elders in the third dimension in a formal way.

We had all been prompted to think the starships may make themselves visible or that we may even be visited by them, but they chose to remain hidden although we were very aware they were around. In fact, three weeks before we arrived, there had been a couple of ships sighted and there 'happened' to be an ABC television crew present who were able to capture the event on film, which I believe was screened around the world.

The starpeople tell us they wish to make their presence on Earth known and will show themselves, their starships en masse, and that they wish to also show themselves as they really are, without illusion. So, while we were there, we were encouraged to see ourselves as aliens, to be aliens, and it seemed to help to break down any fear if we had been confronted by any of them looking so different to us.

I personally made a great breakthrough while I was away when I saw myself once again amongst the Venusians, which I will describe.

Now that I have accepted the reality, rather than the illusion I am actually more ready to accept information they want to give me.

I can even feel myself as I am on Venus. There is a blue/white opalescent light that pervades there; it has a goldness to it, which makes everything sparkle and glow, exactly the same as I was seeing through my new sunglasses when I was at Uluru—the new glasses I have been prompted to buy that made me look like an alien. (*I laughed.*) In fact, the eyes of the Venusians are shaped in much of a similar way.

I feel a great gracefulness in movement, a great fluidity; there is no heaviness as we feel in our physical body. There is very much a flowing, but there is a reality there of a realness. The fingers are very long and slender, as are the feet. The limbs are moveable, exactly the same as ours. There is a torso and a head, all very slim and tall, very gracious to look at. There is a beauty because of the glowing of the light. They do eat, they do rest, and they do drink but not as often as we do in this physical world on Earth.

Sustenance is rather made up of gold light that is directly available, or colour of various energies depending on what one feels or on what energy one needs to strengthen oneself. Food or drink is chosen from that point. It energises the body, the light body and it comes directly from the Holy Grail, which is the Giver of all Life, the fountain of life, which is the monad the centre of all universes. It is partaken regularly so that every thought, every action, and every deed is filtered with that God energy.

The face or the head is slightly elongated; I could say egg-shaped, but that is not quite right. The eyes being the dominant feature on the head, there is no hair. The skin is a bluish white, very clear, but very definite, very real, and it embodies the personality that each God being is. There is ready recognition between everyone. They can dress themselves in different garments just so they can have a little game if they like or be ready for a ceremony or an event.

They are usually clothed in some sort of raiment. Remember they are Creators and are quite capable of creating another being—which they do, and so families are formed. The sexual act is not quite the same as is performed here in this dimension, but there is a concentration and a desire for the little being to be manifested with a 'blueprint' of the personality and the role to play and its destiny, not unlike the little earthlings that are born here on to the physical Earth. It is just that they do not have a body made up of Earth chemistry.

The beings on Venus have great love and concern for each other. They are very ready to communicate with each other, but there is a politeness that exists among all. They do not rush into another's environment, but rather ask permission first.

Because there is a certain amount of eating and drinking that is taken through the mouth and nose if you like, there are apertures, but they are not developed as much as in the physical body of the Earthly being. There is no need for teeth or a jaw.

There is great love. The energy of God is one of love and they look upon one another as a human would look at a baby. They would gently move their head to the side and there would be a gentle glow come over their countenance when they look at the dear little one. This is really how the people on Venus are all the time.

They have that same feeling of warmth and of love and caring and politeness to each other all the time and also to others.

They are of God—they are at one with God.

Their surroundings are very beautiful. There are gardens and water, air similar to that on Earth, just of a different vibration. I am being given an image as if it is like a scene from the film *The Wizard of Oz* when the gentle Lion man, the Tin man, the Straw man, and the young girl walked down a golden path and where in this land that seemed like a fairyland, in fact it is real in another dimension. That story had, of course, been inspired from the light beings on this Earth.

It is strange, I thought, that when I regained the memory of Venus, that I would feel I could not stay here any longer, but in actual fact the opposite has happened. I feel calmer, more at peace, and more patient somehow and I think more ready to accept.

60 28th SITTING

Love is God, God is Love Live in Love,

This is the Way to God

– Baba

Sunday 2.10.1994

I am sitting with the stone and I have been prompted to read 'Revelations' in *The Bible*. It is a little hard to follow at times, but there is reference in the early part to the land being separated.

It tells also of the Fire and the Dragon or Serpent and somehow I am getting the feeling it is linked with the asteroids as they come into the Earth's atmosphere, which would have looked a little like a fiery dragon with many heads, leading to a great catastrophe. It speaks of the greatest earthquake of them all, a sea of fire and giant tidal waves. There was talk of an angel holding stars as well; was this to do with the planetary influence upon the Earth at that time?

Is it not referring to the catastrophe that has already happened on Earth thousands of years ago, and that part of 'Revelations' is not just a prophesy, but is also a revelation of what took place before recorded history.

In the Bible it begins with Genesis, our beginnings or how the Earth was created, and after that it speaks about the Great Flood and Noah. But no mention of when that was supposed to have taken place, and what happened to recorded history before that.

How similar the Dreamtime story about the Great Flood is in the Aboriginal culture. I have been prompted to talk about all of this to a geologist friend of mine, including the possibility of

Uluru being an asteroid and, although he was a little hesitant at first, he now says I have got him thinking and he will do a little research. I will be interested to hear what he has to say—and I will repeat what he says when he gets back to me.

Grenville pointed out that most geologists of today accept the theory the land mass on this Earth was at one time all together. It was a protocontinent called Pangaea. At that time, the South Pole was located in a region that has since separated to form South America, Southern Africa, India, Australia, and Antartica. The equator crossed continental areas that have since separated and drifted north to form what is now North America, Europe, and Asia. The evidence seems to point to a break-up occurring at different times down through the ages.

The first major break-up probably occurred about 200 million years ago with the formation of a northern continent that has been called Lurasia, and a southern land mass, Gondwanaland. (*The name the Australian Aborigines give it in the Dreamtime.*) The theory continues with more land masses separating and new seas forming, and then refers to the sea floor spreading and continental drifts. These theories have since been surpassed by the plate tectonic theory. Most geologists accept the theory of plate tectonics as an explanation for the continental land mass migrations. The plates carry oceanic floors and continents in various directions around the globe.

There is glacial evidence on considerable portions of the Earth that have left unmistakable traces. Evidence of glaciation on the southern continents records patterns of ice movement that can be satisfactorily explained if one assumes these modern continents were once part of the same land mass.

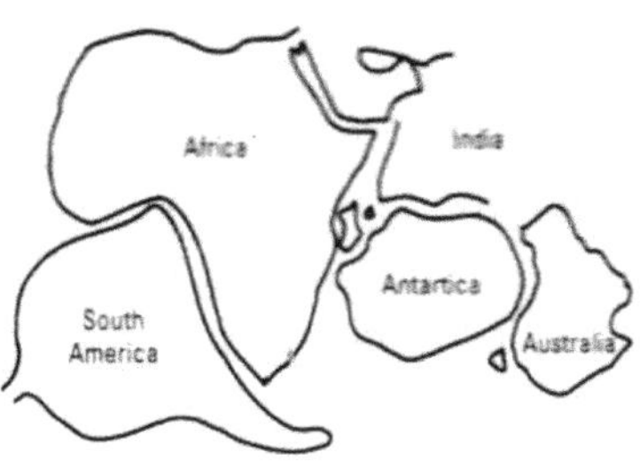

Coal found in many places on the Earth, and there are coal seams known to occur in Antartica. Coal is an accumulation of plant debris and generally occurs in warmer climates. This suggests the South Pole as we now know it was not always cold. There could have been a movement in the Earth's axis at some time, as well as the movement of the plate carrying Antartica to its current location.

When I asked if it was possible Uluru was an asteroid he, like all scientists, was careful about what he said, but spoke about stony meteorites and chondrites and I wondered about the stony-iron meteorites he mentioned. The full cosmological significance of stony-iron meteorites is not well known, but it does have feldspar in it, feldspar being a constituent of the rock of Uluru.

He also pointed out in the book a picture of circular landform in Ontario, Canada, believed to be an ancient impact crater. It probably is an exhumed crater or one that filled with sediments and was later exposed when they weathered away. He was having trouble finding studies made about Uluru, but there would have been work done.

That was enough for me; scientifically it is a possibility.

I was also wondering about Fred Kinnard, a man I happened to meet when at Uluru. I was in the communal kitchen where we were staying when he walked in and put a book briefly on the bench near me; it was about the eternal soul path and I thought, *ooh! he is one of us,* but by this time he had set off quite quickly to his cabin. I found myself chasing him down the corridor and speaking to him and virtually asking him if he was a light worker? I just knew he was.

He was a light worker, very much so, working with astrology, cosmology, and the energy grids all around the Earth, which was much the same as what we were interested in. He lived in New York and was leaving that afternoon.

I will communicate with him because there seems to be a strong understanding the time that was created, or re-created with us being at Uluru, was actually repeating the time when the call to God, or call to Baiame, was answered about 10,000 years ago or so at the time of the great catastrophe, and that the first initiation ceremony that took place then was being re-created now. It is possible he may be able to get information from computer data to establish the same star formation exists now as it did 10,000 years ago. It is worthwhile examining, anyhow. So, at this point in the book I will also enter what information he returns with...

Six weeks later, Fred has not been able to help me. When I met him, he said the area around Uluru reminded him so much of New Mexico and, in fact, he gave me a rock to pass on to a tribal elder of the Pitjantjatjara tribe if I had the opportunity, as he was leaving that day. He, too, had hoped to meet with the Aborigine elders.

I told him what we had been told about Uluru and he found that fascinating—he had been receiving a continual message when looking at Uluru that it was a 'Dreamchild'.

61 29th SITTING

Monday 3.10.1994

I am sitting here with the stone, even though we have an overseas guest staying with us. She has in the past lived in India and was speaking about the original people of India, known as the Dravidians, and how they are so much like the Australian Aborigines to look at. Genny is Australian, which is why she made that comparison.

In light of what has been coming out, I felt very interested in the Dravidians, to find out more about them and their mythology.

The Harappa culture and the ancient Indus civilisation is believed to be the beginnings of the Indian race. Studies have shown the skeletal remains of some of the Harappans were people of the long-headed, narrow-nosed, slender Mediterranean type found all over ancient Egypt and the Middle East and forming an important element of the Indian population at the present day. A second element was the Proto-Australoid, with thick lips and a flat nose, related to the Australian Aborigines and to some of the hill tribes of modern India.

India was a meeting place of many races. The modern South Indian is usually a blend of Mediterranean and Proto-Australoid, the two chief ethnic factors in the Harappa culture. I do not think Sai Baba would mind if I remarked on his physical appearance as being similar to the description of the Proto-Australoid.

It has been suggested the Harappa folk were Dravidians, and there have been authorities who have tried to read their script, claiming their language was a very primitive form of Tamil.

There has also been a study made of the Institution of *Gotra*, which is still very important to the orthodox Brahman to this day.

All Brahmans were believed to have descended from one of the rsis, or legendary seers, after whom the Gotras were named. The chief importance of gotra was in connection with marriage, which was forbidden to persons of a common gotra. The Australian Aborigines had a very strong taboo about marriage within their tribal groups.

This seems to be another link that at some time Australia was attached to the continent known as India before the great cataclysmic explosion took place at the end of Atlantis or when the asteroids hit.

It reminds me of when I had the interview with Sai Baba in India. I felt very confused, very happy, crying all at the same time and making a complete spectacle of myself while he was speaking with me, and then Baba invited one by one each group separately into another smaller interview room where he had private conversations.

I was thinking to myself there was no way he was going to invite me in there alone, forgetting he could read my mind. But he came out and extended his arm towards me with the palm of his hand showing and with a big grin he said, "Australia, come." I thought about that many times later. It is well known that whatever Sai Baba says in an interview always has great significance.

I see now that Australia, as we know it, was at one time attached to the Ancient Holy Land. It was part of the Holy Land known as Bharat.

It explains what appear to be pyramids on the Australian continent and also evidence of what looked to be Ancient Egyptian Hieroglyphs, but in actual fact it would have come from the ancient time of Atlantis, a very advanced civilisation. When it was about to be destroyed, there were many that left and moved to the land of Egypt, and the Americas such as Mexico and Peru. In actual fact, it was from the Ancient Atlantean times the understanding and advanced knowledge of the pyramids was taken to Egypt and these other places.

It makes sense, it fits. It gives understanding why there is evidence of a much more advanced civilisation from various artifacts that have been found around the Earth, the origins of which have been put in the 'too-hard basket'.

Believing such an advanced civilisation may have existed seems incredible. Laser technology was used readily and would give understanding of how there were such finely honed artifacts existing from an unknown time. (*We have come to understand that starpeople used to regularly visit Earth in their starships before the Great Cataclysim of when 'Atlantis Fell'.)*

There was a misuse of power at that time, it seems. We are given the understanding by the Starpeople the Earth had to be allowed to recuperate, recover from that almighty blast and shake, and the civilisations had to regrow, as they did. Information and technology was inspired through to this dimension, but a lot of the previously known technology has been held back until man proves he can be trusted with it, because they say that never again is man going to be allowed to destroy or nearly destroy Earth as happened before—for that mighty impact, in nearly destroying the Earth, also reverberated into the universe and affected many other planets and stars.

It was apparently quickly contained by the starpeople, but the decision was made by the Universal Government that it was not to happen again. That is why they have been monitoring the Earth and its development and the peoples upon it, and assisting their development.

They have tried to assist in every way they can so that development would take place with the understanding of universal intelligence or with the understanding of God.

The Earth is now on its journey through space and is moving into a higher vibration. I think all will readily accept there are changes taking place and that consciousness is rising. There are many now wanting to know more of psychic matters and the understanding of God, with or without religion.

This is no coincidence. Inspiration is being poured forth onto this Earth and it is up to man to accept that inspiration and accept it into their daily lives. Many are doing just that; it filters through to inspire people to re-think what they are eating, what they are drinking, and what they are breathing, and how they can help to look after and heal Mother Earth.

It inspires people to re-think about the way they are thinking. It inspires people to tune in and accept there are other dimensions and allow themselves to be guided from a different consciousness, from the God consciousness that is within them.

Many people on this Earth are riding with the changes taking place without fully understanding. It is creating a turmoil, but in the long term it is releasing all that is unwanted and will allow all to move forward, including Earth herself, free of all the damage, the hurt, and the fear.

We are hurtling through space with movement and the changes are quickening. It is like a new birth. It is a new birth that is taking place on this Earth and all who live upon her.

As governments change, the business and money worlds change, the medicine and ways of healing change, laws change, and society and the way we deal with society change. We will all move forth with more understanding, more strength, but with decisions that will be made for the good of all, rather than for the good of the few.

There will no longer be any hunger on Earth, or suffering, or crying out in fear or want. All will unite and understand Earth's place within the universe and will understand all other forms of life that exist within the universe. There will be a happiness and a feeling of calm that will come upon the Earth and within the Earth, and all will be once again restored to what Earth was meant to be.

It will be the (*prophesied*) Golden Age.

62 30th SITTING

5.10.1994

Today is a dark moon and when I started sitting with this beautiful stone it was a full moon.

I am being told it is the last time I will be sitting with the stone with regard to readings for the book. I am a little sad in a way because I rather enjoyed these sessions, but I am told the readings will expand as I put it on the computer and work with it. It is the bones of the book that has been given and I thank Sai Baba for his help, and all those others from the Other Side who have worked to help and guide me and to teach me.

I have read *Revelations* and the description of the fiery serpents with many heads, earthquakes and floods, and earth separations—it seemed to be not in the future, but rather it was revealing what happened in the past. Earth has already experienced this gigantic upheaval and enormous loss of life. ...*deep sigh*...

Recently, when the asteroids were noted to be like a string of pearls on their way to Jupiter, it was a replay of what had taken place here on Earth thousands of years ago. And when the asteroids, the string of asteroids, entered into our Earth's atmosphere they would have looked like fiery balls joined together that could be described as a fiery serpent. ...*deep sigh*...

It remains now for science, in its many aspects, to accept this has already taken place, and as the Earth starts to shift into another vibrational level, it is releasing its memories of that past cataclysm.

For this reason, on Earth now, she is releasing the memory through volcanic eruptions and Earth quavering, but nowhere near what she experienced that Plato spoke of as the Atlantean time.

Earth will heal, and many on this Earth who experienced a past life in those times will also start to release the memory, the sadness, the quaking, and the quivering that took place. The loss of life, the enormous loss of life, but not really for they rose again like a phoenix from the ashes and took wings into the higher realms, with an expanded understanding and an expanded knowledge. ... *deep sigh...*

Mother Earth needs loving thoughts and healing energy given to her to help her through her past-life memory, as she realigns herself to her place within the solar system. Thus, the galaxy, thus the universe as she was and is meant always to be.

Man needs to stop abusing her and start treating her with love and respect, giving her back the love, respect, nurturing, caring, and support she has always given us, for without her where would we be?

When I started this book, I had no particular interest in the past, in the possible existence of Ancient Atlantis. But information has been sent to me without asking for it, and I know it is the starpeople orchestrating the situation. Obviously, they would like more thought given to the existence of that time before, because it was so catastrophic and so painful a memory that it has been buried in many soul memories, refusing to surface because it was too painful a memory. There are those on Earth now who contributed to the downfall of Atlantis at that time.

There are no records readily available from that time—it is as if the record has tried to be removed and never existed.

On Australia alone, there is said to be an ancient pyramid at Gympie and also Egyptian like, hieroglyphs written on stone near Gosford, New South Wales and in South Australia.

There is an ancient site that has been described and known as 'Stonehenge' in South Australia near Maralinga that was first written about by Len Beadell in his book, *Blast the Bush.*

Bruce Cathie picks up the story in his book *The Pulse of the Universe, Harmonic* 288, and he has kindly allowed me to repeat the description of the site as having individual slivers of grey, water-impervious shale, protruding three feet above the surface of a plateau rising six feet or so above a claypan.

> *'The slivers looked a little like fence posts, perfectly straight, measuring four inches by three and very rectangular. There were about sixty of them about two yards apart. As well as that, there were clusters of the same posts in circles. The raised plateau suggests that the stone platform under the sand is the top surface of a construction, which is at least a few feet high and possibly of something buried deeper in the drifting sand.'*

The stone platform under the ground has a small area exposed, by wind or man, showing small sections of paved surface. The paving stones were large and rectangular in shape and several inches thick. Very accurately cut and fitting together in an extremely precise tessellated pattern. Primitive tools from an ancient native community could not have constructed this, but rather a find like this would be expected in Greece, or Rome, or Ancient Atlantis?

With the images I was given, seeing the centre of Australia as a huge crater and then filling with silt after the Great Flood, I really wonder what could be buried at that site. Is it a Sphinx like the stone was telling me? The site is not that far from Uluru. Or was the image of the Sphinx purely symbolic?

When I was walking into the canyon at Kata Tjuta, there is a steep incline to a point where you can see across the desert towards distant mountain ranges and one mountain had a perfect point looking like a pyramid. I thought that was strange.

I plan to visit India soon. Sai Baba has been communicating telepathically with me and assisting me with this book. At no time in the third dimension has he asked me to write a book, so I go with some trepidation as to whether he will acknowledge me and ask to see the manuscript. There are always thousands of people at the Ashram, from all nations around the world, and I have only met him personally the once, two years ago. At all other times, I have felt I was communicating with him in a different dimension.

At that time when I met him, he asked me, “What do you do?”, and I was completely tongue tied. How could I say I was a medium and do some healing to the greatest medium and healer of them all, the Avatar?

63 SUMMARY

21.12.1994

I have come to understand that Uluru, as an asteroid, came to Earth at another time before man was here. The action helped to stir up and create, and then manifest. The outer Earth itself at that time was going through many changes; time as we understand it does not really matter. The energies that came with Uluru came from another galaxy, from a time immemorial.

Over the millennia of time that this Earth was taking form, many comets or asteroids have hit the Earth. They have virtually stirred up the mixing pot, so to speak, and helped Earth to develop. At the time the rock known as Uluru hit the Earth, a great crater, *which is the Great Artesian Basin*, was formed in the land now known as Australia. At that time, a different climate existed.

In more recent times, after Earth was inhabited, another massive asteroid hit Earth, known as the time of the Fall of Atlantis. Being almost directly opposite Uluru, on the other side of the Earth, the impact sent a wave of energy through the Earth and I see it cushioning or substantially lifting the rock known as Uluru. It is interesting the area known as the Bermuda Triangle and its associated mystery and unstable weather patterns is so close to where that later asteroid was said to have gone down into the sea.

There has been much talk down through the ages about the existence of an advanced civilisation on this Earth, that the starpeople once inhabited this planet and that a race of peoples evolved on Earth from them. The so-called Ancient Atlantis seemed to hold many keys, but it was destroyed and the Earth and the peoples that survived from that time had to undergo a rebuilding and evolvement with new understanding and allegiance with the Universal Law of God. This is still happening.

A medium known as Azena actually leaves her body for a short period, allowing a light being from the Universal Council of Light to present himself as St Germain, taking over her body and speaking through it with much clarity.

With permission of Triad Publishing Pty Ltd in Cairns, Queensland, Australia, who published the book *Earth Birth Changes*, Peter and Carolyn Erbe have very kindly allowed me to quote St Germain's graphic description of The Fall of Atlantis.

> *"There was a celestial body, an asteroid, and it came into an orbital alignment, which was in the evening of time, at dusk when the heavenly bodies that you call Earth, moon, and Venus were aligned. This asteroid was deflected into the orbital pattern of this Earth. It was indeed enhanced through the gravitational fields of Venus and the moon, towards the deflection in the Earth's orbital pattern.*
>
> *Now, these scientists upon Atlantis, the technologists, they were aware of this uncommon phenomenon, and they were desirous of establishing their crystalline technology on this asteroid and therefore intended to capture it with what you term tractor beams. Allowing it to be brought forth into alignment, to hold still, as it were, and be captured into an orbit of the Earth, likened unto another moon. That was the desire of the Atlantean scientists. They felt their laser power was powerful enough to capture this asteroid body to encircle the Earth and place their instruments of war upon it so that the entire Earth planet would be at their submission, would indeed be their kingdom. This was their hearts' desire in that moment. It was a grand one.*
>
> *There were many who were aware of what their desires were, shrouded as they were. And they counseled them and laboured to bring forth wisdom and love of their brothers, to exits without interference, without dominion. But yeh, these entities voiced power lust and their desire to rule the empire*

of the world, and, indeed, it was at the threshold of their fingertips, so they felt.

So, they set up their grand instrumentation, which was experimental. It was not, shall we say, a laboratory in nature. Therefore, there was no trial. They felt, therefore, that this was to be a great maiden journey for their new laser technology. The dolphin in that period of time was embodied in a different fashion, but it was the same sort of consciousness. They came forth and counseled and pleaded with the entities to give forbearance unto this asteroid and allow it to continue its journey in the celestial heavens. They said nay to this and went forth with much confidence and strength of conviction that they were now the new rulers and masters of the Earth plane.

Your brothers, the Pleiadeans of the mountain of Atlas, the Atlantis of your new era to be born yet again, held counsel among themselves. They understood what was to occur. They also understood beyond the understanding of these scientists that there was to be a deflection of the laser ray, that, when encountering the asteroid, it would be deflected and collide with Atlantis itself in addition to the asteroid. They counseled whether or not to alert the Atlanteans about this oncoming disaster.

However, they decided to allow the scientists to understand the wisdom about interference and they went forth and brought many of the records of wisdom into the temples of Egypt. The wisdom of the ages encoded in hieroglyphic form, a terminology not understood of your day, not understood of the language of that time, in that era, because they desired not the same occurrence until the wisdom was captured. This counsel was allowed and aligned and so they extended this understanding unto the entity called Noah, to go forth and craft himself a grand ship, a grand ark, as it were, and to go forth in the shining light of his own essence and be patriarch of the new land, to bring the genealogy of the Atlanteans and the Lemurians into the new continents to be dispersed.

This was done and the casting forth of the laser rays, it also was done. It deflected the light of the laser ray and indeed, the asteroid was damaged, it captured the blast, and it brought forth its essence into the atmosphere of the Earth plane in grand fashion.

The asteroid was about six miles in diameter and it was travelling at a rate of about eight miles per second (8 miles = 28,800 miles/h or 46,080 km/h). When it encountered the atmosphere, it lit into a grand blaze. The blaze was blinding. The energy coefficient of it was 18,000 degrees Fahrenheit. The sun's surface is about 10,000 degrees Fahrenheit. That will give you an idea of how blazing the light came to be upon the plane.

It was a flash that existed for about two minutes of your time, and its explosion into two pieces lasted about the same time. It came down over the Atlantic Ocean and embedded itself in the ocean floor near the Puerto Rico plateau. There are two grand holes there, about 23,000 feet in depth. This is the impact.

The continent of Atlantis was quite in shock. There was much disarray. They frenzied, panicked, and there was some fleeing. Indeed, there was some flight by ship. The impact brought forth the rubble of the smaller structures travelling behind the asteroid.

Because the impact was loaded with so much heat, so much tremendous potential power, everything it touched immediately vaporised and therefore there was an enormous vapour of gas emission in that area beneath the surface of the Earth. Tremendous sub-terrestrial power was released throughout the Earth plane.

The Earth's crust was brittle and fractured, and all this power created rumblings beneath the surface of the Earth throughout the globe and there were risings and lowerings of the Earth's crust in this fashion all over the Earth. That is why there were many Atlantises, the submersion of many continents in some fashion or other, in this timing, until the platform of the islands and the continents gave way, and indeed brought forth a grand volcano, which spewed forth fire into the air.

The impact caused a tidal wave of grand fashion—2,000 feet (610 m) in height were the waves. But before they could reach the coastal areas, there was the emission of the volcanoes in that area. There was a torrent of magma spewing forth into the heavens. A tower of light, a pillar of fire, going forth beyond the Troposphere into the Ionosphere. It was of such impact that about 480,000 cubic miles (480,000 miles = 1,966,080 km) of magma were emitted from the volcano of this area called Atlantis. As it spewed forth, there was the crashing of the waves and the hissing of the steam quenching the fire and this occurred all over the Earth plane, but in particular in Atlantis.

The magma that spewed into the atmosphere was carried by storms and torrential tornadoes as they enshrouded themselves in mushroom clouds of steam and ash and dust emitted from the volcanoes. What was of volcanic action was set off in a chain reaction. Every volcano on Earth became active to release the pressure from the gases beneath your subterranean understanding.

As this came forth into the air, it was swept into massive clouds that became black as night with amber glow because of the ash and the dust. Massive indeed, and they accumulated their size in tremendous speed. They became the size of continents and hovered low across the continent. It was overcast. It was dark as night. Your land, the Earth plane, your beloved Terra, was shrouded in fog for 5,000 years after this. There was no sun to bring warmth into the land.

The tidal waves crashed into all areas of the Earth plane and funneled into the glens and valleys and flooded the forests, and then came the cold.

The asphyxiating gases travelled across the Bering Strait and were followed by arctic cold. This continued for 5,000 of your years, until the warming occurred due to the dispersion of the mists, the shroud of gases, dust and ash. The ash of Atlantis was funneled through these clouds to all areas of the Earth, so if you, in this day of your time, pick up a clod of clay, it could have been touched by the dust of Atlantis.

The platform of the island of Atlantis sunk 10,000 feet (3 km); not only the land itself but the bottom of the Earth floor that supported the island sunk 10,000 feet. It was a gradual disappearance. This occurrence lasted about one and a half of your days and this translates into about one inch per second of your time.

Now, through the impact of this asteroid body, the Earth's axis experienced a rotational polar shift of about two degrees, and this is still so in your understanding of this day. So, the temperate primordial forests were brought forth in the south, and the pole of north came northward. The cold was of the northern hemisphere.

The pulse and blast, they were two different ones. The first one caused the jarring and rending of the continents from one another. Until this time, they were all connected, they were all unified, harmoniously joined within their essence. The impact brought about their severance. They were ripped and torn from one another and they went eastward and westward, separate. That is where the separate Eastern and Western philosophies came from. That also began the polarities in this fashion, of alter ego and divine ego, in the manner they are represented upon this plane in your now.

Now, the separation of continents, the continental drift, as it is called, originated from the Atlantean destruction. The second blast went in the opposite direction. It was an echo of sorts and indeed the shock of this created many fragmented islands around the nations because the Earth was brittle in the crust and therefore created a fragmented appearance. The second blast caused the widening of the Atlantic Ocean, for it was much narrower in that day of your time. The wailing and mourning on the Earth plane could be heard many, many dimensions from this one. It was the mourning of humanity for a lost civilisation of God.

Then there were the storms, the rains, the heavens breaking open their hearts and allowing their tears to run from the breast of the Earth and allowing Mother/Father principle to mourn for Mother Earth. And indeed, she did. The tidal waves and the torrential rains, in their union, they brought forth much flooding and destruction and damage upon the plane. The sea level around the Earth plane rose approximately an average of about 300 feet (approx 100 m) worldwide.

Also, the glaciers shifted and broke apart. This was caused in part by the polar shift. However, they did not melt right away in your time, not immediately. It was about 5,000 of your years before they dissipated, when the breaking of the dawn came, and the warming of the temperature. The Ice Age was really the Atlantean age. The present era is the birth of a new land of golden warmth in the understanding of God divine essence within the Ice Age of your now.

The ice is not apparent upon the plane now. The ice is within your hearts, and it can be melted and merged with, very much like the snow and the fire melt into one another. The fire within your breast can merge with and melt the ice of another's heart, and that is how you become unified. That is how the manipulators become one with God divine essence. Their ice is melting.

Now, many of you remember, but you do not remember. This event of cataclysmic proportions has been engraved upon the hearts and memories and souls of all humanity. But they have forgotten. It haunts them. They have dreams about it. There are relics and echoes and shadows within their experience whispering about it. But they do not understand these whisperings of wisdom. This is brought forth before you this day in your time for you to understand, for you to embrace it, for you to capture what it is that you have experienced, and indeed, enlighten, inflame the world with your newfound knowingness, with your new understanding of what be you and what be your Earth plane, and what be this new Atlantis.

Indeed, to bring the fire of the mountain of Atlantis (Mt. Atlas) and the golden glow of it, to bring it forth for all to see and understand for your own divine example. Burnish yourself with this wisdom and you shall be indeed the refined gold of God."

I see a great crater existing where Uluru stands, but before the Fall of Atlantis there was civilisation and it seems to account for the existence of ancient hieroglyphics and manmade (*or Starman made*) structures that were later buried by silt and water at the time of the great flood. Scientists know it to be the Artesian basin and an inland sea, which is what it was. Because of the climate changes due to the shift in the Earth's axis, it became extremely hot, and water evaporated and left just the sand or silt, although that table of water is still there and bores can be put down into it.

It is interesting also that the Australian Aborigines say the weather patterns go around in circles in the red centre of Australia and that has been confirmed by pictures of the land now received by satellite; this information was shown in a museum at Alice Springs.

Since writing the above, I have been prompted to sit one morning, realising only afterwards, that the day, month, and year added up to 33, which has been used by *Upstairs* as a signpost for me—like, 'Take note, we want you to remember this.' Alcheringa wanted to speak more about the new energy coming through a gateway on to this Earth that is lifting consciousness of not only every being on this Earth, but every form of life and the Earth itself. He speaks of the gateway coming through the central sun and the line of energy and influence being known as the energy of the Lion.

ALCHERINGA speaks:

"I am very pleased to be here, my child. Thank you for inviting me. It is true I wish to speak to you. I have not spoken to you for some time. You have been wondering about the energy from Uluru, which also could be seen as the energy of the Lion, which is why you have been given the image of the Sphinx. Does this help you, my child, do you understand? You may remember you were prompted to see Uluru also looking a little like a Sphinx.

"It is true the energy that has come through from another galaxy at another time filters through into the Earth and comes to various points at the surface of the Earth. What you call Egypt is one of them and it is at those points that pyramids were built on many of those places. These too were also built at another time.

"It allowed the starpeople that came to Earth at that time to use the energy to manifest and to create. It was a network that filtered through the Earth. It is no coincidence that the rock known as Uluru came to this Earth. We as the starpeople actually brought it to this Earth to bring that energy and to help make changes upon the Earth so that it developed. This was at a time before humanity. I myself as an aspect of a star being have remained in the Astral (dimension) to help with the changes and the understanding to be filtered through to humanity until a time that the Earth reaches back to a dimension that existed when the rock first hit this Earth. (The sound of his voice changes here.)

"I am purposely holding my energy back a little, my child, because I want you to realise and understand that the energy infiltrates you more than you realise and at times you will be speaking and it will not be readily seen or heard, but the influence is there. This may happen to you at times when you are speaking publicly.

"It will sound like your own voice and I am doing this and telling you this on purpose, because I want people to know and understand that we do influence many on this

Earth, without them readily realising and understanding. At another consciousness, they know this and have given us permission to do so.

"For your own understanding, Alcheringa is an aspect of Sanat Kumara and it is really Sanat Kumara that speaks with you at this time. I am part of the Council of Light. I want you to understand this, my child.

"You are asking about the energy being known as the Lion energy? It could also be seen as a play on words. It is a particular line of energy and influence that comes upon this Earth from another galaxy altogether.

"There is also the CAT that is envolved, and the HAIR. This is from the level of the cosmic consciousness, which you understand is where the starpeople exist. There are different dimensions, different light energies, different shapes and forms. The HAIR was introduced onto this Earth in the form of a mammal. Up until that time, it had been a reptilian form. The time of the dinosaur, and yes, your feeling that when Uluru hit this Earth it was a time of the wiping out of the reptilian form, the dinosaurs, that had manifested to a point where it was out of control. It had to be re-constructed.

"It will help you if you think of energy as influence. The energy and the influence is what was created here on Earth into a form. It is very simple really—but of course, the form that took place is very complicated and in many forms.

"It was experimental from the starpeople's point of view. We were creating what is called, or what we call, the Garden of Eden. We were able to reproduce these forms because of the vibration that existed here on this Earth. At a later time, the humanoid or the form of man was created and evolved so that senses were experienced because of that heavier vibration. There was a separation between the positive and the negative and the sense in between could be felt. In the World of Light, the energy seen as negative and that of positive operates together so that there is no separation, but there is power. The power was lost to some degree when the

form took place on this Earth in this dimension, where the separation existed.

"But with the slow vibration, it allowed the form to take a heavier existence. This could be experienced in a way that we were not able to experience in the World of Light.

"It is unfortunate that there were those that chose to pull away from the will of God and the Universal Law and so the development and the evolvement upon this Earth went astray, against God's Law and the understanding.

"When it all ended at the time of what you call the Fall of Atlantis, which was not altogether an accident, it allowed that form, that energy, that vibration that existed here on this Earth to evolve into what was meant to be on this Earth.

"The formation is now coming into being and it will herald the New Age and operate within the will of God and the Law of the Universe. It has been an edict from the Council of Light that only those that choose to walk with God and that energy will be able to walk forward into that New Age. All that goes against God or chooses to walk in a different direction will be defused or re-placed.

"Remember all that exists in this world of yours is of a created energy and form—it is not the reality."

In 1994, I had visited Sai Baba in India now four times over the last three years. When I first went to see him, I felt called and knew it was time to go. John was making a business trip to South-East Asia and suddenly said would I like to go to see Sai Baba. I said, well that was strange because I had just heard that day there was a group going to see him from this area.

So he immediately asked me to find out the dates they were travelling to India and it fitted exactly with the times he was proposing for me to be there and later join him in Malaysia. So the day, the month, and the year I was to meet with the group added up to thirty-three, which has always been an important sign for me and when I did go to see Sai Baba at that time I was only able to stay for five days.

The day before I was to leave the Ashram, I had been prompted to dress in a white Sari for the last blessing and had received a message from White Eagle he would send me flowers, and much to my surprise that last morning a young girl did give me some flowers for my hair, jasmine flowers, which was lovely.

That last morning I was there for Darshan, which is when Sai Baba walks amongst the people giving of his light and blessing, he stopped. He looked directly at me, our eyes were locked, and I stared straight back at him; it was as if time stood still. I later realised he was working on my skin. For no other reason other than he just looked at me, within hours my skin began to itch and react and as the days passed, my skin became quite visibly inflamed and painfully itchy. The lesions increased and it was as if the disease was being thrown off—it was quite painful and covered a good part of the body. After a period of time, it did calm down and although it didn't go away totally, it certainly improved.

On that same trip, on the way out of India and due to plane delays, I missed the connection to Malaysia and had to spend the night at Madras on my own. I stayed in an Indian-owned hotel, which I later discovered was run by a Sai devotee, although I did not know that at the time. I felt Baba was with me in his subtle form and was looking after me, so I wasn't nervous at all. In fact, I felt I was being prepared to travel in and out of India on my own, which happened on following trips.

The next day, the flight to Kuala Lumpur, Malaysia, where I was to meet John was Flight MH33. I saw that as a good sign.

Also, just before I left Puttaparthi, where the Ashram is, I had been given a leaf, which the Seva Dals had said was a gift from Sai Baba symbolising Shivarathri. I thought *how lovely*, but knowing I could not take a live leaf back into Australia, I pressed it between some tissue paper and put it inside a book as a keepsake. However, when I finally arrived home, I found it was still alive even though it was about five or six days later and I was prompted to put it in a pot of soil. It actually grew, which surprised me no end. Then another leaf sprouted so I had two leaves looking at me. All year I watered it and talked to it, but it didn't die and it didn't grow, it just looked back at me.

Then around a year later, John again was making another trip into South-East Asia, and asked if I would like to go and see Sai Baba.

The dates John had allotted, I found that day the month and the year added up to thirty three and the day I was to leave India also added up to thirty three. I saw that as a sign Baba was calling me, so I said I would like to go, and overnight I found a new leaf had grown in the little pot. The plant was now three leaves looking at me, which I thought was quite extraordinary.

On my way into India, I stopped off at Singapore and was given by a friend a small photo of Shiva, which showed three small leaves above the forehead, along with three lines and a red dot that I now know to be the symbol of Shiva. One way or another, I found myself being given a deeper understanding about Shiva and the Shiva energy.

It was the second trip I was blessed with an interview with Sai Baba at Brindavan, another Ashram just outside Bangalore. On the first morning, I went to Darshan he gave me the green ring.

It was then I became very sick, but I understood what was happening. Baba soon let me know he was present in his subtle form by rapping on the table if I didn't follow his instructions. I ran the gamut of the sickness, refusing all medication for Sai Baba had, in the interview, told me not to take any medicine. I only realised later what he had meant—I had asked him would he heal my skin, but I felt I was being healed on many levels.

Sixteen days (*double eight*) later when it was time to go, I was still very weak and had to return home in a wheelchair and even though I was alone, I felt and knew Baba in his subtle form was with me, for events happened and fell into place that I knew I was being taken care of.

The second year, or third visit, although John had said that was the last time I was ever going to India, because he did get an awful fright seeing me so sick, he said would I like to go to see Sai Baba again?

I said to him later I was surprised because I thought he had said there was no way I was going again, and in actual fact he agreed, and he couldn't believe he was saying it either. It was like Sai Baba was talking through him.

For the third time I looked again for the signs, and the date I was to go to India again added up to thirty-three and the date I was to come back also added up to thirty-three. I saw that as a sign and very joyously returned to India. Remember, 33 is symbolic of cosmic consciousness.

I was not sick this time, but I was fascinated about the leaves—I seemed to be searching for them everywhere. I couldn't find them. I tried to talk to the Indian people about them and they did have sacred leaves, which they showed me, but they were not the same.

As it turned out this time (*although not planned*), I was actually at Puttaparthi for the Maha Shivarathri festival. While meditating and looking at Sai Baba, dressed in a yellow robe walking among the crowd, I suddenly felt he was dancing with me, spinning me extremely fast in large circles in the air. I started to get the feeling Baba was playing a 'leela' (*cosmic joke)* with me and that it was a little like the story of Hanuman (*the Monkey God*) being sent by Rama's physician to the Himalayas where there is a hill between Mt. Kailasa and Mt. Rishabha to bring back a special herb that was the only leaf to heal the injury Rama had sustained from an arrow.

When Hanuman arrived at the Himalayas, he could not remember which the herb was or leaf, so he brought back the whole hill to Rama and Lakshmana.

Symbolically is that the message Baba was giving me? Is the leaf a 'Soma' leaf, which is not of this dimension? Does he want me to bring back the whole mountain? Somehow, it seems to be connected with the water—I find the leaf is happier growing in the blessed water. It is strange I have often had the positive thought, "It is possible to move mountains."

A discourse was given by Sai Baba in the Poonachundra on the day of the Shivarathri Festival. I was there alone, remember. Although there were over 30,000 people present for the festival, it could have been more.

Baba was sitting on a tall narrow-backed white chair, which was marked with the Shiva symbol. The symbol was just like the photo I was given in Singapore the year before. Behind him was like a mini-ferris wheel of lights going around and around that I felt symbolised a star system or maybe the internal movement of an atom.

In front of him was a huge, very simple and clean-cut white desk, which seemed to be made from a strange material that I couldn't help feeling was as if he was sitting on a starship. I was surprised as I expected a desk in wood, heavily carved, and also a carved wooden chair as you would expect to find in India.

It was only the following year I discovered that I might have been the only one seeing the above scene.

The fourth time I wanted to see Sai Baba, I had a deep need to take this manuscript to India in the fervent hope he would call me for an interview and acknowledge the work. I felt it would be like earthing the information into the third dimension, the information that had been received from another dimension.

Strangely, a group from the area where I live were again going to India, led by Sue, and John this time encouraged me to go with them as he was nervous about me travelling in India alone.

There were seventeen of us and I must commend Sue on making it quite clear what she expected from each person, which led to a willingness by all to adhere and become a very unified group.

It was obvious Baba was very pleased, he actually said so...

We all dressed in white and wore emerald green coloured scarfs that captured much attention. They were metallic looking, I suppose you could say, but I see them looking really like light, the same colour of the ring Baba gave me. That colour, I was led to understand, symbolised the Shakti energy (*the gentle aspect of the Shiva energy*) that is coming onto this Earth from the central sun and ringing the changes that will lead us into the Golden Age.

Somehow, we all had a presence about us, especially when we stood up to go for the interview in front of 10,500 people. The men had said how remarks had been made that the 'metal' looking scarves suggested a spaceship or space age.

On the morning of *7 February 1995*, which adds up to thirty-three, Baba invited us to the interview. There was much laughter. What a wonderful meeting we had with him. There was another Indian couple called also and the man in his enthusiasm in telling of his experiences with Baba actually kept cutting across Baba's words.

Baba sat back in his chair, looking like God, with his eyes rolled up (*playfully*) towards the heavens and feigning exclusion, but his eyes looked like bright lights under the partially closed eye lids. Amazing.

When he was speaking with us, his eyes sparkled like bright diamonds. It was easy to see he is a light being.

There were a few in our group who were quite new to the understanding of Sai Baba and I think for their benefit he played with manifesting a ring for that same Indian gentlemen I have already mentioned. It had an Om symbol on it, and then taking it back between his forefinger and thumb he said maybe he would like a diamond. He blew on it and before our eyes it became a diamond. He encouraged the ring to be passed around so that everybody could see its authenticity and then he took it back and blew on it again while we were watching and it changed back to the Om symbol. He then gave it away.

He finally put me out of my misery as to whether he would acknowledge the book or not. He said where is my green ring? I laughed and he took my hand—I hoped he didn't want to take the ring back. But he laughed and then put out his hand in a gesture for me to hand him the manuscript. He put it on his lap and opened it. "*The Book of Love*," he said. "God is Love, walk with God." Then he said, "It is not finished," teasing me, of course, because he knew what I was hoping to write about on the last page. I thought telepathically, "Baba will you help me?" and he said, "Yes," acknowledging he knew all about its contents and that he would continue to help me. My cup runneth over, I am full of joy.

The changes one experiences in oneself in the presence of Sai Baba are just that: an experience. It is very hard to explain an experience—it is a feeling and a change in perception; it is a change forever.

Twice when sitting in lines waiting to enter the Mandir before sunrise, I saw starships in the outer atmosphere. The first time I thought it was a satellite, but as I was watching the ship suddenly veered off at right angles, and I know satellites don't do that.

The second time I noticed I had lost a charm in the shape of a 'V' from a bracelet John had given me and then too I kept noticing Vs on the ground made from grass or straw. The following morning, I was looking up at the starry sky and there was a 'V' formation of five starships moving quickly across the sky; it was so perfect and as we watched they rolled over into a different formation and went back the way they had come, disappearing out of sight. **I FELT LIKE A STARLADY**.

Baba again '*set me up*' one day, not long before we were to leave, where he was observing some building extension work near the Mandir. There were 10,500 people behind him and as I hurried to join them, I found myself facing him with nothing between us but a space of thirty feet or so. I stopped in my tracks and wondered if I should fall to my knees, but he just stood looking at me and it was if time stood still. I could not move. Telepathically, he asked me to note the signs around him. He was standing next to a very large bell.

*****

Now, in 2019, I realise when Sai Baba said, "*The Book of Love is not finished*," and that he would help me, he meant with the writing of the third book *Alcheringa, When the First Ancestors Were Created*. He was referring to the missing manuscript that John the Divine had written as *The Book of Love*.

Conclusion

64

If I speak in the tongues of men and of angels, but have not love, I am only a resounding gong or a clanging symbol.

If I have the gift of prophecy and can fathom all mysteries and all knowledge, and if I have a faith that can move mountains, but have not love, I am nothing.

If I give all I possess to the poor and surrender my body to the flames, but have not love, I gain nothing.

Love is patient, love is kind. It does not envy, it does not boast, it is not proud.

It is not rude, it is not self-seeking, it is not easily angered, it keeps no record of wrongs.

Love does not delight in evil but rejoices with the truth.

It always protects, always trusts, always hopes, always perseveres.

The First Epistle of Paul the Apostle to the Corinthians, Chapter 13v.1–7

PART THREE

'Alcheringa' 65

When the First Ancestors were Created

Sri Sathya Sai Baba said to me, "It isn't finished" in 1994 when he blessed the manuscript for the 'Book of Love', written when sitting with the Aboriginal sacred stone from the stars.

The following year, I began work on the manuscript *Alcheringa, When the First Ancestors Were Created*. Many people were sent to me, by our star mentor, to contribute to the story. I am reminded of when White Eagle spoke to John for the first time in Chapter seven.

It was quite a while before the manuscript was finally published. It explains the 'missing link' to the creation of the human race. The animal man: becoming the first human or light man.

It is a story of fifty thousand starpeople coming from the Pleiades in a giant starship, named The Rexegena, to found the human race on Earth, 900,000 years ago. It is not a simple story but one filled with intrigue, deception, and the planned destruction of a mission that left only ninety survivors to be cast upon the Earth.

Part of the story was about their survival on a planet whose atmosphere they could barely breathe, a sun they could not expose themselves to, and a dangerous and poisonous environment that took many of the survivors' lives.

Their struggle and success in creating our human race is the miracle they brought. It is our past and they are our heritage.

John and I visited the Ashram in India, with the second manuscript about the attack of our beautiful mothership. It was the day after the Twin Towers World Trade Centre was attacked and destroyed in New York. Only a few planes were flying, except the one that took us to India after that terrible occurrence on 11th September 2001. Now, I read the same World Trade Centre had previously been attacked on 26th February 1993, and then attacked again and destroyed eight years later.

I find it an extraordinary coincidence that our mission story leading to the attack began in 1994, and finally was not published until 2002. Eight years later.

Sri Sathya Sai Baba personally blessed this manuscript also and called it 'The Booku'.

Alcheringa has told us it is the same subject John the Divine wrote in his manuscript held by the Cathars—the past life John and I have experienced as Cathars. And it is the reason we are karmically asked to re-introduce the knowledge from the Starpeople back to this dimension on Earth.

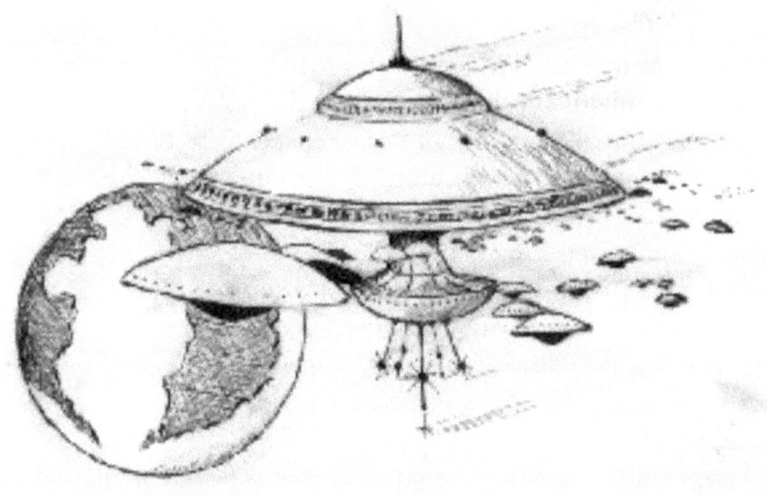

A Vision Persisting From a Time Beyond Conscious Memory

The concept of reincarnation is accepted by Eastern and Indigenous cultures. As time goes forward, it is also being accepted by many of our Western cultures, where there is a belief that our spirit, our soul, lives on after death and returns in a new body to continue its journey of character building until enlightenment. This is referred to as 'past-life memory', of being another personality in a past life. It is written in our soul history.

The Ancient Greek philosopher Plato wrote of the psyche, the soul, and soulmates, as did Aristotle and Socrates. Aristotle quoted, 'Knowing thyself is the beginning of all wisdom.'

In this story, we have found many people reach an initiated state of conscious where they experienced 'past-life memories' of living in another body, but the consciousness reaches into their soul to release the memory of being from other worlds, from other planets. For the people written about in this story, the transition into cosmic consciousness was relatively easy, their memories sparked by looking at symbols that communicated within us at a deep level.

Carl Jung, the famous psychologist speaks about the collective unconscious. This is particularly illustrated with many artists portraying archetypal sacred geometry in their work. Sometimes hypnotherapy is used to access this hidden consciousness. For our spiritual aspirants the knowledge, the memories, came from merely looking at and feeling the simple symbolic glyphs cut into a stone wall. The hidden knowledge within each, released spontaneously.

This leads us to know there was a 'hidden hand' at work guiding us all to release one segment of the story after another that is from a collective consciousness—the story of when the upstanding ape-like creature was elevated into a human being. This is our story. How it unfolded is true.

We have used only some of the audio tapes recorded from the different people sitting, holding photos of the glyphs and remembering that time in Earth's past history. We have changed their names to protect their identities, but many agreed to allow a group photograph to be published. Until the taking of the photo, many had not met one another.

67 Mothership Reunion

To be held at ALCHERINGA on Sunday June 11th 2000

All who have memories of the event that took place 900,000 years ago are welcome.

The invitation is extended to the partners and children of those with the memories.

Please land at 11 am–11.30 am and bring lunch to share We plan to have a professional photographer join us about 3 pm to take a group photo of those who choose to be involved.

The photo will be included in the book that is shortly to go to the publishers. A big thank you is sent to all who are willing to be documented and/or photographed to help validate the whole story.

Ph: 48 789 304
Fax: 48 789 305

John & Valerie Barrow

The author with the late Gerry in the middle and Helen on the left

The mothership Rexegena reunion at the property Alcheringa, Canyonleigh

The author with three of her four long-lost star children from the Rexegena explosion, and husband John

68 The Overview

The mothership was raised on the 8th planet of the Pleiadian cluster in the constellation of Taurus.

It was built, in our terms, quite differently from what the earthling understands at this time. It was a crystalline body. It had a consciousness because of the crystal; a consciousness that had been imbued into it by its builders. It actually grew. Liquid crystal is used in many ways to make many things in the starpeoples' dimension.

The huge mothership was formed and then mounted by the appointment of a commander in chief known as Alchquaringa. His wife was named Egarina, they had four children travelling with them. There were other commanders on the ship—there were divisions of command within the ship. Those that came on the mission had love and compassion in their hearts.

They came because the hierarchy, similar to your United Nations, put out a call for help to be taken to this corner of the Milky Way galaxy where dark, heavy negativity resided. There were many volunteers from other planetary systems who came with their families, knowing their journey would be a long one.

The objective of the mission was to bring new beings to this Earth; to help raise the consciousness of the earth. They had hoped to breed among themselves and that the progeny from the starpeople would be introduced genetically to intermingle with the up-standing apelike man creature who already existed upon the earth.

Genetic engineering was well-known and understood by the starpeople. The mission was to save the animal people on this earth, who were under mind control.

The mind control came from beings not of love and compassion. They were known as the Reptilian people, for they were genetically connected to snakes, lizards, and dinosaurs as we know them. The Reptilian people controlled the consciousness of the up-standing ape-like creature and used them at their will.

The objective was not only to free the animal man from slavery, but to stop them being used in sacrifice to Draconian Gods. There had been those appointed as diplomats from the hierarchy of the World of Light, to come to speak with the Reptilian Kingdom and try to find a way for them to release the animal man. It was the hierarchy's understanding the Reptilian Kingdom had agreed to hand over the Earth to the people who came on the mission. They in turn would leave. There had been an amount of discussion and concessions made, but this was the outcome; at least that is what was agreed.

And so, the 50,000 people on the mothership came, fully believing the Reptilians would leave. A handover ceremony took place, but it was a complete sham. The Reptilian people had no intention of leaving the Earth, nor did they have any intention of stopping the slavery and sacrifice that existed upon this Earth. The starpeople could not believe people could say something and not mean it.

When the mothership arrived with the new race, the Reptilians attacked it, even though it was completely defenceless, blowing it out of the sky. There were only a few who managed to escape. Those that survived established a small community in the Southern Hemisphere.

The mothership exploded above the area that exists now around Jerusalem. There was to be a Jerusalem established by the starpeople. Jerusalem means the starpeople were to intermingle with the slave-like people and teach them love and compassion. A dualism. The starpeople, the survivors, found it too difficult because of the heavier atmosphere, their difficulty in breathing and finding the sun far too hot. They tried to introduce genetic change to their own progeny, with hair on their heads, stronger lung systems, and stronger digestive systems to avoid disease.

These children did not live; the gestation period was not long enough in the new atmosphere.

The starpeople decided to genetically engineer the up-standing ape-like creature. Genes from the starpeople were intermingled with the animal man embryo, then implanted into the females. The babies were born with a larger skull and a little less hair, which went on to evolve so that the more children born, the less hair was manifested.

It was the time the scientists speak of as the missing link. It was a time when the starpeople first introduced fire and showed the animal-like being, now the human, how to cook food to lessen their vulnerability to disease, to teach them the knowledge of the Creator of All. To teach them more about the starpeople, how they live as family, and how they married.

They taught them how to communicate telepathically, and some other clever things, similar to the starpeople. They also taught them to honour and care for their Mother Earth. This original race was known by the starpeople as 'The Chosen Ones' who were the ancestors of the indigenous people. The Australian Indigenous people still carry this knowledge and understanding in their mythology.

As the original numbers grew, the starpeople took them out around the Earth and told them to multiply with other upstanding ape-like creatures who were still brutish and weapon wielding. The change from the animal man to hu-man began to uplift the consciousness of those beings along with strict marriage laws so that they did not interbreed. The starpeople eventually died, but not before telling them that they would one day return.

And they have.

The Mothership Technology

With the starpeoples' technical ability, they were able to make the mothership grow into the magnificent 'state of the art' piece of equipment. Inside the mothership Rexegena, everywhere is white—very clean cut and not much furniture. Just long, rounded, smooth to touch molded seats, slightly shiny, along the side of walls, again all white.

There are rooms off corridors in the 'sleeping section'. Everything is very quiet—inside the room, lights and furniture are available by waving the hand over a small point on a wall, like a light switch with 'thought in mind' opening the bed section for instance or turning on a soft light. The sleeping bed appears as the section of the wall opens. It is more like a cylinder the starperson climbs into, after removing boots, and mentally closing the see-through cover over their body.

The air inside is stabilised into an atmosphere that allows the starperson to sleep for whatever time chosen. It could even be for the full time of travel until the destination is almost reached. The starpersons' mind is then linked with the mothership so as to assist its pre-programmed course. There are always certain numbers of starpeople that are on so-called 'watch', meaning they are in a suspended state of mind to focus only on the movement of the mothership.

Fifty thousand people are on board with never a feeling of over-crowding. At the top of the mothership is the command deck, about twenty people moving about purposefully. It operates with extremely advanced computer equipment. The deck itself is large and almost completely surrounded with a magical window view of the galaxy outside. Large movie screens hang like thin pictures on the remaining walls, which light up on command, showing star maps of where the ship is, where it has been, and where it is going.

To operate these star screens, there are what look like coloured desktop directional control mechanisms. Some of these are buttons are similar to what you would use on a computer; others are like a half globe coloured light set into a console, that when the starperson passes a hand over, it adjusts the pathway of the mothership on its journey. There is a circular shelf used as a desk, linking all the technical lineways within the ship right around the window area surrounding three-quarters of the circular command platform.

At the back of the command room, and in front of the star screens, is a large white molded desk where the commander in chief sits. His seat has a narrow, rather high back showing the

Shiva symbol in red and black. The huge desk also doubles as a kind of boardroom seating for his other commanders when they meet to discuss issues about operating the mothership or other matters. There are eight robots that converse with the crystal consciousness on the ship. I see one of them seated on a molded white seat in front of a panel, placing disks, like CDs, into slots at eye level. This also has an influence on the maintenance of the ship and its programming.

The robots have an eye only for a face, which can move in all directions. The body is like coiled rope of a satin stainless steel-looking material. It has arms, with a tiny hand and long fingers. The legs taper onto a circular platform. The robot glides slightly above the floor. Each robot is operated by a communication crystal at the instruction of one of the commanders. The core of the mothership is flowing liquid crystal, which virtually powers the ship, also allowing the starpeople to regenerate their own body atoms.

The ship could be described as organic. On the lower floor of the mothership are gardens, plantlife that looks more teal in colour than green. There are bathing pools, waterfalls, playful lights, and soft sounds to induce relaxation, and parklands as well as heavier forestation. All of this is to encourage the starpeople to relax and intermingle, for not all onboard are from the same planet, although they all come voluntarily with love and compassion in their heart.

One floor onboard is devoted to genetic research; the rooms are white and sterile. The starpeople are not subjected to bacteria or fungus. There have been some children born. They are placed in an upright cylinder, with a controlled atmosphere, allowing each child to develop fully. The parents nurture their child with telepathic communication and love, as well as mother's milk. There are starwomen who devote their work to midwifery. Care is taken to analyse the newborn children in their progression, both physically and consciously, before they are mature enough to leave the cylinder.

The development of botanical research is carried out on another floor. Taking up a lot of space and grown as we would understand hydroponics, the water being a flowing liquid crystal, giving off a fresh smell and a gentle humidity.

Another floor of the mothership deals with maintaining the mechanics of the ship. Most of the starpeople are dressed in junior navy-coloured boiler suits and boots or pearl silvery-white boiler suits, and boots depending upon their race or position. Other floors are lounge rooms, large gathering halls for celebrations or events, and a kind of film library.

Food is taken by starpeople, mainly liquids but some like sweet cake-like food, which is never overeaten. There are no overweight problems—people know and understand what their body needs to be sustained. There is more body contact and interaction than one could imagine with aliens. Communication is telepathic, with a lot of body language as well. Permission to speak is always asked first. From our Earth point of view, their physical body looks anorexic, but it is a perfectly healthy body.

There is also a hospital on board. Light and sound technology is used for healing as well as genetic engineering. Use of this technology is an everyday occurrence but only ever with the view of transforming a body with permission from the Creative Source. The ship has a childcare centre as well. Dancing occurs with people holding hands, like the Greeks or Jewish people dance, moving the feet so they skip quite fast at times, moving around in large circles, according to the music. These dances are enjoyed and happily shared. From the outside, not much emotion is witnessed but from the inside the starpeople actually experience emotion much more acutely and strongly than the earthlings.

On meeting, one hand is placed across the chest as a greeting. Closer friends may raise their hands and actually give what we would call a 'high five'. Intimate relationships stand in front of each other—palm to palm of both hands, fingers touching so as to connect with all of each other's meridians. This is always exciting and pulls at the heart. It is not uncommon to put one's arm around another or even give each other a hug.

A floor is used as a storage area. It has vast supplies that are to be used when the fifty thousand people eventually establish the new settlement on Earth. There are also flight decks that hold different kinds of flying ships. Many ships are used as surveillance vehicles. They can hold as many as fifty people. Others are smaller and are used to traverse more difficult areas or landing locations. There are also fifty hand flying scooters. There is also a kind of chute, which is used to offload material from the ship onto land—they are operated by one person in a small rocket-looking flying ship—or pod.

There are no weapons of destruction on board—the mothership is completely defenceless.

There are other flying ships used by the Leonine people and also the Reptilian people. These two races are sworn enemies. Both have weapons of destruction. The Leonine ships are larger than the Reptilians. The light onboard is not bright white like the starpeople's mothership. Their technology is not as advanced as the starpeople, although by earthling standards that exist at the present, their technology is far more advanced. The ships are described as untidy compared to the bright white mothership. Furniture is on display and covered with skins—not tucked away as designed on starships. Both races dress in military-style uniforms.

They both have ray guns that can 'freeze' whatever life they point it at. They use sonic equipment to destroy, the same way a high-pitched sound can smash glass. Only the sonic sound is entrained so that it continues to destroy objects until they no longer exist. This is what happened when the Reptilians set out to destroy the huge mothership. Portions of the mothership were destroyed, blow after blow, but it did give time for the starpeople to move quickly to the surveillance ships, enabling them to escape.

When the fleeing ships left and tried to fly away, they were attacked also. Only a few ships managed to get away from the Reptilian line of fire. One of the robots was rescued and survived along with ninety other starpeople.

The starpeople had what was called a laser rod. It did everything. It enabled us to lift or levitate, make changes in work, shape, and burn—not with heat that would harm; it would solidify or liquefy, make something softer, and transform material into another material. It was also what was used to cut into stone. Very useful. I know also they had a boomerang-shaped instrument, which of course was explained to and used by the Cherished Ones.

All of these events operated in the fourth dimensional frequency of Earth time. It was only later in Earth's evolution—about 10,500 years ago at the catastrophic time of the Great Flood or the Fall of Atlantis—that the Earth fell into the third dimensional frequency.

A Green Crystal...the Moldavite Stone

In earlier days, when we first moved to the Southern Highlands, I was awakened from a deep sleep and asked by a voice from *Upstairs* to 'find a green crystal'.

This experience was in 1986, and it was not until I received the Aborigine sacred stone in 1994 and the stories that followed from then, did I realise the message I received, '*I was going home*', was referring to a memory from my soul being a starperson and coming from the Pleiades in the huge mothership Rexegena. That story told of fifty thousand starpeople coming to Earth in peace—to hold divine light on this Earth and to assist in creating hairy men into a hue-man—meaning a 'light man.'

My recent research suggests the Moldavite stone is also known as the 'grail stone' or 'starborn stone'.

Scientists say that millions of years ago there was a meteorite shower, and this rare, bottle-green crystal was the result. It belongs to a group of tektites, which are fragments of extraterrestrial objects such as meteorites and the ensuing melted combination with terrestrial rocks when they crash to the earth. Moldavite is named for an area of Czechoslovakia in which a large crater field was discovered. They are among the rarest minerals on earth, rarer than diamonds, emeralds, or rubies, and prized by humans for thousands of years.

According to legend, the clear, deep green stone in the Holy Grail was Moldavite and anyone who touches the 'Grail Stone' will have a spiritual transformation. This stone activates the 'dream states' and is said to induce positive life changes and also help widen our cosmic consciousness. It is helpful for personal and spiritual growth, and to release old habits that you know, deep down, need to go.

I certainly have gained cosmic consciousness and now I am able to assist others to connect to theirs.

I have a memory of the mothership Rexegena and had a dream when I witnessed it exploding, portion by portion, after it had been attacked. In my memory, and many other people's memory, the mothership was stationed on the outer atmosphere of this planet earth. The ship was organic. With the starpeople's technical ability they were able to make it grow into the magnificent state-of-the-art piece of equipment when it was raised on the eighth planet of the constellation of the Pleiades.

The explosion in my dream looked like a nuclear explosion—hotter than the sun, causing the mothership to melt. Many perished on board. *THE REMAINS OF THE MOTHERSHIP WOULD HAVE FALLEN TO EARTH and this is what is now named the Moldavite stone. Our memory tells us some of its remains went into water and some onto land,* mainly around Bohemia and Moravia of the Czech Republic. This word comes from the Greek word tektos, which means '*melted*', and was first employed by the geologist Franz Sues in the year 1900.

When I was first awakened by spirit and asked to find 'a green crystal', I had no idea they existed, let alone the story that has since unfolded about the mothership Rexegena and it now being the Moldavite stone holding the raised consciousness of Light from the Pleiades and the Seven Sisters.

Czech Moldavites hold an especially significant position among other tektites. They are the only tektites that are transparent—glass-like—and stand out with a variety of green shades. I do not find it difficult to accept the mothership melted and fell to earth, and the dating of the Moldavite stone could be confusing unless it was accepted that the stone was starman made, hence needing a different approach in Earthman's scientific expertise.

Understand that the dimension on which the mothership existed would be the fifth dimension with frequency adjustments made to the fourth dimension as the ship passed through the gateway of change on its way to the fourth dimensional Earth or *Mu* as it was known. Our Earth later fell to the third dimension after the 'cataclyism of Atlantis.'

As starpeople, Egarina and Alchquaringa were 7ft and 8ft tall, with long hands and long feet, long necks and skulls that extended to the back, no hair, and what looked like large black eyes, and small noses, ears and mouths. They came from the galaxy Andromeda M31, and had to reduce their light to work in the Milky Way galaxy and in particular the mission from the Pleiades.

The Kariong Glyphs

We were taken to visit the Kariong Glyphs by our new friend Gerry, the Aboriginal healer and medicine man. He came to us after *The Book of Love* was published. It was on that day, 10 October 1995, that the esoteric story of *Alcheringa: When the First Ancestors Were Created* began to manifest to many people who remembered being Starpeople and who remembered being on the mothership Rexegena.

Alcheringa told us that he was very pleased we had come and that the glyphs would mean many things to many people. For our esoteric story about the mothership Rexegena, the glyphs were giving many of us spontaneous memory of being starpeople.

Alcheringa also said a doorway had been opened and he would release keys for the story to unfold. That was from 1995 until 2002 when the book was first published.

From Top Left: *Pregnant starperson receiving crystal energy from robot - Entrance to cave and the estimated 250 glyphs - The author pointing to star glyph - Wall of glyphs at Kariong.*

Chapters One and Two of 'Alcheringa, When the First Ancestors Were Created'

69

I was assisted by a professional writer Bill Oliver to tell the story *Star People Revisited, Past, Present, and Future* and many others who could remember part of the story. We give our thanks to them all. How the story unfolded is a true story. We later changed the title of the book to *Alcheringa, When the First Humans Were Created,* to honour the Australian Indigenous people.

We are sharing the first two chapters here in the hope it will prompt you to want to read more.

Chapter One: Past, Present, and Future

It's a little overwhelming when I think about what took place. Aborigine Gerry raced his battered pickup truck down a dirt trail towards the highway. My friend Rachel sat beside him, her white knuckles clenching the dashboard. As Gerry drove, he admired an unusual pink crystal he had just bought. Approaching the highway, Gerry brought the truck to a stop. The dirt trail ahead was covered with huge concrete pipes.

A construction crewmember, laying them in the deep trench that ran across the trail, noticed the truck through a cloud of brown dust. All he could do was smile and shrug his shoulders. Another way would have to be found to the highway. As Gerry searched for an alternative, his truck neared the road that leads to the happy place my husband and I call home. Rachel pointed at the road, "That's where my friend Valérie lives, her home is called Alcheringa."

Gerry slowed the truck and then stopped at the crossing. For a moment, he looked intently down the narrow lane. He turned to

Rachel, "Then we will go and see her." The attraction of the name Alcheringa was about to pull in yet another new acquaintance.

In my little study, I sat with the Alcheringa stone having a small celebration. Today, the first copies of *The Book of Love* arrived in Australia. I was happy and content. Through the window, I could see an old pickup truck approaching the house. I recognised my friend Rachel in the truck along with an Aborigine man. As I saw his face, I felt a strong rush of excitement that I was unable to justify.

I had never met a 'Koori' or 'Murri,' as they like to be called. When I say this, I feel sad. I was born and raised in Australia, yet never took the opportunity to meet the Koori socially. This is the same for many white Australians. It is hard for them to take the initiative. There is a great need to have communication and understanding between all races at a social level. My chance had just arrived and I decided to make the most of it. Rachel beamed as she introduced me to Gerry.

I looked through his dust-covered eyeglasses to see the warmest pair of brown eyes I had ever seen. His smile was gigantic and sincere. There was a feeling of love and niceness about him. I instantly connected with him and felt warm to his energy. As I did, he looked deeper into my eyes than anyone ever had before. I made lunch, and as we sat at the table, I intuitively felt that Gerry knew the Alcheringa stone was in my care. My gaze moved to Rachel for a clue, but if she had told Gerry about it, her face was certainly not revealing anything to me.

We talked socially for a while, and then Rachel asked Gerry to show me the crystal he had just bought. As he reached into his pocket, Rachel told me that Gerry used crystals in his work as a healer. Gerry brought the pink crystal forth and held it out to me. He looked right into my eyes. "It's a magic stone, is it not?"

I almost fainted.

"You know about the Alcheringa stone," I blurted out, gasping for air.

Gerry shot back at me, "It's men's business."

My mind raced, looking for something to say. Gerry was still looking into my eyes. They were warm, yet they seemed to search for something inside me. For what seemed like an eternity, I was unable to reply. My eyes kept darting about the room. Finally, I gathered my wits and tried to speak calmly, 'Yes, but you see the stone has never been unwrapped while in my care, I hold it in great respect. I use the stone in my work as a medium, and uh... the voice that comes to me with the help of the stone is a male voice.'

Gerry leaned back and laughed, "Well, that's good." We all laughed and the atmosphere became light again. He slipped the pink crystal back into his pocket. I could not resist,

"Would you like to see the stone?" There was fear in Gerry's eyes as he declined the invitation. My brain went blank. I wasn't quite sure what to do. I should be halfway down the hallway by now, bringing the stone to the kitchen. I had to say something,

"Speaking of stones uh, you know at the last spring equinox, I visited the giant mystery rock Uluru. I really loved the place, and I agree with the Koori that it is sacred. I chose not to walk on the rock out of respect for the Aboriginal people."

Then I described how Alcheringa had presented himself through me at the rock. Gerry's eyebrows shot up. He leaned forward, "One of my Koori friends has an unseen being who speaks through him, calling himself Alcheringa."

In that tiny moment, I felt as one with the Koori; my credentials had been established. Then, Gerry gave me the strangest look, "Do you know of the hieroglyphs at Kariong, near Gosford?"

"Yes, I've heard about those, I'm told they're Aboriginal," I replied.

"I've been there many times, and the hieroglyphs are not Aboriginal. I would like to take you there to see them. Do you think that Alcheringa might talk to me if we go there?"

I said yes, without even thinking about it. Suddenly, I felt as if I was going to be initiated. Alcheringa had told me over a year ago that he would one day speak through me to an Aborigine.

We went to Kariong the following week. The day was very special, the tenth day of the tenth month. My friend Karen joined us. She overheard me talking about the trip, and insisted she go with us until I gave in. We arrived late afternoon after a four-hour drive. Walking ahead of us in the bush, Gerry occasionally threw small stones to inform the spirits we were coming, so as not to surprise them. He told us it would be icy cold at the site, but for me the weather felt quite pleasant.

Gerry instructed us to eat some of the tips of the young leaves of the gum tree to become 'one' with the landscape. Then he asked the spirits and elementals for permission to enter their area. As for our contribution, Karen brought a video camera and I had my 35mm still camera. Well, we are hi-tech white girls, what can I say?

We climbed towards a huge rock that seemed to have broken free from the mountain to form a narrow chasm with a flat but rough floor. The back third was roofed in by a large flat rock. As we crawled through a tiny opening into the chasm, I was stunned by the images that lay before us. The rock walls were covered in breathtaking hieroglyphs. Karen and I were amazed. There were hundreds of them. The chasm was a time capsule carved in stone. Many of them looked Egyptian. I'm no expert, but I clearly recognised a carving of the Egyptian god Anubis. Others looked like symbols or pictographs of some event. Moving to one of the walls, I gently touched several of the hieroglyphs. My fingers tingled as they ran over the ancient images. Some of them seemed to evoke distant emotions I couldn't quite place. As I began to take photographs, I noticed many of them were very clear and deeply cut.

"These were cut into the stone by a laser rod," I said. How could I have known that?

Karen was busy videotaping with her camera. In the centre of the chasm, Gerry stood with his eyes closed, as if in deep meditation.

Then Karen let out a small gasp. I turned to see her pointing intently at a glyph of a pregnant woman. I felt a sense of detachment.

Gerry seemed to sense the change and led us to the top of a rock overlooking the chasm. We sat facing each other. Karen started her video camera as Alcheringa spoke through me.

"Greetings, my friends, I am Alcheringa. I have waited a long time for this meeting to take place. It is my pleasure to be here.

I have known each of you many lifetimes before, you see we are all connected to the worlds of the stars. Many are curious about the drawings carved upon this rock. Each of you has a feeling that they were cut by beings from another world. Indeed, many of them were. For millions of years, beings of other worlds, other stars, even other galaxies have visited the little Earth. Many have influenced the genetic evolvement of living creatures on the Earth such as fish, land animals, and insects. It is a living planet with life forces in every part of it. But then, you are aware of this.

"There are many things to speak of, but this is not the time. Much of the information will unfold gradually, for we have a greater plan. Each part will come together so that a larger picture will be recognised and understood by those who live on the planet Earth.

"There is a great need for all on this planet to understand the mother that you call Earth, the mother who looks after you and nourishes everything that lives upon her. There is a need to love and respect the mother Earth, to nurture her. I know that each of you understands this deep within and will help us to spread that understanding. One of you has a question."

Gerry spoke up, "Is there anything else we should know about this site, does it need protection?"

"This place has been protected all along. We will continue this protection until it is time to come forth in a public way. This ancient place holds keys to a larger picture. These images will unite, open up, and evolve many who will remember. The time now is too soon, it will happen in a time not far ahead."

Gerry asked, 'Is there anything you want us to do?"

"In actual fact, my son, you are already following our inspiration. You have allowed yourself to guide these people. Not just at this meeting place today. We desired this to take place. There will be many times when you realise that unseen hands are at work. There is nothing for you to worry about, we know that you are willing to be of service.

"Be aware, my son, keep yourself alert. Deal with each problem as it is put before you. Many work with you and give assistance. We will sometimes push you a little further than what you are used to. This is done knowing that you have the ability to work from that point.

"As each of you takes a step in life, know that we are with you. We come from the world of light. We come to you with love, from a point of God. We ask that you be not afraid.

"We come to assist and are ready whenever you call upon us. In some way, help will always be given to you. There is really nothing more to say at this time other than to keep up the good work. I will take my leave now. I thank you for welcoming me here. It is no coincidence that we are all here today. More will evolve very soon as you shall see. God bless you all."

Alcheringa's presence departed, yet I still felt a warm energy around me.

Gerry stood up and asked us to follow him. We walked further up the mountain to Whale Rock, a site that overlooked the Brisbane waters and Broken Bay beyond. This was a large flat rock with distinct cobblestone markings cut into it. As we walked onto the rock, both Karen and I lowered our heads. Each of us had the distinctive feeling that we were walking under something. We looked up in unison. There was nothing of course, just our overactive imaginations—*or was it*? Karen and I had both experienced identical reactions to this location. My heart began to beat faster. Gerry said he had been to this place many times, using it as a healing rock.

He motioned to the area around the rock, telling us that Aboriginal families used to live here, eating their meals at the exact spot where we were standing. To one side of us was the men's business site, to the other, the women's business site. He showed us a part of the rock where a formation had been gouged out, like a cradle. Gerry told us in the old times, Aboriginal women had used it as a birthing canal. Karen decided to lie in the rock cradle. Moments later, she appeared to go to sleep. Then her eyes began to move as if she were in REM sleep, a dream state. I watched her curiously, for what seemed like minutes. Then she sat upright with her eyes opened wide.

"What did you feel?" I asked.

Karen look confused, "The ecstasy of childbirth. At the same time I was also feeling abandoned, and yet I knew I was there with others."

Gerry moved close to Karen and looked at her intently with eyes that were suddenly huge, "What about the baby?"

Karen seemed stunned by his question. "I, I don't really know," she replied in a voice that wavered.

Here I began to feel a kind of detachment from reality again, similar to what I feel before I communicate with Alcheringa, but different.

Gerry walked to the edge of the rock overlooking Broken Bay. It was just starting to get dark and twinkling lights were beginning to appear in the town below. He turned and motioned for me to come closer to the edge, then pointed towards the water. There was a dreamy look in his eyes.

"See where that little boat is down in the middle of the water, I think that is where the ship went down. Just focus on it, Valérie."

A rush came over me. I felt my hands reaching out towards the water and was suddenly overcome. A sense of deep sadness wrenched my whole body. I could hear the sounds of terror; there was crying and wailing. I had to release the pain, the fright, and the overwhelming sense of loss that was overtaking me.

Suddenly it was broad daylight. The land looked different than it does now, more tropical and denser. It was extremely hot and I was having trouble breathing. The air was thick and liquid, as if I were breathing under water. Each breath was painful. My outstretched arms were long and thin. The skin on them was a blue-white colour, almost transparent. My head felt elongated.

I experienced an overwhelming feeling of total disbelief. My husband, children, and many friends had all been killed. How could this have happened? The feeling of disbelief was replaced by a sense of betrayal. Then came the rising of anger, an emotional experience that the person I was experiencing had never known before. I recoiled from the impact of her anger back into what I thought was normal reality. Beside me, Karen and Gerry were gasping and on the edge of crying. We appeared to be sharing some kind of group experience.

Whale Rock seemed to be in another time. Then the veil was torn away and the memories began to rush in. We had all come in peace from Pleiades-Lyra, and another place before that sounded like Altaah. I collapsed to my knees as the white-hot daylight and choking atmosphere returned. There had been a desperate attempt to get away from something. We had come in peace on a mission of God and were attacked by those who were not of the light of love. Far below, a saucer-like starship lay broken in the waters of the bay. The occupants of the ship were badly injured and traumatised. Their fear and pain echoed into my mind as if I were sharing their consciousness. Dolphins appeared, reacting to their unspoken pleas for help, pushing some of them ashore. Another saucer ship, the one on which I had arrived, hovered over the crippled saucer picking up those in the water.

Those already on the shore, exposed to the searing light of the sun above, screamed in pain as they sought cover from the intense radiation. Some had sustained terrible injuries, the agony of which I was directly sharing.

My senses reeled and I turned my head away. Others stood behind me, viewing the scene with the same horror. They were all aliens, not of this Earth. I looked down at my arms and body. My God, I was one of them.

I looked up to see Eleura amongst the group, remembering her face and name as if I had known her for centuries. Her large black eyes looked back at me and I connected with her experience. Her husband Ujeshet was pinned by a metal beam to the control console of the saucer ship lying in the water below. He was taking a long time to die under the waters of an ocean he had never known before.

Eleura carried his unborn child, and was conveying the consciousness of the tiny being to Ujeshet as he asked her, “What about the baby?” I sought out the consciousness of Ujeshet and connected with him, sending my love and concern. As my husband’s brother radiated his love back to me there was a loud pop, and I was back in the twilight air of Whale Rock staring directly into the eyes of Gerry.

For a brief instant, Gerry and I connected by mind, just as I had with Ujeshet. Yes, that was it. Gerry was Ujeshet in that distant time. I turned to Karen and had the same connection. Karen was Eleura. We looked at each other and realised why we had come to this place. We had come back to remember, this was the time. We reached out to each other and moved into a tight embrace of reunion. Old friends had come back to live out lives on Earth for this moment in time.

The twilight air was icy cold, yet I felt washed in the warm love of God that was around us and in us. I felt eternally blessed as the three of us joined hand to wrist to form two triangles, one above the other, in an ancient form of greeting, the source of the Star of David.

We raised our interlocked arms out to the stars in thanksgiving. Far above, the soft light of the Pleiades shone down upon us, caressing our faces and drying our tears like a loving mother who had found her long lost children at last. In the exquisite moment of that soothing embrace, we were healed.

Chapter Two

It seemed as if we raced through the fading twilight back to the car. Now we were three people with a very different relationship than we had just moments before. My whole life had suddenly changed. Huge questions posed themselves in my mind. What had just happened on that rock? Who was I when I experienced being that alien person? Who and what am I now?

The first part of the journey back home was in silence, each of us involved in our own thoughts about what had happened. Karen looked troubled and seemed to be making an effort to hold back from crying.

Gerry finally broke the ice. "When I was sixteen, I had a particularly vivid dream. I thought about it for many days afterward because it seemed so real at the time. There was a certain dynamic about it that made me feel as if it had actually happened. In the dream, I was on board a huge spacecraft in orbit around a blue and green planet. Everything on the ship had a bright sheen to it, particularly the uniforms of the people. There was lots of hurried activity, coloured lights were flashing, and bells were ringing. Everyone was in a hurry following certain procedures, as if there were an emergency. I was seeing everything through the eyes of a crewmember, perhaps a pilot or navigator. I felt an urgency to get my family together before some imminent event occurred.

"The scene changed, and I was on board a smaller craft escaping from the mothership. As I looked out the porthole, I became aware of two things, the planet we were heading towards, and the mothership we were leaving. The mothership was an immense saucer or mushroom-shaped silvery craft with hundreds of smaller ships leaving it, one of them containing my wife. They were all heading away in every direction, trying to escape as quickly as possible. Suddenly there was a blinding flash and the mothership blew up. The impact on me was so overwhelming that I woke from the dream.

"Tonight on Whale Rock, I re-lived that dream on the small ship as it hurtled towards the planet. My craft had been crippled in an explosion and I was frantically trying to get it under control. The planet was rushing towards us very fast. As we broke through the cloud layer, I saw the surface below, all green and blue, so beautiful in contrast to the fear that filled my heart. I saw a small bay filled with bright blue water and struggled to focus my mind on bringing the ship to a gentle landing on the shore. I sensed the ship trying to respond, but it could not slow quickly enough. We struck the water. I could feel the bulkhead behind me collapse and pin my body to the control panel.

"The ship began to fill with water through the huge hole that was torn in its side. I signalled for everyone to get out. Several people tried to free me from the control panel, but the water pushed them away. As the ship turned on its side and sank, I tasted the salty water of a strange ocean. All I could think about was my wife and unborn child."

Karen's face seemed both beautiful and sad as she looked at him, "I was your wife."

Gerry turned to her, "Yes, and you gave me such comfort in that moment, bringing me the consciousness of the child that was within you. You gave me hope that our kind would survive in that strange and beautiful world. Our love was so strong, you were with me every moment during the four days it took for me to die. Our bodies were different then, charged with so much energy. But our people could not get to me in time, and so I passed on."

Karen's eyes filled with tears, "Three days after your death, I gave birth to our child, lying in the cradle of rock that was cut for me by the laser rod. He was the first of our people born on the Earth. We called him P'taah of the rock. He fought so hard to live. We all worked to save him. The poor child could not breathe the air. We were all choking on the thick damp gas of the planet. When he died, we all knew that we would have to struggle to survive as a people in that beautiful but deadly place."

I had to stop the car, I couldn't see the road anymore. We all got out to take a breath in the cool night air. The sense of betrayal and anger I felt earlier began to rise within me again. I turned to Gerry and Karen, "What is going on here? Who are we, and why is this happening to us?"

Karen stabbed her finger at me, "Who are you?"

I snapped back, "I am Egarina, the communicator. My husband is the commander in chief of the starship Rexegena. We have come in peace on a mission from God to take this planet back from the Reptoids. They are not of the light and must leave!"

I stopped, gasping for breath. *Where did those words come from?* Karen looked at me quizzically, "What's a Reptoid?"

I felt detached from reality again, like I was back at Kariong. I sat on a nearby rock and sighed, "Damned if I know."

Gerry seemed to understand what was happening, "All of us must have been together before in some other life, but we were not human, at least not human as we know it. Now we have come back together to remember, which we are definitely doing. All we can do is continue to remember and see what happens. I have the feeling that you are some kind of messenger, Valerie, and that we are here to help you."

I looked at him with a frown, "Why do you think that?"

"A Churinga is a message stick or stone used by the Aborigine to send word from one tribe to another. Alcheringa means messenger, as in the one who carries the stick or stone. You have the Alcheringa stone. Even your home has that name. That is why I first came to see you."

"But why me?" I replied weakly.

"You just told us why, you are the communicator."

There would be no sleep that night.

Six am, I lay in bed staring at the ceiling. In my mind, I ran over and over the events of the previous day, trying to understand what had happened. It was real, not some imaginary event. I shared it with two others who confirmed it. Each time I thought about it, something new would come in. I was spontaneously remembering little fragments of a distant past. I got up from the bed and put on my robe. In my study, I lifted the Alcheringa stone from its box. I sat cross-legged on the floor holding the stone and tried to still my thoughts. Softly I called the name Alcheringa, and then felt the familiar sense of detachment.

"It is I, Alcheringa. How may I help you, my child?"

The question had burned in my mind all night, "What was the mission of the Rexegena in coming to Earth?"

"The mission. Ah yes, the mission! Very good dear one, you proceed quite quickly, just as we had hoped."

"This was a very exciting project in the star worlds at that time. We looked forward to achieving what the hierarchy had set before us. The mission was to take many volunteers on a massive living starship to the planet Mu, as we called the Earth in those days. The idea was to set up a base so that a new race could be established, a race that came with the energy of love, harmony, and good will to all. This new energy was to influence what was already taking place on Mu. An aspect of myself had been appointed commander in chief. It was quite a responsibility, but I loved the challenge. My wife, who in that life was you, and our four children, accompanied me. You were all very willing to join me in that journey."

My eyebrows crept up, "I was your wife?"

"Yes, and I loved you dearly, I do so even now. Let us continue. The Rexegena set off from the eighth star of the Pleiadean group with fifty thousand on board. We were going to a place we had never been before. The fifty thousand were from various places within this galaxy. Everyone mingled well together, and all were interested in knowing one another. There was a tremendous sense of excitement and expectation.

"The corner of the galaxy into which we were heading was occupied by races that were not of the same belief patterns as we.

Different belief patterns exist in the star worlds, just as they do on your Earth. Our mission was to change those belief patterns, not with force, but with the influence of love energy, so that these people would come to experience the crystal light. Then these races would understand and know compassion, and how it feels to interact with those of love, light, and joy.

"Now we must travel back to an earlier time so that you will understand what took place. Billions of years before, the Earth itself had come into development, a place that would be suitable for occupation by the hierarchy of which we had come. In those early days, the planet's surface was flat and lifeless. We planned the Earth to become a Garden of Eden. The word Eden comes from a sound, which breaks through the molecule and the atom, helping to create the form.

"The plan required the crust of the Earth to change its shape. Comets and meteors were allowed to hit the surface so that there was created an up and down. Eventually, there was an exchange of gasses and water was introduced onto the planet. With the water, forms of life could be introduced that would be nurtured.

"The hierarchy sent things to create life and help it multiply. Many things were planted in the early stages of the Earth's development. We sent spores and other life forms that could grow and develop on the planet. The changes taking place on the Earth actually fired these elements and substances to create various living forms. The hierarchy created a grid around the planet to help stabilise it, allowing more growth to take place.

"Little forms of life such as fungus, mollusks, and others of low development began to grow and multiply. Many from the hierarchy and the Angelic Realms worked together to help this take place.

"It was at this time that there was interest shown by many of the cultures throughout the cosmos, in particular the extraterrestrial beings that already existed in this corner of the galaxy. They began coming and going to the Earth, showing much interest in the place. These beings came to Earth many millions of years before the journey of the Rexegena. They were created by a different hierarchy, one that came more from the point of self and power. While the energies in these beings were of the light, they did not possess the energy of love and compassion. They were the Reptoids, and as their name suggests, they were reptilian. We say once again, while they understood the light and had the intelligence that goes with it, they did not understand love. They did not have that created within them in the first place.

"There were other races created as such in this corner of the galaxy, including the Dinoid, who also came to the Earth. Because of the missing element of love, dissension eventually arose among them. This resulted in competition and even wars. This was not unusual; it happened in many places in the universe during those early times hundreds of millions of years ago. You must understand that these races had been created by others who had turned away from the light of The One.

"Those of the Angelic Realms who had been working to create this Garden of Eden came from the Elohim. Some were caught up with what was taking place on this Earth and were concerned about the visitations by the Reptoid and Dinoid races, who were starting to claim the planet for themselves. The Reptoids and the Dinoids were also beginning to create many life forms themselves on the planet Earth. They created through genetic engineering, for they were very good at it and enjoyed it immensely.

"While the Reptoids and Dinoids were actually different races, there was a similarity in their nature that allowed them to live in a sort of uneasy way together on the Earth. They both had abilities in genetic engineering and between them created many different life forms. Look at the face of almost any frog in your time and you will see the natural face of the Dinoid.'

'The two races began to work together and started creating, almost like an artist's brush, many different life forms. It became a sort of competition to see who could outdo the other, for they rather enjoyed this.'

"The dinosaur was created by them. This was a Dinoid as well as Reptoid influence, although the dinosaur bore the name of the Dinoid. Through creative competition between the two races, the dinosaurs became larger and more ferocious. As they became larger, they became full of teeth and very dangerous.

The animals continued to breed with one another, and the numbers increased dramatically. The foliage was being eaten very quickly, and in many places the Earth became desert-like. Waste materials from the creatures and their dead bodies littered the landscape.

"A way was needed to have these materials fall back into the Earth, so the Reptoids and Dinoids created virus, bacteria, and parasite forms to assist this process in taking place.

"Many millions of years passed with all this activity on Earth. Other visitors came from different star worlds to visit. They did not stay for very long because of the danger that filled the place. The Earth was overrun by Reptoid and Dinoid creations. This did not fit with the plan of the Elohim, and there were some who sought to try and take it back. This was more difficult than first thought, so the Elohim decided to monitor what was taking place on the Earth. They sent beings that changed their form and entered the waters to become what you know as the whale. In this form, they were the first and only mammal upon the Earth. In fact, they were the only mammal for a long time.

"The whales were able to hold the light and the plan within their consciousness. They helped the Elohim to continue their work and influence upon this planet, even though the Reptoid and Dinoid races were busily going about their own plans. The form of the whale, operating in the waters, did not interfere with what was taking place with the Reptoids and Dinoids on the land. They all lived in reasonable harmony. The Reptoids and Dinoids were not aware that the Elohim were allowing it to take place. There was an unwritten agreement allowing two developments on the Earth at the same time.

"There was a greater plan, one that this planet could be used as a base by people who came with love and light to influence those in this corner of the galaxy where there was so much darkness. Events were scheduled that would change this, events that would eventually allow the Rexegena to set off on its great mission."

"When did the Rexegena come to Earth?" I asked.

"That would have been nine hundred thousand years ago."

"Nearly a million years ago, that's a long time," I noted.

"Not in the star worlds. Someone is coming to see you. There are some things we want you to do."

"But I'm not expecting anybody," I said, as the phone rang. I answered to hear a woman's voice. "Valerie, my name is Pamela Goddard. I came to see you about a year ago. You may not remember me, but I'm getting very strong messages to call you and I don't know why."

"Um, yes I remember you," I replied somewhat thunderstruck. Pulling out my address book, I found her name. Next to it, I had written *clar.* Pamela was a clairvoyant.

My mouth automatically said, "Well, perhaps we should get together sometime and talk."

"Oh good," she replied, "I can be at your place at two o'clock, sound okay?"

"Uh, sure why not, see you here at two." I hung up the phone, "Is Pamela Goddard the one?"

Alcheringa replied, "Yes, that's the one."

Pamela's car came up the driveway at exactly two o'clock. My eye caught the wall clock in the kitchen and I noted her promptness. As the second hand swept past twelve, the phone rang. The caller was my friend Rachel. I had been struggling to help Rachel through a crisis. She was either getting a little carried away with psychic experiences or there was something very wrong with her. The doorbell rang. I recognised Pamela immediately and invited her to have a seat on the lounge while I finished my phone call.

I returned to the phone to hear Rachel talking as if I had never left. Rachel was confused and unsure of herself. She felt that the two of us might have a 'karmic' thing together. She wanted to meet with me and 'work it out'. I stammered out that I had a guest who had just arrived and promised to call her back later. An instant headache settled over me; I felt depressed. Apologising for my mood, I offered Pamela some hot lemon tea.

As we did the little ceremony, Pamela tried to calm my nerves. "I understand just how you feel. I have an acquaintance I'm trying to help who is doing the same thing to me. She has some 'special' things she has to do, and at the same time, she feels unsure of herself and needs constant assurance that she is on the right path. On top of that, Rachel is..."

"Rachel?" I interrupted.

"That's right," Pamela replied. "Rachel is..."

My eyes narrowed, "Rachel O'Meara?" The tiniest fraction of Pamela's composure slipped as she let out a small gasp. We stared at each other in silence for a magical second before breaking into laughter.

Pamela shrugged her shoulders and sipped her tea. "Okay, Valérie. I'm here, what do you want with me?"

We laughed a bit more as I looked at the package of pictures from Kariong sticking out of my purse, the ones I had rushed to the photo shop that morning to have developed. "Well, let's see," I said. I moved to the bookshelf, picked up the Alcheringa stone, and walked over to Pamela in one smooth movement, "Do you mind if I set this in your lap?"

I sat it on her lap before she had a chance to answer. She looked at it a bit askance, "No, I guess not. What is it?"

I took the pictures from my purse, "It's a stone."

Pamela eyed it a bit closer, "Oh, what's that stuff covering it?"

Sitting back in my chair, I removed the photos from the envelope, "It's the bark of the paper bark tree." Pamela touched the texture of the bark, "It's, it's so..."

"Aboriginal," I interjected. "Would you please look at these pictures?" Pamela took the photos.

The phone rang again. It was Karen and she was unhappy.

"This is terrible, I looked at the video, and everything on it is all jerky. I can't make any of the hieroglyphs out. We have to go back to Kariong."

Pamela gave the photos a cursory glance, "Hmm, these rock carvings look Egyptian."

"Go back, what do you mean by jerky?" I asked.

Pamela continued, "This one is Anubis, the god of the underworld I think." Karen continued to complain, "You know, the picture bounces back and forth between glyphs. It only stops for a second and then bounces away again. I can't see a thing."

"Didn't you take that video Karen?"

"I've always wanted to go to Egypt," said Pamela.

"Of course I did Valérie, I know that. You never touched my camera. It doesn't matter. They're no good, we have to go back."

"When did you go there?" inquired Pamela. I pulled the phone away from my ear and looked at Pamela, "Those were taken at Kariong yesterday."

"Kariong?" "Yes, near Gosford, about four hours from here."

I returned to the phone, "You can look at my pictures Karen, they're all nice and sharp."

John walked in and introduced himself to Pamela. Karen seemed to calm down, "Oh, well I'm coming over right now to look at them."

"Karen, I can't see you right now, I'm in a meeting. How about tomorrow?" "Tomorrow? Well in that case we should go back to Kariong."

"Do you seriously want to go back to Kariong?"

"Yes."

John turned and looked at me in amazement, "Are you really going back to Kariong?"

Pamela smiled, "Oh, can I go with you?"

Things got fuzzy for a moment; John was never interested in Kariong before. "Well, okay if you like."

John shrugged his shoulders and walked out. Karen was delighted, "Fantastic, I'll be there at five am, we should get an early start. Bye."

"What?" I replied. Karen had hung up. It all happened so quickly. Pamela looked at the photos, "These look real to me."

I sat next to her, "They're real, Pamela. Look at the pictures carefully, see if there is anything in them that you recognise or get a feeling from."

Pamela began a closer inspection of the pictures. At first, she had no reaction, flipping through them slowly, regarding each one calmly. She stopped at one, held it closer, and stared at one of the rock carvings. Pamela's face began to change, her calm demeanor falling away as a tear tumbled down her cheek onto the picture. She closed her eyes and a look of horror came over her face. "Oh no, I don't want to remember this, there was too much suffering."

"It's okay," I replied. Taking the pictures, I wiped the tear away and looked closely at the frame she was staring at, "Pamela, what did you see when you closed your eyes?"

"The ship, I saw the ship, the same one I see in my dreams. It's always that ship, the one that brought me here. It was so big and solid, how could they have destroyed it?" She began to cry. A memory in Pamela was being triggered by one of the pictures.

"Pamela, I have those memories too, and I know others who do as well."

Pamela wiped her eyes with her hands, "What is happening to me?"

"I'm not quite sure, you're the first person I've shown these photos to. I remembered the ship at Kariong along with two others. All we know is that these rock carvings are some kind of message that seems to awaken memories."

Pamela allowed me to slowly lead her back to that memory. In a manner that ranged from panicky and desperate to calm and lucid, Pamela let out the pent-up emotions of the ship in her dreams.

"I'm stuck here on this planet, we have nothing and can barely breathe the air. I only came here because my family wanted to come, and now they are all dead. What am I doing in this terrible place? I have to help the injured ones, there is no time to suffer the loss of my husband and children. I have fifty things to do, and everyone is going crazy. How could this happen?

"We are devastated, except for our emergency rations there is no food. We don't know what we can eat on this planet. Even the water is dangerous, filled with tiny creatures we have never seen before. I am exhausted, working day and night. Everyone is asking me questions because I have the knowledge of healing.

"Now it's evening and I am down by the water. We can come out in the open when the sun is down. I'm walking along by myself feeling a bit tattered. There is work all the time, healing bodies and putting them together again."

I asked her to describe herself.

"I'm quite tall, willowy I would say. I don't think I have hair. I have big eyes, my skin is very smooth, pale and transparent, kind of whitish, grayish, blue.'

"What about your head?" I asked.

"It feels long, kind of flat on the back. Oh, I still have my laboratory cap on. Ah, I do have some hair, it's bunched up under my cap. Hmm, the cap feels just like skin."

"What do you do in the laboratory?" I asked.

"I'm there with the test tubes and bottles, nothing too fancy because we have a shortage of them. In the beginning, we had what seemed like a first aid kit, now we have a sort of laboratory. We are matching genes for inter-breeding."

"Interbreeding, what are you interbreeding with?"

"We are interbreeding with the upstanding ape creatures from this planet. Everything must be done quickly. Otherwise, the new race will be lost. That's what we came here to do, so it must be done. Things will not keep in this atmosphere, we have no working refrigeration. It's all so new to us."

"Wait, with apelike creatures? How do you do this interbreeding?"

"I am one of the volunteers who will be artificially inseminated, many of the other women have volunteered. We are the ones who will carry the new race into being, a race that can survive in this place."

"But why are you doing this with apelike creatures from the Earth, was this the original plan?"

"No, but we cannot survive here as we are, our newborn children die. It is very difficult, everything has to be very precise. I still have trouble with breathing. I have learned a lot from a Reptoid who joined us. He is very helpful and honest, completely turned around in his ways. I like him very much and can feel his humour. He has shown us how to use vegetation for food and medicine."

"But what happens with this interbreeding thing with the apelike creatures?"

"Some women give birth one after another. This goes on for a while. The women give birth very easily as no pain is involved. The children are very well looked after. Later, they begin to breed amongst themselves."

I must admit that I was in a little state of shock. Here were survivors from a starship, cast onto the Earth, attempting genetic engineering from a first aid kit. "Does the interbreeding with these apelike creatures succeed?"

"Some of them don't turn out quite right, some of them do. There is still much genetic engineering work going on to match the people."

I gasped, "What do you mean some of them don't turn out quite right?"

"It is all for a good purpose. The whole idea is to bring love, light, and peace to the Earth, so that people don't make judgments of others, so that we don't get caught up with wars, hostility, and anger.

"I am old now. I have all this research and knowledge inside of me. I do a lot of teaching to the new ones. I teach about my work with plantlife. It seems I know an awful lot of things.

"The first part of my life was secure, I had a good family. Then I was stranded here and I lost everyone. I never saw my home-world again. I can feel that loss now, it's terrible. I pushed it all down inside of me, so very deep.

"This influenced all my other lives, and it explains my lives of solitude. I've had so many just on my own. Rather than face the hurt and pain, I have lived my life as a nun, or lived by myself. It's all because of the fear of letting my emotions go. Now I have gone and done it again in this life."

Pamela opened her eyes and the tears began to fall anew.

"Isn't that interesting?"

Pamela put her head on my shoulder and cried.

In 2002, it was believed the story 'Starpeople Revisited' still wasn't ready for the mainstream reader. So, it was first released under the name *Alcheringa, When the First Ancestors were Created*, to honour the Australian Indigenous people who are not only the oldest race on Earth but the First Humans. Or the hue-mans blessed with divine light from the Source of All Creation.

In later times, down through the ages of human development, various benevolent starpeople succeeded in upgrading the human's DNA to whom we are now.

70 Prophecies, Myths, Legends & Lost History

I have been advised by my Oversoul, Valoel, an androgynous being from the Angelic Realms in Andromeda M31 that I am commissioned by an edict to bring this story as a messenger, to Earth peoples. John has agreed to assist me.

The Return of the 8th White Sister (*plus the Seven Sisters*) from the Pleiades—Dreaming stories held by the Australian Aborigine of their return when the time was right.

We know her as Egarina, wife of Alchquaringa.

The sign of the WHITE creatures large and small manifesting around the world and in particular the White Buffalo. A legend told by many of the American Native Indian tribes and prophesied great change on Earth. Our past life as American Red Indian links us with this prophecy.

It is interesting, Andromeda Val advises, that all the wild animals are white in Andromeda and are all friendly. It is no coincidence that there are many WHITE animals and birds born onto Earth at present.

White Eagle also said, in his first introduction to me, "That a group of souls on Earth would help to manifest a manuscript that had been written 2,000 years ago, by John the Divine and known as *The Book of Love*. God has asked John the Divine to 'eat it' at the time and by that I presume God meant he was to hold it back.

Somebody then coordinatedly gave us a book about a legend, *The Sign of the Dove* by Elizabeth van Buren.

The legend reads of John the Divine's manuscript *The Book of Love* held by the Cathars, saying it would be found South of France under the sign of the white dove. It would reveal marvelous revelations, at a pre-ordained time, by a predestined being of perfect innocence and absolute purity.' See https://www.valeriebarrow.com/?p=179

John and I incarnated as brother and sister elders in the Cathars on Montsegur. The Cathars referred to themselves as '*The Pure Ones*' and held the manuscript written by John the Divine for over 1,200 years.

We have now been made aware the original manuscript held by the Cathars was consumed by fire at Montsegur in 1244.

White Eagle has advised us that my John was connected to him in a past-life memory, of him being John the Divine, the author of the lost *The Book of Love* and that I was John's sister named Judith in that life over 2,000 years earlier. That was the family of Jesus and the Essenes. Coordinatedly, my second name in this life is Judith.

We have recorded four past-life stories from the South of France—that includes the Cathar perfecta brother and sister elders from Montsegur.

Our visit to the Bay of Marys in Gaul led us to unexpectedy witness the Evocation, the landing of Jesus' family and those in danger after he was crucified, and our connection to the legend—and to our oversoul.

The story of Jehanne d'Arc, who used to call herself 'La Pucelle', The Pure One, who tried to teach of one's internal spirituality and...'The Voice Within'.

Pope Clement V, who tried to stop the terrible Inquisition by the Catholic Church but died with deep unhappiness...seeing the white dove guide him home upon his death. He also wore a green ring exactly the same as was given to Valérie in this life, by the Avatar in India.

The last part of the prophetic legend speaks of the manuscript being found in a cave South of France. And so, the prophecy has come to pass...who would have thought the lost manuscript is glyphs written on stone walls in a cave in Kariong, north of Sydney in NSW, Australia?

Many psychics have now visited the glyphs at Kariong near Gosford. Just looking at the glyphs (*even in photos*) people have remembered their part in coming from the Pleiades to establish a civilisation of light in this dark corner of the galaxy, The Milky Way. After having read the book *Alcheringa, When the First Humans were Created*, they have healed and drawn comfort from the story. Thousands have contacted us since and still do. We were advised by our mentor that everyone in the universe heard of the story, but not all were involved.

It is no coincidence that the *The Book of Love* and the *Alcheringa book, When the First Humans were Created* (*that was the rest of the story*) have been personally blessed by the Avatar of the Age in this, I am advised, preordained time.

When John and I were travelling to sacred places in 2010, we were asked to write another book about the many, many past-life memories we have shared together. This was when we were standing on the Great Pyramid at Giza, Egypt. The book *Two Soulmates, Walking through Time and History* has been published. That led us to joining all the dots and understanding our mission and the reason we have come.

Now the work has been requested by my spirit benevolent mentors to gather all the books into one book as a permanent record under the title *Starlady, the True Story of Valérie and Mr. Dickens*, and other lifetimes spent with John Barrow.

As we all come from the world of divine light as souls, the Holy Blood is within us all.

Egarina Speaks

71

Here are some of our working notes when working with Egarina, the wife of Alchquaringa, the commander in chief of the huge mothership Rexegena.

As already told, the ship was raised on the 8th planet of the Pleiades in the constellation of Taurus. The leaders were originally from Lya, a planet that exists in the galaxy Andromeda M31. However, they had to reduce their light frequency to work from the Pleiades and planet Earth.

These are sessions Valérie had in the year 1999 telepathically with Egarina, who came to Earth as a survivor of the mission of the starship Rexegena. She was the wife of the commander in chief, remember...

"I am Egarina. I have come this day to present myself to you. Do not be afraid. Many from the star worlds are here.

"See the ocean, the way it moves in and out. There is movement in everything. Even the mother Earth moves. Her breath comes in and out just as the tides. There is a constant movement of energy. Take this energy into you, breath it in and out. There is a wonderful flowing gentleness, and if all is well within you, nothing will obstruct that energy flow.

"You come and you go much the same as the breath. *Do you understand*?"

Her voice was soothing and I relaxed, "*Yes, I think so.*"

"There is another aspect of you, as there is with everybody. From that point, you operate with more knowledge and understanding. The body is transitional, it has a very limited life. A personality, however, is a line that is descendant. It really does not matter what dimension it operates in. The knowingness and the knowledge will still operate, whether it is through the personality that you are now or another. You come from that point of knowingness, so there is no limit."

Egarina laughed softly.

"But not to rush out because you hear of other things, my dear, stay where you feel right within your heart."

Even her humour entranced me, this woman with a manner that was so gentle.

"I am here to remind people of who they are and how they are connected with the cosmic races. While the body they walk in is the race of the earthling, it is not all that they are."

"*Why do you do this?*" I asked.

"This is the completion of an agreement I made nearly one million years ago, a promise that one day I would come back when the time was right. This was given while leaving my body at that time. I had begun to see and understand what the bigger plan was all about, in creating a race with warmth, love, and peace in their hearts. It is they who will help to change the energies upon this Earth.

"A new race was created, born with a more evolved brain, with increased intelligence and psychic gifts to a degree. The new race was more aware of ceremonies and energies. They were aware of the Creator and his love. This made them different from the brothers and sisters that had been created by others before them. This meant the Reptoid and Dinoid, races that did not naturally have love and compassion built into them, had an opportunity to incarnate into a new race and experience these emotions. This is because we built the crystalline energy or, as you know it, the Christ energy into the new earthling bodies.

"This put them on a path that allowed them to evolve. Now they could come and go, experiencing down through the ages, and then return to their cosmic races, taking the energy with them. The process will continue until this corner of the galaxy becomes evolved with divine energy, love, and compassion."

I shuddered, "Doesn't that mean a lot of people on the Earth are incarnating from Reptoid and Dinoid worlds, and doesn't that kind of make them like, Reptoids and Dinoids?"

"Yes, it does Valérie."

"The Earth will soon enter into a new Golden Age, one of love and peace. On that day there will come a final choice. Some people have spoken of it as The Judgement Day."

"This is correct, but it is a judgement of the self by the self. It is the last opportunity for the self to make that choice. A choice must be made to follow guidance from the love of all or that which is good for the few. For many, it is a simple choice.

"There will be those who will not agree. When that last choice comes, they can move with us all or they can be assisted to another place. This is not a threat. It is up to each little earthling to decide. There is no judgement, but there are some whose energies are different, and they are not yet ready to move into the Golden Age.

"I have made my presence known to you, please be aware of me. I work to assist with the transition. You must help me in this work. All you need do is write the events taking place into a book. This will be received with love and compassion."

I laughed. "Well, I've already done that."

"That one was for practice, to familiarise you. Now others will help you to write another one that tells the whole story, some already have. This one will reach many to reawaken memories. Do not worry about the outcome. You are merely here in service. Deep within your soul is knowledge that this is reality. Are you understanding my dear?"

The room was spinning. "I, ah..."

Egarina whispered, "I thank you, and I take my leave."

Valérie: It is quite strange. I feel as if I am sitting in a bubble. I feel it pushing against me and if I lean forward, it pushes me back. It is pushing against my face. I have to come out now.

72 Egarina the 8th White Sister

Who has Returned...

Valérie channeling Egarina:
Egarina speaks about the Eighth White Sister.

"Almost a million years has passed for the evolution of the little earthling since I first came to this planet. There has been influence down through the ages to help with their evolution.

"When I left my star being body, I returned straight away and walked into one of the new creatures. I was able to take on a role as mother and continue to do the work of light and love because the new creatures had been imbued with the crystalline energy. I was very much the 'wise woman' of the tribe. I taught the new ones how to work with the psychic energy that increased knowledge and wisdom, and to use telepathy to communicate.

"The new people did not have the ability to understand technical knowledge. It was easier for them to understand concepts like the lizard people, the snake people, and others that were connected to the reptiles. The furry animals were linked to the race from which they had come. They were all told stories from that point, a little like you would tell stories about animals to children.

"It was from there the myth of the white sisters was established. This lore was given to the Aborigine people to help them remember their source. The original story was that the sisters had come from the Pleiades and when the family of the original ones died they returned to the Pleiades. They weren't given the full details of the galactic families or races in the earlier days. They were just told that the seven stars represented the Pleiades group.

"The little Aborigine people could look to the sky, point to the Pleiades system, and see seven stars. They understood the number seven. We taught them this. They even made up their own little stories. They kept the story going amongst their storytellers in various tribes. At times, I would manifest to them as a reminder.

"They were also told that one sister from the eighth star would return, the star that was just out of their sight. The idea of the Eighth White Sister returning was to update their knowledge of understanding, to remind them once again of their beginnings from the Pleiades, and at the same time spread the story and the knowledge of the original mission to Earth.

"This was promised to happen when the time was right, and that time is now. Of course, in the bigger plan, the story was to be released not only to the Aboriginal people, but to all those who have their ears open, and are ready to hear."

Did the mothership in fact originate from the eighth star?

"Looking from the Earth, yes.

"About the time the myth was being told to them, the starpeople were also teaching the Aborigine people about the energy of crystals, which they have always used. The crystalline energy protected the starpeople, and we wanted the Aborigine people to understand that they too were protected by the crystalline energy that was imbued in them. They didn't have the technology or the knowledge as a scientist to understand the structure of crystalline energy, and so we showed them crystals and connected to it that way.

"Mt. Warning was then an active volcano. The people came to know and understand that crystals existed on Mt Warning and that crystals came from the inside of the Earth. It was easy for them to understand that other crystals would still be under the great mountain, and so it was told to them that the sister lay asleep inside a crystal under the mountain. It was just a way in helping them to understand that she was with them, and that she would come forth, when the time was right, to help them to understand their beginnings.

"The Aboriginal people were very good at holding the original story, but sometimes they got a bit carried away and embellished it. They expanded the story to some degree, which is why there are a number of them that differ. But their common line is that a sister from the eighth star will come back for when time is right to release knowledge. The Aborigines are aware, and they wait."

How will this knowledge be known?

"It is to be through your book, my dear one, for I am the eighth white sister. My message is one of hope, one of love and compassion for one another in all races. The people of the world will join together knowing that they are all the same. There will no longer be a reason for them to fight amongst themselves, and there will be peace. My message is of the love from the Source that imbues all.

"The future walks by itself separately, yet beside you. The future can be many different things depending on which track one walks. The future is how you think and feel, and how you imbue the love into yourselves and each other. If all walk with love and compassion for their brothers and sisters, no matter what the colour of their skin, they will create a race of harmony and goodwill.

"Everyone will choose the path on which they walk. They will make the decision individually. There will be those who walk one track and those who walk another. The individual will only walk a track that suits their frequency. At all times, the choice is theirs. With the knowledge of the eighth white sister returning, they will hopefully give serious thought to the direction their steps will take, on what track they will choose."

How does one know they are on the right track?

"There is no such thing as the right track, it is one's choice about what one feels happy about. We hope our story will help people to make the choice, and realise and gain inner strength. It is up to them.

"There are many ways to find the God consciousness within. This book is not designed for that. The eighth white sister returns to bring knowledge of the existence of many galactic races that are connected to the Source, and to bring knowledge to the races that have been victims and do not know and understand the Source. Egarina challenges them to find the God consciousness within.

The Golden Age is coming, a rising of frequency amongst all the beings upon this Earth. It is the same for the mother when she is about to produce a child. This is what is happening to Mother Earth. Her frequency is being raised, she is about to give birth to new children with raised consciousness."

Sacred Wollumbin—where the Eighth Black Sister from the Pleiades sleeps

73 Egarina Speaks: 2002

From Betrayal and Destruction...to the Golden Age

Valerie can actually see Egarina sitting on the box that holds the crystal in the command room of the mothership Rexegena. Like her children, she also liked sitting on that box and observing the command room. It was quite big, people moving around quietly, calmly observing.

It had a huge unlimited view, looking out into the universe. It was a spectacular view. It is understandable that the children should like watching. Egarina liked watching also.

(*Egarina changes the time and view.*)

Betrayal and Destruction

"I am actually back on the land surrounded by complete destruction, the mothership Rexegena had been destroyed. My brothers and sisters are in agony with severe pain and loss. I myself feel that loss, the loss of my husband and four children. But this also only comes after a period when we all helped each other to try and recover, after the surveillance ship had gone into the water and after we had all so frantically followed it. We knew it would need assistance as soon as it hit the Earth.

"We were able to land reasonably close to it in our escape vehicle, so we quickly gave assistance to those who had crashed into the water. The dolphins had already brought some to the shore. The ones brought to shore were in such a sorry state, many needed help, and many needed to be looked after. There was no time to think much about what had happened. It was a war-like scene, there was total destruction."

Dolphins helped the starpeople to shore

"It is only after some time passed that we were able to make shelter for ourselves, to gather together to draw strength from one another, and to try and get some sense into what happened and why it happened. It was quite clear that the Reptoids had gone back on their word. They had no intention of handing over the planet Mu, they had deceived us into believing that they would leave. There had been an edict from the Galactic Council that they were to leave. They were given a choice, they could leave quietly and in peace, or they would be hunted off the planet. They had no right to stay; they had come in the first place, millions of years before, against the will of the Galactic Council.

"But now they had been told to leave, and they had agreed, or so we thought. But they had gone back on their word, something we could not understand, we just could not believe that someone could go back on their word. What they said was not what they meant. **It was not what they meant at all.**

"Instead of that, they sent out warships and attacked the mothership Rexegena that had taken so long to prepare and to grow into its shape. And then to travel with those fifty thousand people on board from so many different races from the cosmic worlds. The families, the children, so many were lost. There was no time to dwell on that any more, we had to make the best of what had happened. We were left without any of the technology we had, we were left with great difficulty in surviving. We knew that we could no longer survive the way we were used to, we would have to find new ways."

Survival on a new planet

"We soon discovered that even when we drank the water it made us sick. We tried to eat food from the foliage, but some of that made us very sick, in fact it killed some, it poisoned them. We lost more in anguish. We were still suffering from the trauma of what had happened. There was no time to be sorry, we had to really make the best of what we could to survive. We had come on a mission to bring light into this corner of the galaxy, and to this planet, and survive we would.

"We were determined to survive, we would find ways, we would find out how to live in this harsh but beautiful land. It was difficult. Then some of our enemy came and joined us. These reptilians wanted to help because they were so upset about what their own people had done, what their king and queen had done. They didn't go along with what had taken place. They liked us, they knew we were good people, that we had something in us that they wanted to be part of. They asked if they could join us so that they could help us, and we welcomed their help.

"We forgave them; we forgave the race that they had come from. There was no time, no point in holding grudges. Not all of their race were bad people, it was quite obvious, and so we accepted their help and they showed us different ways of clearing the water with certain leaves, and showed us food from the foliage that was safe to eat, the seeds that could be ground and made into little cakes. We had enough sustenance; we didn't need very much. We were never used to eating very much.

"Thus, we all gathered together, decided to stay together. There were a few that we knew had come to Earth in a different place. We tried to get them to come with us, but they decided not to. They did not survive very long, but we did because we stayed together and supported each other. Some interbred with each other, it was not an unusual thing to take place after losing their own families. But we found that the newborn did not survive."

The Need for Genetic Engineering

"So, we had to find a way of adjusting or genetically changing the babies so that they could survive. We knew the starpeople babies would never survive and so we drew from the experience and knowledge that there were these ape-like creatures that had been constructed and made by the reptilians, using genetic material from the Leonines, who were a warm blooded race that we were familiar with and friendly with. We knew that was a starting basis.

"The dugong had served as their mothers also, and had that energy in them. It was a good start, so we decided to blend genetic material from them with the female eggs of the starmothers who had volunteered. These eggs were implanted back into the starmothers. They saw that as a great honour, for they felt that they had permission from God. This was why they had come, to bring light to this area, to establish a community, and this is what they were going to do. Nothing would stop them, they were determined it would succeed, and when the babies were born suffering so badly with too much hair that was strangling them, the starmothers were very distraught, not knowing how the babies would survive, and sadly they did not survive."

Dugong

"They were determined to have another try at genetic engineering and used the eggs of the upstanding ape creature, and implanted genetic material from the starpeople. This time, the babies survived. They had a larger skull shape, as we had. They had skin that was a little tougher; it was certainly darker. The hair, of course, was still there, but it had fallen away slightly, which was a result of the genetic work we had done. The starpeople were quite used to using genetics for interacting and creating, it was not an unusual thing at all. The babies survived quite well. Some were malformed. This saddened us, and we assisted them and helped them.

"We brought them into our fold and adopted them. They loved us also, for the energy was exchanged, and the energy from the starpeople was interwoven into these new little creatures. Our families became one. This made us happy, this is what we felt was what the mission was supposed to do, and in some way we didn't know at the time how, but this was definitely the way that it was going to work. These little creatures would be able to hold the light from the divine source, hold it within their bodies, and spread it."

Inner Happiness with Light and Love: The REAL Mission

"This was what the mission was about. We began to realise and understand the mission *hadn't* worked the way we thought it was going to, but in our determination and courage we did succeed. We were very pleased with ourselves to some degree. There were still many things to overcome. We managed to make settlements and housing of sorts to take shelter, for the sun was unkind to our skin and our head. The new little ones with hair on their heads and a skin that was more suited to the environment, thrived.

"They were loving creatures, loving to one another, and loving to us. We thrived from the energy that had finally been born onto the planet Mu (Earth). We felt that we had succeeded in our mission. We continued to make genetic improvements to the eggs in other ways as more children came, until we found that the best way of producing children without any malformation was to encourage them not to breed with each other. We established encoded symbols so that they would understand that they could not interbreed with brothers and sisters. They needed to be sure to breed only with those that were far enough apart genetically as to not cause malformation.

"The little community thrived. Those that survived lived for quite some time. The children grew, and a decision was made that they should go out and multiply, to continually spread the new knowledge that we had taught them, the energy that came from the starpeople, and the rituals and ceremonies that we had also taught them. They needed to spread that information. It was time for them to go out and multiply with the other upstanding ape like creatures that were still brutish and weapon wielding.

"This they did and after a time we also felt they could be taken out further. We did have an airship that still could be used. We had tentatively explored the area around where we were settled. However, we were not aware, nor sure, as to how safe we would be, if we ventured too far. Although the ship was crippled for lack of power, it was able to travel to some degree.

"After a time, we set a course out past the coasts and moved onto other lands, and eventually spread these new creatures who possessed starpeople genes and understandings along with psychic abilities to different places on the planet. We encouraged them to establish settlements of their own. This continued long after the starpeople had died."

The Return of Egarina and the Golden Age

"I myself, as Egarina, said to the ones that looked after me so well (*for we looked after them when they were children—they, in turn, looked after us when we became old*), I said to them—I assured them, that I would return when the time was right. I have returned now, for the time is right. Now we are moving into change, the Earth, the energy, everything around is changing whether we realise it or not.

"There are new energies coming onto the Earth that are of a golden nature. It brings with it wisdom, compassion, and love, as always has been available to everyone that is on the Earth. Now it is coming in waves that are much stronger and people will know, understand, and accept this new knowledge. They can experience and feel for themselves changes happening around them. Where it does not flow, where the energy of goodness which is of God is not present, then structures fall apart such as banks, such as societies that are controlled with police or harsh regimes, or with dealings with anything within that society.

"Society itself is changing. There are some outbreaks of war, for people still disagree and think that hitting one another with weapons is the only way to solve problems. But, of course, if they accept the new energy that is coming onto the Earth, and imbue themselves with it, they will realise and lift their consciousness to understand and know they can solve and resolve any problems. It does not matter what is the problem among people, there can always be a solution in some way without fighting."

Egarina, as I speak through Valérie, has returned.

"I have come back to remind people of their beginnings and remind them also that we are in a time of great change, a turning point which will come, in a decade, to lead them into the Golden Age. The future of the Golden Age will be one where genes will be able to be changed, so there will no longer be disease or malformation. All these things will be corrected, and the information and knowledge will be given once again from the starpeople.

"This is the time, this is what all are moving into. I am very happy to be back, to say that it is time. Please listen, please move with the change, please come to know the spirit and the energy of God that presents itself now on the planet. Accept it, allow yourself to be imbued with it, and rise to become the children of God. That's it.

"Our galaxy, our solar system now receives energy from the central sun of all universes—bringing forth a Golden Age on Earth."

*****

It is here I would like to mention that my John and I first came together in the star worlds on this mission. He was a starman from Sirius—he had many lives as a Leonine, but when we met at the time the Leonines and the starpeople came to rescue us, it was John, as a starman from an all-male planet who had come, as the commander, on a Leonine Ship to rescue us. His name was Himel. He looked more like us, as starpeople. He was very tall and his skull rose up—whereas we had skulls that tended to grow out from the back. He was the one who had handed Egarina the sacred Alcheringa stone from the stars—that was like a 'little piece of home' that held so much of our story from Alcheringa. The starman who was the commander-in-chief of the huge mothership Rexegena that had been destroyed. He had sent it to us, via Himel. It brought an upliftment of love and compassionate energy that we, the survivors, had thought we had lost.

Egarina Speaks: Survival and the First Hue-mans

74

Egarina—An Angelic Being

Egarina is now an angelic being who has been involved in the 'seeding' of planets in many universes.

Egarina: My mission as an angelic being never ceases, for I have great love and compassion for all that exist upon this earth and other worlds. I have no limitation as to who is or who isn't, my love at all times is readily given. I have worked as an angelic being in my fullest state many times before and on many occasions, I have been involved with this planet Earth, and many times within the galaxy, within the universe, and other universes.

Egarina has come to Earth many times. In Egarina's time, Earth was known as 'Mu'.

Egarina: I was involved in its earliest conception. This is a role that the angelic beings take in helping planets to be birthed into a being of one that is planned for use by cosmic races.

When the angelic being takes form, a limitation occurs.

Egarina: I was an aspect of that angelic being. I actually knew and understood that at the time, but what took place and what happened to the body called Egarina at that time was blocked from her understanding to some point, to some degree. Egarina as an aspect was limited.

Valérie goes on to explain how Egarina feels about this episode, for Egarina has strong feelings:

Valérie: I feel Egarina's presence and she was upset. She was upset even while she was on the ship, because she had a deep feeling that mission would not succeed. She tried to talk to her husband Alchqaringa (Alcheringa), but he told her not to worry, that all would be well, and so there was nowhere to turn. So, she put it out of her mind and got on with it. So that deep down, when she was thrust onto the Earth, it really wasn't a surprise. Although it was very difficult, very traumatic, it angered her. They had been let down, they felt they had been betrayed. I felt I had been betrayed.

The Betrayal and the Robot

Egarina: There was a realisation that all along it wasn't going to succeed, and it doesn't really matter what was said, it was a feeling of betrayal. In the beginning, I voiced it to my husband Alchqaringa (known to us today as Alcheringa). Everybody was so happy and excited that it was very easy to be put off, to put the fears behind me, not to worry any more, and to just go along with the mood that prevailed on the ship.

Egarina shares that there was a 'changeover' ceremony with the Reptoids. They were to leave and allow the Starpeoples of the mothership Rexegena to settle on Earth. There was a communication crystal, which Egarina used to report back to the Elohim (the hierarchy) of the steps taken in the mission.

Egarina: The crystal was always available for communication while I was on the ship, and I did come ashore for the ceremony. At that time, I was a little uneasy, we felt an air of mistrust, and we felt that energy amongst the reptilian people. We felt that something was not quite right. Also, we were reassured by the hierarchy that existed, by the king and his queens that all was as it should be. Yet, they seemed confused, saying one thing and then contradicting themselves in another. It was like it was not a totally committed agreement in the way that we work. We put it down to them just being a different race, and there was nothing to worry about, at least that is what we hoped. We returned to the mothership and it was not long after that the mothership was attacked. After the changeover ceremony, when we returned to the mothership, I gave a report using the communication crystal. It was time, yes, it was something that was done as a matter of process that always took place in times of the whole journey. There kept being reports made, so that after the handover ceremony took place it was important that feedback of what had taken place was given so that it could be chronicled.

Egarina: It wasn't long after that the ship was attacked. The ship started to shudder. It was a huge ship, so that the shuddering didn't fit. It was something, I suppose the way people would feel like when they experience an earthquake, and it didn't make sense, it didn't fit at all with the experience of being on the ship. The ship was very stable and of the highest technology. It did not take very long to realise, of course, that we were under attack.

When the mothership was being attacked, Egarina was returning to her accommodation quarters. Immediately after the attack, Egarina went to a scout ship and took a communication robot with her.

Egarina: I had actually left the command station and was walking towards accommodation for some reason, and the ship started to shudder. I was on my own, away from the family, away from my husband, and so I was caught in a part of the ship where it was not easy to make contact with the children or my husband.

Egarina: Everything was happening very quickly, and people were very nervous and moving very quickly. They had been trained to abandon ship, the same as happens now with ships that have life drills. This applied onboard the ship also. Although, no one expected anything to go wrong. However, there was training given should that ever happen, which is interesting when you think about it. We just moved to the nearest station, where there was a smaller ship that was available to leave the mothership. Orders had been given to abandon the mothership. A bell sounded, there were explosions, we had the ability of remote viewing, and we could see the mothership starting to break up.

It was instinct that I invited the robot to come. The two scout ships ejected from their launch pods and landed in what is now known as Broken Bay, NSW, Australia. This is on the eastern seaboard coast of Australia.

Lion Island, Broken Bay, NSW, Australia

Lion Island is a river island located at the mouth of the Hawkesbury River. The island is thought to be part of the Central Coast. It has a descriptive name as it resembles a Sphinx, a mythical figure of a crouching lion.

Difficulties in Communication at Home

Egarina: Everybody was in a state of trauma, there were many dying, there were many injured who needed assistance. There was no time to think about anything, other than to help our fellow brothers and sisters. We were also under slight attack, which the men dealt with. The females that survived quickly moved to bring care and assistance to those who were suffering and injured. We were aware that there were some reptilians still around, even where we had landed. They were soon sent away.

There was a problem, the emotional trauma of leaving the mothership, the atmosphere of Earth, and the harshness of the sun on the skin of the different Starpeoples. People found it even hard to breathe. People expected that help would come.

Egarina: The only way to make communication was through the robot as it turned out. The robot was not able to make clear communication. It seemed to be more as one way. We were not able to return the communication through the robot. It was difficult, it was a time when we really had to make decisions for ourselves, rather than calling on orders.

The robot was trying to deal with many questions that were coming from many of the survivors who were in panic mode. It was hard to calm everybody and encourage them to return to the state of being that they were used to onboard the ship. They were thrown into a different atmosphere; they could not breathe properly. They could not operate their psychic abilities as well as they could on the ship. This was a completely new experience to them and they panicked to some degree within themselves. They did not outwardly show panic, it was within themselves, and they started to experience tumultuous feelings. It was very new to them.

Egarina shares that it was not possible to contact the hierarchy. The communications robot was damaged to a degree and could not function as demanded. It was not a 'two-way radio', so to speak.

Egarina: Communication managed to come to the robot to assist the robot to operate and be active to some degree, because the robot was not thrown into tumult as the starpeople were. So, it was possible to receive messages from the hierarchy into the robot. That is as far as it went. Instructions were given through the robot and the robot struggled to try to find answers in its own computer-like way. It would almost be like the computers that operate in your now, in that if they cannot find an answer they would say, 'I cannot compute.'

With the attack, there is a general perception of total failure of the mission of the mothership Rexegena. Egarina has a surprising insight to share.

Egarina: The mothership itself brought light into this corner of the galaxy. That was achieved regardless, even if there had been no survivors. That was a big jumping point. The survivors, at another level, yes, had agreed, but they did not realise this at that time. They were very angry, they were very upset, they were not clear in their communicating with higher guidance, and they were not able to see the bigger picture. It was only later when they had calmed themselves, which came many years later, that they came to realise they had set themselves up for that mission and what role they were to play in that mission.

It would seem that the hierarchy (out of time and space) were aware of the possibility of betrayal, and perhaps, the presence of traitors onboard the mothership Rexegena. From the angelic point of view, and from the point of view of the hierarchy, who oversight many galaxies, many universes, many star systems being birthed, and the crystal consciousness BEING imbued in the life forms in this universe and millions and millions of other parallel, multi-dimensional universes—this was a possibility that was accepted. The mission of the mothership Rexegena was to bring light to this corner of our galaxy, in what we call the Orion Arm of our Universe. The Reptoids were there on Mu and had agreed to leave.

The Reptoids and the Mission of the Mothership Rexegena

Egarina: The mothership arrived into this corner of the galaxy and settled just outside the atmosphere of Earth. The smaller ships were able to move into the Earth's atmosphere because at that time it operated in a slightly different frequency. It is important to understand and know that difference, for it is quite difficult for airships to enter into this atmosphere in the now. The time then, the ships entered, and were coming and going. They were preparing to offload a quite a lot of material, provisions, and seedlings, many things that were brought by the mothership, and that had been prepared, even plantlife that had been growing on the ship. That had been brought to the Earth to begin to establish a settlement.

Egarina: The Reptilian people had come to Earth a long time before, and they had taken over the pyramids. The pyramids had been used previously by light beings, who had come to the Earth, and the pyramids had been established to be used as points of light to feed into the planet and create the crystal grid.

On the journey to Mu, we were not aware of any Reptoids nor Draco peoples onboard. There was some dissension on the mothership on its journey towards the planet Mu, and it concerned us. It concerned my husband Alchqaringa, who was the commander in chief, and his other commanders were concerned. They didn't understand why there should be dissension, when all should have been coming from like mind. But they were of different races and so allowances were made, and believed to be cultural differences. But they well hid who they really were. It was only later that we discovered they were not of our races. They hid their identity behind another image. We recognised there were differences and there was a problem. It did not occur to us that there could be such deception.

The Starpeople that were on the ship that lost their lives also played a role. They brought the ship to this point, which as I have said, brought light and love and compassion on its journey to this corner of the galaxy. When the ship exploded, it did actually melt and become pieces of that memory on the Earth, which helped to spread out that light and change of consciousness. This happened with many people down throughout the ages because they chose to collect the pieces of the mothership, although they call it a stone that has come from the stars, a green stone that has come from the stars.

We have come to know it as the Moldavite stone—or Grail stone.

Egarina: The Starpeople—the survivors—knew they would live their lives here and end their lives here. They were not able to return home, so they knew they would eventually lose their lives in that body on the planet Mu.

The Environment

Egarina: There was great difficulty in breathing for all of us. This was a very real problem. It was far too hot, it was humid, the air was thick and heavy to us.

The sun that radiated the planet Earth was far too hot for us, and not what we were used to. We had to take shelter where we could. We were unable to take the rays of the sun. It took quite some time for the survivors to fully recover from their trauma; they were in total shock. Some actually seemed to, for a while, lose their minds, in that they could not think at all. They were zombie-like in some ways. There were others that could think but still suffered very greatly, although they tried to help their brothers and sisters.

While there were supplies and equipment placed near the pyramids, the survivors had some doubt as to whether they could safely return to that place, and what was left. We had been partially attacked, and that was taken as danger, and if we ventured further around the planet Earth, we could be destroyed. We were very vulnerable, we no longer had the technology we had on the mothership, and even the smaller scout ship, because some of the functioning was not operating as it was supposed to.

The primary focus was raw survival.

Egarina: We had to recover our wits immediately and to count as many as we could as to who had survived, and to gather them together, because we felt there would be strength in us all staying together. There were some who chose to take a different path, and they went in a different direction.

They chose to settle elsewhere. There was actually another settlement established, slightly north to the bay we where we had settled. They were of a different race, which is why they didn't readily connect with us. There were some of their race that did stay with us.

That settlement eventually did wither and they did not survive. That was later. They suffered because there were fewer of them, and because in a gathering of like minds there is more strength and power. We had more power because we stayed together. Those beings of a different race, slightly north of us, we went to talk with them. I was one that went along with the others, and we tried to encourage them to join us. But they chose to stay.

Egarina: There was one that seemed to survive, in some way, it was like a scout ship. The others had survived from our ships, and they made their way to rescue them. Understand that we still had abilities to connect and know, on this planet, of our own people from a distance. We were still able to communicate and contact. We still had the ability to remote view. This was a way of us knowing we would be safe if we stayed where we were, for we knew that the reptilian races had all left and decided to leave us alone because they believed that we would not survive. They were also worried that there might be repercussions, so they left.

Egarina: Some Reptoids, a few, came to help us. They could not understand why we were attacked. We forgave them because they were very concerned and upset about what had taken place. They wanted to learn more from us and they knew if they could they wanted to help us survive. There were not many, I think about six. I say I think because there were some who came but had to leave again. They were actually sought out by their own kind. So, they had been seen as deserting, which of course they had. This was frowned upon by the reptilian races.

Genetic Engineering: The Up-standing Ape-like man

In order to survive on Mu, the sensitive, light-skinned Starpeople had to make adaptations, especially for their offspring. There were Reptoids who befriended them, helped them, and even showed them how to do genetic engineering.

Egarina: Genetic engineering of eggs—this was actually information given to the starpeople by the reptilians because they were very clever at genetics and had a lot of knowledge and understanding of the process in the planet's atmosphere. There was a feeling of gratefulness that they were willing to help. There was certainly no judgement, for we knew they had only been carrying out orders and they were truly sorry. We recognised this in them, and we accepted them for that. So, we accepted their help.

At first, there were a number of the female survivors who volunteered. They felt they had permission from the Source to take into them a genetically modified egg, their own egg, using some adjustments so that the new little one would be able to breathe better, to have hair so that the head would be covered, and they would not burn so easily. The skin was also to be a little tougher than what the starpeople had, so they could live in the planet's atmosphere without suffering.

The new creature was more like the genetic material it was taken from, rather than the egg that was used from the starmothers. This actually upset us all greatly. We still viewed the new little beings with love and compassion, and they were assisted and taken into the fold. It was seen also that there would be problems with their survival. Then it was done the other way around, the fertilised eggs were transplanted into upstanding ape like creatures, the females. The children born from those were much stronger and able to survive.

They had inherited some of the psychic abilities of the starpeople and their heads were larger. They had loving and compassionate qualities that were taught to them by the starpeople. That was also connecting to the Leonine genetic material that existed in the ape-like creature. But there was an element of brutish energy that still was inherited in them. This was encouraged to be mastered. This is why the children were imbued with crystalline energy that was given to them from the robot.

We continued with these births—with starpeople eggs genetically engineered and placed in the females of the up-standing apes. There were some abnormalities, which we tried to correct. There were more adjustments until a time came when we considered that, with the engineering and changes, enough had taken place. It was then we decided that mating should be encouraged between the new little ape-like creatures that had grown into young adults.

They started to grow to a point where they could mate with each other, but we realised if they interbred there would be problems with the genetics that existed. We discouraged them to mate with certain ones if they were too closely related. This was understood because we always imbued love and compassion to them. This energy infiltrated them and they gave that back to us. As such, they were ready to accept our direction and our teaching.

We had our successes and our failures. It was from trial and error we found a race that could survive with the genetic material from the starpeople. As they grew, they were encouraged to interbreed, taking note they could not interbreed with brothers and sisters. As they grew in number, there came a point later where some were taken and placed further from the settlement, and eventually further and further away.

Eventually, they went out and multiplied with the other ape-like creatures that had been left to their own devices. The plan was that they would interbreed with them and the starpeople's genes would infiltrate into the ape-like creatures that existed around the Earth.

Valerie: The starpeople have continued to assist the evolvement of the human down through the ages.

Andromeda Val has advised the above all happened 900,000 years ago...and 200,000 years later, there was a need for the Angelic Realms to expand their Great Plan with assistance from the United Planetary Nations within our Solar System and to monitor what was happening to the new breed of Humans on Earth. 700,000 years ago, an edict was called, deciding there needed to be a Karmic Board established to act like a stage or jumping off point from The World of Light, where **souls would birth into every little human baby** born onto this planet.

The souls would come from many different star races and experience life on Earth. All souls would then have the opportunity to grow and evolve, returning eventually to their own race in other worlds and influencing them.

There was another major upload of consciousness to the human race when the Blue people from Venus (this was when the Earth was still in 4th /5th dimension, before the Fall of Atlantis) came to Earth in Atlantean times and mated with the cromagnon race about 300,000 years ago.

They went on to evolve into the Race of Atlan. The Atlanteans. They had advanced abilities and knowledge. They played with their ability of genetic engineering and began to create all the strange shapes of animal and man together. The images have been recorded in Greek mythology.

Atlantis Fell

After the Earth nearly died, dropping from 4th Dimension to 3rd Dimension, the Ancient Egyptians held a lot of the knowledge of the Starpeople. The Royalty were not actually Starpeople, but they genetically held the genes of the Starpeople with elongated heads and the shaped body of the Starpeople.

They understood the Pyramids. The Pyramids were built long before the earth nearly died. The Ancient Egyptians built over them.

The pyramids were points of light that held the connection of the earth's energy in direct alignment with the 'core' of suns linking with the center of creation of all—The Absolute.

After the fall of Atlantis, there was a shift in the alignment. After that, the pyramids were a little off key—for the key was holding the Earth's alignment—to the 4th and 5th dimension, heralding the Golden Age.

The Golden Age existed on Earth a number of times before. There have been advanced civilisations upon Earth a few times before the existing civilisation of the human race.

Natural transmutation of the humans has evolved to the humans we are today as the new energy coming on to this planet raises consciousness, closely linking to the benevolent starpeople.

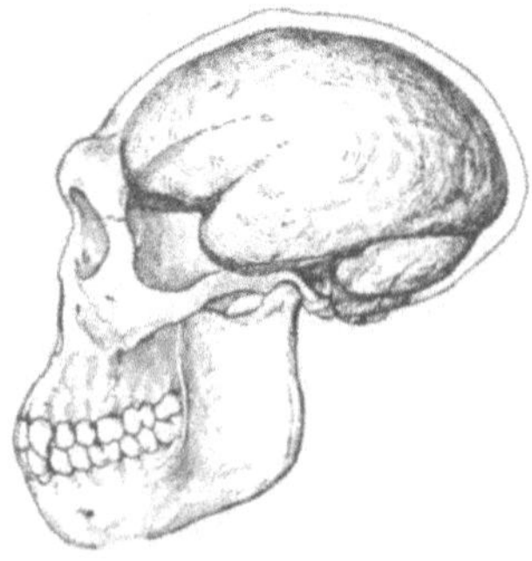

Java Man-800,000 years when the skull was enlarged

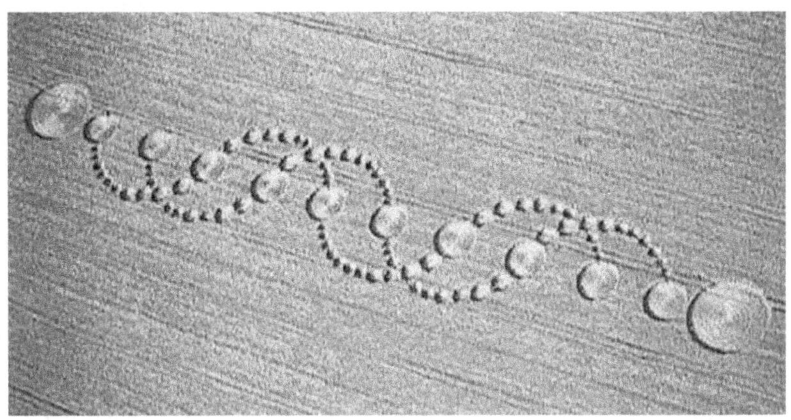

DNA crop circle at Alton Barnes – Reminisceint of 12-strand DNA. Appeared on 17 June 1996

The same time we began the Alcheringa story when the first humans were created

75 Egarina Speaks: The Evolution of the Reptoids

Egarina turns to the nature of the Reptoids, their character, and what drove them to behave as they did. The Reptilians had their own instructions, their own hierarchy, and their own gods. They had lost the way, and the starpeople had come and imbued the crystal light from the Source; the en-Christing of the upstanding ape-like man to the first humans.

How did the intelligent Reptoid beings come to Earth?

Egarina: There was a time when the beings had the form of the Mako—there was a time they needed to leave where they existed: they were brought by the Draco, by mind suggestion, to this planet. They came, and in fact it has been written about as the tribes of the bird people. They came at a very early stage of the development of this planet.

Egarina reveals aspects of the Reptoid culture and how they stacked up against the intellect of the starpeoples. Although they were cold-blooded creatures, they associated together and reproduced. Whereas they remain on Earth today, they remain for a higher purpose that has been given for their higher en-lighten-ment (imbued with light) and evolution.

Egarina: The Reptoids had a culture that was one of control—in that they had to follow and do as their leaders told them. The Reptoid leaders were following the orders of the hierarchy, which for them was the Draco. Though they were allowed to conduct their lives in their own way, there were points they could not surpass or they would be annihilated, so they were operating from fear. They had abilities, they communicated telepathically, but they did not have the consciousness of thinking and reasoning the starpeople had. They followed instructions given telepathically from the Draco, from their hierarchy, from their 'gods' as they believed.

Egarina: There was a certain amount of affection, but it actually came from mere need to procreate, and the respect for that in one another to proceed. They knew that unless they respected the other, they would just drift away or run away. They reproduced extensively and remnants of the reptilian form are still present to this day on this planet. The reptilian races operate in a different dimension, and they are around in the sense they are still attached to an aspect of someone who has come into a physical body. But this has been allowed to hopefully—with guidance (there are many from the star worlds working very hard and diligently at helping them)—to rethink and redirect and understand about the ways of God and the Source, the Source and God that is one of love, compassion, and heart. The god that comes from the good of all...where they had been used to coming from a god that was only for itself.

It is known the hairy, upstanding ape-like man were created by the Reptoids and have Reptoid DNA within, in addition to being mixed with other DNA matter—mineral, insect, and plant DNA. Egarina relates how the Reptoid DNA still influences the human today—by way of thought, word, and action. Impulses from within may emerge and be acted out without emotion, and without thought and intellect, nor any evaluation of the consequences.

Egarina: The first influence of the reptilian action, of course, is one of attempting to consume consciousness, and this is done through a misuse of power. This attitude is one of control, one of fear, and manipulation of others, in that if you step out of line you could be destroyed. This still happens. There are still places on Earth where others will kill someone for a misdemeanor. This is not the way of the benevolent starpeople.

There were other influences on the Reptoid creatures, their own origins, their own history, and although they had chosen a path, a road, there was still buried deep within a yearning for the peace that comes through the love of Source.

Egarina: The reptoids, in fact, inherited a leaning towards an understanding that all was not quite right from the hierarchy or the gods they followed because inherent in them, from the genetic structure of the bird people, was an influence. Not strongly, but it was there. The bird people themselves had been created from angelic beings that had strayed. If you can picture in your mind that although the angelic beings had strayed, they did still have the love of God deep within them.

How could one so aware stray in the first place?

Egarina: It was a little by accident. In other words, sometimes people—from lack of knowledge—can actually fall into a situation where they find themselves completely out of control. A little like somebody who perhaps would be partaking of drugs and find themselves in a situation where they had lost reality and were no longer in control of themselves. It was not their true nature. In the beginning it was an accident. There were forces around them that caused them to lose the way.

Questions then arise about other influences of the reptilian races within the human. While there are some aspects of the Source within them, they do have less emotional response within. The evolvement of the hairy, upstanding ape-like man to being imbued with the crystal light or the Christ light within levels the playing field and allows for evolution of the reptilian influence within the human.

Egarina: In the hue-man you are asking about, in fact the eyes of the human have a reptilian aspect. You would remember that the eyes of the starpeople are different. You also ask about social aspects of the reptilian...there were in some ways, but remember, the reptilian races and even the Draco have aspects of the Source in them, and their creation of what they do is really replicating what the starpeople do. It is to do with intent. If a sport venue was arranged and it became an ugly scene with arguments and hitting out with a weapon, such as the hand, they are going against the way the game would be played in the star worlds. In the star worlds, that would not happen. There was a simple lack of love and understanding, the light of love within them is all that separated these two cultures. That is why the little ape-like creature was chosen to absorb the light and genetic material that came from the starpeople, to help, shall we say, level the playing field and allow evolvement to take place.

Egarina: If you can look at it in a different way, these forms in the cosmic worlds were lost in darkness. They needed assistance to be imbued with light from the source. This was a way that was considered to help bring light into those races. There were many from the star worlds that came, and also incarnated into the little new forms to help engender that light to be spread. There are many around this Earth who do just that. They have committed to totally devote their life to spread cosmic light and love from the Source.

Valérie: I would like to add here about a time, not long after the Second World War and into 1960, 1979 or so, when there were a lot of reports from humans claiming to be abducted by aliens and suffering experiments upon them against their will. I mentioned in Part One of this book a two-year initiation I experienced—and reading Whitley Streiber's *Communion, Encounters with the Unknown: a True Story*.

I found out much later the experiments were examined by the benevolent Starpeople to find cures for disease and so on, with genetic engineering. Various Souls had agreed to this before they came into human bodies. They also wanted to create the Adonis race that looked like humans that would be able to communicate with us and not cause fear.

In 2017, after meeting Andromeda Val, I came to understand that I had lost an embryo in a miscarriage and that embryo had been rescued by the benevolent Starpeople and was the future Andromeda Val, 6,000 years into our future. Sai Baba had referred to me meaningfully when he looked into my eyes and said, "And what is your name, Val?" This was when he gave me the green ring made by the Starpeople, 25 years before I actually met her.

Unfortunately, at the same time, some Reptoid people still living on Earth decided they would experiment also and began abducting people without their permission. Because they are a cold-blooded race and have little feeling, they were actually causing the humans chosen to feel pain and terror.

So, the whole programme was ceased by the benevolent Starpeople and pressure placed on the Reptoid race to cease their intrusion.

Alcheringa and Egarina Speak: The Origin of the Reptoids

76

Alcheringa joins the conversation. He was asked to come and help with the background and story of the Reptoids and the Draco and how they came to Earth, which was then called Mu. Egarina then takes up the story of the reptilian remnant within the DNA of the human, and evolution of the earthling into a Buddha-like being living in the Golden Age. All have the source of light within from the Creative Source of All.

Alcheringa Speaks on the Story of the Reptoids on Mu

How did the Reptoid race come into existence? Are they from another planet, like the Draco?

Alcheringa: The Reptoid race was actually created genetically by the Draco, who lived on this planet at another time completely. By that I mean it was a different dimensional situation.

So, the Reptoids were created on this planet—not as we know it with its continents and oceans, rainforest, and plains?

Alcheringa: Indeed so. The reptilians were created in different forms to assist the Draco in jobs that they wish to be done.

So, the reptilians were created as servile creatures themselves, much like the upstanding ape-like man was created by the Reptoid to be of service?

Alcheringa: Indeed so. In fact, they were consumed by the Draco from time to time.

They acted as a food source as well?

Alcheringa: Indeed so.

And the Draco would have consumed their consciousness as they did with the upstanding ape creature when they came to Earth?

Alcheringa: In their whole physicality at times, much like the human being consumes the cow, or the chicken, or the dog.

Was the Reptoid an entirely new creation by the Draco or was it a modification of some existing life form?

Alcheringa: Some of the genetic material was used from other creations of the Draco; the Mako is one. I must add here that the Draco created many different forms within the galaxy, particularly this corner of the galaxy.

This brings an important question to mind. How were the Draco created?

Alcheringa: This is a good question. The Draco were actually pulling away from God's creation. They chose to evolve a different way than the path if you like. The Draco continued its evolvement and became more and more of its own creation, in other words, it did have the Source built into it, but it almost lost it because it was coming from a point of turning inwards at all times, and consuming almost itself. For this reason, it started to consume other forms to survive. There was a point where the Draco did evolve from turning inwards at all times to become what it is and what it still is.

If I can persist with the question, who originally created the Draco as a race? Was it an act of the Creator?

Alcheringa: It was actually a pulling away of some of the angelic beings that God created.

So, there were some angels who existed before the Draco and they had pulled away from the Creator?

Alcheringa: Indeed so.

Were these angels—who had pulled away from the Creator—the ones who were involved in the creation of the Draco as a species?

Alcheringa: They were, but not consciously. It was almost accidental, but it happened because their choice to pull away and follow a path of their own, rather than one that was directed by the will of the Source.

Why did these angels who existed earlier, why did they pull away? What was their reason for that?

Alcheringa: They did not have any reason, as I said it was almost an accident.

So, the Draco originally conceived of and created the Reptoid races. This would have been in some other location than Earth, is that correct?

Alcheringa: Indeed, yes, there were other planets where they were placed. The Draco had the ability to move from one planet to another, and they also had ability to move from one dimension to another.

Was this a result of their habit of ingesting powdered gold?

Alcheringa: This is true; it is a chemical of transmutation. This was used more by the reptilian races, but it was, in earlier days, used also by the Draco. The Draco, when it consumed other forms, they would also ingest whatever the other forms had ingested. In other words, they became what they ate. In their consciousness, they became the consciousness of what they ate. It was as what they took unto them they became and were responsible for.

In what shape, form, or fashion were the Draco and/or Reptoids attracted to the planet Mu?

Alcheringa: The planet Mu, in its very earliest beginnings, was actually planned to be used by the angelic races that needed a place to create a Garden of Eden in this dark corner. They had plans to populate, to be able to bring the energy of the Source into this corner, and so spread that energy. The greater plan, of course, was in their minds, but it would have been a long time to evolve. The Draco was attracted to this new planet. They actually wanted to use it. They were coming and going, and they planted reptilian beings, in their smaller form such as you see here today, like snakes and lizards and other reptilian forms that exist.

Would some of these reptiles have been intellectually advanced as well?

Alcheringa: No, these were like pets that had been created. They were actually found and consumed.

Was the planet Mu as a form of bait for the Draco? Was the Earth as seen as a source of food?

Alcheringa: The Draco were attracted to it. They came from their worlds, as I have already said. They came, they found these smaller reptilian creatures, and they ate, they consumed. The reptilian creatures had been created on Earth in the image of the Reptoids.

Did the hierarchy simply allow our planet, Mu, what we now call Earth, to be a source of food for another species, the Draco? Was this the plan, to attract these creatures who had pulled away from the light?

Alcheringa: No, but when they did come they were allowed to stay because it could be seen that, in actual fact, their presence could be of assistance in eventually infiltrating all these beings with the light of the Source.

There came a time—later—when the Reptoids were ordered to leave the planet.

Alcheringa: Indeed, it was because they had already been using genetic engineering and creating forms that were out of control. These, at another time, had been destroyed. But then they could not help themselves and they were beginning to create larger forms that were out of control again. (Dinosaurs.) There were millions of years between what I am speaking of. You are talking about this council that existed in your time, just a million years ago, in the evolution of the planet Earth.

Egarina Speaks on the Coming of the Golden Age

How will everything be transformed into the energy of love and compassion?

Egarina: Everything is energy, and if the energy can be brought to a point where the syndrome of the 100th monkey operates, everything will collapse like a pack of cards into the warm blood of love and compassion, and the fire of God's light. So, talking of numbers and a toll of how many may be of Draconian and Reptilian races, it would be better to think in a positive way that the energies can be changed if all upon this Earth can help one another to bring that love and understanding to each other, then the energy will change automatically.

Are you saying that those of Draco and Reptilian origin will have the experience of everything collapsing like a deck of cards? They would shudder at the realisation that this is their basic nature and this is what they have come from.

Egarina: I am saying that the energy that pulls away from God could collapse like a deck of cards and change into the stronger energy of love, light, and compassion. It will change overnight, or in the blink of an eye. There would be no judgment on one another, for I would remind you the little earthling carries some reptilian aspect with it from its creation that existed before the starpeople engendered the genetic material to make and lift the changes of consciousness of the upstanding ape-like man creature.

So, we all have a bit of reptilian nature? Is that what attracts the reptilian in us?

Egarina: This is true, like attracts like. This is what was agreed on by the Elohim (Angelic Realms) at the meetings. The galactic foundation has agreed this is what was needed to help bring change, if ever change was going to happen. So, you can understand the reasoning from the light beings in being so willing to volunteer to help bring those changes. It required courage and they came with courage, under the auspices of the Archangel Mikael carrying his sword of light to cut though the darkness.

Is there a time when this process of change will take place on this planet?

Egarina: There was a turning point in the year 2011-2012, but this does not mean it will be the total change, for change has a way of transforming over a period of time, so that all will not necessarily change at the same time, if that makes some sense. However, the turning point brings great influence into the change that leads into the Golden Age. We speak of the Golden Age, for the Golden Age also brings an aura of golden light, which is connected to the Buddha or the Buddhic way, the golden light of enlightenment. All those that exist on the Earth in the Golden Age will be as Buddha. They will be enlightened beings with golden auras and they will have the wisdom, the knowledge, and the understanding of compassion that goes with that energy.

The Golden Buddha

Will there be people who will not choose the golden aura, who will not be capable of making this transition?

Egarina: Yes. These will be assisted to go to another place in another dimension. There are always worlds upon worlds upon worlds.

And will these people all begin the process again?

Egarina: They may be, they may not. This is something that will be decided upon by the Creator.

Egarina: Spirit surrounds everyone, every being on this Earth. The weight and the measure of each spirit of the aspects that exist on the Earth will be given opportunity for whatever growth is needed. We hope with this great plan that the light will brighten this corner of the galaxy. I am sure you are feeling and knowing this is happening. As I have said, light attracts light, and it is the strongest energy that exists. It is very easy for the strong light to touch those that are weak, and in so doing, it will help make the change to a brighter light.

*****

The Eighth Black and White Sister Connection to the Pleiades

77

I would like to share more about the initiation we experienced when we visited Uluru in 1994, while I still had the sacred Alcheringa stone in my care. I have shared the story in how Goolagaia, the Black Giantess initiated me at Mutitjulu Waterhole at Uluru, the heart centre of Australia and the Rainbow Serpent energy.

Then, at another time, Goolagaia visited us again, this time in 2002 when we were holding a meditation in our healing room at our Canyonleigh house, in the Southern Highlands, NSW.

Alcheringa came as usual, spoke for a while, then made me sit like a stone Buddha inviting people to communicate with him telepathically, saying he would answer their questions. He also asked me telepathically if I would allow Goolagaia, the Black Giantess, to incorporate my body and speak with everyone. I willingly said yes.

Her presence came in and was awesome. So loud. "*Aaaaaaaaaah*!" And then a great drawing in of breath.

"*I am here...Ah! Ah*!" Everyone laughed.

"*Yes...and with great joy, for this is a propitious time*." Her arms were fully extended out and forward from the body.

"*The eighth sister has returned and I have been hooooolding the energy for all these years, so that she could come, so that she could return. This is a reminder to the earthling body, the body that you walk in, huh, huh, huh. I do not walk in it, I am too big.*" She was still talking loudly.

"*But I hold the energy—this was my purpose, this was my reason, and I have been very happy to do this. To be this for the enlightened ones for they came, they came to this planet to assist the little earthling—as they were at that time, and still confused to some degree, as they are now. I have others with me and they enjoy the work. I am too large to enter into Valerie's body, but I surround her..."*

She was looking around at everyone and lent forward with a cheeky laugh and said, *"I surroooooooound all of youuuu so do not be afraid. I said I come with looove and compassion, my dear ones. We know much and we serve, like all of you. I will away noooooooow...hmmmmm...ooooooh...ahhhhhhhh!"*

And then she was gone. Just as she left, she showed herself to me in my inner vision, looking like a beautiful black angel. A visitor sitting in our meditation circle named Bob Wright said, "Goolagaia also protected tribal children if they wandered too near swamps or water if their lives were in danger. She would show herself in a fierce way to frighten them so they would run back to their tribe. She had enormous love. She was huge. She was beautiful. She played with me like a puppet. She had such a wonderful sense of fun. She is very strong, protective, caring, and all-powerful."

Bob our visitor had lived in the outback at Uluru and heard about her from the indigenous people a long time ago. He told us he had seen a painting of her by a tribal artist and it showed her extending her arms out and over everyone, just as she had done today.

The day after our meeting, I was prompted to call on Alcheringa to make his presence. I said to him that yesterday was a lovely day. "When you came you introduced us to Goolagaia, when she made her presence, she said it was a propitious day. May I ask what that was about?"

"Indeed, my dear, indeed. It was a time that you and she were to meld. For she is the eighth Black Sister in Earth form and you, my dear, represent the eighth White Sister, the starperson. So, with the two of you coming together, this is the moment that will move forward with everything that you have come to do."

Cave Hill Dreamtime Story

78

CAVE HILL holds the Dreamtime story of the seven sisters from the Pleiades—100kms from Uluru. The following is a spontaneous memory John had of the Leonine Race at the time the asteroid Uluru was brought to Australia approximately 65 million years ago.

After John returned from flying over our property with a friend in a small bi-plane, he said, "While flying over the absolute wilderness near where we lived at Canyonleigh, my reality changed momentarily and I could see myself as a Leonine-looking person with paws that controlled a flying panel of a spacecraft."

I was surprised, although he knew about the story of the mothership Rexegena. He added that he has had glimpses of that for a few years. He agreed to try a regression.

John frowned and sat back in our tall-backed armchair and spontaneously went into an altered state of consciousness. All the time, he was sitting in the position of 'The Thinker' with his arm resting on the arm of the chair, his head bent forward, and his fingers rubbing his forehead. So, I said quietly, "Tell me about the Leonine race who you have said are a warrior race?"

"Most of the time they think they are right."

I chuckled, "So that would be a Leonine trait, eh? Did you say you were on a mission somewhere?"

John became agitated, "We are going somewhere, but I feel in limbo. I don't know where we have come from or where we are going to."

"That's okay," I assured him, "just relax, allow yourself to go deeper into the memory. Do you know why you are warriors? Are the others aggressive also?"

"They are like lions, they have a huge lion energy. These half-man and half- animal bipeds come from different planets. I've always thought that cats and dogs come from a different dimension."

"Are there biped beings that look like dogs?" I asked.

"Yes, but they are lesser beings. You only have to look at the cat family to see that they are superior to everybody else, or so they think they are. Even domestic cats believe they are in charge, at least from their standpoint, whereas dogs are servile, generally speaking."

I had no idea where this was going. I asked him to move on his memory, to when he arrives somewhere.

"Of course. Before me are the controls of the ship. They are crystal, pyramid shaped, with light around them. They steer the ship, but I have no idea how. As I look out the window, I see deep black space filled with stars. Arrayed around me is what is definitely an attacking force. I am aware of these reptiles, dinosaurs below. These Reptoid beings also have a high intelligence and technology. They are suppressing other beings and that is why we are here, to sort them out. We are the governors of space."

"Who is this other force suppressing?"

"The Reptoid race have created a very bad situation here on Earth. Our mission is to go and fix them, to wipe them out if need be. The other ones they are suppressing are the up-standing ape-like creatures. They created them to mine gold for them and called them in via mind control when needed. We wanted to protect them because DNA material from our Leonine race had been used to create them, along with their own Reptilian DNA material."

John wavered for a moment, then continued, "If we have to, we will use our technology to annihilate these Reptoids because they are causing far too much trouble. They're not just on one planet you know, there are other places where they have created their dinosaurs. They all have to be brought to heel. We have the power to direct meteors, which is like our artillery, our bombers. We have laser beams you could equate to infantry. These beams can petrify the Reptoids into fossil instantly, or any other creature for that matter."

He was asked how they caught the meteors.

"The command ships in this Peace Corp are very small."

"Whom do you answer to?" I asked.

"No one at all, not that I can perceive. We are definitely the Lords of Space. We have tremendous power and a total sense of right and justice. Perhaps we are God."

"Do you believe in a superior being?" I asked.

"There is a high being, probably God, above all this but I can't define it. I do know exactly why we are here, though. We are Cosmic Cops. The Reptoid people have the capability of retaliating. What I can see in my heart is a huge ship that was destroyed by the enemy. You talk about nuclear bombs and missiles on Earth, they are peashooters compared with what goes on up there."

He also added that they were still around. All the time John was speaking of the Leonine race in the cosmos, I could see in my inner vision strong warrior-looking bi-peds with long coats of fur, just like lions, but they are people, and I knew them well. They were dressed in protective clothing, strangely a little like the Ancient Roman gladiators.

What John was regressing to, in this last cosmic memory, was being part of a Leonine race who had been instructed by the cosmic hierarchy to destroy the dinosaurs. They were eating all the vegetation and some of them were very large and extremely ferocious. They were killing each other, and the huge carcasses were slow to deteriorate back into the soil. Consequently, our planet—the beautiful Garden of Eden the hierarchy had worked so hard to create—was being despoiled, leaving behind a very bad odour. Without trees and plants, the atmosphere was losing oxygen.

Thus, an asteroid was 'captured' by the cosmic Leonines and cast upon the planet Earth about sixty-five million years ago. Its main body landed on Earth to become what is known as Uluru, pushing the seabed up into high mounds known as Kata Tjuta. Other fragments breaking from Uluru entered Earth's atmosphere and were cast elsewhere around the Earth.

I have found when working with people who relive memories of their star selves in the cosmos, they can easily jump from one time to another without realising it. That is what John had done in his more than one lives as a Leonine. They came from Sirius.

When he came to rescue the survivors of the Rexegena he was not from the Leonine race, even though he was in charge of the Leonine batallion. He came from an all male race, also from Sirius, looking much like Egarina but much taller at nine foot. His skull was shaped higher from the brow, instead of Egarina's skull that pertruded to the back. They became partners in that life.

His name was Himel—he was bitten by a snake and was furious that the Reptilians were able to bring him down so simply. However, Egarina nursed him back to health and he decided to stay and help the survivors on Mu, and as I have said he brought from home the sacred Alcheringa stone for the survivors.

I was recently invited to travel with three other light workers to visit Cave Hill. It is a five-hour journey there and back to sacred Uluru in Central Australia. We travelled through the desert on a rough red, sandy soil road, passing Mount Conner, one hundred and fifteen kilometres from Uluru to Cave Hill.

It is very sacred to the local indigenous people who ask that no photos be taken of their cave holding their Dreaming story of the Seven Sisters from the Pleiades. The rock art on the ceiling of the cave is said to be carbon dated twenty-four thousand years old.

We were enthralled with the majestic art, seeing circles in a row that to us represented a core of suns our solar system was aligning to. We saw drawings of Wandjina-looking beings said to be starpeople. We also were excited to see a drawing of what we believed was a Draco-Reptilian biped. A Reptoid upstanding with very heavy legs, with four toes on each foot, heavy hips and thinner torso with tail, thin arms with three fingers on the hands, a stout neck and head with a long snout-like face and small ears. It was a similar image of being attacked by the Reptoids that many of us had been given in our memory as starpeople from the Pleiades.

These Reptoids had lived on this planet for a long time and had genetically created the race of the various dangerous reptiles and dinosaurs without permission from the Source. It was obvious to us that whoever drew the picture on the cave roof so long ago knew of the same knowledge we had been given.

As soon as we arrived at Cave Hill, we could see it was the same feldspar rock as Uluru. When the asteroid came from the stars, a piece had broken off, landing a hundred kilometres away from where Uluru now stands.

There are indigenous Dreaming stories telling of their ancestors coming from the Pleiades, or Seven Sisters as they see the stars when they look to the night sky. As I have said before, there is also another Dreaming story speaking of the eighth Sister from the Pleiades returning. Dreaming stories are really oral historic records as are their rock art historic pictures—they once communicated telepathically, just like the starpeople.

The starpeople told them they would one day return and now they have.

While we were in the cave, we were visited by Alcheringa in spirit, who, as mentioned previously, resides at Uluru. Goolagaia, the Black Giantess who holds the energy of the eighth Sister on earth and the eighth White Sister from the Pleaides, gave messages through me.

Later, sitting alone, I was given understanding this cave was where the Afghan Cameleer had originally found the Alcheringa sacred stone. He had been attracted by light shining and coming from Cave Hill when the setting sun hit the feldspar in the rock. He wanted to give it to the indigenous people, but they were frightened of it. It was held by his Afghan family for decades until it finally found its way to me to tell its story before it was returned to the indigenous people.

When our Aborigine friend Gerry took us to the site of the ancient glyphs at Kariong near Kuringai National Park, it was the tenth of the tenth 1995. When our journey ended at Uluru after our visit to Cave Hill, it was the tenth of the tenth 2011—sixteen years later.

10.10.1995 adds to 8 and 10.10.2011 was 16 years later = double 8 = 16. Always an important sign for me.

The Aborigines know they began here in Australia and spread out from here; there is evidence of Australian Indigenous presence in many places around the world—they did not come from elsewhere.

Not only are they the oldest living human race, their ancestors were the first humans. It was the time when the skull increased in size, there was less hair on the body, and indigenous people had developed extraordinary psychic abilities, the same as starpeople. Their ancestors always communicated telepathically.

They are the first astronomers on Earth. They also knew and carried out important ceremonies of dance and song to nourish and balance energies in Mother Earth; they learnt this from the skypeople.

Geneticists are misled as to the beginnings of our humanity and in particular the first race as humans, hence the Australian Indigenous people. If they are examined, the DNA still exists within all humans from inheriting the Reptilian/animal DNA created within the upstanding ape-like creature known as 'man', by the Draco/Reptoid race. This DNA was raised by the blending genetically of the starpeople's genes and within that, the light from the Source, which is still changing and raising consciousness within our human DNA at this time on Earth. There is new energy coming onto this Earth, all the time leading us to a Golden Age that is automatically raising consciousness in everything. Geneticists need to be aware of this.

Message from a Group of Light Beings – Announcement

79

Benevolent Beings of Light from the United Planetary Nations

At our house in Moss Vale, a number of visitors gather for a meditation meeting and are seated in a circle in our blue healing room. As I always do, I light a candle requesting all present connect their minds to the Source of all Creation. I do not plan how the meeting is to unfold. I ask everyone present to allow themselves, in the name of God, to become peaceful with loving thoughts. This particular day, I heard a voice ask me if I would be willing to receive direction from a conglomerate of light beings, allowing an address to take place. I willingly agreed, although a little curious, as I haven't done this before. I felt a peaceful energy overtake my energy field and begin speaking through my voice box.

"The one that comes through speaks on behalf of the light beings. They have always been here to hold the energy of the crystal light in whatever form they present themselves. As they have said so often, all you have to do is ask for guidance and/or assistance and they will come.

"It is from the World of Light that the energy is coming. The World of Light is where souls return to, to a sea of souls. Souls are aspects of light beings. The energy of the soul is never lost.

"There have been many races created and evolved on Earth and in the cosmos. The beings of light are here now to assist the little earthling to raise the consciousness of the Earth body. The Earth body continues to multiply and hold the energy in its cells of the ascension that has taken place at various times through its beginning and will continue to ascend. This light energy is held in the eggs of the earthling race and continues to be held with each new generation of babies. It holds the signature of the Earth being and so the race of the earthling is always infused with the light in the World of Light.

"There are two major upliftments of the earthling race. In particular when the infusion began from the animal man into human, the light was imbued into the form of human. The other was when babies were born to Earth women who had been infused with light from the blue people of Venus. This is what has been brought to the earthling's understanding so that they may be aware of their beginnings and continue to have understanding of their source and their connection to their source of Creation of All.

"All the beings of light who were here at Atlantean times are back here now, assisting with this uplifting of the earthling. Those who were part of the race that were progeny of the blue people who fell to a degree are here, but so are the light beings that have never broken away from the Source of Creation of all. They are here to bring that strength, that courage, and that initiation into the earthling that exists here now.

"The earthling is imbued with many different energy forms and light forms. The blue crystal light is the one that will take them into the future of the Adonis race—which is a co-habitation and image of energies that have been used down through the ages to create the future form of the earthling. This is where the earthling race will move into.

"There will be two paths. There will be a path where the earthling will move into the Golden Age and be part of the Adonis race, and a path where the race of the earthling who is not ready to move into the Adonis race. They will continue to live on Earth as Earth is presented at this time to evolve and mature until they are ready to move into the future race of the Adonis."

"The Adonis race, to look at, is very similar to the earthling. A very good-looking race, the eyes are not as large as those that are seen in the extraterrestrial, but they do have large eyes—more as was seen with the ancient Egyptians. They have hair, they have well-shaped bodies and balanced auras, a very graceful movement, they are free of disease, and are free of imperfections when unions take place and the new little embryos are formed; imperfections will no longer exist. They will carry the energy of the Adonis race as each form is recreated at the coming together to produce the little ones. It is an act of God. It is an act that has total permission from the Source, and therefore no pulling away in any distorted fashion from the World of Light or from the Source.

"The people are kind and generous in thought—big people, caring people, loving people, considerate to one another—and always, if there is a difference of opinion, honouring that difference and finding consensus to overcome a problem.

"This is the new Earth. There are two Earths. One operating in a different dimension. Those operating in the new Earth of the Adonis race will not be aware of the other race that is operating on the Earth. Nor will those Earth people be aware of the Earth's Adonis race—they will operate independently but within the same sphere.

"Some have spoken about two suns and in actual fact that is true. But they are independent of each other. It is a different world. **A world upon a world. It is separate but in the same place.**"

"I speak on behalf of the beings of light who have come and are always here to assist in any way that they can. To reach the point of separation where those that have chosen to move into the Adonis race, they will be welcomed with open arms. Those that choose to stay in a different dimension will be assisted and allowed to evolve. It is no judgement—it has been spoken of as at time of 'wheat being sorted from the chaff', an allegory only, of what we are speaking about.

"Thank you, my beloved. Thank you for allowing us to come—we bless you—we are always with you. Our hearts are One. God bless."

The message, I believe now, is we are all Creators and it is time to devote ourselves with prayer to God—the Creation Source of universal love—to anchor the energy of change for the good of all.

*****

On the 16th July 2019, morning—on the day of Guru Purnima—praise with love to our teacher, Cosmic Sai Baba had announced to Isaac Tigret that the most amazing event had taken place that morning when he was shown a beautiful golden stairway that had opened up a doorway that had been closed for thousands of years and was now opened for the very first time on Earth, making it easier for everyone to move into a higher consciousness to merge with God.

Historic Revelations that Unfolded on Our Sacred Journey

80

Jehanne d'Arc was born of royal blood. The templars have always known. Plus, the story of Joan of Arc's ghost.

Missing 'Book of Love' written by John the Divine, held by the Cathars—now found.

The three Marys who walked with Jesus; Mother Mary, Mary Magdalene, and the Third 'Mary' is Judith of Judea, who was sister to Jesus and John the Divine.

'Mystical' photo shows where Mary Magdalene's remains really were.

Pope Clement V found innocent of conspiracy against Templar Grand Master 700 years later.

Nuns burned at the stake by priests at Mount Saint Michel, Normandy—no official record found?

Ellen Ternan's true relationship is above reproach with Charles Dickens and his mistrust of women.

What happened to Nerfetiti, wife of Akhenaten during the age of Amarna in Ancient Egypt—the truth is revealed.

The Story of Uluru and its true Source given—the Australian Aborigine have always known.

A sacred Alcheringa stone that comes from the stars reveals cosmic memories—evolution of earth and two major asteroid hits—originally found at Cave Hill.

The Return of the Spirit of 8th Sister from the Pleiades as written in Aborigine Dreamtime stories.

The energy from the Egyptian-like hieroglyphs drawn on cave walls at Kariong reveal many stories, but the main story is of starpeople coming from the Pleiades and the beginning of the human race—the Australian Aborigine.

Hieroglyphs written on rock walls at Kariong show Ancient Egyptians visited the east coast of Australia 4,500 years ago.

Understanding given that the green crystal Moldavite (tektite) is the remains of the mothership in which the visitors came from the Pleiadean cluster.

The hierarchy from the cosmic worlds' great plan for the return of the Garden of Eden on this planet.

Isaac Tigret talk at Guru Purnima celebrations 16th July, 2019 at Muddenhalli, India: https://www.youtube.com/atch?v=5Z_kxEqk6vc

About the Author

Valerie Barrow was a businesswoman for many years before moving with her husband to country New South Wales, Australia, to be closer to her grandchildren and nature. She has worked in the Australia, Hong Kong, and Singapore regions teaching, conducting groups, and giving public talks.

She has been interviewed on television in Hong Kong and Australia, and on radio in New York, Texas, and Australia. The author is highly regarded for her mediumship and wise counsel.

Photo by Gillian Young

Several visits to India and conversations with Sri Sathya Sai Baba helped her understand she receives information by divine illumination. Since 1982, she has worked with unseen beings that speak with her or over-light her body and speak through her.

In 2018, 36 years later, she has been introduced to her oversoul from Andromeda M31 who speaks through her, sometimes using star language. Valérie is advised that Andromeda Val works from the highest order 6,000 years into our future.

She has written three books, but now her mentor has requested that she write ONE BOOK, her Tome, bringing all the information from two books and an overview of the third book, and more, into one volume. The Alcheringa Story of when the first ancestors were created will be published on it's own.

Valérie can be contacted through her website: *https://www.valeriebarrow.com/*

Notes and References

Preface Outline of Past-Life Memory and Altered State of Conscious
Introduction to Andromeda Val from the Galaxy M31
http://narayanaoracle.com/?p=1845#more-1845
Chapter 1 Refer website www.valeriebarrow.com
Chapter 4 Our Journey to Central Java, Indonesia
Borobudur, Marzuki & hearty – Penerbit Djambatan. Indonesia
Siddhartha Guatama – Founder of Buddhist Teachings
Chapter 6 A Green Crystal
Moldavite Research www.e-moldavite "about Moldavites and their origins," - "About moldavites" on the same website.
Chapter 7 Property named 'Alcheringa' Canyonleigh, N.S.W. Australia.
Where I was trained as a 'Direct Voice Channel'
Chapter 8 The Ghost of Jehanne d'Arc - Walking her Journey of Birth, Life and Death in France
www.fordham.edu/halsall/basis/joanofarc-trial.asp
Chapter 9 The Ghost of Jehanne d'Arc and her Real Birth
http://en.wikipedia.org/wiki/Charles_VII_of_France The Dauphin
http://en.wikipedia.org/wiki/Charles_VI_of_France The Dauphin's father
http://en.wikipedia.org/wiki/Louis_I,_Duke_of_Orléans The Dauphin's uncle - his father's younger brother - the 100 years war
1990 Peter Ramster, The Search for Lives Past,Somerset Films and Publishing
Chapter 10 Continuing the Ghost of Jehanne d'Arc - Mont Saint Michel.
http://en.wikipedia.org/wiki/Mont_Saint-Michel -history
Chapter 11 Interview with a Knight Templar
Ref: The Book of Jubilees. http://en.wikipedia.org/wiki/Jubilees
http://en.wikipedia.org/wiki/Sathya_Sai_Baba
Chapter 12 More Story of the Ghost of Jehanne d'Arc – Scotland Judith of Judea – Half Sister of Issa (Jesus) – a Previous Life.

http://en.wikipedia.org/wiki/Catharism
www.russianbooks.org/montsegur/montsegur3.htm
www.essenespirit.com/who.html
http://en.wikipedia.org/wiki/Vézelay_Abbey
http://en.wikipedia.org/wiki/The_Holy_Blood_and_the_Holy_Grail
www.sacredconnections.co.uk

Chapter 13 The Ghost of Charles Dickens
Staplehurst Rail Crash – Charles Dickens – Ref: Wikipedia
The Mystery of Ellen Ternan - The Violated Letter - Copyright © 1997-20172015
David A. Perdue, All Rights Reserved. URL:
http://charlesdickenspage.com/the_violated_letter.html

Chapter 15 We are on a Mission –
Photos of Dr Charles Leadbeater and Dr Annie Besant -India
http://en.wikipedia.org/wiki/Charles_Webster_Leadbeater
http://en.wikipedia.org/wiki/Annie_Besant

Chapter 16 Les Saintes de la Mer, The Bay of Marys on the Mediterranean Camargue Coast, France. – The Evocation.
http://en.wikipedia.org/wiki/Camargue
http://en.wikipedia.org/wiki/Camargue_horse

Chapter 17 The Basilica of Mary Magdalene at Saint Maximin La Sainte-Baume Region, France
http://en.wikipedia.org/wiki/Saint-Maximin-la-Sainte-Baume
http://en.wikipedia.org/wiki/Sainte-Baume The Cave of Mary Magdalene at La Sainte-Baume
http://en.wikipedia.org/wiki/Sainte-Baume
Mystical photo given by spirit showing Mary Magdalene's remains in cave.

Chapter 18 Glastonbury Abbey and the Tor - England
http://en.wikipedia.org/wiki/Glastonbury_Abbey
Leaflet given on entry into the Abbey.
http://en.wikipedia.org/wiki/Stonehenge
http://en.wikipedia.org/wiki/Avebury
www.hintsandthings.com - permission given for article written by John D Trueman about White Horses
http://en.wikipedia.org/wiki/Avebury -West Kennet Long Barrow - Silbury Hill.

Chapter 19 Rennes-le-Chateau and the Valley of God - France

http://en.wikipedia.org/wiki/Rennes-le-Château

http://www.sol.com.au/kor/7_01.htm

Refer book Holy Blood, Holy Grail by Baigent, Leigh and Lincoln

Letter written by Father B. Sauniere, 1903

http://campus.udayton.edu/mary/resources/marianshrineinpakistan.htm

http://www.jesusfamilytomb.com/back_to_basics/alternative/kashmir_tomb.html

http://en.wikipedia.org/wiki/St._Thomas_Mount

http://www.sol.com.au/kor/7_01.htm

Chapter 20 The Aude Valley, Esperaza Dinosaur Museum

Dinosaur Country – Red earth connection to Uluru

DVD "Guide to Rennes-le-Chateau and the Aude Valley." By Henry Lincoln

Vitruvian man. - http://en.wikipedia.org/wiki/Vitruvian_Man

http://en.wikipedia.org/wiki/Dinosauria_(museum) -Esperaza

Finding 2 keys at Mt. Bugarach – unlocking our Past-Lives.

Chapter 21 Montsegur, Languedoc, South of France – The Last Bastion of the Cathars

http://en.wikipedia.org/wiki/Montségur

http://en.wikipedia.org/wiki/Catharism#Consolamentum

Photo of 2 keys on door to Museum at village of Montsegur

Chapter 24 Past Life memory at Montsegur

The 'whereabouts' of the Lost 'Book of Love.'

http://www.cathar.info

Chapter 22 The Palais de Papes, Avignon – Vaucluse, South of France

http://en.wikipedia.org/wiki/Palais_des_Papes

http://en.wikipedia.org/wiki/Pope_Clement_V

madmonarchist.blogspot.com.au/2011/09/papal-profile-pope-clement-v.html

http://www.theinsider.org/news/article.asp?id=2623

http://www.reuters.com/article/2007/10/12/us-vatican-templars-idUSL0934223200710l2

Nothing has given me more inner peace than to read the formal apology given by Pope Paul ll for the misdeeds done by man and the church in the name of God.

Double Keys given 3 Times on Our Sacred Journey to Unlock Past-Life Memories.

Chapter 23 Cairo and the Pyramids of Giza, Egypt.
http://en.wikipedia.org/wiki/Cairo
en.wikipedia.org/wiki/Cairo_Citadel
Art & History, EGYPT book. English Edition 5,000 years of civilization.
Text & Drawings by Alberto Carlo Carpiceci – EB Bonechi

Chapter 24 Visit to the Famous Cairo Museum - The Amarna Story.
http://ngm.nationalgeographic.com/2010/09/tut-dna/hawass-text/1
National Geographic Magazine September 2010 –King Tut's DNA – Unlocking family secrets.
http://en.wikipedia.org/wiki/Amenhotep_III
http://books.google.com.au/books?id=VIycXJHjMgIC&pg=PA124&lpg=PA124&dq=immaculate+conception+-+Luxor+Temple+-
http://en.wikipedia.org/wiki/Akhenaten
http://en.wikipedia.org/wiki/Tutankhamun
The Secret of Nefertiti is Revealed
http://en.wikipedia.org/wiki/Nefertiti
http://en.wikipedia.org/wiki/Myth_of_Osiris_and_Isis
http://en.wikipedia.org/wiki/Solar_deity
Crop-circles
http://www.cropcircleuniversity.com/2016/05/08/2016-05-6-east-kennett/

Chapter 31 The Sacred Aborigine Alcheringa Stone -
Refer to full story in my first book 'The Book of Love by a Medium.'
The Mission of the Mother Ship Rexegena from The Pleiades
Refer to full story in second book 'Alcheringa, when the first ancestors were created.'

Quote from Uncle Rueben Kelly, a Dhungutti (Kempsey) Elder and last man in NSW allowed to carry out initiation ceremonies for boys. "Our legends tell us we came to your planet in a space ship made of energy. When it hit the atmosphere it turned into crystal." Ref: https://www.newdawnmagazine.com/articles/the-first-race-out-of-australia-not-africa

Chapter 60

In 2011 I have since written an article with Alcheringa 'The Story of Uluru and its impact crater,' on my website https://www.valerie-barrow.com/?p=53

Suggested Reading & Viewing

The Joy and Power of Your Eternal Self – by Dr Anthony Emmett. Published by Joshua Books - Australia.

'Moldavite: Starborn Stone of Transformation' by Roberty Simmons and Kathy Warner. Published by Heaven & Earth RRI, Box 25 Marshfield, VT 05658 USA. Ph: 1-800-942-9423

'Forgotten Origin' by Steven Strong and Evan Strong. Published by University Press of America – 2011.

'Many Lives, Many Masters' and 'Only Love is Real' by Dr. Brian Weiss

'All Books' written by Dolores Cannon – Ozark Mountain Publishers, P.O. Box 754 Huntsville, AR 72740-0754

'Joan of Arc' The Mystic Legacy. By Marcia Quinn Noren published by Gold Fields Press USA.

'Dickens' by Peter Akroyd – published by Minerva

'When the Earth Nearly Died' by D.S. Allan & J.B. Delair published by Gateway Books U.K.

'Holy Blood, Holy Grail' by Michael Baigent, Richard Leigh and Henry Lincoln.

'The Da Vinci Code' by Dan Brown

'Vision of Albion' Key to the Holy Grail. by Barry Dunford – self published.

'The Sign of the Dove' by Elizabeth Van Buren – published 1983 by Neville Spearman Limited, Spirals PO Box 13157, Oakland, CA 94661

'Our Ancestors came from Outer Space' by Maurice Chatelain a NASA expert confirms man's extraterrestrial origins – published by Pan Books 1979

'The Gosford Files' – UFOs over the NSW Central Coast by Moira McGhee & Bryan Dickeson published by INUFOR

'Extraterrestrial Presence on Earth'– Lessons in History by Judy Carroll

'Hybrid Aliens' by Daniella and Bruce Fenton

'The Sasquatch People'

https://www.psychicsasquatch.com/sunbow/
Remember who you are by Gail Nicholls. ND.DipCliHyp.LBL -Balboa Press Div of Hay House.

'Ghost' – The movie with Whoopie Goldberg, Patrick Swayze and Demi Moore.

Isaac Tigret talk at Guru Purnima celebrations 16th July, 2019 at Muddenhalli, India: https://www.youtube.com/watch?v=5Z _kxEqk6vc

Lightning Source UK Ltd.
Milton Keynes UK
UKHW021003081020
371228UK00005B/375